The car was a 1965 Cadillac aqua-blue hardtop convertible. As we neared the car I noticed two things: the strong odor of gasoline got even stronger, and the red bedspread hanging out of the open driver's side front window was covered with a darker red material that looked like blood to me . . .

## *CRIME SCENE*

"I need three things to write a novel: inspiration, something to write on, and Larry Ragle's *Crime Scene*. . . . A fascinating read for anyone with an interest in the amazing world where science meets crime. I highly recommend it."

T. Jefferson Parker

# CRIME SCENE

### FROM FINGERPRINTS TO DNA TESTING— AN ASTONISHING INSIDE LOOK AT THE REAL WORLD OF C.S.I.

# LARRY RAGLE

AVON BOOKS
*An Imprint of HarperCollinsPublishers*

AVON BOOKS
*An Imprint of* HarperCollins*Publishers*
10 East 53rd Street
New York, New York 10022-5299

Copyright © 1995, 2002 by Larry Ragle
ISBN: 0-380-77379-1
www.avonbooks.com

First Avon Books paperback printing: October 1995

Avon Trademark Reg. U.S. Pat. Off. and in Other Countries, Marca Registrada, Hecho en U.S.A.
HarperCollins ® is a registered trademark of HarperCollins Publishers Inc.

Printed in the U.S.A.

10

*To Nina,*
*it's all for you*

———————————

# Acknowledgments

Investigating a crime scene is an art as well as a science. All the scientists in the world could not bring a criminal investigation to a successful conclusion without the involvement of the artists—the detectives who link the components of a case into a complete package. In this book I introduce a mere handful of the brilliant investigators who I was fortunate to work with over the years. They were wise, compassionate, tenacious, and had an insatiable curiosity that left nothing unquestioned.

While writing some of these crime scene descriptions I relied on the help of some of my friends from the Costa Mesa Police Department: Investigator Linda Geisler; Sergeants Sam Cordero and Larry Bersch; from the Orange County Sheriff-Coroner's Division, Jim "Toe Tags" Beisner and Sandy Smith; and from the crime lab, Bob Cravey, Margaret Kuo, Frank Fitzpatrick, John Hartman, Gary Jackson, Sharon Krenz, Sandy Abrams, Laurie Crutchfield, Mary Hong, and Loren Sugarman. Thanks as well to the other members of the laboratory staff who are mentioned in *Crime Scene*.

Finally, my thanks to my editor, Sarah Durand, copyeditor, Peter Weissman, and all the people at HarperCollins who worked to make this book look good.

On a sad note, two of my associates who are prominent in this book, Dr. Bob Richards and Bob Wagner, passed away recently. Their contributions to Orange County's criminal justice system were countless. They are missed.

# Contents

# Introduction

*The body of Eileen Jane Snow, twenty-eight, lies on the bed of her apartment. She is nude and has been posed with splayed legs, like a pinup girl. The electric cord of her iron is wrapped around her neck, leaving deep ligature gashes. It appears the victim was dealt three or four overpowering blows to the head with the iron, forced to ingest sodium amytal, and subjected to object rape. Her attacker left ejaculate [mixed in ketchup] on her clean sheets.*

Ted Bundy?

Richard "the Night Stalker" Ramirez?

Nope, that's *CSI: Crime Scene Investigation* via CBS, viewed by millions of people every week. This is the biggest quasiforensic scientific show since *Quincy, M.D.* It's always in the top ten rated prime time shows. Where is *my* agent when I need him?

A few years ago I wrote, "People seem to have an insatiable appetite for the grizzly details of murder, sexual violence, drugs, and anything else that deals with crime." That was a gross understatement. You can bet NBC, ABC, and Fox will have *CSI* clones on the air by the time you read this.

In the past, fictional TV detectives only referred to forensics as an aside: "Get the lab guys in here," or maybe some guy with CRIME LAB in letters on his back might be seen pondering some prop in the background. Now, TV viewers see more gore than some real cops will see in a career. Where else can one look through microscopes, identify bugs on dead pigs, match pieces of toenails, bash blood-laden plastic heads with golf clubs, find ketchup in semen, or see close-ups of slit throats and decapitated heads? It's gory, but people are captivated by it. The point is, TV is transforming forensic scientists into celebrities.

However, celebrity can lead to problems—not for the fictional scientists, but for the real ones. Perhaps this is the time to pose the chicken and the egg question: Who's mirroring whom? Before the fictional characters in *NYPD, Hill Street Blues*, or *Columbo*, did real cops run around dressed funny and get into all kinds of trouble? They do now.

*Quincy, M.D.* was a hit in the 1970s. Up to that time, I never saw real forensic pathologists issuing press releases or mouthing off on television about anything. When they sought equal time—that is, celebrity—they became targets and a bunch of them fell, big-time.

TV as a role model worries me. Are the real criminalists and forensic scientists next to take the bait? For example, few, if any, real criminalists carry guns. Yet everyone on the *CSI* cast carries huge semiautomatic eighteen-shooters, and they point them at people. Real crime lab people don't interrogate suspects. Somehow *CSI*'s criminalists always seem to end up on the inside of the mirrored room trying to trap a lying suspect with their forensic facts. They also get to accuse other actors of heinous crimes, and they have a dumb boss. I know for a fact that the criminalists who worked for me didn't have a dumb boss. TV cops always have dumb bosses. Except for *Barney Miller*. The first clue will be when real crime scene scientists start emoting like the *CSI* staff. Somehow, somewhere, I'll bet it has already started.

The influence of shows such as *CSI* has as much to do with the audience as the producers. People are no longer satisfied with just the news that someone was killed. They want to know every detail, its importance, and how that information will be used by both sides to reconstruct the events of the crime.

Today's fascination with crime scene investigation—in both fiction and real life—has not only increased dramatically, it has matured. Sherlock Holmes may have been the first to expound on the potential evidential value of a tiny chip of wood and a feather removed from a suspect's pocket, but that was just a beginning. Perhaps when Holmes described his endeavors to Dr. Watson as "Elementary," he was predicting the complexities of modern forensic science rather than feigning humility. Indeed, recent writers, following Sir Arthur Conan Doyle's lead, have introduced the reader to all sorts of sophisticated scientific investigation.

And there lies the rub.

The media, in every form, bombard us with their rendition of scientific crime sleuthing. Real-life examples of scientific investigations using computers, lasers, and DNA are constantly in the news. Occasionally they are portrayed accurately, but in thirty second sound bites. In the world of fiction—novels, television, and movies—there are specific instances when forensic scientists at work have been portrayed properly. Some screenwriters and novelists take the time to be accurate when exposing audiences to their versions of forensic science, while others seem to have little interest in or regard for facts. *The problem is, the public—and even some people in the business—can't tell one version from the other.*

For example, the special effects used in films to represent gunshot entrance wounds, a violent eruption of blood at the point of entry, are so prevalent that the general public, and I fear some officials, believe that is what really happens. You will see in the chapter on firearms evidence that, with one rare exception, the only time the typical film version of an entry wound occurs is if the weapon is held in tight contact with the victim's body.

For years, fans of fiction were led to believe that if the police found a fingerprint at the crime scene, it would immediately identify the unknown source. This wasn't true until the 1980s, when automated fingerprint searching systems became a reality, and there still is no guarantee of a hit. The fingerprints of the person who left a print at the scene have to be registered in the computer for it to work at all.

The fact is, real forensic scientists can't compare to the fictional ones who never fail to produce an abundance of astonishing information, often from a tiny speck of debris. Real forensic scientists operate under handicaps; for one, they can't write the script. More important, most of them don't have the opportunity to go to the crime scene and collect the evidence. It may be collected by untrained police personnel, investigators who lack knowledge of the value of physical evidence, or officers who just don't care. In these situations, physical evidence can be left uncollected—overlooked or dismissed as unimportant—or collected improperly, compromising its potential value. For example, collecting dry blood by wetting it, a standard procedure, but then leaving it moist or unfrozen, can destroy most of its definitive characteristics.

If collected, the evidence may be stored and examined only in the event of a trial. If the evidence is analyzed, the laboratory information is often misused by expert witnesses and the attorneys on both sides. Words used to add credibility to an examination such as "matching" or "consistent with," or "within the limits of this examination," may be misleading unless they are defined or challenged. An attorney can ask an expert a leading question, such as, "Did the hair found at the crime scene match the defendant's hairs?" The witness need only answer yes. If the answer is unchallenged, the jury is left to believe the hair came from the defendant. A hair, however, can't be individualized without DNA.

Even if everything has been done properly, it remains for the jurors, who may have no scientific savvy, to incorporate their collective interpretation of the testimony into their decision of guilt or innocence.

This book is, in effect, a compilation of forensic science information, providing straightforward answers to the very basic questions asked of physical evidence—its relative value, by whom and how it should be collected, and what levels of information it provides decision makers and triers of fact.

This book will take the interested layman to a new level of expertise, including the latest techniques and advances in forensic science.

I am what you'd call a very lucky guy. After high school and a short tour of active duty in the Air Force Reserves, where I was assigned to the Air Police, I decided I wanted to study scientific crime investigation. I lived in the San Francisco Bay area, in the town of Albany, at the time. I soon discovered that the only university-level program in the world that taught criminalistics—the study of the application of chemistry, physics, and other sciences to physical evidence, and the course I wanted—was offered at the University of California, Berkeley, less than ten miles from my family home.

At U.C. Berkeley, I majored in criminalistics under Dr. Paul Kirk, a world-renowned pioneer in forensic sciences. While a student, I was hired as a patrolman for the city of Berkeley, which at the time was a model of community policing. After graduation, I was hired as a criminalist for the Orange County Sheriff's Department by Jack Cadman, another renowned pioneer in forensic science. I was a generalist for sixteen years. That means I worked every kind of case submitted—drunk driving, dope, burglaries, sexual assaults, and questioned deaths. We took turns on call, responding to major crime scenes when they occurred. This involved hundreds of scenes, mostly homicides, mostly at night. When Cadman retired, I was promoted and became Director of Forensic Sciences. My responsibilities included the crime lab, toxicology lab, ID bureau, CAL-ID, and the Coroner's Office.

For the most part, the experiences related in *Crime Scene* happened to me or around me during twenty-nine years in Orange County, California, or were shaped by my education and work in Berkeley.

This book is for anyone who wants to learn what goes on at a crime scene and what happens to the evidence from that point on. It is also for police officers and attorneys interested in expanding their knowledge of scientific evidence, and for crime writers, who should understand the value as well as the limitations of physical evidence.

Finally, students looking for a career could not find a more interesting or rewarding vocation than one in forensic science. I hope my accounts entice them to explore the educational and job opportunities in the field.

# Seventeen Years

Think about the events of your life between your fifth and your twenty-second birthday, or about everything you have done in the past seventeen years, say back to 1985. If you could write down every single thing that happened, it could take another seventeen years, or longer if you type like me.

This case is the story of a man who could write it all on a single piece of paper. It might say:

> Every day for seventeen years I sat in my cell
>     wondering why I was here.
> I awoke wondering,
> I ate wondering,
> I worked at my assigned job wondering, and
> I slept wondering.
> Why?

This is why. On the night of September 30, 1979, in Tustin, California, Kevin Green was a little horny. He was at home, as was his wife Dianna, so under normal conditions his being horny was a good thing, a solvable problem. But lately things were different. The wife was pregnant—really pregnant—and sex was a no-no. This baby was so due she was ready to blow out some birthday candles. She would never get that chance.

A man's urges are hard to control, and when reason fails, the urges are known to get men into trouble. So Green made a move on his wife, and needless to say, she didn't like it. A screaming match ensued during which each one made their point. Her message—"Don't even think about it"—prevailed. When a man's sexual urges are so totally rejected, there is only one thing that can calm him down—a cheeseburger.

Green's account to the police of what happened that night included a cheeseburger and seeing a dark-skinned man. One of the first officers to arrive on the crime scene made note of a Jack in the Box bag and its undisturbed contents, still warm to the touch. Green's account also included a twenty minute period it took to drive to the Jack in the Box and back. A receipt was found during the crime scene search that identified the specific location of the fast food restaurant. The investigators later verified that it was indeed a ten minute one-way trip. However, from the beginning they questioned why Green had not gone to another Jack in the Box much closer. Green wasn't new to the area. Why did he go that far out of his way?

Kevin Green, a corporal in the Marines, was on active duty, assigned to a nearby base. His story to the police didn't sound too original. He described a dark-skinned stranger with an Afro lurking outside the apartment building, and added that the stranger saw him leaving. When he returned, he said, he caught a glimpse of the same man getting into a white van and driving hurriedly away. When he reentered the apartment, his first impression was that his wife was asleep. When she made no response, he realized that her head, apparently crushed, was in a pool of blood. He called for help.

The paramedic quickly discovered that Dianna was still alive, and rushed her to the closest emergency hospital. It was clear she had been the victim of blunt force trauma causing severe brain damage. She did not regain consciousness and was put on life support systems. Regardless of her perilous condition, a sexual assault kit was collected from Dianna at the hospital, and not a moment too soon. The timing was critical. Had the baby's delivery been vaginal, natural or induced, any evidence of seminal fluid would have been destroyed. But the baby was dead.

The crime scene was searched for physical evidence, with little results. There was no apparent forced entry, no evidence of burglary, and no obvious weapon. There were no unexplained fingerprints or shoe tracks, no evidence to indicate any uninvited intruder. There was no blood apparent on the clothing Green was wearing. The sexual assault kit was all that remained unexamined, and it was the last hope to find incriminating evidence.

In 1979 only two systems of genetic markers—ABO and PGM, an enzyme—were discernable from semen. Blood was tested to determine ABO and PGM types, and saliva was tested to determine secretor status. If the ABO type showed up in the saliva analysis, as it does in about eighty percent of the population, it would also be present in the donor's semen. The PGM markers would be present in any case.

When a spouse is murdered, the mate is always a prime suspect, at least in the minds of the investigators. Because of Miranda—the right to remain silent warning—investigators must tiptoe around prearrest interviews of the mate before accusations, if any, are made. However, they can request certain samples for elimination purposes. For example, the blood types of consensual sexual partners must be identified before any meaningful interpretation of test kit results can be considered.

Blood and saliva samples were obtained from Green, in the event semen was found in the rape kit. Finding a husband's semen in a sexual assault kit could be expected. However, if semen (spermatozoa) was found in the victim's vagina that lacked any of his or his wife's ABO/PGM markers, it could absolutely exclude Green as the source. Any other marker would indicate a third person.

Kevin and Dianna had the same types, O, and Kevin was a secretor. The kit tested positive for sperm, and the results matched Green's types. The crime lab's results failed to exclude Green, meaning he could have been the source of the semen. There was no clear evidence of a third person. A serologist would testify that the sperm could have been donated by any man of type O and the same PGM markers as Green, or from any nonsecretor with the same PGM markers.

What would you do if you were the investigator? You have at least one murder and one attempted murder, and maybe a burglary and rape. The surviving victim is near death in a deep coma. You have a spouse who admits having an argument with his injured wife, an alibi about going out for a cheeseburger, and a story about a dark-skinned stranger lurking in the bushes nearby. The only physical evidence, the semen, matches the husband. There's one addition: A neighbor claims to have seen a dark-skinned stranger about the same time Green said he saw him. In this case the investigators played it cool. They waited.

Weeks later Dianna came out of her coma, but it would be many more weeks before she could be questioned as to exactly what happened. The damage to her brain was severe, affected her ability to speak and, to some extent, her memory. When the time finally arrived and the doctors allowed a few questions, the investigators were not taken by surprise when Dianna said: "Kevin did it!"

Kevin Green was arrested on December 1, 1979, and charged with the murder of his stillborn baby and the attempted murder of his wife. Green's trial began on September 22, 1980, a week and a day short of a year from the day of the crime. As murder trials go, this was a short haul. The jury was picked, Dianna testified, family members testified of tales of past abuse, and a neighbor said he heard a cry, "Please don't hit me again!" The investigators testified, the serologist testified, and the prosecution rested. What the jury zeroed in on was Dianna's statement, "He attacked me because I refused to have sex," and that the argument was the last thing she could remember.

Green's defense was slim. He testified, offering his proof that he went out for twenty minutes for a cheeseburger. And a neighbor testified that Green's car was not in its parking space during the time he said he was gone. Big deal; everybody knows Jack in the Box doesn't deliver! But there was the neighbor who testified that he also saw the dark-skinned man lurking in the area. Nevertheless, none of that diluted Dianna's description of what happened a year earlier. On October 2, 1980, the jury found Kevin Green guilty of murder in the second degree of his unborn child and attempted murder of his wife. On November 7, 1980, he was sentenced to prison for fifteen years to life.

He would spend the next seventeen years wondering why.

Kevin Green was not the only person wondering. Others were wondering about the numerous "who-done-its" across Orange County, California. All law enforcement agencies have unsolved crimes. Murders are the type of crime most likely to remain unsolved, for an obvious reason—the best and perhaps only witness is dead. This is why there is no statute of limitation for the crime of murder. Unless a major blunder occurs, all of the physical evidence from murder cases, solved or unsolved, is retained as best as possible.

The Orange County Sheriff's property room is full of evidence from murder cases, some dating back to the 1940s. However, most items—for example, dry stains—were stored at room temperature, while liquid degradable items were refrigerated. Human tissue and other solid degradable items were frozen.

Kevin Green may not know it, but he owes a great deal of gratitude to a suspected child molester from Northern California by the name of Nation, a Costa Mesa police forensic scientist, and the diligence of the Orange County laboratory serologists. In the *People* v. *Nation* (1980), the defense requested a reexamination of a microscope slide, collected from a child, suspected to contain seminal fluids. The slide could not be located. The defense challenged the admissibility of the prosecution witness's testimony to the identity of the fluid since the defendant had no opportunity to examine it. The outcome of the case favored the defendant. The high court stated that every effort must be taken to preserve the natural properties of any type of evidence. In the case of biologicals such as blood and semen stains, that meant freezing them. In murder cases, that meant forever. The crime lab staff gathered all such evidential items that were not already there, and stored them in the laboratory freezer.

Tustin is a small and old town by Southern California standards, with a population of 60,000. Indians, and later the Spaniards, settled there because of natural springs. In 1979 a good part of the population were Marines assigned to El Toro Marine Corps Air Station, three miles south, or to Tustin MCAS. You would never know you were in Tustin unless you noticed the city limits sign. The county is really just one big city, and Tustin is almost in the dead center of the county, six miles south of Anaheim, home of Disneyland. It's eight miles down the I-5 freeway to the Pacific Ocean. Costa Mesa is on the way to the ocean.

From the 1970s to the mid-1980s there were several serial killers terrorizing Southern California. Four of them—William Bonin, Kenneth Bianchi, Patrick Kearney and Randy Kraft—targeted only men. One, Richard Ramirez, murdered anyone in his way. But one series involved young women, aged seventeen to thirty-one, all in Orange County. Of the seven cases connected by M.O. factors, five had been raped and murdered, one was beaten and raped, and one had only been beaten. All seven lived in apartments, all seven were asleep alone, there was no forced entry, no fingerprints or shoe tracks, and all seven suffered blunt force trauma to the head. The weapons appeared to be whatever was convenient—a two-by-four, a rock, and in some cases no weapon was ever located.

The terror began in Anaheim. It was the only crime scene north of the I-5 freeway. The press, quick to establish titles, called these the "Bedroom Basher Murders."

April 1, 1979, Costa Mesa, female 25, murdered in bed in her apartment

May 24, 1979, Costa Mesa, female 25, beaten while asleep in her apartment

July 21, 1979, Costa Mesa, female 29, beaten while asleep in her apartment

September 14, 1979, Costa Mesa, female 31, murdered in bed in her apartment

October 7, 1979, Tustin, female 24, murdered in bed
   in her apartment
October 21, 1979, Costa Mesa, female 17, murdered
   in bed in her apartment

At that point the series stopped.

Dianna Green was beaten while asleep in bed in her apartment on September 30, 1979, and Kevin Green was arrested December 1, 1979. Because of her certainty that "Kevin did it," this murder was classified a violent domestic dispute, a family matter and nothing else. The police never considered Kevin as a suspect in the "Bedroom Basher Murders." And, since the Green murder was closed, it was never connected to the Basher series.

On the afternoon of February 15, 1980, in the city of Tustin, a thirteen-year-old girl was walking to her home after buying a belated birthday gift for her mother. The day had been all bad to that point: it was the day of her father's funeral, two days after her mother's uncelebrated birthday. She had hoped the gift would bring some comfort to her mother.

She would testify nineteen years later that she saw a van stopping next to the curb ahead of her and saw the driver exiting. He appeared to be repairing something on the van, but as she passed by, he grabbed her, hit her in the face, and threw her into the van. The driver drove north to an isolated area in Westminster, where he forced her to disrobe and then raped her. He kept her captive until it was dark and then drove back to Tustin and released her.

Her account to the police that night led them to arrest the owner of a similar van, a sergeant in the Marines, named Gerald Parker, a dark-skinned man.

In the blink of an eye, Parker plead guilty and was sent to prison. In retrospect, it seems he wanted out of Orange County as quickly as possible. Out of sight, out of mind, as the saying goes. However, there was one detail over which he had no control. The state of California had enacted a requirement that certain felons were required to give blood, specifically for typing to profile ABO and polymorphic enzyme/protein markers. Parker had to comply. His sample was shipped to the state laboratory for typing and inclusion in a database of convicted sex offenders.

A database was an idea years ahead of its time. The idea was that evidence from an unsolved case could be compared to all the prior arrested felons. There were two problems with this. First, the markers available were nonspecific, making searches difficult. More important, the legislature, although well-intended, failed to provide funding for the project, leaving thousands of samples untested. Fortunately, the samples were property preserved. Parker would be in and out of prison three more times, all for nonsex-related crimes. He would have been paroled in 1984 but he assaulted another inmate and spent three more years in prison. He was out from 1987 until 1993, when he was convicted of burglary. He was scheduled to be released July 6, 1996.

By 1996, DNA profiling was fully established. The legislature atoned for their oversight and funded a fully automated DNA database, and personnel to process the stored samples. Motivated by the opportunity, the Orange County District Attorney, Sheriff's Office and other local law enforcement agencies began a process of looking at cold cases, and in specific murder cases where evidence involved blood and/or semen. The "Basher" cases were on top of the list.

Some evidence, once examined by the Orange County Sheriff's laboratory, was returned to the investigating agencies for safekeeping. Costa Mesa PD criminalist Bruce Radonski, a man with an eye for fine detail and well-aware of the delicate nature of biological samples, stored the sexual assault kits from their cases in their freezer long before the Nation case mandate. When the "Bashers" cases were reexamined seven years later, Radonski provided the key evidence—an ideally preserved specimen of the Basher's semen. Of significance, this sample from one of the nonfatal cases was past the statute of limitations. Nevertheless, Radonski had recognized its M.O. connections to the murders and maintained its integrity.

In June 1996 the sheriff's DNA lab completed their analysis of the Basher sample. All of the samples had common

DNA markers indicating a common source. The sample preserved by Radonski provided the most complete profile for Basher, and it was relayed to the DOJ database.

There was one match: Gerald Parker.

The state criminal records indicated that Parker was in custody at Avenal State Prison, a facility off the I-5 freeway, approximately two hundred miles north of Orange County. Investigators from Tustin and Costa Mesa, armed with the DNA information, made the trip prepared to interrogate Parker regarding the murders. Parker must have anticipated this eventuality; he freely admitted all of the Basher cases.

Satisfied with a job well done, the investigators were surprised when Parker added an unexpected confession: "I've always felt bad about a guy who was blamed for what I did. I think he's on death row. He didn't do it, I did." In his statement, he gave details that only the killer could have known. He described the Greens' apartment and the victim. Green was released from prison based on Parker's confession.

At first, some wondered if somehow Parker and Green, in the prison system at the same time, had corresponded. Had Parker agreed to take the blame for Green if and when his identity as the Basher came to light? One more murder wouldn't make him die any quicker. Without DNA results, one could ponder that thought.

The Tustin investigators requested that Dianna's assault kit samples be reanalyzed for DNA and compared to Kevin Green's and Parker's. In fact, Parker's ABO/PGM type was already known—on file from the assault that sent him to prison the first time. It was identical to Green's and to the test results from Dianna's kit. However, the DNA profiling of the kit, when completed, matched only one man—Parker.

Considering DNA results and Parker's confession, almost everyone was convinced that Green was totally innocent. But one was not swayed—Dianna. To this day, and perhaps forever, she maintains, in her mind, Kevin's guilt. The last thing she remembers was him standing over her screaming and, she adds, hitting her on the head with his keys. She doesn't believe the DNA results, and perhaps never will.

"Kevin did it!"

Cold hits, à la Basher, are common now that a national system is in place and the base continues to grow. DNA miracle cases are well-publicized. Now, I wonder. Parker had to have been wondering himself, anticipating the day he would be identified as the Basher. Prisoners get the same news we do. They know about the reexamination of cold cases using DNA and automated fingerprint systems. You can bet some of them spend their days and nights wondering not why, but when.

# chapter one

## The Concepts of Forensic Science

### Introduction

Forensic science is the business of providing timely, accurate, and thorough information to all levels of decision makers in our criminal justice system. The cops, district attorney, defense attorney, judge, and jury don't want a bunch of scientific hocus-pocus, they want straightforward information to help them decide what to do.

The information they need is derived from the examination of physical evidence collected at the scene (or scenes) of the crime. Cops and the general public are used to hearing about guns and blood. Actually, there is no limit to the nature of physical evidence. But there is a limit to our ability to recognize, collect, and analyze it.

Physical evidence can be anything that is tangible, any material thing that can be seen or measured, with or without magnification. It can be in the molecular form as an odor or a drug dissolved in the blood. Someone must be clever enough to recognize the evidence's potential value and trained to collect and preserve it, and the scientist must be capable of analyzing it.

I offer the following case, a gruesome murder provoked by anger, passion, and greed, to illustrate the scope of a scientific crime scene investigation and the relevance of a physical evidence in reconstructing criminal behavior.

## CRIME SCENE:

### THE KEY TO THE CRIME

Big-time crime scenes always seem to be discovered at night. I was told that a body had been found in a vehicle parked on Cabot Road, just off the I-5 freeway exit at Oso Parkway. In 1972 it was considered a remote part of Orange County. Few people used Cabot, particularly at night, since it came to a dead end just south of Oso, so it must have looked like the ideal spot to get rid of a body. The bad guys in this case had a pretty good plan to make things difficult for the investigators. They actually wanted us to find the body, but on their terms. Ignorance and chance, in that order, spoiled their plans. It made out job a hell of a lot easier.

As I pulled up to the crime scene, in the last seconds of the flood of my headlights, I could see the sheriff's ID truck and several cars, one parked off the pavement between the road and the Southern Pacific railroad tracks. Several people were standing nearby. One of them started walking in my direction.

I hadn't taken five steps from my parked car when I noticed the first hint of physical evidence. Simultaneously, one of the deputies assigned to protect the scene cautioned me, "If you are thinking of having a smoke, don't." Even at fifty feet the smell of gasoline was unmistakable. It was obvious that there was a lot of loose fuel somewhere nearby.

The car was a 1965 Cadillac aqua-blue two-door hardtop convertible. The window on the driver's side door was down all the way, and a large dark red cloth, which turned out to be a bedspread, was hanging out the window all the way down to the ground. As we neared the car I noticed two things: The strong odor of gasoline got even stronger and the red bedspread was covered with a darker red that looked like blood to me.

A closer look revealed the presence of some small chunks

of beige gelatinous matter clinging to the cloth. This stuff could have been some flavor of Jell-O, but the scene didn't look like a picnic. I was betting on splattered brain tissue. The cloth extended inside to the backseat and was covering something fairly large. I worked my way to the open window by shining my flashlight onto the ground and taking small steps one at a time. This way I could be fairly sure that I was not going to step on any evidence. I was now able to put my head inside the vehicle. The smell of gasoline was so strong, my eyes were burning and I couldn't keep looking for very long. Regardless, I saw enough. There was a foot sticking out from under a bedspread. My trained scientific mind had already assumed that we had a problem here. But nowhere near that of the guy in the backseat.

I did take time to notice that there was a single key in the off position of the ignition. The coroner had been called and was on the way to the crime scene. Legally as well as practically, bodies aren't searched or moved until a deputy coroner arrives on the scene. This little wait gave me time to learn what the other investigators had found out and what they believed had happened up to this point.

I continued to look around the car as homicide investigator Bill Johnson related the events that led the deputies to the scene in the first place. Deputy Mike Phoenix and his partner had been parked less than a mile north on the west side of I-5, on Cabot at La Paz, expecting to rendezvous with another South County unit for a coffee break. The second unit had exited I-5 at Oso and was northbound on Cabot. About halfway to Oso these deputies were surprised to see two cars parked off the road in a dirt area next to the railroad tracks, as well as two people moving around outside. Except for teenagers drinking and drivers with car trouble, it was unusual for anyone to park along Cabot.

Although it doesn't take too long to stop a car traveling fifty miles per hour and get it turned around, it must have seemed like an hour and a half to the two deputies. To the two men on foot at the scene, those same minutes must have seemed like seconds, leaving them no time to complete their perfect crime.

The Japanese have a proverb, "Of the thirty-six plans, flight is the best." These two suspects had only two more parts of their plan to carry out, but with survival their fundamental interest, they chose to flee instead. By the time the deputies were back at the scene, the two guys had made it to their car and were burning rubber southbound on Cabot, headed toward Oso and the freeway. The deputies, slowing only long enough to see that no one else was standing around outside the parked car, radioed for backups, gave the best description they could of the fleeing car, and followed it south onto the freeway, the direction they believed it had taken. Deputy Phoenix, north of the scene, was in a position to see if the suspects were headed his way. They never showed, so they had to be traveling south. Moments later Phoenix was dispatched to the Cabot scene. Everyone on the air wanted to know why these guys were in such a hurry.

Within minutes other units of the Sheriff's Patrol and the California Highway Patrol positioned themselves to observe the freeway. A vehicle that matched the description was spotted southbound on I-5, exiting into the town of San Juan Capistrano. Several units got in position before the lead unit put on its red lights. No one in the line of emergency vehicles was too surprised when the driver of the suspect vehicle used his left hand to give his pursuers the bird and his right foot to slam the gas pedal to the floor.

The chase lasted about fifteen minutes, around and about San Juan and finally north on Pacific Coast Highway. As the entourage approached Laguna Beach, the suspect driver tried to make an abrupt turn but lost it, and slid uncontrolled into a concrete retaining wall.

The suspect vehicle, our second crime scene, was now under our control. Because the suspect's vehicle was out of view for a period of time, however, we needed a good deal of physical evidence to prove, beyond a reasonable doubt, that the uninjured suspects were the same two guys seen standing by the Cadillac. The felonious act of flipping off a peace officer, compounded by the lesser offenses of reckless driving and evading arrest, wouldn't keep them in jail too long.

Johnson explained that another criminalist, Jim White, had been called out and asked to cover the crash scene. Jim is the criminalist's criminalist. His entire life has been surrounded by mystery. His father, William Anthony White, under the pen name Anthony Boucher, created a classic style of mystery writing. Jim, on the other hand, elected to solve real mysteries and studied criminalisitics at U.C. Berkeley. He grew into one hell of a laboratory and crime scene investigator. Searching the overturned and somewhat messed-up interior, Jim didn't need much time to find a potential connecting link.

By the time Johnson had completed his account of the events, I was close enough to take a good look at the beige gelatinous stuff on the bedspread. My suspicions were correct, it was brain tissue. The more I looked, the more pieces of brain I saw, and it wasn't all on the bedspread. Some was splashed up on the underside of the car. However, there was no brain or blood on the ground below the vehicle or anywhere else in the surrounding area. The questions were: Where, when, by whom, and—perhaps most important—how did all that brain get way up under the fender? My best guess at the time was multiple blows to the head by a heavy object, an ax or perhaps a baseball bat, while the victim was on the ground next to the left rear fender. Regardless of how it happened, the splattered brain alerted us that we had a third crime scene, the death scene, somewhere else.

The license plate information had been radioed to the sheriff's dispatcher, who in turn requested registration information from the California Department of Motor Vehicles. The vehicle was registered to a resident of Garden Grove, California. Criminal history was then requested on the owner, who, it turned out, had a local arrest record. This was good news. If the body and the registered owner were one and the same, a fingerprint card would be available to make an absolute identification. The victim's residence is always a likely source of vital information, and in this case could well have been the third crime scene. The sooner we verified the identity, the better the chance of finding useful physical evidence, wherever the death scene.

The deputies who first spotted the car came back to the scene and added some information. They described where they believed the getaway car had been originally parked and placed the two people as standing near the trunk of the Cadillac. This helped. A close look at the trunk lid revealed deep pry marks just below the key opening. Although damaged, the lock had held. I was guessing there was something still in the trunk the two guys really wanted. My personal car was another GM product, a Chevy, about the same age as the Cadillac. The ignition key worked in all the locks: ignition, glove compartment, doors, and trunk. So perhaps we could use the key I'd spotted earlier.

There would certainly be some sweet irony if the key did work in the trunk. The bad guys had a perfect plan, it would seem. Drive the body to a remote location, cover it and the interior of the car with about two gallons of gasoline, remove the prize from the trunk, and then with a single match totally devastate the crime scene. If they had tried the ignition key and it had worked for them, they, and the crucial evidence at the scene, would have been long gone by the time our deputies happened on the scene.

But we would have to wait awhile to get to the key and the body. First we had to make the scene as safe as possible. Because of the danger of the gasoline, we needed the county fire department to stand by before anything could be removed. A spark could easily ignite the gasoline-soaked bedspread and interior. Also, after the fire department arrived and before the body could be removed, the front seat area of the vehicle had to be examined for fingerprints and more photos taken.

In the meantime I searched the area between the trunk and where the getaway car had been parked on Cabot Road, picturing what the two suspects had to do to get from one place to the other. More good luck. The entire area was dirt and there was a depression between the two locations. It had rained two or three days prior. The depression had held enough water to remain soft, and the resulting mud was a perfect consistency to capture the minute details of impressions of feet, shoes, or tires.

You guessed it. There were two perfect trails where the suspects had run. One set of tracks had been made by someone wearing boots, but the other appeared to have been made by bare feet. A closer inspection indicated that the feet hadn't been bare but had worn socks.

Jim White had completed his search of the accident scene. He arrived at the Cabot site with sealed bags of evidence collected from the suspects' vehicle. Among the items Jim had located, three would become critical: a pry bar, a pair of shoes (without mud), and an empty gasoline can. These items would become the links needed to place the suspects at the Cabot crime scene. The pry bar provided the first physical evidence connection. Jim had noted, before he packaged it securely, that there was electrician's tape wrapped around the shaft of the bar. Some of the tape was torn and missing. On the Cadillac's back bumper, just below the damaged area near the trunk lock, he saw a small torn piece of the same type of tape, a possible physical match.

I showed Jim the impressions made in the mud. He had not seen the suspects and was unable to describe their footwear. He did remind me that he had found a pair of mudless boots in the suspects' car. That could explain the sock impression.

Our ID trucks are stocked with everything one would need at a crime scene, including a good supply of plaster of Paris. Jim and I managed to use most of it making the two plaster casts. A day later we would obtain the clothing worn by the suspects. One was wearing muddy boots and the other muddy socks when they were pulled from their vehicle.

With the county fire department standing by, it was time to begin the process of removing the body from the Cadillac. The photos were taken without sparking anything but a little gasoline fume nausea on the part of the photographer. No useful fingerprints were found. I put on rubber gloves to deal with the bedspread. The larger chunks of brain clinging to it were removed and placed in a glass jar before the spread was folded and sealed in a plastic bag, a procedure that would preserve the volatile liquids but could destroy the character of the biological materials.

Mixed evidence—in this case, blood, brain, and gasoline, as well as the bedspread—requires an important decision. Which has the greatest significance in the case? They are not all preserved and stored in the same manner. That night it seemed that the source of the gasoline and the bedspread was the most significant question. Why? The blood and brain most likely came from the body, but the source of the gasoline and bedspread could possibly implicate the suspects. Furthermore, if it because necessary to establish the suspect's intent to destroy the evidence, it would be helpful to prove by laboratory examination that the odor was indeed that of gasoline. If that proved to be the case, the gasoline can White found could contain enough residual liquid to compare to the gasoline in the bedspread.

Removing the bedspread finally made it possible to view the body closely. The victim looked to be a male, based on size and clothing, and most likely a Caucasian. He was face-down with his head toward the driver's side. His legs were bent at the knees and pulled back as if hog-tied. The clothing was good news because it could contain a wallet or other forms of identification.

With the driver's door opened, we could see a plastic bowl on the left rear floor positioned under the victim's head. The bowl contained more pieces of brain. The outer rim appeared to be crusted with dried dog food. As each new item of evidence was discovered, more photographs were taken.

All the team members agreed that it was time to remove the body from the car. Once the body was removed, the source of the brain matter was no longer in question. The entire rear section of the victim's head had been pulverized somehow. In gross appearance, it was visually similar to a case I had recently worked in which the victim had been knocked to the ground, facedown, and repeatedly beaten with the working end of a heavy-duty automobile jack. Whatever the cause here, there was a lot of tissue and bone unaccounted for, and that added to the potential value of that undiscovered third crime scene.

Unfortunately, the deputy coroner found no wallet or identification when he searched the body. The body was placed in a body bag and readied for transfer to an autopsy site. With no central morgue, we would have to do the autopsy in a make-do arrangement. But a local funeral parlor would not be adequate, since full-body X rays were an absolute necessity. An immediate autopsy was scheduled at the UCI Medical Center because they had the only X-ray equipment available to us at that time.

There was only one job left to do at this crime scene. Would the ignition key open the trunk? I verified that we had a good close-up photograph of the key still in the ignition, then the key was dusted quickly, but no prints came up. The key was inserted in the trunk lock and a turn brought a satisfying *click*. Raising the trunk lid fully, we discovered the first evidence to establish a motive for murder: drugs. A large box was filled to the top with red capsules. The container was removed and packaged as evidence. Later analysis identified the drug as secobarbituric acid, commonly called reds or downers. The narcs valued the find at $3,000 to $5,000.

The autopsy was performed by Dr. Robert Richards, Orange County's first board-certified forensic pathologist. We received the X rays before beginning the autopsy. Some spots showed completely clear on the developed film. Something that dense had to be metallic. They could be fragments of a bullet or metal that had broken off a pipe or bar. Heavy metal would explain the destructive nature of the wound.

Within minutes of beginning the autopsy, Dr. Richards had located a round hole in the victim's skull. The hole was slightly larger than an inch, and there was heavy sooting on the tissue and bone. There is only one explanation for this trauma: A shotgun was held in tight contact to the victim's head when it was fired. All that burning gunpowder, nitrocellulose, creates a mass of hot expanding gas. When held in tight contact, the gas enters the wound and expands inside the cavity, in this case the skull. At the critical point of stress, the bone and scalp give way, and you've got one hell of a mess. But there was a mystery. Why didn't we see any shot in the X ray?

Also, the victim had to have been on the ground with his head within inches of the left rear fender, almost under it when he was shot. This information meant that the third crime scene would be covered with blood, brain tissue, hair, and perhaps some scalp.

To this point it was an intriguing autopsy, providing meaningful information to all concerned. But the next finding only confused us at first. With about the same fanfare as a magician when he pulls a rabbit from his hat, Dr. Richards produced a bloody package of cigarettes from the deepest area of the wound. Three people simultaneously reacted, "How the hell did that get there?" and I was one of the three. A closer look revealed that the pack was a Lucky Strike package, white with their famous red bull's-eye logo. Although bloody, it was still possible to see that most of the bull's-eye was missing. A hole slightly larger than an inch. Maybe it was symbolic, something between the victim and his killers, but my guess was that the shooter had used the pack as a target, placing the pack between the muzzle and the victim's head.

We collected the standard autopsy specimens, a set of the victim's fingerprints, the victim's clothing, the cigarette package, the bone surrounding the entrance wound, and some other pieces of the victim's skull. We were done with the technical stuff. The body could now be released to the next-of-kin for disposition. As the autopsy concluded, I half jokingly advised the lead investigator, "Look for a house with an enclosed garage where you will find lots of blood and a very hungry dog."

At that point in the investigation, time became the enemy. We needed to locate the shooting scene, the sooner the better. Some leads started to pay off. The autopsy fingerprints were compared to the file prints of the vehicle's registered owner. A match!

Later the same day, Investigator Johnson interviewed the victim's closest next-of-kin, his sister. Her address was the same as the one on the Cadillac's registration information, a corner house with the front door on one street and the garage door on the other in a nice neighborhood in Garden Grove.

She agreed to talk and led Johnson into the kitchen. He explained some of the circumstances of her brother's death but left out most of the details. She acknowledged that her brother lived there on occasion, but she knew nothing of his whereabouts for the past few days. Johnson noticed a dog but no food bowl, but didn't bring up the subject. At the conclusion of the interview, Johnson, who had entered the house by the front door, asked if he could leave by the kitchen door that exited out through the garage. He had noticed that the two-car garage was empty and the door was open when he first approached the house. He made reference to where he had parked to explain why he wanted to use the side exit and started out, not waiting for her to answer.

There was a small washroom connecting the kitchen and the garage. Johnson said later that the minute he walked into the garage, he saw a lot of what looked like blood to him on the concrete floor, with the heaviest concentration very near the laundry room door. With no search warrant, he elected to walk out, acting unconcerned and unaware of the potential evidence.

Bill was a better cop than he was an actor. His body language must have betrayed his excitement. You can bet someone was watching him very closely as he walked to his car. Someone, it would seem, who had a lot to conceal but very little time to do it.

Johnson drove to a telephone immediately and contacted his office to begin the two- to four-hour process of obtaining a telephonic search warrant. Jim and I were briefed and asked to stand by. The final warrant listed all areas of the house and property, and specified items that related to what we knew up to that moment—for example, blood, tissue, a shotgun and ammunition.

The team, led by Johnson and Les Leber, along with White, myself, and an ID tech, were all at the house, search warrant in hand, within three hours. The garage door was closed. The sister was at home and accepted the warrant at the front door with no emotion. Leber and crew entered the front of the house. Johnson, Jim, and I went to the street entrance of the garage door and opened it quickly. We should have had the photographer ready to take a picture of the expressions on our faces.

There was no longer any visible blood on the concrete floor. Instead of blood, we found a floor still tacky with fresh black paint. An empty can of automobile tire dressing sat near the garbage can. This could turn into a disaster. The sister, when asked, explained that her live-in boyfriend had spilled something and decided to paint the floor. Was this a confession?

That day may have been the first time that I recognized a very important human trait: Bad guys, in a panic, think in only two dimensions. Whoever painted the floor was. Although every spot of blood on the floor had been thoroughly concealed, the painter had forgotten the walls and ceiling.

Finding key evidence when a scene had been altered requires some extra steps. I find that visualization plays an important role in reconstructing a crime scene and in understanding where to look for evidence. I can replay in my mind, over and over, all the possible scenarios of how something like this could have happened. I considered what I knew already: first, the explosive nature of the contact shot fired by a shotgun; second, the brain tissue on the underside of the left rear fender of the Cadillac; and third, the concentration of blood Bill had seen on the garage floor near the laundry room door.

If the Cadillac was parked in the normal manner, front end first, the right front tire would line up with the area of heavy concentration Bill had described. That's the wrong fender. This meant the Cadillac had to be backed into the garage. That would put the victim's head less than five feet from the rear wall of the garage.

Kneeling down in that location, I could see a heavy splatter of blood and tissue that looked like brain on the studs and oil paper that covered the unfinished rear wall. The heaviest concentration of debris was only a few inches off the floor. The splatter pattern indicated my position as a likely origin of the debris. This material on the wall was not painted over and had gone unnoticed by the panicked painter. I found one small area on the wall where no splatters were visible, indicating something had shielded that space at the time of the shooting. Later, a plastic bucket stained with what appeared to be blood and tissue was found in a closet in the washroom. It had to have been in the garage, between the victim's head and the wall at the moment the trigger was pulled. The bucket created an effect called "shadowing." (This is discussed in Chapter 6.)

It all fit. I was about satisfied I had seen everything important when something else caught my eye. The thing was stuck down in a seam of the concrete floor where it tied in with the driveway. If the garage door had been shut, it would have covered the evidence. I knelt down and realized I was looking at a relatively big piece of metal. It looked like a huge lead slug, like the kind fired from shotguns by big game hunters who want to get real close to their prey. So close they can't miss.

Jim White was busy searching the inside of the house. No shotgun had been found in any obvious storage space. Eventually, Jim noticed an attic crawl hole, and like a kid looking for hidden Christmas presents, took a peek and found the shotgun. This caused enough excitement to get me out of the garage for a look. It was a twelve-gauge shotgun heavily stained around the muzzle with crusted blood and chunks of tissue that looked just like brain. In addition, the whole mess was covered with small feathers that were stuck in the dry blood.

When searching a crime scene, always remember to look up. One tends to look down and around, considering the effect gravity has on most evidence, but there is an *up*. When we went back to the garage, we looked up and saw a military-style foot locker—a large metal suitcase—perched between two rafters directly above where we had stood before. Once it was opened, it was apparent that someone had used the foot locker as a fireplace. But several pieces of paper were only partially burned, one of which contained the name of the victim.

Also included in the burned debris was one piece of material that didn't look like the rest. It was slightly charred but too thick to be paper. I picked it up and recognized it as bone. A relatively big piece of bone, more than an inch long and an inch wide. It was thick, too, at least an eighth to three-sixteenths of an inch thick, and it possessed convex/concave surfaces. The convex surface was covered with a membrane of blackened tissue. Regardless of any fire damage, this was clearly a piece of skull, and it was my bet that it was human skull. And it didn't require a psychic to visualize who had been its previous owner.

It was a hell of a find; however, the sight of the bone sent a shiver of panic down my spine. Call the coroner! Call Dr. Richards! Call the mortuary! We had to know where this piece of bone came from. And there was only one way to be absolutely sure.

The quick call to the deputy coroner, and his quick call to the mortuary, saved the day. I made arrangements to leave the scene and headed for the mortuary. Dr. Richards and I arrived at about the same time. We found the victim's body on a gurney next to the mortuary's crematorium. The fire was burning full-bore. The body had been scheduled to go into the flames at almost the same time the piece of bone was found. The phone calls had fortunately stopped the process.

Dr. Richards worked quickly to reexamine the victim's skull, removing every loose piece of fractured bone. There were more than a dozen pieces that we would be able to work with. To my knowledge, no one in a criminal investigation had ever attempted to reconstruct a fragmented skull from one source and then physically match it to the rest of the skull recovered from a remote location, the ultimate jigsaw puzzle. And the ultimate evidence to place the violent action in the garage of the victim's sister's house.

There was something else matted up in the remaining blood and tissue, small particles of stuff that didn't seem to belong there. I removed a piece and spread it out flat. It was a feather! For the most part, the crime scene work was complete. Now the work of analyzing and interpreting the evidence would begin.

Let's stop for a moment and consider the list of physical evidence collected to this point.

**Crime Scene One: The Abandoned Vehicle**

1. Body and attached clothing

2. Bedspread contaminated with suspected brain tissue, blood, and gasoline

3. Dog food bowl containing suspected brain tissue

4. Transfer electrician's tape removed from the trunk area

5. Suspected controlled substance (drugs) removed from the trunk

6. Suspected brain and blood tissue from the lower left rear fender

7. Two plaster casts of impressions in mud

Numerous photographs taken by the department's crime scene photographer also became evidence representing the scene before anything was altered.

**Crime Scene Two: The Overturned Vehicle**

1. Gas can

2. Pry bar

3. One pair of shoes (no mud)

**Autopsy One**

1. Pieces of skull indicating the charred entrance hole

2. Blood-soaked Lucky Strike package

**Autopsy Two**

1. Remaining pieces of fractured skull

2. Feathers

The key issues to be established in the case were:

*Identity of the victim.* This was verified by comparing the inked prints obtained from the corpse to the ten-print card of the vehicle's registered owner, Steven Brush.

*Location of the killing.* The Cabot location of the vehicle was definitely not the place of the killing, nor was the inside of the car. The blood and brain splatter pattern inside the garage of the Garden Grove house plus the fragment of human bone that fit into the reconstructed skull of the victim placed the killing at that location. The matching of the skull fragments is discussed below.

*Cause and manner of death.* The autopsy established the cause of death as massive cerebral damage due to close-range gunshot wound.

*Weapon used.* The shotgun located by Jim White in the Garden Grove house was identified as the murder weapon based on the blood and feathers found adhering to the barrel. The feathers on the shotgun barrel and in the debris of the skull provided associative information to assist in reconstructing the events of the crime. The victim's blood type information matched the blood on the barrel. Both the blood and the brain found in and on the Cadillac and on various objects in the garage and house had matching class characteristics to the victim's blood type based on several classification systems in use at the time. Although the blood and brain could have come from another person, the nature of the victim's trauma and the distribution of the blood and brains at both scenes provided convincing evidence that no other victims were involved.

*Person(s) responsible for the killing.* The two subjects apprehended after the chase were charged with the murder of the victim. They were placed at the scene by their impressions in the mud between the two vehicles and the similarities of the two sources of gasoline.

Prior to the trial, I compared the suspect's boots to the plaster casts made at the first crime scene. All the class characteristics were present. The size and style of the boots matched the impression. Although the boots were well-worn, no accidental markings were visible. There was however, a transfer of information that established individuality.

These boots were the type issued by the government, called jump boots. They were high-top, calf-length. It was a tedious job for the wearer just to lace and unlace each boot, so it became common practice to have a shoemaker install a vertical zipper on the inward side of each boot. I had done the same thing when I was in the military. The boot would be sliced open by hand and a zipper sewn in place. The exact placement of the shoemaker's handiwork was random, as opposed to a factory installation.

The boot impression had been made in soft mud and was two or three inches deep. Jim White and I had filled the entire hole with the plaster mix. An examination of the appropriate location on the cast revealed the replica of the zipper, in the precise location as on the boot. This was a great lesson on the value of making a plaster cast, since the zipper marking wasn't visible in the close-up photograph of the impression.

The second cast was compared to the second suspect. Only the size was similar, but nonetheless the information was useful in reconstructing the events of the crime. The presence of gasoline on the bedspread and inside the Cadillac that had matching characteristics to the gasoline in the gas can found inside the getaway vehicle also helped establish the suspect's intentions.

Jim White connected the suspects to the victim's car by matching the electrician's tape found on the Cadillac's (the transfer piece) bumper to the larger piece wrapped around the pry bar found in the getaway car. The transfer piece visually matched the tape still on the tool in color, texture, and composition, all class characteristics. More important, the transfer piece fit back into the torn edge of the tape still on the pry bar. Two matching borders are individual characteristics, and the fit is absolute proof of a common origin. It is circumstantial evidence, in that it doesn't establish a specific time or place (the car could have been anywhere) when the transfer of the tape actually occurred, but it does place the pry tool on the bumper and implies physical force sufficient to break the material apart.

The second physical match involved an individual human identification. I predicted that the small piece of bone found in the suspect's garage had at one time been a part of the victim's skull. The reconstruction of the skull could establish a single source for all the pieces (see Photo 1).

Since it was my idea, it was appropriate that I got to do the work. I followed a process taught to me by Dr. Judy Suchey, a forensic anthropology professor at California State University at Fullerton. Suchey spends most of her free time assisting the coroners in Southern California in identifying skeletal remains. I took all the pieces recovered at the autopsy and cooked them slowly for several hours in a solution of ammonia and water. The ammonia dissolves the fats and tissue in and on the bone.

Once the pieces were dry, I was able to glue them back together. I felt I was doing a good job. The big pieces went together quickly. I was able to reconstruct the entrance hole and surrounding area with no problem. But I still had a lot of little pieces and the one piece from the garage that didn't fit. I worked on it for a long time but still could not figure it out. Judy Suchey agreed to take a look. I felt a little better about it when she admitted it took her a while to match it up, and she had a colleague working with her.

After all that work, the defense objected to the introduction of the skull into evidence on the grounds that it was inflammatory. The judge agreed and would not allow the actual skull into the courtroom. I was able to demonstrate the reconstruction and fit by using photographs.

All this physical evidence along with the deputies' observations and the circumstance of the chase and their arrest in the area virtually assured the suspect's association to the Cabot crime scene.

Considering the entrance wound characteristics, the gunshot debris associated inside the victim's wounds, and the observations at both scenes, it was possible to form an opinion of what occurred inside the suspect's garage.

*Other evidence*

The drugs were analyzed to establish them as a controlled substance. This fit the information the investigators received from associates of the victim and the defendants, Michael McNabb and Joseph Ruschak. They were all dealing drugs together. The defendants suspected Brush was cheating them. They never explained what happened, but they may have simply asked him to open his trunk so they could verify his proclaimed innocence. Apparently he refused.

A few days after the initial search of the house, the investigators learned from informants that the violence actually started in the living room. Brush was struck from behind with a tire iron and knocked to the floor. From that point he was dragged through the kitchen and the washroom, and into the garage. One of the two went outside and started his motorcycle, sans muffler, of course, drowning out any sounds from within the garage. You already know what happened next.

McNabb and Ruschak were convicted of first-degree murder.

## FORENSIC SCIENCES

Forensic science is an all-inclusive label that covers a variety of technical disciplines that are applied to investigations that may end up in a court of law. Investigations are not limited to criminal cases since evidence is also introduced in civil cases in essentially the same manner.

The word *forensic* means "related to debate or argument." A forensic team is found in most schools but it is not a group of expert crime scene investigators searching for clues; it is the campus debating team. The latest definition of forensics includes the phrase "suitable for the courts." Apart from the consequences to the loser, there is very little difference between a debate and a courtroom trial.

## The Advocate System

The advocate system, that is, representing a single point of view, gives the opposing attorneys the freedom to select witnesses who they believe will testify to information that supports their contentions. Under this system, no attorney need call a witness to the stand who could hurt his point of view. When critical physical evidence is involved, it is not unusual for each side to call its own expert. One expert says yes while the other says no.

This raises the question: How can two scientists look at the same piece of evidence and form completely opposing opinions? This question has many answers, so for now, consider that one value of the advocate system is what is referred to as "check and balance." There can be two sides to a story, or two interpretations, or one witness could have made a mistake, or one witness could be giving false or misleading information. In this system it is the judge or the jury that makes the final decision, believing who and what they want to believe.

Forensic science testimony is generally presented in an advocate manner in the United States, but it may also be given by an individual selected by judges who, for reasons of their own, believe that a clarification of facts is required. In this situation the witness is acting as a friend of the court. The friend's testimony may be challenged by either side. This form of neutral scientific testimony is preferred in some countries, such as England.

## What is Evidence?

Evidence can be anything. For example, it can be the eye-witness account of an event. Or it may be a substance, such as a tiny speck of blood or a ton of marijuana. Evidence of either type can be used by investigators to conclude that a crime was committed, to make an arrest, and to seek a criminal complaint against a suspect. Further, such evidence can be used by prosecuting attorneys as they attempt to convince a judge or jury that the defendant committed the crime charged, while defense attorneys may use the same evidence or additional evidence to show their client's innocence.

When a witness states, "I was robbed by that guy!" under oath in a court of law, and then points out the defendant, the words and the identification are considered direct evidence. Unless challenged successfully by the defense, the spoken word of the victim is considered proof that a crime was committed by the defendant and justifies a guilty verdict.

Evidence that does not directly prove a fact is called *indirect*. Circumstantial evidence is used to imply an event. Almost all physical evidence is circumstantial. For example, a fingerprint is considered evidence that someone touched the host surface. That fact alone may imply some circumstance about how a crime was alleged to have been committed. Eventually, learning the owner of the fingerprint and how it could or could not have been deposited at the scene may narrow the possible circumstances to a single conclusion. Lacking a believable account to explain otherwise, the trier of fact, judge or jury, can conclude the suspect was at the scene.

Some physical evidence, however, may be considered proof of a fact. For example, possessing a controlled substance, once its identity has overcome any challenge, *is* the crime. Certain laws specify per se proof of a crime. For example, in many states a driver with a blood alcohol level of 0.08 percent weight volume is per se in violation of driving under the influence.

## EVIDENCE:

### CLASSIFICATION AND IDENTIFICATION

The process of classification and identification is at the very core of all the forensic sciences. In almost every situation, the primary role of forensic scientists is identifying an object and/or connecting it to a source. We do so by studying the object's characteristics. Someone once said, "If it waddles like a duck, quacks like a duck, and smells like a duck, then it is a duck!" Unfortunately, all evidence is not so easily identified.

Remember, forensics means "debatable." There are two sides to every trial. Two or more forensic witnesses may not *interpret* characteristics exactly the same way. It is possible that either expert could be wrong. And even the best investigators, under pressure or just making a quick identification, can overlook something important, even if it's right beneath their eyes, like Poe's purloined letter.

To be as thorough as possible, then, the process of forensic identification should always begin with something like the duck test. For instance, we discover something in a suspect's closet, examine it, note its characteristics, and place these characteristics in different categories. Thus, we decide it is a shoe, but not just any shoe: This is an athletic shoe.

We have just made our first critical inclusions and eliminations. When we call it an athletic shoe, we place it in a different class than all the other kinds of shoes in the world. For example, this is definitely not a dress shoe, unless you live and play in Southern California.

We can see additional class characteristics: the color, the size, and the specific pattern of the sole, which may include the brand name or identifying logo. Color is not a factor in comparing this shoe to an impression found at the crime scene, but the other three observations significantly reduce the number of potential suspect shoes. Now we must compare this shoe to the mark found at the scene and, ideally, to an unused sample of the same brand and model of the shoe. (The process is explained further in Chapter 4.)

All forensic identification ultimately involves comparative analysis. Any fingerprint found at a crime scene is useless unless it can be compared and matched to prints collected from a known individual. Blood spots on a suspect's clothing have to be compared to the blood collected from the victim, the suspect's own blood, and blood from anyone else who is known to have had something to do with the incident. Even a sample of powder that is a suspected drug will be submitted to tests that develop charts and graphs that are then compared to charts and graphs obtained from known chemical compounds.

Because forensic scientists are humans, and humans have been known to make mistakes—and if a forensic scientist makes a mistake, an innocent person could be jailed or a guilty one set free—modern forensic laboratories have many built-in programs that assure the quality of the laboratories' results. Such programs involve *duplicate testing*—a second analyst independently repeats the test process on the same material; *peer review*—two scientists independently examine and interpret the results of the same test, and *supervisor review*—a senior scientist studies the entire process of identification for accuracy and completeness.

All chemical or physical procedures should also include numerous quality control samples, which are analyzed along with the questioned samples using all the same reagents and equipment. These quality control samples are made of known materials in various concentrations that will react predictably, and blank samples that must not react at all. Any unexpected reactions with the control samples alert the examiner that a problem exists with the process and all results are in doubt. After the problem is discovered and corrected, the samples must be reanalyzed to the satisfaction of the quality assurance standards of the laboratory.

To be considered a valid test, a new method must pass a proficiency test; and all methods, on occasion, should be revalidated by proficiency samples. A proficiency test may consist of known samples or may be submitted for testing blind—a mixture of positive and negative samples submitted in a sequence unknown to the examiner. Double-blind tests are submitted to the lab from an outside source. Answers are available after results have been filed with the source.

## The Value of Physical Evidence

Attorneys consider the significance of a piece of evidence its "probative value," that is, the level of proof the evidence provides either to prove or to disprove a crime has been committed or that the defendant was the one who did the deed. Different types of evidence and varying circumstances influence the eventual probative value.

Evidence may also have an associative value, that is, its usefulness in placing a suspect at a location, proving the suspect handled evidence or came in contact with another person.

## The Product Rule

The association of one thing to another is intuitive in the sense, for example, that a getaway car was red and the defendant was stopped in a red car. However, before that evidence and any other form of physical evidence has probative or true associative value, it is necessary to understand the frequency of the occurrence of the characteristics being considered. If the only reason the defendant was arrested was because he was driving a red car, then the likelihood of other red cars in the area during the same time period must be considered. Likelihood translates to probability. Probability of an event is calculated by considering all the facts known and applying a value for their frequency of occurrence. When all the values are considered together, the process is described as applying the *product rule*.

The product rule applies to *any* series of independent characteristics. Once the independence of a characteristic is determined, then the frequency of one can be multiplied by that of the next and so on. For example, consider the defendant I described above and factor in some more information. Pulling numbers out of the air for illustrative purposes only, suppose that one out of every ten passenger vehicles on the road is a Ford, one out of every twelve passenger vehicles is a station wagon, and one out of every eighteen vehicles is red. The product rule would tell us that one out of every 2,160 vehicles on the road is a red Ford station wagon. That is: $10 \times 12 \times 18 = 2,160$.

Now let's consider two more characteristics: one out of two vehicles on the road has four doors, and one of 1,100 has simulated wood paneling on each side. Is the product now 1 out of 4,752,000? No. The last two characteristics are not independent characteristics to true station wagons. All true station wagons have four doors, and wood paneling on station wagons is common. Consider that wood panels are on one out of three station wagons. The product is one out of 6,480, not 4,752,000.

In this situation it is unlikely that a second red Ford station wagon would be in the area. If the fact that a man was driving is factored in, then the chance of two men in red Ford station wagons driving in the same area is even more unlikely, *but not impossible*. To prove or disprove this concept, go to any part of town. Count and categorize three thousand cars by their characteristics. Then go to three other parts of town and repeat the process and send the numbers to me. Then I won't have to guess at these numbers anymore.

The more independent characteristics, the more improbable it is that there would be two such occurrences. What is not considered in my simplified example is variations due to subpopulations. For example, the frequency of station wagons would likely vary at different times and locations, as on Saturday night at the heavy metal/grunge concert hall, versus Monday afternoon in the vicinity of the local grade school as school is letting out.

In some forms of evidence, the spatial relationship of the random characteristics and their likelihood of coincidental duplication can be calculated using the product rule. For instance, the fine detail in fingerprints and accidental marks on tools are considered random independent characteristics.

To place physical evidence at the appropriate probative or associative value, I will use two terms, *class characteristics* and *individual characteristics*. A class characteristic is an identifiable quality that is common to a group of objects; for example, any kind of button. An individual characteristic is a quality or combination of qualities that establish the uniqueness of one item or one person, allowing the conclusion that it is one of a kind. To some extent, individualizing items is an everyday occurrence in everyone's daily routine. It is how you know at a glance that you are looking at your car or your shoes or your friend. Technically, the number and location of independent or random characteristics provide the discriminating examiner with the information to separate one item from a group of similar specimens.

## Types of Physical Evidence and Their Potential for Individualization

I offer a list of the following types of physical evidence as a starting point to understanding the potential for individualization, beginning with the items of the highest probative value.

### Friction Ridge Transfer Impressions

This category includes fingerprints, palm prints, and bare footprints. It has the highest probative value because it can often be identified to a specific individual (see photo, insert page 2).

This type of information is frequently found at crime scenes in one or more forms: latent, visible, or plastic (three-dimensional). Latent means hidden, so latent prints must be made visible by some physical or chemical process. Friction ridge information found on finger and toe tips can be divided into classes of patterns, loops, whorls, and arches, or they may be composites of the patterns. A closer look reveals that the patterns are made up of ridges that divide occasionally, bifurcation, and ridges that end, occasionally. These events collectively are called minutia or Galton points, and are class characteristics. A closer look at the ridges in the photo reveals some small white dots that are pores, the openings of sweat glands. Some examiners rely heavily on pore distributions, a science called poroscopy. What makes the ridges and their minutia of great value for the identification process is that there is no predictable reason for their spatial distribution. There are hundreds of them in small areas of our skin, as on each fingertip, and the distribution is entirely random. Even identical twins who may have similar patterns and loops on each finger have different minutia.

The basic fingertip patterns with their minutia points and pores can be directly registered and classified by one of several types of automated fingerprint indentification systems (AFIS). Standard inked ten-print cards (rolled) or paperless systems (live scan/direct read) can be used to register the data. Live scan methods use a digital camera to capture the same detail seen on an inked card. So-called ten-print classifications are uniformly accepted as personal identification.

Investigators seldom find more than partial ridge information at a crime scene. However, a detailed examination of the relative location of minutia, bifurcations, and ridge endings clearly show that these characteristics can be individualized. If a crime scene print is clear enough to show ten or more points of connecting minutia, and the minutia points match those of a print found elsewhere, it can be stated without compromise that the two prints have a common origin. (The specifics of fingerprint science are described in Chapter 3.)

## Physiological Fluids and Tissue When Examined for DNA Genetic Types

DNA—deoxyribonucleic acid—is unique to each individual, except identical twins. Each person's chromosomal DNA is a product, based on genetic principle, wherein half the factors are inherited from the mother and half from the father. Discharged blood, semen, vaginal fluid, saliva, skin, hairs pulled with the root follicle attached, bone marrow, tooth pulp, and other fluids containing nucleated cells—all materials often found at scenes of violent crimes—are potential sources of DNA, chromosomal and/or mitochondrial.

Our bodies are made up of many different types of cells, but for the purpose of discussing DNA, there are only two types—nucleated and non-nucleated. DNA is found in the cell's nucleus. The DNA in blood is contained in the nucleus of white blood cells and platelets but not in *human* red blood cells, since they are non-nucleated cells. Some animals—for instance, fish and birds—do have nucleated red cells. Epithelial cells are nucleated. They compose our outer skin and the lining of most of our body cavities, such as the mouth, nose, vagina, and urethra, the conduit inside the penis. Epithelial cells, not blood, are the source of DNA in skin, root follicles, saliva, vaginal fluid, and seminal fluid from vasectomized or otherwise aspermatic males.

The application of DNA information to crime scene interpretation originated in England in the mid-1980s. As more background information is developed on the frequency of distribution of selected genetic markers within families and races, the elimination factor increases, enhancing the potential for the individualization of the sample. (The forensic application of DNA is described in Chapter 7.)

## Physical Matches

During violent activities, things tear or break apart unexpectedly or may be intentionally torn or randomly cut by a tool such as scissors. This type of evidence can also be labeled as a jigsaw puzzle match. The test is: Do two pieces of similarly appearing material, one from the crime scene and one found in the possession of the suspect, fit back together. (Physical match evidence is described in Chapter 4.)

## Impressions

Impression evidence is created when one object comes in contact with another and patterns are transferred or embedded from one surface to the other. Occasionally, information is transferred from one object to the opposing object, for example, when automobiles collide. Three types of impressions are included in the category: two-dimensional, three-dimensional, and striations.

A two-dimensional impression is like a rubber stamp transfer. Three-dimensional impressions occur when the receiving material is pliable and softer than the source, as when a suspect steps in mud or a tool is used to pry open a window or a door. Striations are linear scratches. Riflings are striations made in a bullet by the lands and grooves cut into the harder steel of a gun barrel.

Impression evidence can often be individualized when accidental or random defects are identifiable. Misinterpreting factory marks as accidental marks can be the consequence of uninformed evidence examiners working in a system without a quality assurance program or any form of critical review. (The difference between accidental marks and factory marks that may be mistaken for individuality is discussed in Chapter 5. Impression evidence is described in Chapter 4.)

## Physiological Fluids

The individualization of blood, semen, and other body fluids was rarely possible when relying on what some people now call the classic or conventional systems that predate DNA. Crime scene blood is usually dry and certainly seen out of context. Red blood cells are seldom found intact, so certain typing systems are not used on crime scene blood. The most noted is Rh. Whenever you read a novel in which the scene blood is typed A positive, for example, you know the author didn't do his or her homework. While reporting any of the ABO system types remains possible, Rh factors (positive or negative) have been considered unreliable since the 1960s. Serologists, after comparing results on simulated crime scene samples, discovered they could not duplicate their results consistently.

Nevertheless, an amazing amount of information can be derived from a single drop of blood, dry or not, properly collected at a crime scene. The probative value of the ABO typing system when combined with information from what serologists call the polymorphic proteins and enzymes, circa 1973, all genetic markers, can be very convincing depending on the circumstances. (Physiological fluid evidence is described in Chapter 6.)

## Trace Evidence

The word "trace" describes evidence that is small, often too small to see, and always too small to consider attempts at physical matches. The use of force during the commission of a crime—such as breaking and entering, assault, hit-and-run, and arson—results in items being smashed and is responsible for the production of these tiny particles of evidence. Chips of glass, paint, metal, and plastic and particles of soil whose origin is the crime scene are frequently carried away by the unaware perpetrator. The residue of a flammable accelerant can be recovered from arson scenes and matched to a few drops of fuel still in the arsonist's gasoline can.

A single item of trace evidence is characterized by its chemical and physical properties, and because we are talking about mass-produced commodities, it always has a limited probative value. But consider an arsonist who breaks a window to gain entry to a building, pours gasoline around the structure, and gets mud on his shoes as he exits the scene. If he is apprehended soon after, three types of matching trace evidence could associate him to that scene. I call this a trail of trace evidence. The more matching items identified and associated with the scene, the longer the trail and the higher the probative value of the accumulated evidence. (Trace evidence is described further in Chapter 8.)

## Fibers and Hairs

Fibers can be naturally occurring or can be man-made. For example, cotton and linen are plant materials, while wool and silk are animal products. Examples of man-made fibers are acetate, rayon, nylon, polyester, and orlon. Within these groups, there are numerous variations, depending on the intended purpose of the fibers. The same synthetic product may be formulated for different functions, such as textile fibers for clothing or rugs, and fibers for rope and string production. The appearance of the fiber may vary dramatically in microscopic appearance and cross section. A skilled fiber examiner can distinguish one from another and provide considerable information about the fiber source to the police investigators. But that's the end of the good news.

Fibers are made in bulk quantities and distributed internationally. Finding an out-of-place fiber on the clothing of a suspected rapist that matches the fibers of the victim's sweater, for example, has very limited probative value, because there are thousands of other potential sources for the same kind of fiber. A case in point: Red wool fibers were removed from the clothing of an infant who had been kidnapped and murdered. An individual wearing a red sweater made of fibers that matched those found on the baby's clothing was located and was considered the prime suspect. But the source of the fibers came into question when a red wool blanket was discovered in the victim's crib. These fibers also matched those on the victim's clothing and were a likely source of the evidence fibers. Nevertheless, on occasion fibers can still be powerful probative evidence. (I will discuss cases where fibers became key evidence in Chapter 8.)

Unattached hairs that have not been forcefully removed or are found without roots can be classified by their color and morphological characteristics, that is, variations in form and structure. These variations are class characteristics and are common to large groups of people. (See Chapter 7 about mitochondrial DNA.)

To further complicate the evaluation of hairs, there are variations within the variations. For instance, a person whose natural hair is considered blond actually has a gradation of colors that may range from medium brown to almost white. The composite color looks blond. But if only one hair is found at the crime scene, it may not be representative of what we anticipate the suspect looks like. In fact, it could be misleading. In any event, a single hair doesn't offer much probative help. Additionally, hairs growing on different parts of the body have their own morphology.

Most animal hair is obviously different from human hair. It is usually not a problem making the distinction since the morphology is grossly different. With a few exceptions, animal hairs grow to a specific length, then fall out, usually on the couch. Sheep and some dogs, poodles and bichons frises, have hair that continues to grow and must be cut occasionally. Their hairs could be misidentified by an unaware examiner.

Most animals have two distinctly different types of hairs on their backs: guard hairs and down hairs. The guard hairs are often coarse and multicolored. The down hairs are very fine and much softer. Animal hairs can be classified by species, as in the type used for fur coats or those named as endangered creatures. Animals have their own unique DNA.

**The Bottom Line**

The value of physical evidence varies from type to type and case to case. In some investigations, its potential may never be fully appreciated. In some jurisdictions it is a matter of the availability of trained personnel who can respond to crime scenes and collect the appropriate evidence. In the following chapters, I describe an assortment of crime scene investigations in which the value of teamwork and the value of the physical evidence are put to its best use.

**chapter two**

# The Crime Scene Team

## Introduction

The purpose of investigating an incident is to determine if a crime has been committed and, if so, to bring to justice the person or persons who committed the crime. The investigation begins the moment the incident is reported, by either a victim or a witness, or by an officer who comes upon a crime by chance. It ends with the final verdict of the court or jury.

Fictional heroes always solve their cases. For instance, the lead character of CBS's hit program, *CSI*, Gil Grissom, managed to perform most if not all of the jobs of the usual team players. If the screenplay had been solely about the day-to-day work of a forensic scientist, most of the audience would have been sound asleep about six minutes into the story.

A real crime scene team is a group of professional investigators, each trained in a variety of special disciplines needed to form a complete team. The common goal of the team is to locate and document all the evidence at the scene, and each member must be allowed to work the scene independently of the others' influence and to challenge the others' assumptions. It is presumed that other members of the criminal justice system—other investigators, attorneys, judges, and jurors—will at some future occasion need to understand the scene and the evidence collected as intimately as if they were present during the original investigation.

The success of an investigation depends on many factors. A crime may be solved by good timing or pure luck, such as when an officer catches a suspect in the act. Some factors are unpredictable and often uncontrollable: the weather, the time of day or night the crime is reported, the location of the incident. But the most important factors to successful investigation are planning and teamwork. The investigative agency must have personnel trained in crime scene procedures with a crime scene protocol to follow and access to the proper equipment. In the investigation described below, luck was a factor—some amount usually is—but the case was solved by good teamwork.

## CRIME SCENE:

### "NOW I LOVE HER, NOW I DON'T"

My phone was ringing again. It was 3:45 A.M. It seems, unfortunately, that most crime scenes are discovered at night. The caller, Larry Bersch, a Costa Mesa detective, wanted my presence at the scene of a homicide. He gave me the location, an apartment complex in Costa Mesa at Eighteenth and Wallace, and I assured him I could be there within twenty minutes. The quicker you can investigate a scene, the better.

As I drove into the parking lot, I saw two uniformed officers shining their flashlights into one of the many parked vehicles in the lot. They turned, realized who I was when they saw the badge in my hand, and pointed in the direction of a narrow walkway leading toward the apartment complex.

"This is her car, 10–28 confirms it. But you can't see much inside," said one of the officers who was trying to shine his light through the dew that had formed on the outside of the windows. A 10–28 is the radio code for a vehicle registration inquiry with the California Department of Motor Vehicles. I noticed the cars parked on each side of this one were much wetter, if that meant anything.

I walked down the path between two garages that opened to a common driveway. On the other side of the driveway, about thirty feet across, were two more garages facing the same driveway. Someone was taking photos, lighting the entire scene momentarily with the flash. I saw Bersch standing near a small black purse that was lying on the walkway. Detective Gary Thompson was writing or drawing something in his notepad as R. C. Johnson, a sheriff's crime scene investigator, took the photos. I was close enough when the next flash went off to see a pool of red liquid that turned out to be blood. Bersch saw me, then glanced at his wristwatch long enough to make a proper subtraction. It was four A.M. I made it in fifteen minutes.

"It looks like she got this far and then got zapped. At least two to the head, according to [Tom] Walezak [the deputy coroner], and one in the hand. He went straight to Hoag E.R. She was DOA, by the way. Don't ask me why they transported her," Bersch said. It is not unusual for bodies to be removed from the scene even though there is no sign of life. It screws up the crime scene, but if one in a million victims is saved by some heroics, it's worth it.

"One of our units was about three blocks away," Thompson said, "motor off, and heard four shots. The victim's boyfriend was waiting for her in their apartment, and he heard the same four shots; two, a pause, then two more. Nothing to indicate much of a struggle. Her purse is here, no robbery and nothing to indicate much of a fight."

"She lives here?"

"Yes," Bersch answered. "She worked at a bar in Fullerton, got off at two or a little after, and from what we know up to now, left alone about 2:15 on her way home. She has a car, parked in the outer parking lot."

"I saw it as I was driving in. Your guys were looking it over."

"The gunshots were right around three A.M.," Thompson said, "so it looks like she drove straight home. She could have made a quick stop, milk, something. But look around. There is nothing here."

I did look around. There were marks on the pavement that outlined where the victim had been. The blood on the sidewalk appeared to be primarily from her head and perhaps her hand. The pooled blood had already started to dry around the edges and congeal in the center. The small amount of blood indicated that she died soon after being shot or the medics had arrived very quickly. I was guessing the shot to the head stopped her vital functions—specifically, the brain directing her heart to pump. With no blood pressure there is not much bleeding except drainage due to gravity. There were no shell casings. Unless the shooter took the time to pick them up, which wasn't too likely, we were talking revolver.

R. C. had photographed some keys—hers, as it turned out. She probably had them in her hand ready to unlock her apartment door. He pointed out a pair of earrings loose on the dirt within a few feet of where she was shot.

"Was her purse opened when you got here?" I asked.

"No, we looked in it for her ID," Bersch said. "Found who she was and a business card for a bar where she worked. The place was closed but Fullerton PD had an emergency phone number for the owner. That's how we got the skinny on when and how she left work. There's money in there. No robbery. Wallet. The usual lady's stuff. Nothing appears to be missing."

R. C. called out. He had found something important. As he took his photos, he had worked his way a few feet south of the blood toward the victim's apartment. There was a vehicle parked next to the path. R. C. was pointing at a chunk of metal directly under the left side of the bumper. It was a bullet, badly damaged. R. C. was down on his knees.

"There is hair stuck in this thing!" he said.

It is not unusual to find material embedded in a lead bullet. Anything in its path is torn or broken, so small particles can be stuck in the lead. Maybe there were other bullets to be found. I walked back toward the victim's parking area shining my flashlight down into the bushes, looking for anything of interest. There was a narrow planted area bordering each side of the walk. No shoe prints, no bullets, nothing.

I hadn't gone far when I realized how dark it was between the buildings. This hadn't registered earlier, when I had walked in. I looked back at the scene and beyond and saw other night lights, all on. You'd think there would be a light for the pathway between the body and the parking area. I was looking at the side of the building and may have said out loud, "There should be one here." There was, about six and a half feet above the ground, but it was not lit.

One step off the sidewalk and I was directly under the fixture. The lightbulb was in place, but when I touched it near the socket with the tip of my fingernail, it was loose. "R. C., we need a photo of this!" I said.

"Looks like the shooter was lying in wait," Bersch said. Lying in wait to commit a murder is a capital offense in California because the killer has time to plan the crime, and more importantly, has time for a change of mind. Premeditation and malice aforethought are, thus, a given. A loose lightbulb, one that should be working, could demonstrate the killer had a plan and had laid a trap—a dark walkway where the killer would have all the advantages.

After the photograph, the bulb was unscrewed in a manner that would protect any fingerprints on the area normally touched by someone placing or removing a bulb. If the killer did what we were thinking, fingerprints were a possibility.

Neither Bersch nor I could think of anything else to do. It was now almost seven A.M. Bersch had asked for an immediate autopsy. In a case like this, with an unknown killer on the loose, the investigators need leads. The autopsy may be a better source of information than the scene, so when every minute counts, you cannot wait for a pathologist's office hours. This autopsy would be conducted at a local mortuary, a practice that continued until 1981, when the county agreed to construct its first forensic morgue.

At daylight, Bersch had assigned two detectives to start knocking on doors, in the event that anyone other than the RP (reporting party) saw or heard anything that could be helpful. Bersch, Thompson, and I headed for the mortuary. R. C.'s tour of duty was almost over, so he would stay at the scene and finish taking overall photos and measurements but would be replaced by another crime scene investigator who would work the autopsy. This is a bad practice. I think the same people who work the scene should also work the autopsy whenever possible.

The mortuary, West Cliff Chapel in downtown Costa Mesa, had no X ray, inadequate lighting, no ventilation, and little or no room for the crime scene team to participate in the process. The only good news was that the pathologist, Dr. Richard Fukumoto, and his assistant were there ready to get started. Andy Anderson took R. C.'s place. Costa Mesa investigator Arnie Appleman and the ID investigator, David Leighton, also joined the team at the autopsy. It was a crowd but a good crowd.

A cursory examination of the victim, still fully dressed, provided new information. She was dressed in a skirt and a pullover sweater with a matching cardigan. Her nylons were in place, but her shoes were missing. Nothing had been obviously torn or even pulled up, down, or out to indicate a sexual attack. There were *two* apparent entrance holes in her sweater, both gunshots, that had not been recognized while at the scene. One was on her left breast and the other on her lower left side just below the last rib. Muzzle debris was present on the skin of her hand and on the left side of her sweater, indicating these shots were close in, within inches. But there was no debris on the sweater over the breast. Close-up photos were taken of all the defects.

"This is strange," Dr. Fukumoto said. "Have a look." He was studying her sweater where it covered her left breast. "The sweater appears to be embedded in her breast, like it was poked into her."

The pathologist was right. The sweater was twisted from within, as if it had been pulled in from a point on the backside and turned repeatedly, like one would wring out a washcloth from its center.

After the initial photo had been taken, Dr. Fukumoto began the process of extracting the sweater. He pinched the cloth between his thumb and forefinger with each hand and pulled outward. As the cloth slid out of her breast, the twisted sweater unwound, turn by turn. When the cloth was spread flat, there, nestled in the final indentation, like an egg in a bird's nest, was a shiny metallic object.

"It's a goddamn bullet," at least three people said simultaneously.

It had been polished clean, buffed against the wool of the sweater as it spun to rest, twisting and taking the sweater with it, but the sweater held together. There was no hole in it.

"It's the hand wound. One shot, through the hand and into the sweater, most of the energy lost so it couldn't get all the way through the material," Fukumoto said, holding his hand in front of his chest as if he were about to be shot.

"It looks like a .38," I said, "but I'll tell you one thing for sure, it's not going to help much. There are no striations left on it."

Fukumoto pulled the sweater up to examine the wound in the breast. The victim was wearing a bra that had apparently also been pushed into the wound.

"Penetration, but not more than one to one and a half inches into the fatty tissue of her breast. It didn't even make it to her ribs," Fukumoto said.

With the sweater up for the first time, the wound on the left side was fully visible. Fukumoto moved to the right side to look for an exit wound. There was none. He touched her right side with the tip of his finger, directly opposite the entrance wound.

"I don't believe this, it's right here," he said, pointing to a large bump.

I touched the spot. It was very hard. After the area was photographed, the pathologist made an incision less than an inch wide and a quarter inch deep just below the bump. With one hand cupped below the cut, he pushed with the other just above the bump. A bullet popped out.

Two bullets had already been recovered from the body and the autopsy hadn't formally started yet, in the traditional manner with a Y-incision. Fukumoto gave me the bullet. This one was pristine, with clearly visible land and groove marks.

From this point on the autopsy would conform to the standard procedures of all forensic postmortem examinations. The remaining clothing was removed, and oral, vaginal, and anal swabs were collected in the event sexual activity became a question. Her pubic hairs were combed out and all loose hairs were packaged. Representative head and pubic hairs were pulled, to include the roots, and packaged as standards. The debris on the back of her right hand was swabbed with cotton, to be tested for gunshot residue if needed, and the undersides of her fingernails were scraped, producing nothing noteworthy.

This involves a thorough examination of all parts of the body, locating anatomical trauma, establishing methods of injury, and collecting toxicology specimens and stomach contents, all to determine the medical cause of death. Any natural causes of death must be eliminated by direct and, later, microscopic examination.

Now Fukumoto made the Y-incision. To picture this process, stand in front of a mirror and place your index fingers on your upper chest, the right about two inches above your right nipple, and the left above your left nipple. Now move your fingers downward at an angle so they meet about six inches above your navel. From that point move one finger down to just above the hairline of your pubic area. The next step following the Y-incision (don't try this) is to reflect the skin, that is, pull it open to reveal the rib cage, and then cut and remove the entire front section of the ribs. This opens the abdominal cavity and exposes the viscera, the vital organs, and associated tissues. Before altering the relative position of the viscera, Dr. Fukumoto followed the path of the bullet that had entered the victim's left side.

"There is damage to the liver but no major blood vessels were damaged," he said. "Relatively speaking, this wound caused almost no damage. Treatable . . . nonfatal . . ." The search for a cause of death would focus on the head.

Two entrance wounds, inches apart, were visible on the right side of the victim's head. One was just in front of the earlobe. The second wound was in the right temporal area, just above the ear. There was what Fukumoto called singeing and smudging on her skin around these wounds. He was describing muzzle blast debris, which means the weapon was in close proximity at the time it was fired, within inches. (See Chapter 5 for details.) Dr. Fukumoto rolled her head slightly. There was evidence of an exit wound on the left side. After photos, he began the process of opening the head. The high-pitched sound of the head saw almost masked the ringing of the phone.

It was for me. "We found something out here that looks important, can you come back to the scene?" a police officer asked.

"Now?"

"Well, it looks like blood, and it was you, I think, who said in the crime scene class that you shouldn't let blood lie around. The sun is coming up now. Didn't you say that it was bad for blood to stay in the sun?"

I didn't actually know which CMPD officer was talking to me but he was absolutely right. People *do* listen in our classes on crime scene processing.

Before I left, Fukumoto showed me the trajectory of the shot to the temporal area. It had an upward direction of 20 to 25 degrees and exited in the upper left temporal area. This was the bullet that was found at the scene. As he described the extensive avulsion (forceful tearing) of the brain and massive hemorrhage caused by the two projectiles, he removed a badly damaged metallic lump and offered it to me. This brain damage was clearly the cause of death. She hadn't lived for long after these shots.

The autopsy was over, for the most part, so I excused myself and headed back to the scene.

Coming from the mortuary, I approached the scene from the south side, driving west of Eighteenth Street, and saw Detective Strickland standing just off the sidewalk that led into the apartment complex. Earlier that night I had entered the scene from the north, as did the victim and the other members of the crime scene team. I parked and walked toward Strickland, who was pointing down at a reddish spot on the concrete walk.

It is amazing what you can reconstruct merely by looking at blood spots like these. We walked back, north, into the complex a short distance, and Strickland pointed out more spots. These spots were large, bigger than a dime. From the point where I started, the spots were about three feet apart. Big drops close together would indicate some fairly heavy bleeding. The drops were almost round, with just enough secondary splashing motion toward the south to indicate the bleeder was heading in that direction.

Sergeant Bersch arrived back at the scene in time to join in the observation process. Two facts were puzzling. First, the spots were farther apart as we walked back into the crime scene, and second, the initial drop was at least two hundred feet from where the victim had been found. The bleeder was headed south in no hurry, but bleeding more heavily with each step. Bersch and I walked past Strickland, past the curb line and out into the street. The spots, even closer together now, angled across the pavement to a point about ten feet from the south curb. At that point there were many spots close together, in fact overlapping, and here the trail stopped. Looking down at the pavement just to the east, I saw two heavy black rubber marks. "Looks like he decided to leave in a hurry," Strickland said from across the street. "I already checked at the nearest house. The guy who lives there heard someone peeling rubber just after three A.M. Even better, he told me what kind of car it was. Didn't see it but he heard it. He's a mechanic and restores Chevrolet Corvairs, so he knows the sound of the rear engine. It was the same sound, he's sure of it."

"I'll get a man on this right away," Bersch said. "We'll check every hospital in the county, if we have to, whether it's our guy who's hurt or whether he's nailed someone else. I've already checked the other departments. No one else is working a shooting as of 7:30 A.M."

By law, if anyone wounded by a firearm seeks treatment from a doctor or hospital, the doctor or staff must notify the local police. The police then investigate the shooting to determine the what, where, why, when, and how of the incident. A teletype was sent to all Southern California law enforcement agencies describing Costa Mesa's case and requesting information on any such investigation. No one replied. This could mean the suspect had treated himself without professional help, or if he did go for help, the nature of whatever caused the bleeding didn't arouse suspicion and simply wasn't reported. Detective Arnie Appleman, a recent promotee, got the tedious job. There are a lot of hospitals in Orange County.

Three days had passed with no news. I was at the lab when I got word that Bob Waganer, our firearms examiner, was looking for me. He had good news.

When I walked into his lab, he was holding up an enlargement of a photograph of what looked like a bunch of scratches. "You're looking at the bullet removed from her side," he said. "It's the only one with any detail. It's a .38 Special by weight. The other three bullets are dinged up but I'm sure they are also .38s. There's enough there to indicate that there was only one weapon. Here's the zinger. These land and groove marks were not made by a .38 Special weapon. Their number, direction, and angle of twist indicate a .380 Webley revolver, a British-made weapon that's pretty much obsolete. You ask, how can a gun fire a different caliber round? A .380 is a true .38, that is, .3800 of an inch in diameter. Our .38 is .3570. Their ammo will not fit in our .38s but our .38 ammo can be chambered and fired in their .380 revolvers. If you do so, though, the smaller round will have what I call a 'Webley wobble.' A lot of hot air will slip down the barrel before the bullet makes its way out. It loses a lot of its velocity and energy because of this. But the big problem is that not every round will necessarily pick up the same land and groove marks. I may have to test-fire a lot of rounds to reproduce the bullet you recovered."

"You just answered the $64,000 question, or at least one leading to it," I told him. "Your explanation of the lost energy explains why the chest slug didn't enter her body and the side shot didn't exit her body. I'll call Bersch and let him know what he's looking for."

Appleman was working his way toward the north end of the county, interviewing the intake staff at each hospital that provided emergency or walk-in service. One week after the shooting, Bersch called me with good news.

"Our guy walks into the Martin Luther Hospital in Anaheim at zero dark hundred the same morning of the shooting while we were still at the autopsy. The E.R. guy knows what to do. He calls their PD. They send their night dick. Our guy tells the cop that he was cleaning his gun and didn't realize it was loaded. Pop, he shoots himself. Guess where?"

"In Costa Mesa?"

"No, smartass, in the back of his left hand, with a .380 Webley."

"Anaheim bought his story?" I asked.

"Hook, line, and sinker. When their cop's at the hospital, we're still working the scene, so he doesn't know what we're doing. He goes back to the PD, files his report, and is off duty."

"But no follow-up, no nothing? Why?"

"It may have been our suspect's uniform. He's a security guard. A rent-a-cop, a wannabe, he has an ID, a little badge, and a big gun; he's even on a department's list for hire! I think they may pass over him."

Bersch asked me to meet him, Thompson, and their captain, Ed Glasgow, in Fullerton, a block away from the suspect's apartment. Along with two Fullerton Police Department detectives, they had been watching the apartment building from this vantage point.

"There's a bar down a couple of blocks on the other side of the street, the Orangefair," Bersch said, pointing in the direction of the establishment. "That's where she worked. She is, was, a waitress there. Worked that night until 2:30. Did I tell you the only vehicle registered to our suspect is a Chevrolet Corvair?"

The apartment building, a two-story structure, was anything but fancy. Not a dump but very plain, drab even. The suspect, Levester Coley Jr., lived on the second floor. Bersch asked one FPD officer to cover the back of the building while he took Thompson and the other FPD officer with him to Coley's door. The captain covered the front steps. Bersch told me to wait on the ground floor until he called me. That sounded more than fair to me.

Bersch approached the door while the others positioned themselves to each side of the door, out of sight should someone use the peephole. I could hear Bersch knocking on the door. A faint voice responded, something I couldn't make out.

"I'm a police officer. I need to ask you some questions," Bersch said loudly.

There was a pause that seemed long to me, but I'm sure it seemed a lot longer to Bersch. Then the door opened slowly. Everyone's reflexes were primed. The FPD officer had removed his weapon from a concealed holster. I couldn't see what Bersch or Thompson was doing but I would have bet they were doing the same thing.

Coley looked relaxed. He was smallish, he wore glasses, and if I was asked to describe him based on that moment, I would have said he looked regular, except for the heavily bandaged left hand. He was looking down the stairs toward me when he spoke.

"What do you need to know?"

"It's about your hand. I want to know exactly how it happened and I'd like to see your weapon," Bersch said.

"You haven't heard. I reported it to my boss and to the police." Pointing to a small area of damage on the door frame, he added, "Someone broke in here and stole my service revolver. Actually, it's the company's weapon, not mine."

"May we come in?" Bersch asked. He waved me up the stairs.

Coley didn't respond verbally but he did step back and turn toward his living room. We all took this as a tacit invitation and followed him inside, Bersch first, watching Coley's unbandaged hand closely. Bersch hadn't mentioned to Coley that he had both an arrest warrant and a search warrant specifying the type of weapon and any and all ammunition.

"I read the police report regarding the shooting. Where were you when it happened?" Bersch said.

"In there," Coley said. He pointed while starting to move in the direction of his bedroom.

"Hold it, please. Just let me look," Bersch said.

Bersch stepped ahead of Coley and looked into the room. He said, "Okay, show us where you were, but first there is something I need to tell you."

Bersch took this moment to advise Coley of his Miranda rights, the right to remain silent and so forth. When he was done with the recital, he added, "I realize you are trained as a special peace officer, Mr. Coley, and you are aware of all these technicalities. So if it's still okay with you, why don't you go ahead and tell us what happened."

"I was on the bed, cleaning the weapon. Do you want a reenactment?"

Bersch nodded. Coley knelt on the bed and held his right hand as if he were holding a weapon. He placed his bandaged hand on the top of the bed with his right hand, index finger now outstretched like a kid playing cowboy, pointing first at Bersch, then at me, and finally down toward his left hand.

"I started to stand up and as I pushed off, like this, and, bam, I shot myself."

I walked toward the bed and lifted up the bedding. When I lifted the mattress cover, Coley said, "See, there's the hole."

There was a hole. Bigger than it should have been but a hole for sure. I acted as if I were about to lift the mattress to follow the course of the bullet, but before I could, Coley said, "You won't find it. I dug it out to take to the hospital, in case the doctor wanted to see it."

It was not a very likely story, due to the lack of blood anywhere on the mattress.

"Where is it now?"

"It got lost, somewhere at the hospital. I have no idea where."

At this point Bersch informed Coley that he was under arrest and showed him the documents authorizing a search of the premises. He summoned the FPD officer, who was by now in the front room. Coley was cuffed and the three of them disappeared, leaving the apartment, momentarily, to Thompson and me.

Bersch was back in a flash and hot to find the gun. He

started looking at obvious places in the living room, kitchen, and bathroom. He didn't find the weapon or any ammo.

I was spending my time in the bedroom. I checked the contents of a wastebasket that was next to the bed, removing the trash piece by piece. Papers mostly, and at first nothing interesting. Then, at the very bottom, under all the junk, I found something that clarified a critical point of the crime scene puzzle. This item accounted for the mystery of the blood trail. The lack of blood between the victim's body and the bloody trail on the sidewalk two hundred feet away hadn't made sense, until now.

The item I was looking at was a blood-encrusted handkerchief, dried in the telltale shape of a makeshift tourniquet. The dried blood was acting as glue, holding the cloth in the same shape that, it turns out, Coley made when he wrapped the handkerchief around his wounded, bleeding hand. He had wounded himself somehow, and then acting as his personal paramedic, stood there over the body rendering first aid to himself before beginning his escape. The tourniquet had held the bleeding until he had walked some two hundred feet through the apartment complex. But that first drop of blood gave him away, for if he had a more absorbent handkerchief, we would have had no idea he was wounded. No hospital checks would have meant no identity and no arrest.

Bersch was looking out a small bathroom window. When I was close enough, I could see what he was looking at. There was a Chevrolet Corvair in the parking lot behind the building.

"The Corvair next," he said.

The key had been obtained from Coley's possessions upon his arrest. Once the car was opened, it was apparent that he kept it in immaculate condition or had recently cleaned it meticulously. There was no visible blood, weapon, or anything else of interest in the passenger compartment. The trunk of the Corvair, located in the front, was still lined with the original factory-issue felt-covered cardboard panels. It was possible to remove the panels without damaging them. We began with the right side. Nothing. Then we removed the left side panel. Maybe we should have been shocked at the sight of a small leather bag, similar to a man's shaving kit. I'm sure all four of us standing there looking at the bag knew exactly what we would find inside. I broke the silence.

"Let's peek."

I pulled the zipper open less than two inches. It was enough to see the butt end of a revolver, grayish-silver in color, with the characteristic lanyard ring of a .380 Webley.

"Maybe we should get some photos of this before we go any further," I said.

Coley pleaded guilty to murder.

It turns out he had been conducting a one-sided love affair with the victim. He spent every available moment at the bar where she worked, conveniently near his apartment. He wanted to talk with her, but like many men in similar situations, could never find the nerve to speak to her. He apparently never had confided in anyone about his obsession with the victim. Later, when asked, no one at the bar, employee or regular customer, had even the slightest hint of this one-sided attraction.

He began repeatedly following her home, stalking her as she parked and walked to her apartment. Until the moment of the shooting, she was never aware of any of his activities. That night, he left the area of the bar before she did, assured that he could predict her route. He waited in the shrubbery next to the path. His only activity, other than planning his surprise, was to unscrew the nearby night light, giving him another advantage. She appeared on schedule, walking directly toward him.

His plan was simple. To speak to her. To explain his attraction to her. To break the months of silence. To ask her to make love with him. He apparently felt more secure during this icebreaker moment by pointing the .380 Webley at her when he spoke. Whatever he said, "I love you" or "I want you" or "Let's screw," didn't have the expected reaction. He then grabbed her right breast. That made matters worse. She grabbed his hand and screamed a scream that only he heard. He pulled the trigger first time, shooting her in the back of her hand, the one gripping his. The bullet didn't care. It smashed through her hand and his hand and then, still spinning, into the layers of her sweater. It stopped there only because its power was handicapped by the "Webley wobble."

Coley would say later that the second shot was instinctive, but when he realized what he had done, he knew he had to finish her. The love affair ended abruptly with the two near-contact shots to the victim's head.

## Epilogue

I selected this case to emphasize the importance of teamwork. Everyone involved—the police investigators, the pathologist, the photographers, the scientific investigators, and especially the firearms expert—made a timely contribution that led to the suspect's identification, arrest, and successful prosecution. The discovery of the blood trail led us to realize that the suspect was injured, and that led to the hospital. The preliminary firearms identification was remarkable, as were the follow-up comparisons. It takes a lot of talented people, dedicated to their work, to make *any* case.

It is true that, even without the hospital records, Costa Mesa PD might have solved the case, perhaps by some other means. For example, a lucky break, a tip, or tedious work, like checking all Webley revolvers registered in California, could have led to Coley's identification. In any event, he would have had a lot more time to destroy the physical evidence, perhaps all of it. Even the wound to his hand would have healed, and perhaps been unnoticeable after a few weeks. One frightening fact remains. Coley might have escaped detection if not for the remote trail of blood and all the excellent follow-up work by the team.

## INVESTIGATING A CRIME:

### THE TEAM APPROACH

The team approach to crime scene investigation begins well before the inevitable crime. The planning begins with a procedure agreed upon by all the team members—the police, the scientists, and, when a death is involved, the coroner. Training for each member is a must, but perhaps more important is an understanding of exactly what is expected of each member at the scene and at the autopsy. The scene procedure can vary depending on the agency and the crime. In any case, the plan must anticipate problems and provide answers to specific questions, such as:

- How do you define a crime scene?
- Is it legal to conduct a search?
- How many scenes can a single crime have?
- How big is a crime scene?
- Who should be at the crime scene?
- Who is in charge?
- What should be done to process the scene?
- Who should do the work?

## The Scene of the Crime

The scene of the crime is thought of as the place where the crime was committed. But a single crime may have numerous locations to search where events took place. Consider the first scene where evidence is located the primary scene, even if it is not the most significant, and other subsequent locations as follow-up or secondary scenes.

### Legal Issues

In general, the primary crime scene can be legally searched if the crime is committed in a public place, if the resident calls for help at his or her dwelling, or if the evidence is in plain view while an emergency condition exists in a dwelling or place of business.

All other situations, including many secondary scenes, may involve a right-to-privacy issue and require careful analysis by the team before they proceed with a warrantless search. For example, if the public place is a business and the investigation begins to acquire information indicating the owners or employees are suspects, there is most likely an expectation-of-privacy issue, at least in part, if not all, of the establishment.

The police may respond to a citizen's calls for help in the home or business, only to discover, as the investigation progresses, that it looks as if the reporting party committed the crime. Their welcome to search most likely expires the moment the investigators begin to suspect the reporting party. This reporting party is not required to verbally withdraw permission, but can do so at any time. Rather, the team leader must verify the permissive search and, ideally, obtain the suspect's written permission to search. If the suspect refuses for any reason, or is not available to give permission, a search warrant is mandatory. Evidence seized up to the time of the admonishment should be admissible unless it appears the team ignored the obvious and failed to give a timely warning. Stupidity or naiveté is no excuse. A judge hearing a motion to suppress the evidence will rule on how the investigators should have reacted under the circumstances.

The same process applies once an emergency in the home or place of business is over or under control. Although legally inside the scene, the team has to reexamine its authority to search for anything other than what was in plain sight of the exact point of the emergency. For instance, a weapon in a room where the emergency team has responded to treat an injured person can be legally seized if it is consistent with the wounds or if, by government code, it is illegal per se. But the team cannot legally look into other rooms or places unless there is sufficient cause—for example, a trail of blood leading into other rooms indicating other possible victims.

The right of privacy may be an issue even when the victim is deceased. For example, a landlord calls to report a murder in an apartment rented to the victim. Before evidence is seized, the landlord should sign a statement indicating there are no cotenants and giving permission to search. If there are cotenants, they must also give permission. If they are not available for any reason, a search warrant is required since the cotenant may turn out to be a suspect in the crime.

## A Crime Scene Defined

A working definition of the crime scene, primary and secondary, is anywhere evidence may be located that will help explain the events. All the evidence could be in a phone booth, but more often it is spread out. It is not unusual for investigators to travel to other cities, counties, states, or even neighboring countries to search for evidence. A body may be found in one location but may have been kidnapped from another place and murdered in a third area. Frequently, the suspect's vehicle, home, and place of business are also scenes. In any death investigation, the autopsy should always be considered a scene to be attended, ideally, by the same investigators who worked the original scene.

## The Size of the Scene

The physical dimensions of a crime scene are often determined for the wrong reasons. When the crime was in progress there were no out of bounds markers. Perhaps only the person committing the crime knows exactly how big the true scene is. The first officer at the scene must decide what to protect. Unfortunately, this decision is usually arbitrary and may in fact be made simply because convenient places are available for stringing the standard yellow plastic ribbon, such as street signs, poles, or car radio antennas. As the rest of the team arrives, the scene appears protected. In fact, as soon as possible, someone must search outside these preliminary boundaries to assure that all evidence is protected.

## The Crime Scene Team

As a group, the crime scene team will assure the documentation of the scene by:

1. Their written or electronically recorded notes

2. Photographs of the scene and all observed evidence

3. A scale diagram, a drawing, of all the pertinent items at the scene

4. Collecting, marking, packaging, and preserving all the items collected

The following is a list of potential members and a description of their individual duties in their logical order of appearance (when required). The team will consist of members depending on the nature of the crime and the availability of the experts in specific localities. If there are two significant concurrent locations, as in "The Key to the Crime," a second team should be called out to collect the evidence there before it is compromised.

*The first officers on the scene* must determine the nature of the crime, if any, and in the case of injuries, summon the proper emergency medic. Almost simultaneously, they must detain any suspects, protect the scene from further change, interview the victim or witnesses, if available, and make notes, at least mentally, of the conditions of the scene upon their arrival. Subsequent investigators must be told of any changes that had to be made to the scene; for instance, moving the victim or a weapon or opening a purse to check for identification. They will stay at the scene to provide such information to subsequent team members. They may also be required to provide continuing security for civilian team members as needed.

*The medics* may be first on the scene. Their primary function is to save the life of the injured. They should be trained to protect a crime scene but unfortunately seldom are.

*The investigator* should be the team leader. The investigator is in charge and should have an understanding of who else might be needed at the scene. The investigator must keep the scene protected from further change until the documentation process begins. Before the scene is relinquished, the investigator should verify with each team member that all the documentation has been completed.

**The deputy coroner or deputy medical examiner investigator.** If a death occurred, this person's primary job is to step into the shoes of the victim to assure that the victim's best interests are looked after. In addition, the deputy coroner's training should include the ability to recognize changes in the condition of the body following death and to determine the time of death as closely as possible. The coroner must be able to understand medical terms, interview the deceased's physicians, and locate and review the deceased's medical records to determine what recent medical history may mean in determining the cause of death. (A more complete description of the coroner's function appears in Chapter 10.)

**The field evidence technician** may also be called a forensic specialist, crime scene investigator (CSI), or identification technician. The FET's role is to perform most of the technical functions that document the evidence at the scenes (including the autopsy). These tasks include taking photographs, examining the scene for prints, dusting for prints, searching for evidence, measuring and diagramming the location of the evidence, and collecting and packaging the evidence. The FET performs the same work at an autopsy.

**The criminalist** or forensic scientist should be trained in overall scene investigation, including recognizing specific types of evidence, reconstructing the activities of the suspect and victim based on scene conditions such as blood patterns or bullet holes, and collecting and packaging of evidence. The criminalist is also trained in laboratory analysis.

**Other specialists.** Depending on the evidence, analysis of some scenes may require the knowledge of a specialist, such as a firearms examiner, arson and explosive expert, serologist, toxicologist, forensic odontologist (dentist), physical anthropologist for studying skeletal remains, and the pathologist who will perform the autopsy. Since the primary purpose of the autopsy is to determine the cause of death, there are numerous occasions where seeing the scene and the victim's body unaltered would be of great help to the pathologist.

*A prosecuting or district attorney.* If legal issues arise, such as the need for a search warrant, the local prosecutor's office may be represented.

A complete crime scene team working a complex death investigation scene should consist of at least five or more of the previously mentioned individuals. Realistically, some jurisdictions don't have all these experts available to them for a timely scene investigation. In some smaller jurisdictions one investigator may be required to perform several jobs. This may not be a problem if the individuals have been adequately trained and, perhaps more important, recognize their own limitations.

*Press information officer or press liaison.* The media has a need to know. However, there is a limit to the type and quantity of information to be released. More important, the department head or other upper management staff may want to be kept informed as the investigation progresses. In any event, if the media arrives at the scene expecting a story, the information they receive may be restricted to facts approved by the team and transmitted by the press information officer. No one else should release case-related information unless the team approves it.

### Naming the Teams

Depending on the crime, there may be three phases of a scene investigation: the emergency phase, the investigation phase, and, in the case of death investigations, the autopsy phase.

*The emergency team*, the first officers on the scene, and perhaps the medic if there is an injury, have the difficult task of controlling and evaluating what often is a tumultuous scene. For example, the suspect may still be in or near the scene, and/or an unruly crowd may be present. Pretend for a moment that you are a police officer. Consider what it is like to enter a dark and unfamiliar alley knowing you have a vicious killer armed with a semiautomatic weapon on the loose in the area, dead or wounded victims, blood and guts strewn about, hysterical witnesses, and a crowd watching your every move, teetering on the brink of a full-blown riot. Your job is to somehow quickly transform this scene into a calm and safe environment where a controlled, methodical crime scene investigation can be carried out by the investigative team.

*The investigative team*, which may include all the individuals listed previously, often has the advantage of time. By the time all members arrive at the scene, the turmoil should be under control. They can go about their work in relative peace.

*The autopsy team,* if a death is involved, is made up of essentially the same members as the investigative team, with the addition of the pathologist and staff. Since their work continues that done at the scene, ideally the same criminal investigator, deputy coroner, FET, criminalist, and other experts who are familiar with the scene will participate in the autopsy.

## Processing a Scene

Eleven steps are required to document a crime scene. The sequence, as listed here, is ideal when all conditions are favorable or at least controllable. The team leader, using his expert judgment and considering input from the other team members, will determine the need to vary the sequence. Injuries to the victim or suspect requiring treatment or their removal is justification to vary the sequence, as are weather conditions—such as wind, rain, or snow—that are destroying the evidence, or an unruly crowd throwing rocks and bottles at the team members.

There may be other reasons to expedite any one step of the process. As long as all the members of the team agree that the quality of the evidence is not compromised or the legal admissibility at a subsequent trial will not be affected, there are no limitations on moving the steps around. Nevertheless, all steps must be completed eventually.

### Step One: Evaluate the Nature of the Scene

Someone, usually the first police officers to arrive, must make the initial determination of the seriousness of the incident. The questions they must address are: Is anyone in danger? Are there injuries? Is it most likely a crime? If so, what class of crime? How can the scene be protected? Is a suspect still at the scene? What kind and how much assistance will be required?

The evaluation begins with the first officers, but it is actually an ongoing process, continuing each time a new team member arrives at the scene and ending only when the last one leaves.

### Step Two: Protecting the Scene

The process of protecting the scene is not merely to keep everything safe and orderly. It has a far-reaching purpose: to establish and protect the *integrity* of any evidence located at the scene. To the criminal justice system in general and to the trial court specifically, the integrity of all evidence is crucial.

Before any item collected by the crime scene team is admitted as evidence, it must meet four standards. It must be *legally obtained*; it must be *relevant* to the crime charged; a witness must *identify* the item, describing its origin (the scene, the autopsy, etc.); and the *chain of possession* must be demonstrated—that is, everyone who handled the item in any manner must be available to testify. This last includes finding, transporting, storing, or analyzing the items.

Evidence from the crime scene may never become evidence at a trial because of a court ruling beyond the control of any of the team members. But evidence should never be inadmissible because a team member can't identify the object or because the chain of possession is unclear. Other than the death of one of the team members, there is no excuse for failure in either of these categories. Even with a death, a trial judge would most likely admit the evidence if proper records were presented along with someone to testify to the deceased's signature or handwriting.

Protecting the scene and the evidence it contained is, therefore, a constant process also, begun by the first officer at the same time the scene is first evaluated, and continuing for as long as it is under the control of the authorities. The protection of the scenes lasts until the entire team agrees that there is nothing remaining to do and it can be surrendered back to its normal purpose. Processing a scene may take minutes, hours, or days.

The worst enemy to the integrity of a crime scene is a bunch of well-meaning, insatiably curious police officers and detectives who invade a scene as if it were an Easter egg hunt, each moving freely about, hoping to find the golden egg, the vital clue that will solve the case.

The only way to guarantee that this doesn't happen is a planned procedure. It must be an agency policy that is put into place as manpower arrives at the scene. This includes:

- The first officers must notify the watch commander of the conditions at the scene indicating the necessity for a team investigation or any other issues, such as a search warrant.

- Members of the team are notified of the circumstances of the scene and respond to the location. The team may be a predetermined group of individuals or may be selected from a list of on-call personnel.

- The first police personnel at the scene take control of it and make it clear to all others in or near the scene what they are to do. No one already at the scene should be allowed to leave without being properly identified. The officer in charge of the emergency team must create a list of everyone—police, medics, witnesses, victims, or suspects—known to have been within the boundaries of the scene up to that moment.

- The first officers encircle the scene as best they can recognize it, with a barrier such as protective tape and uniformed officers.

- The team members should establish a command post just outside the entrance and boundaries of the scene. This can be as simple as a card table or as elaborate as a fully equipped mobile communication center and/or laboratory.

- At the command post they must initiate an order of entry form, that is, a sign-in sheet that every person entering the scene signs, indicating time of entry and purpose for being there, and describing all items they located and removed from the scene. This is the first step in the chain of possession of the evidence. They must require that everyone who enters the scene—that is, beyond the command post—write a supplemental report indicating what they did at the scene.

- Everyone other than personnel who are protecting the scene should be escorted to the command post. Ideally, the command post will be equipped with video equipment. One team member can tape a walking tour of the crime scene. The so-called "walk through" traditionally provided for each investigator, supervisor, or higher as they arrive is counterproductive to the integrity of the scene. I recommend a camcorder with a foldout viewing screen that can be viewed by each new arrival, replacing the need for the "walk through." (The tape eventually becomes a part of the scene documentation.) This is an effective way to indoctrinate curious cops, keeping them out of the scene.

- Upon arrival, the investigator in charge, based on all the available information, should determine if a search warrant will be necessary, and if so, begin the process of obtaining one.

- Once all the team members are at the scene, the investigator should brief the group with all the known information, such as changes to the scene made by the emergency team. The team should determine at this point if a larger area should be protected.

- An entrance/exit, the gate, and a pathway in and out of the scene—the path clearly marked with rope or tape—should be selected by a joint decision of the team. The path, as roundabout as it need be, is chosen to avoid traffic through areas of obvious or potential evidence. The path may be altered as new items are located or when the processing in a specific area has been completed to the team's satisfaction.

- The team members entering the scene wear a clearly marked garment distinguishing them from other personnel working around but not in the scene. Under some circumstances—for example, a bloody scene or a clandestine drug laboratory—they must also wear protective clothing and/or necessary safety devices to protect both the evidence and themselves.

- Periodically, the investigator should hold mini-meetings to determine the progress of the team.

- Before the team surrenders the scene, the investigator should hold a team critique to verify that everything has been completely documented.

*Step Three: Surveying the Scene*

The purpose of this step is to gather enough preliminary information to begin the most logical approach to processing the scene. As with the first two steps, the scene survey invariably begins the moment each team member arrives and makes observations from his or her viewpoint outside the scene. But since no two crime scenes are the same, a plan for this specific scene is needed before the processing begins. A formalized period for this survey, by the entire team as a unit, is advised.

Up to this point nothing should have been touched by anyone of authority, unless an injured party had been treated or removed, a deceased victim has been examined by the coroner, or, due to conditions such as bad weather, some evidence had to be collected or moved to preserve it.

With an unaltered scene as a continuing goal (until step six), the survey is best begun at the agreed upon entrance—the gate. The team members should move carefully into the scene on the path to a vantage point where most of the evidence can be seen. At that point an error-free route to specific items can be established. Since evidence is often not obvious, careful hands-off movement is still required as the team members begin their duties. Key questions to be considered by the team at this point are:

- Is there evidence of the suspect's point of entry, point of attack, or point of exit?

- Does the suspect normally have access to the area?

- Was the suspect still in the scene or allowed back into the scene?

- Does information offered by the victim, witnesses, or suspect make sense at this time?

If there are surviving victims available or witnesses who are familiar with the scene, their knowledge of the scene may be vital. Their input should be part of the next stage of the survey process. They should be asked to view the scene from outside the barriers. If a line of sight is not possible, it is permissible to escort such persons into the scene as soon as a safe route is established and clearly marked in order to ask the following questions:

- Can they recognize if anything has been moved from its normal position?

- Is anything missing?

- Is anything present that doesn't belong there?

Under no circumstances should known suspects—or any of their belongings—be escorted into the scene, even if they admit having been there earlier. To do so could negate the significance of existing evidence that could provide information about their presence and their movement and activities at the scene.

## Step Four: Photographing the Scene

Three categories of photographs should be taken at crime scenes:

1. Overall views, looking into and out of the entire scene

2. Orientation views of items of evidence

3. Close-up views of each piece of evidence (discussed in step seven)

These photographs provide a history of the conditions at the scene, a view of the location of each item of evidence, and a method of identifying the items for future reference. The team members will use the photos as an investigative tool to reconstruct the events or to refresh their memory of the scene at a later date. The attorneys for both sides will use them to develop their case, and during the trial the witnesses will use them to educate the court official, the attorneys, the judge, and the jury. The goal is to familiarize these decision makers with the scene to the degree that they feel as if they had been there.

For the overall photographs, the photographer preserves the essential history of the scene at the moment the photographs were taken, capturing both an inventory and the condition of all the visible items. When taken, looking at and away from the scene from multiple points of view, the photos capture all the visible details of the scene, even those that did not seem relevant to the team members at the time of the investigation. For example, photos of a kitchen, although not apparently a part of the crime scene, may yield clues about the last meal eaten, the food served, and the number of people participating.

Eye-level photographs are the most common, but other positions or angles may be advantageous. For example, at outdoor scenes, photographs may be taken either from an aircraft, some convenient nearby building, or from the heights of the fire department's high-rise equipment.

For the orientation photographs, the photographer usually takes eye-level views, since the purpose is to identify the relative location of evidence to be collected. For example, consider the orientation photograph of an apparent bloody fingerprint on a light switch. Light switches all look about the same, particularly in the same building. The orientation photo would be taken from a distance sufficient to include the recognizable shape of the print, the light switch, plus something else to distinguish this light switch from all the others at the scene. The overall photos will show the switch from a greater distance, including the wall it is on. Anything on the wall—a picture, thermostat, or unique defect—will allow the viewer to recognize the light switch involved. Since many light switches are next to doors, the door should be included in the photo, but unless it is different than all the other doors, it can't be used as a point of orientation within the room.

Advances in technology have provided affordable camcorders that can enhance the photo history of the scene with a moving view of the scene on videotape. In addition, computer-developed animated models picturing the participants' behavior, at least from one side's perspective, are now being accepted as evidence in criminal and civil trials. For example, computer-generated reenactments were introduced by the defense in the case against the officers charged with beating Rodney King. At about the same time, the juries in two California murder trials were allowed to view cartoon-like videos created under the direction of crime scene experts. In the future expect to see the use of virtual reality: a computer-generated three-dimensional effect that will allow the wearers of special equipment to wander around in the crime scene as if they were part of the team. The viewers, perhaps twelve jurors, will be able look in different directions, independent of one another. Only the cost of these new technologies prevent their widespread use today. Eventually, as with all new technology, the expense of the equipment or the process will drop and the pressure to provide more definitive information will increase. When the need justifies the cost, the newest technology is made available to scene investigators.

## Step Five: Sketching the Scene

The crime scene sketch is a record of the exact location and relative position of all the relevant items at the scene. The distances recorded by the evidence investigator at the scene may be used later to prepare a formal crime scene drawing to be used to educate decision makers. These sketches and drawings are two-dimensional and are presented in conjunction with the scene photographs. Occasionally, when it is necessary to emphasize an issue, such as line of sight, a three-dimensional scale model is built. The rules for sketching a scene are as follows:

- The investigators must make the measurement carefully, that is, within the limits of the devices used, such as tape measures, rulers, or measuring wheels. It is not acceptable to make estimates, pace off the distances, or rely on someone else's undocumented information.

- North must always be indicated and should be at the top of the paper, the rule of north. It is a mapmaker's tradition to do so, and in many trials other maps or diagrams will be presented. To avoid any confusion, the tradition is followed. North must be determined by the use of a compass at the scene. An ordinary compass that measures magnetic north, which varies from true north depending on where you are on the planet, is an acceptable device.

- The scale must be indicated somewhere on the document, even if the drawing is life-size, as in a one-to-one tracing of a blood pattern.

- The sketch and the drawing must be identified with key information, such as the case number, the location represented, a table of contents (a list of the items shown), the name of the person making the sketch, and, if the final drawing is done by another person or artist, the name of the person who verified all the details. The witness must approve the drawing prior to taking the stand. Correcting errors while explaining the details to the court may confuse the jury or discredit the drawing.

- Irrelevant items are not included in the sketch. The photographs will reveal everything at the scene, so it is unnecessary to include uninvolved items, even if they are in the middle of the place. The simple rule is: If the thing is the evidence or the host of the evidence and will be collected, it goes on the sketch.

- All items must be located on the sketch by measurements from at least two permanent fixed points that can be relocated if the need arises. On occasion it is necessary to return to a scene at a later time, perhaps to look for additional evidence, for further study, or to reenact the events in the presence of the jury. Before some cases actually get to the trial stage, years can pass. It's not unheard-of that this reenactment takes place years later. Combining the information on the sketch with the three categories of crime scene photographs, if need be, pinpoints the original position and, when practical, allows the evidence to be replaced in exactly the same orientation.

The three measuring methods used most frequently are the coordinate system, the polar method, and triangulation. Measurements must be made from some fixed point to the location of the evidence. Anything permanent may be considered a fixed point. Crimes are most often committed within a short distance from a fixed point, the walls of a room, or a curb line near numbered utility poles.

The coordinate system, as used in mathematics and computer science, locates a point within a space using two measurements. Most of these applications rely on four quadrants marked by x, y coordinates. Almost all crime scene sketches are prepared using the coordinate method, relying solely on quadrant 1, the one in the upper right-hand corner (see Figure 1). The center of the system represents the corner of a room with square corners or the right-angle intersection of two curb lines on a roadway.

For some scenes it may be useful to use two or more quadrants. Some rooms, for example, have no square corners or parallel walls, as in a round or oval room or one of a unique design. In this situation two quadrants, 1 and 2 (the lower right quadrant) can be used to position all the evidence, by making all the measurements from the x coordinate. Although the walls would be shown on the drawing as a reference, the shape of the floor plan is ignored. I suggest placing one measuring tape on the floor between the two corners of the room that, as close as possible, make an east-west line. Any two corners will do if you don't have a compass at the time. As indicated in Figure 2, the tape is left in position and the distance between the tape and items of evidence is measured, north or south, with a second tape.

Evidence on a wall, such as a bullet hole or blood patterns, should be drawn as if in quadrant 1, that is, with the

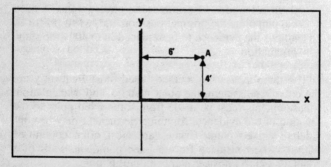

**Figure 1. Coordinate method using 2 fixed walls as X and Y +, +, quadrant.**

lower left-hand corner of the wall placed at the x-y intersection. It is usually convenient to measure from the floor up to the evidence, since a floor is almost always flat.

Face north to measure and sketch evidence on a ceiling, with the x-y intersection in the corner over your left shoulder. Note that when you view the finished sketch, north is indicated pointing to the bottom of the page, the one exception to the rule of north.

Some crimes are committed at locations so remote they lack any fixed points near enough to be suitable for measurements. The polar method provides for the two fixed measurements to be made conveniently by allowing the team to arbitrarily select a center point for their crime scene regardless of the location (see Figure 3).

Say, for example, that body parts are scattered about a scene located more than a half mile off the road in a plowed field (see Figure 4). Although you can see the scene from the roadway, there is an impassable ravine between the road and the scene. The area surrounding the body parts is void of any fixable points from which to measure. It is too far to stretch a tape from the roadway, and the ravine makes it too dangerous to even try. The decision is made based on input from all the team members, selecting a single central point that is closest to all the evidence but not where movement by the team will endanger any item.

A compass is used to locate north. A circular protractor or a staff compass is centered over the selected point with zero degrees to the north. Both a circular protractor and a staff compass—a large open-face compass fixed on a pointed shaft that can be stuck in the ground—are marked with all 360 degrees. Zero and 360 degrees are the same mark.

The left corner of a tape measure is stretched from the center of 360 degrees to the object. The angle from north can be determined by noting the degree marker where the left edge of the tape passes over. The distance out from the center is read directly from the tape. This process is repeated for each item of evidence.

One more critical step is required when using the polar method: some way to relocate the arbitrary center of the crime scene. Ideally, the location is documented by Global Satellite Position technology, which we will discuss shortly. Lacking GPS equipment, the simplest method, where conditions allow, is to measure the distance to the closest fixed object, but in this case the route was blocked by a ravine. Another simple method would be to drive a three-foot-long metal stake (quarter-inch steel) into the ground at the center point. As long as the general area can be relocated, a metal detector can be used to find the stake. When a metal stake is not practical, one method of lo-

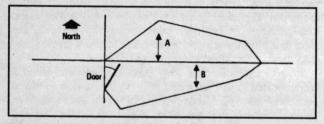

**Figure 2. Using the Coordinate System where walls are not parallel, a measuring tape creates a midline, the x axis. Items A and B are first measured along the x axis. The y distance is measured 90 degrees from the x axis. A is plus, B is minus.**

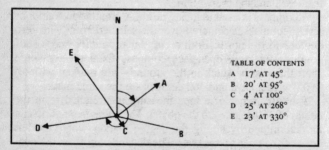

TABLE OF CONTENTS

| | | |
|---|---|---|
| A | 17' | AT 45° |
| B | 20' | AT 95° |
| C | 4' | AT 100° |
| D | 25' | AT 268° |
| E | 23' | AT 330° |

**Figure 3. Polar system using a single fixed point and a compass or protractor for angles. The center point can be any convenient location, and identified with a GPS device.**

cating the center of the crime scene is the use of triangulation.

A basic rule of geometry states that if the dimensions of the base of a triangle and the two included angles are known, the dimensions of the two remaining sides and the third angle can be determined. This same principle can be used to solve the problem of locating the center of the scene when using the polar method. Furthermore, simple triangulation can be used in place of the coordinate method as a matter of preference.

Applying the method to the plowed field scene requires the use of surveying equipment, a transit or surveyor's level, and an experienced operator to do the measurements. This equipment contains a telescope mounted on a circular table marked with a 360-degree scale and should be equipped with a compass.

Two locations along the road are marked. They may be existing numbered highway markers—those white paddle-shaped signs that often contain a reflector—or they may be numbered utility poles. The numbers are important in the event the road is widened or changed in the interim between the scene investigation and the trial. The locations of numbered poles are recorded by the installer—the highway department, or the utility company—and these records are maintained. Their history, even years later, can be traced and the original location remarked.

If no fixtures along the road are permanent, the locations can be determined by the use of the odometer on a vehicle, starting at a major intersection or some other reliable marker. In either event, the two locations should be several hundred feet apart to form the base of the triangle and must

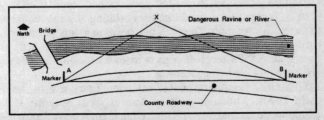

**Figure 4. Triangulation System. Used only if GPS is not available.**

have a clear line of sight to the point of interest.

The two included angles are determined by first having a target (designated x in Figure 4) at the point of interest. This can be one of the team standing on the spot. Then the transit is placed at the location of angle A aligned with zero degrees to the north. Once the telescope is focused on the target, the angle from north can be determined by taking the reading on the scale. The same process is repeated at angle B.

Triangulation can be used at more conventional scenes, such as inside a room, if two appropriate-length tapes are available. One tape can be secured in the southwest corner, angle A, and the other tape secured in the southwest corner, angle B. The tapes are then extended to the item and the two measurements recorded as side A and side B. The south wall is side C for our purposes. Since the base, wall C, is fixed, we don't actually need to measure it. The two tapes stretched to the same reading will only meet at one place in the room. The south wall will nonetheless be measured to recreate the shape of the room (see step ten).

If odd-shaped rooms have two convenient places from which to measure, such as door frames or window frames, triangulation can be applied as previously described.

## GPS Measuring

The method of choice for documenting locations such as remote crime scenes is by the U.S. Department of Defense's Global Positioning Satellite System, known for short as GPS. One of the systems—the geostationary orbit (GEO) system, is a group of fixed satellites orbiting at a rate equal to the earth's rotation. Their relative position to any place on earth never changes. The same satellites are always directly overhead. A GPS receiver detects its exact location, speed, and time relative to the satellites.

GPS-GEO became available for nonmilitary use in the early 1990s. Although military devices were accurate to within inches at that time, civilian equipment received a corrupted signal, introducing an error as great as a three-hundred-foot radius. As of May 2000 the intentional corruption factor, Selective Availability (SA), has been turned off. Now, even inexpensive units ($75 and up) sold at sporting goods stores are accurate within a few feet, perhaps inches. More expensive civilian receivers can be as accurate as the military models. For example, the Department of the U.S. Geological Survey has installed 250 GPS receivers to monitor subtle movement of the earth's outer crust in Southern California and northern Baja California. The system can detect movement of 0.04 inches, or about one millimeter, and is expected to provide an early warning of earthquakes.

The exact location of any crime scene, whether remote or not, can be documented with a handheld receiver, the size of a cell phone, while standing in the middle of the scene. The GPS receives data from three or four satellites identifying the latitude (parallel to the equator), longitude (pole to pole), and altitude by triangulation. There is a built-in compass and clock. Most models display land speed while moving, and the distance traveled between points. GPS is installed in many patrol units and can be used for the same purpose.

Before relying on any receiver, it should be tested for accuracy and reproducibility. A documented location is required to determine accuracy. The U.S. Department of Interior, Geological Survey Office, has prepared a series of geological survey maps (minute maps) for the entire country. Each map covers a small area about 4.5 by 3.5 miles that includes precise latitude and longitude numbers, as do some civilian travel maps. To determine accuracy, locate a documented site on a map and compare it to the receiver's reading. If the accuracy test checks out, the system should also be checked for reproducibility.

To determine reproducibility, start at any convenient spot that can be relocated exactly and record the readings—latitude, longitude, and altitude. Leave, and then return to the same spot and compare the reading. They should be the same. Turn the unit off for a moment and then obtain another reading. Again, they should be the same. Move at least a hundred yards from the spot and then return in the direction of the spot, using the readings as a guide rather than looking for the spot. When the readings match the original numbers, mark the place where you are standing and measure and record the distance to your original spot. Repeat this a few times, and repeat the entire process twenty-four to forty-eight hours later. This will define the accuracy and reproducibility of the device. A line of sight to the satellites is required, so the GPS won't work inside a building. However, they work in a vehicle.

Most units have a *go-to* setting. While at the original scene, select the *way station* setting option. The device remembers that setting and gives it a number. To return to the spot, you select the way station number and the go-to option. Instructions appear on the screen, such as, go three hundred feet NNW—and will fine-tune the information as the original scene is approached. These are the same devices available for automobiles—for example, On Star—and are now appearing in some rental vehicles used to secretly track speed, distance traveled, and destinations. Be advised!

## Other Measuring Devices

New models of lasers, similar to the type used on golf courses to verify distance, can be used for outdoor scenes, and a carpenter's laser can be used for indoor scenes. They must be calibrated before they are used at actual crime scenes. An elaborate (and expensive) device, a total survey system designed for civil engineers, has been used for accident reconstruction and crime scene investigation by some law enforcement agencies.

There are two new computer software programs for producing crime scene drawings, the Crime Zone and Map-Scenes (see Figure 5). Computer Assisted Designs (CADs) can be adapted to any type of scene. However, the basic rules of measuring and constructing the drawings are the same, whether by pen, pencil, or computer.

### Step Six: The Limited Search

After the arrangement and location of all the evidence and the relevant items in the room have been thoroughly docu-

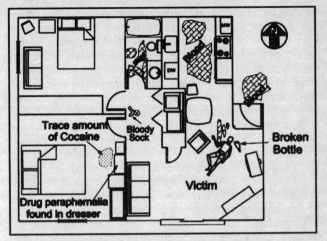

**Figure 5. An officer-submitted diagram of a homicide.**

Diagram created with The Crime Zone, published by The CAD Zone, Inc.

mented, the first nonemergency alterations to the scene are permitted. Perhaps the most common search that visibly alters the scene is dusting or chemically treating areas for prints. The contents of the photographs taken after step six may appear different than those taken when the first officers arrived at the crime scene.

*Step Seven: Close-up Photography*

The photographer takes close-up photos to document the item in such detail that it can be used for comparative analysis. If the photo is to be used for comparative purposes, the frame must include a measurement scale of some type, such as a ruler. The scale or ruler is as important as the clear focused detail. Because comparative analysis requires comparing like sizes, usually one-to-one—which means life-size—the evidence examiner must be able to reproduce a copy of the photo, enlarging or reducing it to the same size as the exemplar material.

All close-up photographs must have a ruler or scale in millimeters or eighths of an inch or smaller divisions. The future usefulness of the photograph depends on such a ruler. The ruler's image on the negative will be used as a guide by the darkroom photo technician to make enlargements, increasing the information on the film to a specific size on the final photograph. For instance, a bloody shoe print must be enlarged to life-size to compare it to a suspect's shoe. Some objects are enlarged many times larger than life—a latent fingerprint found at the crime scene, for example, to be compared to a suspect's prints. A ruler will be included with the photograph of the suspect's known fingerprint, enabling both to be enlarged to the exact same size for comparison and courtroom exhibits.

By this stage of the investigation many items of potential evidential value may have been located. Some of these must be documented in a close-up photograph, since the process of physically collecting them will most likely damage or alter their appearance completely. In particular, details of materials that are attached to or are part of an immovable object, like blood splattered on a concrete floor or bloody fingerprints on a steel wall safe, must be captured on film before attempts are made to collect them.

Depending on the complexity of the case, the associative value of the evidence, and the time available to process the scene, close-up photographs of all detailed evidence, even evidence that is transportable, should be taken. Improper handling or unforeseen mishaps can result in irreparable damage to evidence during collection, packaging, transporting, and storage. The scene photos may be the only source of information.

## Step Eight: The Complete Search

Although the crime scene has been visually examined from the moment the first officers and the team members arrived, nothing has been moved or collected, other than for emergency reasons. At this point every apparent item of evidence has been documented. The complete search is initiated to locate less obvious evidence. This allows each member of the team to focus on the nature of every item at the scene. The value of this dedicated search is enhanced by the diversity of the team members. To some extent, they will see and consider each item differently. What one member might consider unimportant or overlook entirely, another will see.

For indoor crime scenes, there are only three absolute considerations:

1. Always search the crime scene with adequate light. Major scenes deserve to be searched in daylight. The case described in this chapter is a perfect example of seeing evidence in the daylight that was not noticed in the dark.

2. Remember to look in all directions. Look up, look down, and look around things. Don't just look up at the ceiling. Get down on the floor and look at the underside of furniture, such as tables and chairs. Look around at the back side of standing things. Open doors must be shut eventually and the reverse side examined.

3. Always take a close look at the area outside the designated crime scene, at least a few feet in all directions around the outer perimeter. Remember, the yellow tape (or whatever method was used to protect the scene) was draped around the scene somewhat arbitrarily. More important, it is an artificial barrier that wasn't there at the time the crime was committed. Since it didn't contain the criminals, it shouldn't restrict the investigators.

Large outdoor scenes require an organized search. To begin, the scene should be divided into grids—for example, 50 by 50 feet or 100 by 100 feet—and identified by a number or letter designation. Each grid is then searched individually, one at a time. One method favored by many agencies is the line search. The team forms a line, elbow-to-elbow, and walks or crawls, as the case may be, in lanes back and forth until each grid is covered. Moving slowly, each member can look side to side as well as to the front. This provides a diverse point of view depending on the searcher's area of expertise.

## Step Nine: Collecting The Evidence

This step is also the first link in the chain of possession. Each person, each movement, and each subsequent examination becomes an additional link in the chain. During a trial, upon demand, a complete documentation of the chain for each piece of evidence must be presented, establishing the integrity of the item. If the chain of possession cannot be completed, the admissibility of the evidence is in jeopardy. Further, during a trial, each witness in the chain must be able to identify and testify that the item or package is, in fact, the same one they had possessed before.

The courts demand that evidence be presented in its most original form—the best evidence rule. Photographs of objects can be introduced, but if the actual object was capable of being collected, it had better be available for introduction into evidence. Nevertheless, the courts recognize the limits of collecting evidence that is not practical to move. For example, bloody shoe prints on concrete floors can be documented by means of careful photography that establishes the location and the minute details of the evidence. Courts do not expect crime scene investigators to jackhammer a piece out of the floor just to collect the print. (However, although they are attached to a subfloor, rugs and tiles should be collected by cutting or prying out the area of interest.) I do suggest that the film be developed and examined before anyone is allowed to clean up the area on the floor.

If the evidence is found on anything portable, after the series of photographs is completed, the entire object is collected and transported to the crime lab. The extent of disassembling a place of business, a residence, or a vehicle should be a team decision based on the severity of the case and the best evidence rule, that is, the admissibility and relative associative and probative value of the evidence in photographic form versus the actual item. This requires someone on the team to know precisely what the laboratory can do with the evidence. For example, the image of the bloody shoe print, properly photographed, can be compared to the suspect's shoes, but if the source of the blood is also in question, serological examinations require that some of the blood be collected before the scene is surrendered. In crimes of violence, the cost of disassembling part of the scene should never be a consideration if justice is to be served.

If the court agrees with the crime scene team's spokesperson who has testified why it was not possible to collect the actual evidence, the photographs of the evidence become the best evidence.

Identifying the evidence and establishing the chain of possession is achieved by marking both the item itself and the packing material used to protect it, and attaching a completed evidence tag that contains all the descriptive information. Obviously, some things cannot be marked, such as tiny chips of paint or glass, plant material, and bloodstains. The courts recognize that it is impossible to mark some items or that marking would alter or damage the evidentiary value of the item.

### Step Ten: Completing the Measurements

Any measurements that could not previously be made without altering the scene or moving the evidence can now be made.

### Step Eleven: Team Critique

Members of the team individually review what they have done at the scene. If after hearing each member's explanation, the team as a whole is satisfied that nothing still needs to be done, the scene can be returned to its normal use.

## The Bottom Line

Any group of interested people can investigate a crime scene. As the optimist once said, "Put some monkeys in a room full of typewriters and eventually they will rewrite all the classics." The inexperienced can try to do a good job, but success would be a lot more likely with a team, a plan, a leader, and a group of workers with a high level of expertise.

***Not all crime scene teams are created equal.*** My participation in crime scene investigations, as a criminalist or as Director of Forensic Sciences, occurred in Orange County, California. I now realize I was working in a near perfect system where scientists, the evidence technician, criminalist, and coroner's pathologists and investigators controlled the physical evidence at the scenes/autopsies from beginning to end. The team leader, usually a detective, made suggestions but did not give orders as to what to do or not do. There was always a high level of cooperation, but the scientist determined the value of the evidence, whether it helped prove or disprove the investigator's theory of the case. There was never any pressure to *make* the case. The same level of trust applied at the D.A.'s office. The laboratory staff made the decision as to what evidence was to be examined and how far to take it.

It turns out this isn't the case everywhere. In some jurisdictions the crime scene investigators do only what they are told to do and collect only what the police investigator points out. Further, the lab staff may only examine the specific items requested, with the result that they may never discover more meaningful information, incriminating or exculpatory. This is not right. This is not science.

## chapter three

# Fingerprints

## Introduction

For the past century it has been a commonly held belief that no two fingerprints are exactly the same unless the same person made them. For that reason, matching a crime scene print to a suspect's known print has universally been accepted as absolute proof of identity, placing the defendant at the scene and circumstantial guilt, at least when there was no innocent explanation for the existence of the print. That seems logical since it has never been reported that two individuals matched the same crime scene print. Unfortunately, this affects the way typical examiners go about their work: They obtain a list of possible candidates either from investigators or a computer database and begin making comparisons and when a match is found, they search no further.

They stop looking for the same reason you might stop looking for something you've misplaced at home, like your watch. Since you know you have only one watch, you feel confident that you are not going to find a second watch, no matter how hard you look. In the case of would-be experts, they have been taught there can only be one source for a matching print, so when you've found it, why look further?

What if you lost your watch at a beach? Using a metal detector, you may find several watches, maybe one just like yours, before you locate your watch, if you ever do. Unless you look, you have no idea how many other people have lost their watches at that beach. Similarly, the would-be fingerprint expert may be right, but for the wrong reason. The problem is one of blind faith. They had read somewhere or some instructor has made the statement that no two individuals' fingerprints are the same.

A federal court decision, Daubert (1993), has inspired challenges to all types of scientific opinion testimony. Daubert involved a case of questioned document examination. It excluded opinion testimony regarding the examination of forensic evidence because the procedure used, in general, lacked a foundation based on scientific principles. Expert testimony by fingerprint examiners is now the target of defense attorneys hoping to exclude the evidence intended to identify the client. The questions asked are, Do fingerprint examiners use methods based on scientific principles? and, On what do they base their opinion that no two fingerprints are the same?

In this chapter I explain why fingerprints have been accepted by the courts. The case I describe is one of a series of sixty similar deaths of young men that occurred over a twelve-year period. A suspect was eventually charged with sixteen of the murders, all originating in Orange County, California. The individuality of his fingerprint was the key to the trial.

## CRIME SCENE:

### ONE FLING LEADS TO ANOTHER

The roads that lead up to the highest peaks in the Santa Ana Mountains are all unpaved. They wind from almost sea level to a respectable 5,687 feet. These mountains have a history of criminal activity. Gangs of outlaws once used the canyon for hideouts. Black Star, Horse Thief, and Holy Jim canyons are said to be haunted by the men who were murdered there. Folks died, some trying to retake their rustled stock, some over the pelts of grizzly bears that were hunted for sport and profit until the last one was killed in 1908. The discovery of silver in 1877 lured both those who were willing to work for their prize and those who were more interested in stealing it away with as little work as possible.

On the afternoon of January 3, 1976, at about 3:30 P.M., a four-wheel-drive off-road vehicle slowed to a stop near the summit of one of the higher mountains in the range, Bedford Peak. The occupants, two off-duty Santa Ana police officers and their teenage daughters, had enjoyed the cool winter day by picnicking a few miles farther up the road on Santiago Peak, or Old Saddleback, as it is frequently called. A beer with lunch had worked its way through the system of the officer riding shotgun, producing what some refer to as nature's call.

The berm along the roadway had been cleared of underbrush and weeds, providing the officer with no privacy for his mission of relief. So he was forced to seek the cover of the chaparral, a dense growth of native plants that bordered the road about twenty feet downhill to the north. The chaparral was thick at its top, about ten feet tall, blocking out almost all light, but relatively open at ground level. The officer spotted an opening to a narrow trail, most likely frequented by deer. He made his way into the thicket, occasionally looking back until he could no longer make out the shapes of his companions or the vehicle. Forty feet or so into the brush he felt alone at last.

He had only relaxed for a moment before he sensed there was *something* near him. Was he being watched? He made out a human figure some ten feet farther down the hill. Finishing his immediate business, the officer moved in for a closer look. He called out but got no response. The path led down to the left of the figure. From six feet away he had a clear view despite the remaining tree trunks. That was close enough. He knew why he had received no response.

I was home and it was almost dark by the time the watch commander called me. I was told about a John Doe, possible 187 (a murder), and to meet the homicide investigators at the end of Silverado Canyon road. I asked the watch commander to call Frank Fitzpatrick, a relatively new criminalist in the crime lab who had shown a talent for understanding crime scenes. From what I had been told, this scene would be quite different from any he'd been to before. In fact, as it turned out, it would prove different from any scene anyone on this team had ever been to before.

When I arrived at the end of the road, several official vehicles and a few private cars were parked in the small lot just outside a fire gate. The gate is left open after the first winter rains, allowing the adventurous to explore the mountainsides. Fitzpatrick was talking to the two deputies guarding the gate. One deputy had been assigned to drive us up the mountain to the scene. Although the road was passable, it was not in the best condition for regular street vehicles. As we climbed and went in and out of dozens of hairpin curves at certain points, the lights of Orange County sparkled enough to remind me that we were not very far from civilization.

We arrived at Bedford Peak, elevation 3,800 feet, in about twenty minutes. The lights of the patrol vehicle illuminated some other cars parked on a fairly flat clearing, open for a few feet on both sides of the road. As the deputy stopped just off the road, he instinctively turned off his headlights. I realized how dark it gets on top of a mountain, and when I opened the car door I realized how frigid and windy it gets also.

Investigator Willie Stansbury was walking toward us and beckoning me to come his way. Stansbury is best described as a big man with a big sense of humor, Southern-style drawl and all. He'd drive one hundred miles out of his way if there was a hint that some café served good biscuits and gravy. So would I.

"Damn, I thought this was Southern California; we are going to freeze our butts off," I said.

"Up here there ain't nothing between us and the North Pole except a fence in Idaho, and I heard that blew down last winter," Stansbury said, leading me toward the chaparral. "It's a little better down on the hillside. The brush blocks some of the breeze."

A power cable led from the ID truck generator down the berm, and as we approached the edge of the thicket I could make out the light at its end farther down the slope. I also saw the flash of a photographer's strobe. Ed Carson, a sheriff's ID investigator, was already hard at work. Ernie Krey, the deputy coroner, waited for us beside the chaparral.

"The Santa Ana guy walks deep enough into this crap to almost step on the body," he said. "Pure luck that he spots it. Another day or two and every coyote on the mountain would have thought they had died and gone to heaven. Really, this body would never have been found otherwise." Stan led us to the opening in the thicket that had become the path into the scene. It was too dark for me to tell at the time, but it was the only way in.

As the four of us started down the hill, we were joined by Investigator Bernie Esposito, who had been in his unit, staying out of the cold. Once we were in the thicket it did seem less cold—not warmer—but as if to compensate, the overhead clearance dropped to less than five feet. We'd have to hunch over the rest of the way in.

Ed Carson had stretched a heavy rope over the berm and down the path. It helped guide us in the darkness and would be a bigger help on the steeper places on the way back up the hill. The path led us past the left side of the body—made clearly visible by the portable light—down the hill, and then back up to just below the victim's feet. Ed was near the body and still taking pictures when we arrived.

The nude body—a male, based on what was left of his anatomy—was laid out flat on his back with his head on the high side of the slope. His legs and feet were bent back almost over his face and were held in place by the trunk of a small tree. The back of his right ankle was hooked against the trunk, and the left calf was propped on top against the same tree. His face was pointing a little to the right, facing away from our vantage point. His arms were crossed over his chest, the right above the left. There was a long deep slice on his left thigh, beginning behind his knee and extending out to the side and ending near his hip. A pattern of blood and soil was on his face, but nothing to explain how it got there. There was no blood on the ground or weeds to either side of his face.

We were able to move farther down the slope a few feet, hook back, and approach the body from below. The sexual organs had been cut away. Complete excision. Complete emasculation. The margins along the cut edges were clean, indicating a sharp weapon had made the wounds, but perhaps the most alarming observation was the darkening of the margins of the remaining tissue, which meant that there was a vital reaction to the incision. Krey took some time looking over the body, touching it once.

"This guy may have been alive when this was going on," he said, "but I doubt it."

Regardless, the extent of the mutilation made the bitter coldness seem insignificant.

"I don't know if you can see it in this light, but there appears to be something stuck up this guy's rectum," Krey said.

"How long has he been here?" I asked.

"Could be a couple of days, maybe more," Krey said. "He's ice-cold to the touch. It is as cold as a refrigerator up here. Even in the daytime, in all this shade, it's colder than most meat boxes. He could stay pretty fresh for a week or more, assuming the animals didn't find him, and clearly they didn't."

With my flashlight I was able to make out the object Krey had described, but I had no idea what it was. Directly under his anus, in the area between the victim's legs, were leaves and debris stained with what appeared to be blood, but not a lot of blood. Later we would find an excised testicle matted up in this debris.

This would indicate the emasculation and excision of the genitalia had taken place where we were kneeling.

"Does it appear to you that this guy got here on his own?" I asked. "It doesn't seem likely that he was carried down here; there is not enough overhead clearance and I don't see anything that resembles drag marks."

There were marks on his chest, several small circular burns, and it appeared that areas of the victim's body hair had been shaved or cut away but with no damage to the skin. Krey was close enough to realize that both eyes had been severely burned.

"It's the same circular pattern, the left eye more than the right," Krey said.

Numerous pieces of a broken vodka bottle were scattered on the ground, with some large pieces under the victim's buttocks. The label was torn but still glued in place on various broken pieces. The brand was Winner's Cup.

The body had been in this position for several hours. Krey had confirmed the body was in full rigor mortis and faint lividity was present. He indicated that it did not blanch, a phenomenon explained in Chapter 10. The extreme coldness would be expected to slow these postmortem changes, but more than likely the death had occurred within twenty-four to forty-eight hours. The position of the lividity indicated that the victim had been alive or recently killed when placed in this position.

Everything that appeared foreign to the area was collected, including the leaves stained with what appeared to be blood. Carson was carefully picking up the broken glass when he said, "This looks like blood or tissue on the point of this piece."

He was pointing to a fairly long shard of the bottle that had bloodlike material caked on the tip.

"This could be the *tool* used to do some of the cutting," I replied. "It's sharp enough. How about prints?"

"Fingerprints are possible. By the way, does anyone here smoke Half and Half cigarettes? I saw an empty package over there on the ground earlier. I already collected it."

Stansbury, who had left our location for a moment, returned, indicating that he wanted to talk to me.

"The guys up there were talking. We could be stepping on this guy's parts and not know it, it's so dark. What do you think about taking him out of here but leaving the scene under guard until daylight?" he asked.

"You've got my vote. We could miss something in all the shadows. It's happened before. Is the autopsy lined up?" I asked.

"Matter of fact, Krey set it up for tonight, Doc Richards at county hospital. By the time we're out of here he'll be ready."

An immediate autopsy should be an option in all cases of who-done-it homicides. The sooner the victim is identified and the cause and classification of the death are established, the better. Homicide investigators—the good ones, that is—don't take many breaks, even for sleep, during the first twenty-four to forty-eight hours into a case. Timing really *is* everything. Early on, leads are fresh and must be acted upon before a suspect has time to talk to friends and fabricate a story or while associative evidence at other locations may still be intact. To delay unnecessarily is to give the advantage to the killer.

Everything that was obvious had been bagged and tagged. Before the body was wrapped in a sheet in preparation for bagging, Krey rolled the victim over about sixty degrees, enough to see his back and buttocks for the first time. Both areas were heavily scraped.

"It looks like he was dragged down here after all, and these marks look postmortem to me," Krey said.

This made everything we had seen even more puzzling. The first call service—the people, sometimes called morgue attendants, who transport bodies from death scenes to the morgue—did their job of lifting the bagged body, and somehow moved the whole package up the hill to the dirt road. It was time to head down the hill.

The autopsy began at 10:30 P.M. after close-up photos were taken of all the obvious exterior trauma. Dr. Robert Richards started by studying the external trauma we had observed at the scene, in particular the margins of the connective tissue of what had once been this man's penis and scrotum.

"I hate to think about what was going on, but it took several cuts to complete this excision," Dr. Richards said. "I don't see much sign of tissue reaction, so I don't think the cuts are antemortem. There is discoloration along the margins but a lot of that is dirt and darkening as time passed. These circular burns on the chest look like the shape of an automobile cigarette lighter."

"Postmortem or ante?" someone asked.

"Right now, that's close," he replied. "This reddening could be dirt or drying. If there is tissue reaction it is remarkably little. Right now, I'd say postmortem. The micros will help."

The micros are tissue samples that are prepared by slicing the specimens with a Microtone, a device similar to a butcher's meat slicer, but that prepares very thin layers. By using stains, changes in the tissues can be classified as ante or postmortem.

It was beginning to make sense. Had the excision been antemortem and done down the hill, you would have expected a lot more blood under the body than we had seen in the limited light. All the more reason to revisit the scene in the daylight. If the burns were made by an automobile cigarette lighter, the victim had to have been in the immediate vicinity because the lighters cool down quickly. If the burns were postmortem, that would mean the victim had been dead before he'd been taken down the hill.

To this point, we had no cause of death. All the major trauma identified so far that could have caused or contributed to the victim's death had been described as postmortem. But the autopsy wasn't over yet. The brain and heart were normal and the skull was intact. There is always the question of strangulation in violent deaths. Perhaps the most significant source of information establishing trauma to the neck is the examination of the hyoid bone. (This is discussed in Chapter 10.) The hyoid was intact, but while examining the airway, Dr. Richards found an obvious cause of death.

There was a large amount of dirt in the esophagus and the trachea. To recall the sequence of the airway: there's the mouth and tongue, then the esophagus leads to the stomach and the larynx leads to the trachea, bronchi, and lungs, in that order. The farther he looked into the airway, the more dirt he found. By the time he got to the lower trachea at the intersection of the bronchial trees leading into each lung, the passageway was packed solid with dirt. The victim had suffocated.

Dr. Richards was certain about the cause of death until he received the toxicology report later in the month. The victim's blood alcohol level fit right into the list of other startling findings. The level, 0.67 percent weight/volume (W/V), was a stand-alone cause of death. Most people get sick or pass out at levels above 0.20 percent and can die when their levels approach 0.35 percent.

Had it not been for the dirt blocking the lungs, Dr. Richards could have signed the case out as due to acute alcohol intoxication. To avoid any unnecessary conflict, he used both causes on the official death certificate. The exact wording was: "Immediate cause, suffocation with acute alcoholism, due to consequences of dirt in trachea and lungs and massive ingestion of alcohol." The death certificate did not mention that forensic toxicologist Jimmy Turner had also identified a low level of diazepam, a tranquilizer often sold under the name Valium. This finding would later prove to be extremely important to the investigators.

The amount of dirt involved could not have been inhaled accidentally. It had to be forced down the victim's mouth, and may have been washed down with the vodka. From my point of view, the dirt was the murder weapon.

Another critical point for Dr. Richards to consider was the effect the level of alcohol would have had on tissue reaction if any of the trauma occurred as death approached, with or without the dirt. Alcohol causes the central nervous system to slow down, and the slowing of the heart and respiration rate can cause pulmonary edema and death. Blood pressure is very low and the subject's skin feels cold to the touch although the subject is still alive. Even at such a high blood alcohol level, with proper heroics victims have been known to survive.

Trauma inflicted at such a time could show less tissue reaction. Pathologists consider the period between life and death to be very short, a time frame they label "perimortem." This particular victim, suffering from acute alcohol intoxication during his time in captivity, could have suffered trauma while alive that showed little tissue reaction. The net result of all this placed tremendous pressure on Dr. Richards to classify each specific trauma as ante, peri, or postmortem. The crimes of torture and mayhem require the victim to be alive at the moment of the violence.

It was close to four A.M. and the autopsy was over. The last evidence collected was a set of the victim's fingerprints. There are three critical reasons to do this. If a ten-print card was already in the Orange County file, the name of our John Doe would be known by daylight. If any latent prints were found on the pieces of the vodka bottle, the victim would have to be eliminated as a source. And if a suspect was located, any vehicles involved would be examined for fingerprints, which would then be compared to the victim's ten-print card. Once that was done, we all agreed to revisit the scene after a couple of hours' sleep.

Our trip would be fruitless. The main object of our renewed search, the victim's genitalia, were discovered in his rectum, and the chaparral held no more surprises.

The victim's fingerprints were compared to similar ten-print fingerprint cards on file. He was identified as Mark Hall, age twenty-two, a resident of Santa Ana. Stansbury began tracing Hall's last known activities and found that Hall had been a guest at a New Year's Eve party very near the I-5 freeway in San Juan Capistrano, a small city in the southern end of Orange County. He was seen carrying a bottle around with him at the party and was drinking straight from it. No one remembered his actions after the midnight celebration, and although all the people attending the party and Mark Hall's family and friends were interviewed, no new information was developed.

The investigators followed up anything that could be considered a lead. Stores that sold the brand of vodka were contacted but offered no help, even though the brand was uncommon. Ed Carson dusted the pieces of broken glass for latent fingerprints, but only faint areas of detail were identifiable. With no suspects, the print had no immediate value. No one who had been at the scene admitted discarding the cigarette package, but no prints were found on the paper wrappings.

The circular burn patterns on the victim's chest appeared

to have been made by the heating coil of an automobile cigarette lighter. A U.C. Berkeley student, Keith Inman, who was working in the crime lab as an intern, contacted the makers of these lighters in hopes that one brand of vehicle could be singled out. We learned from his research that we could distinguish different patterns, but the patterns were not identified with any particular make or model of vehicle.

Within a few months all leads had come to dead ends—no connections were made to previous cases, either—and the case was left in limbo, although not closed. Unsolved murders are never forgotten, under any circumstances. All the evidence in this case was preserved in the evidence property room. Indeed, the evidence in every homicide in Orange County since 1948, solved and unsolved, is still stored and preserved.

During the next seven years, eleven more bodies of murdered young men were dumped in various locations in Orange County. Other jurisdictions reported similar murders. But as in the Hall case, no one was arrested as a suspect.

On May 14, 1983, at 1:15 A.M., California Highway Patrol officer Mike Sterling was cruising Interstate 5 northbound between Oso Parkway and La Paz. He observed a Toyota Celica directly ahead of him traveling slower than the speed limit and weaving to the degree that he suspected the driver was intoxicated. He made the stop and approached the vehicle, realizing that two people were inside, the driver and a passenger who seemed to be sleeping. As the driver exited, a beer bottle fell from the vehicle onto the shoulder. The driver, Randy Steven Kraft, produced a California driver's license. He told the officer that the passenger was a hitchhiker.

Kraft's overall behavior furthered Sterling's initial suspicions. He administered the standard set of roadside sobriety tests and concluded that Kraft was indeed under the influence. He informed Kraft that he was under arrest and placed him in the backseat of his patrol unit. The passenger was still in the same position. He was seated in the front bucket seat set in a reclining position, and he had a jacket across his lap.

By this time a backup officer had arrived. Sterling touched the passenger but got no response. He felt the passenger's skin, and finding it cool to the touch, he radioed for paramedics. While waiting, he returned to Kraft's vehicle and removed the jacket that had been in the passenger's lap. The person's pants and underwear were pulled down to around his knees. Sterling also noted a wide black leather belt on the floor behind the driver's seat.

The passenger, later identified as Terry Lee Gambrel, a twenty-five-year-old marine, was treated by the paramedics and transported to the closest E.R. room, where he was pronounced dead at 2:19 A.M.

The highway patrol investigates most traffic matters on California's freeways and roadways, but the local agencies usually retain jurisdiction over criminal matters, such as death investigations not related to a traffic incident. The sheriff's department responded to the scene and ordered the vehicle impounded. The first investigators on the scene also quickly recognized the M.O. similarities to previous cases. The special team assigned to this ongoing series of deaths was called out. Investigator Jim Sidebotham and senior criminalists Jim White and Tina Chan went to the laboratory garage to examine the vehicle for evidence pertaining to the dead passenger.

One of the first things White noticed was that the passenger's seat was wet with urine, a fact Officer Sterling had noted after the victim was removed by the paramedics. But White soon realized he was seeing more than urine. A significant amount of blood was matted in the upholstery. Sidebotham got on the phone and confirmed that this victim had *not* been bleeding. Later White and Chan discovered that the blood type found on the seat was similar to that of another victim whose penis had been cut off before he was dumped along a roadway.

During the search of the vehicle, White located a packet of photographs. Some of them were of young men posed in various positions on a sofa and on a living room floor. Many of them were nude. At least five different males were pictured. Some appeared to be asleep, while others appeared awake, and some looked dazed. No wounds or trauma showed in any photograph. Several sheriff's investigators, including Jim Sidebotham, studied the photos.

"Do you see this? Get me that crime scene photo of Eric Church. I can't see the guy's face, but I'll buy you all lunch at Flo's if that's not Church's jacket," Sidebotham said.

Eric Church's body had been discovered four months earlier, on January 27, 1983, at almost the same location, near the 405/605 interchange, where the bodies of Edward Moore and Ronnie Wiebe had been dumped ten years earlier. Church had on a shirt, pants, and a jacket, but his belt was missing. The photo removed from Kraft's car failed to reveal the subject's face, but the clothing in the photo was in sharp focus. A black belt was loose across the subject's lap. (Later, White and Chan compared the photograph of the belt to the belt found in Kraft's car. It was the same belt.) Sidebotham was so familiar with all of his cases, he realized he was looking at the clothing he had seen on Church's body the day it was discovered. He did not have to buy anyone lunch.

Sidebotham and his team obtained a search warrant for Randy Kraft's house, located in Long Beach, California. During the search, the team located key evidence that would be introduced during Kraft's trial. They located additional photographs of young men posed in various positions. It was difficult to determine if any of them had been alive at the time the photos were taken, but many were clearly identifiable as someone who ended up dead.

As the work at the scene progressed, a truly remarkable piece of evidence was discovered: a piece of lined notepaper that contained sixty-one cryptic notations. The list, soon to be described as "Kraft's Death List," was in two columns, one on the far left and the other on the far right. The sixty-one notations included EDM (Edward D. Moore's initials), New Year's Eve (Mark Hall disappeared on New Year's Eve), Seventh Street (Eric Church was found on the I-605 Seventh Street ramp), and Dart 405 (Ronnie Wiebe was found on the I-405 Seventh Street ramp).

*  *  *

As you recall, there was a faint fingerprint discovered on a piece of the vodka bottle we had found at the Mark Hall crime scene. It became a key to the prosecution case against Kraft. But if it was of poor quality in 1976, why was it of value during the trial?

After Kraft's arrest, senior forensic specialist Gary Jackson reexamined the broken glass using a new process called Super Gluing, which had not been available to Ed Carson in 1976. The process is a truly dramatic yet simple addition to fingerprint science.

Jackson exposed the pieces of bottle to the fumes of Super Glue (cyano acrylate), and as the fumes settled on the surface of the glass, they intensified ridge information. Clearly identifiable ridges appeared where carbon dust alone had revealed only faint smudges.

Kraft had been fingerprinted the night he was booked into jail following the California Highway Patrol arrest. Jackson pulled Kraft's card and within minutes located the corresponding friction ridge information.

Sergeant Sidebotham dedicated several years to organizing the cases against Randy Kraft. In all, sixteen counts of murder were filed against Kraft. Some very incriminating physical evidence was offered during the trial to connect Kraft to each count charged; however, the fingerprint was the one piece of evidence that, as prosecutor Bryan Brown would point out during the trial, placed Kraft inextricably in the middle of one of the crime scenes. There was only one explanation for Randy Kraft's fingerprint on a piece of the vodka bottle found next to Mark Hall's body.

On May 12, 1989, Randy Kraft was found guilty of all sixteen counts of murder. He was sentenced to die and is presently in San Quentin Prison. His sentence is being appealed.

## THE BASIS FOR INDIVIDUALITY

Almost everyone agrees, no two fingerprints are exactly the same, not even from identical twins. Disagreements between examiners are usually based on the lack of quality or quantity of information recognizable in the crime scene print. The fact that no two individuals' prints have identical areas has never been proven empirically since not all prints are on record and there is no method presently available to make comparisons of the ones that are. Further, crime scene prints often have limited useful areas. Limited areas of ridge characteristics within different individuals' prints have been shown to match, making it necessary to adopt a technique of establishing individualization. Historically in the United States, ten to twelve matching points, called minutiae or Galton points (sixteen points in England), was considered sufficient to declare that two prints were from the same person.

Edmund Locard's study of friction ridge structure (1914) laid the foundation for the individualization of fingerprints, stating that twelve matching points, or minutiae, with no differences was an identification. The reliance on Locard's observations stood the test of time and remains the standard for some examiners. The obvious problem occurs when there are fewer minutiae. Some examiners believe that unless one can comply with the standard, it is an exclusion—that is, the print was not made by the suspect.

However, Locard also concluded that fewer points, when there is other clear structural forms, could be as conclusive as the twelve minutiae. He was the first to publish a study on the spatial relationship of pores and ridge shapes when present in fine detail. Such detail is attainable in inked, rolled prints but less likely in crime scene prints.

The skin on our hands and feet displays an unpredictable array of fine details that are collectively called "friction ridges." The random nature of these ridges—their distribution, continuity, length, and curvature—explain why, if you look closely enough, one print will differ from all others. Perhaps the most important observation made by the pioneers of fingerprint identification was that fingerprint patterns, down to the finest detail, do not change with time. If the ridges are intentionally buffed off, they grow back as they were. Even deep scarring does not prevent identification. Only the complete removal of the flesh down to the meaty tissue, necessitating skin grafts, will destroy the ridge detail.

Functionally, friction ridges on skin increase our ability to grip objects and reduce slippage. In lower forms of animals the ridges are much more pronounced because friction ridges provide them some of the necessary means of continued existence—grasping, climbing, running, and turning abruptly. As we humans evolved, we developed skills and methods other than flight, such as weapons and tools, and dependence on friction ridges selectively disappeared.

The basic patterns described in 1892 by Sir Francis Galton in his first book on fingerprint classification—arches, loops, and whorls, or their composites—are found on the tips of our fingers and toes. With few exceptions, we all have one or more of these patterns or variations on each fingertip. Some individuals may have the same basic pattern on all ten fingers, while others may have a mix. Arches, loops, and whorls are class characteristics, since many people have the same basic pattern. We have to look further for the quality of individuality.

In addition to the three basic patterns, we all have other groups of class characteristics. For example, individuals who have loop patterns have, as a necessary part of every loop, a core and a delta, and a varying number of ridges between the core and the delta that are counted. Since more than one person has these items and may have the same count, the core, delta, and ridge count are class characteristics. Also, everyone's ridges are fashioned of the same type of fine detail, ridge endings, and bifurcations. Taken individ-

**Arch**              **Whorl**              **Loop**

**Figure 6. Basic fingerprint patterns.**

ually, these points called minutiae are also class characteristics since everyone has them. Minutiae and their relative location to one another, called the spatial relationship, are the basis for individualizing fingerprints (see insert, page 2).

Note that the ridges in Photo 2 are not continuous. The ridge will run along for a while and stop. This is called a termination or ridge ending. Some ridges may continue to a point where they divide into two or more ridges. This is called a bifurcation (two) or trifurcation (three).

Each ridge ending and division is called a minutiae point. Every ridge has a beginning and an ending, depending on how you look at it, but for classification purposes both are called endings. Therefore, all ridges have at least two minutiae points, two endings, and may have more if they contain one or more bifurcations. For instance, a ridge that bifurcates has at least four minutiae points, three endings, and the point of the bifurcation. Patterns, ridges, ridge endings, and forks are all class characteristics, since we all have them in one form or another. The number is important, but it is the relative location of each point that establishes individuality.

To complicate matters, there are many subclassifications of the basic patterns. Even fingerprint experts may argue over how a particular print should be classified. For example, there are two forms of arches, plain and tented. Arches have no core or delta. All loops have a core and a delta. The principle variations of loops are identified by their direction of flow, radial or ulnar. If they open toward the inside of the arm or the thumb, they are called radial loops, as the arm

**Figure 7. Ridge ending.**

bone closest to our bodies is the radial bone. The outside arm bone is called the ulnar, so loops that flow and open to the outside, toward the little finger, are called ulnar loops. Whorls are distinguished by one or more ridges that are continuous, making complete circles, spirals, or ovals. They usually have two deltas and at least one core.

Some composites are called *accidental* prints. Accidentals are visually similar to the basic patterns, but on close examination usually possess characteristics of more than one pattern.

All class characteristics must be properly classified and described if the information is to be used to classify ten-print cards regardless of the file system. Uniformity of opinion from classifier to classifier is critical, since the original card will be filed based on how each finger is classified. If, where, or when another ten-print card is made on the same individual, subsequent searches are often made based on another classifier's description of the patterns. A miscall or difference of opinion about a basic pattern can result in the failure to identify the individual correctly.

The friction ridges also usually contain sweat pores that are arranged randomly along the ridges. Occasionally, the pores are clearly delineated and may be helpful in matching small areas of fingerprints often found at crime scenes. Perhaps more significant, the pores provide the sweat that moistens the hand. The perspiration produced contains chemicals that act like an invisible ink, transferring ridge detail to

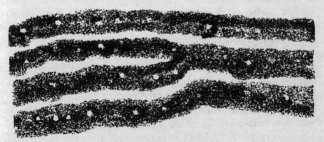

**Figure 8. Bifurcation.**

items touched and thus providing potential proof of one's presence. However, while there are published methods of comparing pore location as a means of identification, some fingerprint examiners rely only on the ridge detail.

## Identification Process

Fingerprint information is universally accepted as a means of personal identification. Identifying individuals by their fingerprints is possible using two different approaches, depending on the circumstances. If an individual is available, exemplar impressions of all ten fingers can be made by applying ink or by applying other chemicals or electronically, to create a ten-print card on paper or on a computer disk, a process called "rolling the prints." The card can be classified by the Henry system—named for Sir Edward Henry, who published *Classification and Uses of Fingerprints,* the basis for modern methods, in 1900—or registered in an automated system and, in either event, compared to other available cards to seek an identity. Or, when fingerprints of unknown origin are collected at a crime scene, they may be compared to known suspects, victims, and their associates, and to investigators or officials who have visited the scene. Known ten-print cards of all these individuals must be available in some form.

The most common use of fingerprint records is the comparison of a ten-fingerprint card taken during a jail booking to a file set of all ten fingers previously recorded under a particular name. This is the ten-print system. In the classic method, fingerprints of this type are impressions collected by a fingerprint technician who, while holding the individual's hand, covers the fingertips with a special ink and then rolls the tips, one finger at a time, across a clear piece of paper. In live scan systems, which we'll get to below, an ink-free finger is rolled on glass placed over a video camera.

In practice, a police officer, jailer, fingerprint examiner, autopsy technician, or clerk does the rolling of prints. The person grasps the subject's fingers, one after the other, and rolls them onto a thin layer of ink spread over a plate of glass and then onto the appropriate space on the card. Most people, even criminals, cooperate, relaxing the arm and hand muscles and allowing the proper rolling motion to take place.

The quality of the ridge information transferred to the card is, no doubt, the most important criterion that controls the success of all systems in use, including the manual search of the Henry system. The person obtaining the card, depending on skill, experience, and attitude at the time, can limit the quality. The behavior of the printee can also hamper the outcome to some extent, if allowed to resist.

And smudges, smears, or just too much ink on either card can obscure minutiae points, resulting in a no-match search even if the person is in the system. Some newer methods avoid ink altogether by placing a colorless chemical on the fingers and rolling them onto a chemically treated paper where the chemicals react and become visible.

The newest methods of recording fingerprint ridge information are the live scan systems. There is no ink and no card. Each finger is rolled onto a glass plate that is placed over a video camera. The ridge information is recorded and translated into digital information and stored on disks. If a card is needed, something similar to an inked card can be produced. It sounds good, but the output of early systems failed to be reproducible. For example, a ridge ending might be printed as an ending on copy number one, but on the next copy the same ending appears to be connected to the next ridge over, forming an apparent bifurcation. Newer systems claim to correct this problem.

Some conditions may be beyond a person's or method's control, such as the condition of the skin on the subject's fingers. People in some jobs, such as plasterers or cement finishers, may have badly damaged skin on their fingertips that obscure detail. A corpse should be fingerprinted at the time of examination to verify identity, but depending on the time and circumstances of death, may represent some unique problems. For one thing, rigor mortis, the muscle stiffness associated with the first forty-eight hours after death, causes the finger muscles to contract—the so-called death grip. This condition makes it difficult if not impossible to get at the fingertips, much less roll them. The technician must loosen the muscles by pushing and pulling on the hand, breaking the rigor. Decomposed or burned bodies may also be beyond printing, but there are methods in use that revitalize partially denatured fingertips.

Nonetheless, the quality of the original card and the search card have to be good. Eventually the card is examined and graded by an expert in fingerprint classification. The quality of the card may be graded as A, excellent; B, good; or C, not good. C-graded cards are unacceptable to master file agencies, such as the FBI and statewide systems. Cards graded unusable for any reason are sent back to the recording agency with instructions to redo them. Criminals may no longer be in custody, and if they used a false name during booking, they may have beaten the system, at least for the time being.

## How the Ten-Print System Works

Every time an individual is booked into jail, a fingerprint card is taken, without exception. If I'm booked into jail and fingerprinted and I say my name is Larry Ragle, a fingerprint classifier will manually compare my new ten-print card to all other cards on file locally under the name Larry Ragle. If the new card matches an existing card, my identity is accepted. Next, my name is checked for any criminal holds or warrants, ideally before I'm released. If there is no card on file under the name given, or if I give a false name and don't match up to anyone under that name, a full file search is begun.

Three types of fingerprint files are in use: manual, semi-automated (IBM punch cards), and automated fingerprint information systems (AFIS). Almost all ten-print classification systems have their roots in the modified Galton-Henry system (usually abbreviated as the Henry system or just Henry), but in an AFIS, the print is stored entirely differently.

Manual systems are searched like an old-fashioned library card system, by thumbing.

With the semiautomated IBM punch card system, the data, according to Henry, are punched into the cards and compared to a batch of cards with similar data. Once the initial search is completed, a fingerprint examiner must search through all the possible matches, which could be dozens or even hundreds of cards. This is a slow, tedious process, but is still used in some jurisdictions.

An automated system takes minutes instead of hours or days to do the same search. Most systems on the market arrange the likely candidates by score. The highest score, in a ten-print search, almost always identifies the matching card. A human verifies the match.

The California System, CAL-ID, 2000, is a network of computers that link major population bases to the main fingerprint files at the Department of Justice in Sacramento, the state capital. CAL-ID also links the files of several western states in a system called Western Information Network (WIN). Nevada, Utah, Washington, Oregon, Alaska, and Idaho are in this network. Each population center has a file of cards obtained locally from arrests and/or bookings, or from job applicants, when the responsibilities of their employment require some level of background clearance. A local system may also contain data from other states or countries of wanted or notorious criminals, but only if some outside agency takes the trouble to send them.

A local search is initiated once the card has been received and registered into the system. A fingerprint expert classifier will make some observation of the basic patterns—per Henry—channeling the card to predetermined files, but an automated video camera does the detailed classification. Most AFIS pay no attention to the basic patterns. Instead, all ridge endings and bifurcations are located and charted. At that point the fingerprint is converted to a field of minutiae points and the ridge pattern becomes transparent in some systems. All the points are connected graphically to adjacent minutiae points. CAL-ID counts the ridges between the points. The result is a complex model somewhat resembling a confused spiderweb. Because the location of the minutiae is random, it is unlikely that any two spatial models will match exactly. The computer assigns a high score to best match. Other spatial models that have sufficient similarity will also register scores. A list is printed and each person on the list is considered by a fingerprint examiner. The first step taken is to obtain a printout of the actual ridge patterns since, at the time of the search, patterns such as loops and whorls were invisible to the computer.

With older systems, the operator will almost always shorten the search by specifying parameters, such as sex, race, or age, if they are indicated on the fingerprint card or other included information. For example, a search could be limited to files that contain only white females between the ages of twenty and thirty with a loop on their right thumb and a double loop on their left. CAL-ID, 2000 is capable of searching without limits.

## Palm Prints

Since 1996 automated palm information systems (APIS) have been available, although few are in service. Nevertheless, suspects arrested for felonies and all sex crimes are usually required to give full flat palms, the butt (the side of the hand below the little finger) as well as the standard rolled tips and the fingers/thumb pressed flat. The registration phase, converting analog to digital information, is based on the same principle as AFIS, as is the comparison process.

CAL-ID, 2000, includes APIS, and the database is in the process of being constructed. In July 2001 the San Francisco Police Department reported the first database hit on a palm print search.

## Crime Scene Prints

Fingerprints located at crime scenes, initially of unknown origin, can be categorized as visible, plastic or latent prints. Unlike the former two, latent prints are not visible, and must be found and made visible with special techniques.

Visible prints are generated because there was something,

such as blood, on the person's fingers when an object was touched. Generally, a bloody print will appear as a positive replica of the ridge information, matching the appearance of an inked print. In some circumstances the impression is a negative image, that is, the blood is concentrated in the furrows between the ridges rather than on the ridges. This can happen when a bloody finger is pressed firmly against a solid surface or when a blood-free finger contacts drying blood. In both situations the liquid blood is squeegeed away by the ridges and concentrated in the furrows. The resulting print can be confusing to the novice fingerprint examiner. For example, when the blood on the ridges forming a bifurcation is squeegeed into the furrow between, that area appears darker and can look like a ridge ending. In fact, it is a furrow ending, not a ridge ending. All visible prints must be considered as both positives and negatives, and no suspects should be eliminated based on minutiae until the nature of the print is certain.

Plastic prints are made when a person touches something soft and pliable, yet permanent enough to retain three-dimensional impressions of friction ridges. Tacky paint, putty, and clay are likely surfaces to capture plastic prints.

Latent prints are two-dimensional impressions representing the friction ridge patterns. They occur when perspiration or sebaceous oils are on the hands of the donor. Sebaceous oils are transferred inadvertently to the hands by rubbing one's face.

There is no guarantee that any fingerprints will be left by the perpetrator at a crime scene even if the person handled many items. Experienced criminals often wear gloves. And, on cold dry days or nights there may be so little moisture or oil on the fingers that there is no transfer. In some cases the surface involved may be incompatible with accepting the prints. An oily surface, for example, may only reveal smears. Perhaps the most important factors in locating latent prints are the experience of the investigators, and the chemicals and equipment at their disposal.

Locating latent fingerprints at a crime scene may be accomplished by selective searching or by full coverage, that is, blanketing the scene. The choice largely depends on the magnitude of the crime, the perceived method and manner of the suspect's and victim's actions, the size of and conditions at the scene, and the experience and awareness of the crime scene investigator.

The majority of crime scenes where fingerprints are sought involve relatively straightforward crimes against property and fit into a common scenario. The perpetrators break a window, enter the scene, and leave an obvious trail of activity as they ransack the victim's house or business. Their point of entry, points of attack, and point of exit are relatively simple to identify, allowing the investigator to select and focus on those points.

Some crimes are witnessed, and the victim or witness lives to describe the suspect's movements and activities. The search team can then focus on those indicated areas.

In crimes of violence or crimes in which the perpetrator's movements within the scene are more subtle, a broader approach is more likely. Experienced investigators may be able to *visualize* and mentally reenact the crime and select specific areas to examine for prints. The problem with that approach is obvious. The investigator can be wrong and a critical source of evidence can be overlooked. Unless the entire area is examined, blanketed, the investigators may never know what they might have missed.

## Finding Latent Friction Ridge Impressions

Searching for latent fingerprints at crime scenes using assorted materials, if used improperly, can be hazardous to the examiner's health (short and long term) and destructive (messy) to the premises examined. For that reason, at indoor locations any portable item should be removed and examined, ideally in a laboratory fume hood, or at least outside if conditions permit. Regardless, safety devices such as dust masks and gloves should be worn. If fuming entire rooms or vehicles (see below), a respirator is a necessity. If the victim is alive and available, they should be advised of any potential permanent damage to their property prior to the examination.

Invisible impressions can be made visible by a number of processes involving physical or chemical means. The oldest of methods, carbon powder dusting, remains the method of choice due primarily to its simplicity. During the 1970s and particularly in the 1990s, innovative approaches to locating prints also became available to investigators. The success or failure in locating fingerprints remains a factor of the experience and tenacity of the investigator and the availability of the items listed on the following pages.

Before doing any field test or examinations on an object, the investigator must consider the entire significance of the evidence. Before proceeding with a field examination, all team members should be consulted to determine the best sequence to follow. More than one type of evidence may be present on the object—for example, fingerprints and blood—and a test for one could harm the value of the other.

Several recent studies indicate that DNA is not affected by routine visualization methods used to search for fingerprints. Nevertheless, before any new chemicals are used to develop latent evidence associated with bloody surfaces, the examiner should contact the local crime lab's serologist for concurrence.

### The Classic Methods

**Carbon Dusting.** Finely ground carbon powder is the original material used for the dusting process. Over the years, various manufacturers have blended pure black carbon with white pigments such as titanium oxide to produce various shades of gray. Otherwise the carbon process has remained unchanged. The carbon powder can be applied to the item or surface by any approach, but the standard method is by brushing on a small amount with a brush made of very soft fibers or with a fluffy feather.

Two conditions must be present for this method to work. First, the material making the impression must consist of transfer debris, oils, or other tacky materials. This debris may be from either perspiration or sebaceous transfer, or it could be a foreign transparent oily or tacky substance. Second, the surface to be dusted must be totally dry, free of other oily materials, and relatively free of other contamination.

The examiner dabs the brush into the container of powder, flicks it to remove the excess, and lightly brushes the remaining powder over the areas of interest. A large area, such as a door and the door frame, can be examined in a few seconds. The powder will cling to any receptive surface contamination. Experienced dusters recognize potential prints and modify their dusting action by moving the brush in the direction of ridge detail, avoiding repeated crossing against the flow of the ridges. This reduces any potential damage to the detail of the print. Any excess powder is lightly brushed away from the pattern to enhance the contrast.

The details of the print are documented first, by a close-up photograph that includes a ruler or scale. Special cameras and adapters are designed to take a one-to-one photograph, that is, a life-size copy of the print. The next step is to collect the print.

Carbon-enhanced prints are literally lifted off the host surface using transparent acetate tape similar to Scotch tape, only wide enough—one and a half to two inches—to cover an entire print. The examiner carefully spreads the tape over the area of interest and flattens it against the surface. The tape is pulled up from one end until completely loose and transferred to a three-by-five card. Cards are available with printed forms for case information and have a black area on the reverse side that will enhance contrast if a lighter shade of gray powder was used.

The timing of the dusting and collection procedure will depend on the nature of the item to be examined. If it is an immovable object, the dusting and the lifting must take place at the scene. Portable objects that appear to have evidential value other than fingerprints are often collected and examined later. Other experts—serologists, for example, if there is blood on the object—can be consulted before testing begins. In addition, alternative visualization methods described below may be available in the laboratory. The convenience of dusting for prints in the laboratory may be reason enough to do it there.

When the print is found on a portable object while at the

scene—particularly if it plays some part in the crime other than a host for a latent print—the object may be collected with the print and tape still attached. The standard process is to place the lifting tape over the print to protect it, and to lift it at a later time, when conditions may be better.

***Magna Brush.*** As the name implies, this device is a magnetic wand that attracts iron dust. When the wand is dipped into the iron dust, the particles align in long fiberlike configurations that look and act like a brush. The application of the iron is essentially the same as for carbon but less messy, and perhaps less destructive to the print. Excess iron dust can be retrieved using the magnet, dust free. A variety of colors are available, including several types of fluorescent powders. The fluorescent powder reflects various types of alternative light—UV, laser, etc.—effectively eliminating background patterns. The fluorescing print must be photographed for documentation.

***Iodine Fuming.*** During the early years of fingerprint science and until the 1970s, iodine fuming was one of two classic chemical methods of locating latent fingerprints, primarily when the surface was paper or cardboard. The vapors of iodine are brown in color and differentially absorb into the debris forming the print, causing the ridge detail to stand out.

Iodine is one of a few chemicals that change their physical state from a solid directly to a gas without a liquid intermediary. The crystals of iodine are placed in a glass tube called a fumer. Human breath is hot enough to cause the transformation from solid to fumes. The examiner blows into the fumer, and iodine vapors are emitted from the other end. If the tube is aimed at a latent print, it will become visible for a short time. A photograph must be taken quickly to document the print. A second application can be made if the print fades before the photo is taken.

The toxicity of iodine, a kin of chlorine gas, is a far more serious problem than the rapidly fading image. To avoid severe headaches, or even dying from the fumes, examiners learned to rely on vapor chambers. Items are placed in the chamber with a small container of iodine. A standard light-bulb under the chamber provides the heat necessary to vaporize the crystals. If the entire process is conducted inside a fume hood, it is relatively safe. Fortunately, the method is seldom used.

*Silver Nitrate.* A somewhat less toxic approach to locating prints on paper relies on the same principle that produces black and white photographs. Silver chloride turns black in the presence of light. One of the components in perspiration is salt—sodium chloride. The process employs a 0.2 percent solution of silver nitrate in distilled water that is used to spray on or saturate the paper, producing silver chloride only in the ridge areas. The paper is exposed to light, and the print turns black.

The big assumption here is that no chlorides are inherent in the paper or present for any other reason. Examiners learned to make a spot test before risking the entire surface of the document.

*Ninhydrin.* A significant event occurred during the 1970s that changed the nature of fingerprint detection on paper. A university scientist in an unrelated field was working with a process that stains protein tissue sections a purple-red color. The scientist knocked over an open bottle of the fluid, a ninhydrin solution, soaking his precious notes. Seeing that the ink was being dissolved by the solution, he hurriedly placed all his wet papers in a laboratory oven that was set 10 or 20 degrees above room temperature. After a few hours, he removed the papers, happy to see most of his notes intact. There was one problem he hadn't anticipated: His notes were covered with dozens of purple-red fingerprints.

He consulted a fellow professor, a forensic scientist, ostensibly to find a way to remove the prints. The second scientist quickly recognized the value of the accidental discovery and they jointly published a paper making the method known to fingerprint and document examiners.

Some problems were reported early on with the application of ninhydrin solution to documents. There was a story, perhaps forensic fiction, of a handwritten ransom note that was examined for prints using ninhydrin. Some prints became visible, but the critical evidence, the text of the ink writing, was dissolved away. This problem emphasizes the importance of consulting with other experts whether certain tests should be done, and if so, in what order. It would have taken only a small modification of the solution to avoid dissolving the ink.

A major advantage of ninhydrin is that it can be sprayed on large surfaces, such as cardboard containers. It may take longer for the prints to become visible if the paper isn't exposed to heat, but the reaction still works eventually. Like iodine, however, ninhydrin is toxic. Applications should take place inside a fume hood or outdoors, with adequate ventilation and breathing devices.

*Super Glue.* Another story of accidental discovery is told about a civilian forensic scientist who was working in the U.S. Army Crime Laboratory in Japan. This scientist used a new commercial product, Super Glue, to repair some loose parts on a camera frame. He returned to find the camera mended, but he also noticed white fingerprints all over the black camera's parts. Since his area of specialty was fingerprints, he required no consultation to recognize the importance of his discovery. Super Glue contains cyano acrylate (CA), the active component that combines with the print. Nevertheless, the household name, Super Glue, is used most often when describing this process.

The discovery of CA was a major breakthrough for crime scene investigators and laboratory evidence examiners. For the first time, latent friction ridge impressions could be located on surfaces that defied conventional methods. For example, plastic materials, and even surfaces contaminated to some extent, yield usable prints in the presence of CA.

Carbon powder is unsuitable for dusting many types of plastic surfaces. The powder tends to smear over the plastic as if the surface is oily. From the 1950s on, plastic has played an increasingly important role in our society, and it has always presented a difficult if not impossible task for crime scene and laboratory examiners. Since the introduction of CA, plastic surfaces such as the interiors of automobiles; plastic bags used to conceal and transport dope, bodies, or body parts; plastic gasoline cans; and plastic tape used to bind victims of kidnapping or murder, yield usable prints. The same is true of some surfaces that are contaminated with material that is sticky, tacky, or even oily. Carbon dust adheres to all the contaminants, while CA is often more selective, producing usable prints.

Of equal importance is CA's attraction to thin prints found on regular surfaces. A thin print is one in which only a trace amount of debris is transferred from the skin to the surface. Although some carbon dust adheres to the print, not enough carbon dust is absorbed to render the print usable. CA has a higher affinity to the transfer debris left by friction ridges than does carbon powder. This means that the same print exposed to CA will be more apparent, revealing more detail than if exposed to carbon dust. One of the most satisfying discoveries in the science of searching for latent prints is that dusting with carbon first does not impair the ability of CA to absorb into the debris. Faint prints made barely visible with carbon dust, too thin to be of value, may become identifiable after they are Super Glued.

## Other Chemicals and Their Uses

Many of the following chemicals have identical or similar uses and are often a matter of personal choice or, simply, availability. Often it is the texture, color, or contamination on the surface to be examined that determines the approach taken. In some cases the material is used alone and physically adheres to the oily fluids forming the print. Common practice is to fume the evidence or, for that matter, an entire room, with CA, and then apply appropriate powders, sprays, or dyes.

Examiners who are not familiar with the powder should always experiment on nonevidence surfaces to learn what works best for them. Before applying any stain or dye to evidence, a very small amount should be added to a swab and lightly touched to the actual surface in an area least likely to be significant. This will identify any unexpected discoloration that could obliterate any possible prints.

Any visible or partially developed print should be completely documented by photography—overall, orientation, and close up (one-to-one)—before any attempt is made to enhance or lift it.

## The Chemicals

**Amido Black.** Like ninhydrin, this is used in histology labs as a stain for protein. It enhances faint blood patterns, particularly fingerprints. It works on porous surfaces, such as paper, and nonporous materials, such as rubber and plastic. A fixing agent is applied to bloodstains prior to applying the stain. Specific products sold for evidence examination come with the stain and the appropriate fixing fluid; an alcohol, for example.

**Ardrox.** This is an industrial dye that absorbs into CA-fumed print. It fluoresces with most of the light sources listed below at wavelengths between 365nm to 480nm.

**Basic Yellow.** Essentially the same as Ardrox but yellow.

**Crystal Violet (Gentian).** A stain used in histology labs (Gram's stain). Enhances prints in the sticky side of tape without CA fuming. Fluoresces with the lamps listed below. Also works on CA-fumed oily surfaces.

**DFO.** Stands for 1,8,diazafluoren-9-one; similar uses as ninhydrin and amido black.

**Indanediones.** Currently, research projects are studying variations of the material in solvents and comparing them to DFO and ninhydrin.

*Leuco Crystal Violet.* A stain that enhances bloody prints. The material is sprayed directly on the stain and forms a purplish image. It is also used to enhance faint bloody shoe prints. Have a camera ready to capture the results, and include a scale in at least one exposure.

*Ray.* I don't know who, but someone has mixed **R**hodamine 6G, **A**rdrox, and Basic **Y**ellow and called it RAY. My kind of chemistry! Maybe with this mix you see the print no matter the wavelength of the light source.

*Redwop/Greenwop.* Redwop is powder spelled backward; cute. However, what's powneerg? They are fluorescent powders and provide a choice of colors, depending on the background color. CA fuming and high-energy lamps enhance the image.

*Small Particle Solution.* A suspension of molybdenum disulfide that can be sprayed on porous surfaces, auto paint for example. It is messy but will wash off since it is often suspended in a detergent. Molybdenum is an element.

*Stickyside Powder.* A product of Japan, hence the trendy name, this is designed to be applied to the sticky side of tapes, duct, etc.

*Sudan Black.* An industrial dye that is absorbed into fingerprint oils and into CA-enhanced prints. A blue-black color is produced.

## DNA in Fingerprint Evidences

The makeup of a bloody print may be all victim, all suspect, or a mix of the print of the suspect and the blood of the victim. Studies indicate these chemicals *do not* damage the DNA necessary for PCR-STR profiling. However, keep in mind that the chemicals that make up a fingerprint—amino acids, etc.—most likely contain enough of the donor's DNA for PCR-STR profiling.

## New Technology

*Nanocrystals.* Many of these dyes and stains depend on fluorescence as a means of optimal visualization, making photography possible. However, background fluorescence due to the makeup of the print's location is a problem one cannot always control. Some powders are available that produce a variety of colors, offering some contrast. The science of nanotechnology offers another solution. Nanocrystals are man-made particles of semiconductor material, a few billionths of a meter in diameter.

A pioneer in fingerprint science, Dr. E. Roland Menzel, is studying their use in detecting crime scene prints that, coincidentally, are on a fluorescent background. The crystals have fluorescent qualities when exposed to specific wavelengths. The observable color depends on the diameter of the crystals. Nanocrystals are unique due to a minor optical fault that forms during their creation. When light strikes most crystals, it either reflects off the surface or passes through, depending upon angle and the crystal's refractive qualities. The nanocrystal's optical fault "traps" the light, momentarily resulting in a photoluminescence or lingering afterglow. The nanocrystals are mixed with organic solvents and polymers for application and react with untreated prints or CA-fumed prints, or after some of the above chemicals have failed.

## Equipment

*Ultraviolet Light.* The effects of ultraviolet light are well-known. A UV lamp, sometimes called a black light because the human eye does not see UV light, is most effective in darkened environments. Lamps are available in three types: short wavelength, long wavelength, and full-range UV. The various levels of radiant energy cause some minerals, pigments, organic compounds, and even some living things, such as fish, to glow in the dark. The short wavelength lamps emit a light of higher energy, while the long wavelengths emit light nearing the visible range. The drug LSD, for example, glows a bright bluish-white fluorescence when examined with a simple shortwave UV lamp.

Numerous fingerprint powders are available that glow under long wavelength UV lamps.

***The Laser.*** Of all the light sources used in the forensic laboratory, the laser is the most powerful. The power is attained when monochromatic light (light of a single wavelength) is pumped into the system and reflected back and forth until it is vibrating in phase, a condition called "coherency." The energy of coherent light is amplified rapidly as more light is pumped into the system and gets into phase. Due to the speed of light, this amplification is, in effect, instant. The beam is emitted at predetermined energy levels, depending on the laser function. For example, it is diffused through fiber optics when used to search evidence but can also be focused to a pinpoint and used in lieu of a surgeon's scalpel.

Portable lasers can be used at a crime scene, although they produce only about one-thirtieth of the energy of a laboratory bench model.

***Alternative Light Source.*** An ALS supplies a powerful light that causes many materials to exhibit fluorescence or luminescence; for example, fingerprints enhanced by CA, fibers, or seminal stains. There are several variations of the ALS but they all serve the same purpose, illuminating otherwise latent evidence. ALSes have some advantages over the more powerful laser light. They are lightweight and self-cooling, making them far more portable than a laser. They are more versatile, providing light in a wide range of wavelengths. This means the crime scene can be examined for various types of evidence with the same light source.

***Reflective Ultraviolet Imaging System***—RUVIS is a unique handheld instrument combining UV radiation, special filters that enhance any fingerprint image, an eyepiece for viewing the image, and a capture device that can take a still or video image. It performs equally well in full daylight as it does in total darkness. No treatment—dusting, for example—is required to locate most prints on nonporous surfaces. However, CA is suggested since it increases the likelihood of locating a print. A UV lamp provides the energy to excite the fingerprint residue, and the filters remove all but the print image. Otherwise undetected prints developed by CA or luminol (see Chapter 6), but still too faint to be useful, are enhanced by this process. It is ideally suited for examining oily surfaces such as firearms. Prints on the adhesive side of tape are revealed in detail with no enhancement necessary. The light reflects off the surface, making the examination of porous material, such as paper, nonproductive, since the light is scattered.

***Vacuum Metal Deposition Chamber.*** VMDC is said to be the most sensitive method of detecting latent fingerprints when all else fails. However, it is also the most elaborate and expensive. Items are placed in the chamber and the atmosphere is reduced. A small amount of gold is vaporized, plating the object, including any fingerprint deposits. Zinc is then vaporized, plating the object except the gold over the print's ridge patterns, resulting in a golden fingerprint highlighted by zinc.

## IDENTIFYING THE SOURCE OF CRIME SCENE PRINTS

The manual comparison of two ten-print cards is usually no problem if they are of good quality. However, crime scene prints are partial prints and can have limited minutiae points and other minute characteristics. There can be unreadable areas within the print due to poor quality, or only a small area of excellent quality. Is it identification if there are less than ten points and no differences? Some examiners would report a match with even fewer points, while others would report exclusion. Is either expert in error?

The Daubert decision directly impacts this issue. It requires the trial judge to screen scientific testimony to determine the admissibility of scientific evidence and to ensure it is relevant while assuring its reliability based on the principles and methodology used. These include:

- Testing and validation
- Peer review
- Rate of error
- General acceptance by the scientific community

Not all state courts are impacted by the Daubert rule, but document examiners in those jurisdictions were forced to rethink their methods, particularly in determining an error rate. Other states have similar admissibility standards. In California, it is a Kelly-Frye hearing.

## Pore Wars

Presently, there is debate among fingerprint examiners over the standards and/or the minimum number of data points required to individualize a crime scene print, a dilemma of great significance. One side, the traditionalists, believes in a minimal number of minutia points, ten or twelve. The modernists form non-numerical opinions based on the overall appearance of the spatial relationship of details. They add value to the consistency of open fields, areas where ridges are lacking minutiae, the fine spatial detail of pores, *poroscopy*, and the irregularities of the edges of each ridge, *edgeology*.

While the choice of standards, numerical or non-numerical, is a personal matter, the International Association for Identification (IAI), a group of examiners who specialize in making physical comparisons such as fingerprints and tool marks, voted in 1973 to drop the requirement for a numerical standard. The changeover has been slow.

A second issue further complicates the debate, also at the federal level. The National Institute of Science's requested proposals (May 2000) to validate "Forensic Friction Ridge (Fingerprints) Examination." Daubert requires a scientific standard, and the NIS request gives the impression that there may be no valid scientific method to compare ridge detail.

Defense attorneys are attacking the science from these two fronts. In the first dozen or so serious challenges, trial judges, including an appellate judge, have ruled in favor of the prosecution and allowed expert opinion. However, it is reasonable to believe that eventually the defense may prevail.

Aware of these issues, many fingerprint examiners are urging the adoption of a systematic approach when comparing prints. David R. Ashbaugh, a scientist employed by the Royal Canadian Mounted Police, designed a method. Ashbaugh, in his publication, *Ridgeology*, describes ACE-V, a system based on all the observable qualities of a fingerprint rather than a set number of Galton points (minutiae).

### ACE-V: Analysis, Comparison, Evaluation, and Verification

**Analysis.** Ashbaugh's first level, begins with the study of the questioned print to determine the overall orientation, quality, shapes, flow of ridges, and any other observable characteristics. The known print is analyzed in the same manner. If the information is consistent, the exam goes to the next level. The exam is terminated if nonmatching characteristics are observed; an exclusion. In the case of an ALPS database search, the examiner would select the next candidate. Unlike a ten-print search, a match is not always the highest score.

**Comparison,** the second level, begins by orienting the two prints in the same manner and selecting a common point in the center of the two prints, or a distinctive point, for that matter. This process can be done using two hand lenses designed for this process, or on a split screen fingerprint comparator. The known is visually scanned for the nearest characteristic and its counterpoint in the questioned print. This process continues until all the characteristics are accounted for and there are no unexplainable differences.

Some differences are expected. It is highly unlikely that two impressions of the same fingerprint directly overlay, that is, superimpose exactly. Crime scene prints, particularly tape lifts, generally include an image of patterns from the host surface, detail such as wood grain or surface scratches. There may be bits of material—paint chips or wood fibers, for example—that are embedded in the sticky side of the lift and break the flow of a ridge. A smudged area within an otherwise clear print, on the questioned or on the known, happens. These differences are to be expected and can explain missing detail or other inconsistencies. However, if the examiner did not personally collect the questioned print, and there is superimposition and no indication of the crime scene surface, I suggest learning more about how and where the questioned print was collected. Evil happens.

*Evaluation* is the third level. All the information to this point is evaluated. An exclusion would be made in the event of a clear difference. A non-numerical identification may be made at this level when the two prints demonstrate numerous matching areas and overall consistency, such as matching areas of open fields. An identification may be made based on the amount and degree of ridge detail. Lacking ridge detail, the third level detail of pore distribution and ridge shapes and edges, if present, is relied on to establish individuality. Regardless of the examiner's conclusion, exclusion or identification, another qualified examiner reexamines the print.

*Verification.* Ideally, the verification is made by an experienced examiner who is not associated in any way with the case, or for that matter has any knowledge of the facts of the case, which could impart bias. If this results in a difference, additional experts must examine the evidence in total.

Even under the most extreme form of verification, errors can occur. I reexamined a case years after an identification had been verified by the FBI and two experts hired by the defense. They all agreed that the print identified the defendant. It did. However, they did not recognize that the print was a forgery. The defendant spent three years of a fifteen-year sentence in prison before the forgery was discovered and he was exonerated.

## IAI Certification/Proficiency Testing

Certification programs are voluntary for all forensic scientists, while proficiency testing may be a mandatory process required for laboratory accreditation or, where it exists, licensing of a forensic scientist. In either event, passing a series of tests demonstrates knowledge and skills while taking the test, but it does not guarantee compliance later, while on the job. The process can be compared to driver's license testing. If people always drove the way they did when the inspector was in the passenger seat . . . You get my point.

To add to the problem, there are fingerprint examiners who learn on the job, train themselves, and have no supervision or peer review. They may seem to do excellent work, but how do you know?

## The Bottom Line

A D.A. once said, "I never met a fingerprint I didn't like." What else can I say?

That's still the case. But what if the fingerprint match may be inadmissible because the fingerprint witness fails to qualify as an expert or the examination did not meet scientific standards? The following is my contribution to the solution. I have been suggesting this approach to my CSI/FET students for the past ten years.

Automated systems, ALPS, have a capability no human has ever had. The computer can locate similar areas of minutiae by searching millions of prints in minutes; more than a human could accomplish in a lifetime. It compares any "questioned" print to file prints, and provides a series of possible matching prints, arranged by score. In casework, the examiner begins the hands-on comparison with the highest scored card, until a match is made. Typically, the examiner then stops looking.

I suggest that they continue to compare some of the other possible matching cards to solidify their opinion that no two people have the same details in their prints. The argument against this suggestion is the belief that no two prints can be the same, so why look any further after a matching area is found? I say, how do you know that if you don't look at the other high scores? If there isn't time to do this during case-work, it should at least be done during the internship/train-ing period. The "questioned" print can be another rolled print or a crime scene print. Any print will do.

## chapter four

# Impressions and Physical Matches

## Introduction

Of all the types of physical evidence discussed in this book, my favorites are impressions and physical matches. Why? Because they are usually simple and direct, and the only elaborate analytical equipment you need are your eyes and your brain.

The potential for individualizing impressions and physical match evidence should inspire investigators to dedicate time at every crime scene searching them out, even when they are not readily apparent. Their one drawback is that they are often made of inanimate material. This may require additional steps to associate the evidence to the suspect. That turned out to be the major problem in this next case.

## CRIME SCENE:

### THE 7-ELEVEN KILLERS

Halloween is the night that monsters come out to play.

My phone rang at 1:30 A.M.

"Fountain Valley has a 187, at a 7-Eleven, corner of Warner and Newhope," said the sheriff's department watch commander. "It looks like a 211 went sour. Their evidence tech has never worked a murder scene, so they want you to act as an adviser . . . to make sure they don't overlook anything. Would you be so kind as to drop by?"

"I'm on my way."

"By the way, no one is in custody. They could still be in the area."

"Thanks a bunch," I said as I hung up the phone, wondering why I had the damn thing in the first place.

A murder during a robbery of an all-night convenience market was what the WC had told me. The street cops have their own names for such stores: Stop and Rob and 2-11. (In California, 211 is the penal code number for armed robbery.)

I drove into the parking lot a little after two A.M. A yellow rope had been strung around the outside of the building for the purpose of keeping people out, and a uniformed officer stood by to check out everyone who approached the store. He was tactfully explaining to a would-be customer why the store was closed, although, other than the rope and his presence, it appeared open for business as usual. When the officer stopped talking, he looked toward me and saw my badge dangling from its leather holder. Waving me on, he said, "They're waiting for you."

Actually, they hadn't been waiting. As I approached I could see a lot of activities, photos being taken, people searching, and so forth. I was greeted at the front door by the ID tech, Carl Lawrence. Carl briefed me on what tasks had been started and what was known at that point. The victim's body was still in the back room. The coroner had come and gone, but had scheduled the first call service to move the body.

The reporting party, also a clerk at the store, was supposed to take over at midnight but had been about five minutes late. He said that when he drove into the parking lot, he saw two people standing at the counter, both pointing what looked like guns toward the victim. He wisely chose to remain in his car, where he had a clear view of what happened next. Within seconds, he stated, he saw the taller of the two people fire a shot at the victim's face. He saw his friend turn and run to the back of the store with the two attackers in pursuit. He lost sight of what was happening but heard more shots. He froze in his seat, not knowing if the two had seen him drive in.

Moments later he saw the two run from the store and get into a sedan that was parked in a side alley facing him and the street. In an instant the car was moving toward his vehicle, then past it and out into the street. They hadn't seen him! He tried to focus on the front license plate but it was too dark to read any numbers. What he did see was almost as good as the numbers, though: a white license plate bordered by the outline of a mountain range. Montana, Wyoming, Colorado . . . it had to be one of the states that makes a living off their mountains. The car was a Chrysler and looked gray. But how many such visitors were driving around California at the moment? Once he told the police what he saw, every police unit in Southern California was alerted to the vehicle and passengers' descriptions.

Carl explained that his department wanted me to supervise what he and the rest of the scene team was doing, to approve what and how they planned to collect the evidence, and to suggest methods of locating, collecting, and preserving the evidence if what they planned wasn't the best approach. In addition, and perhaps most critically, they wanted me to help reconstruct the series of events that happened that night.

This was not the usual request for assistance. Generally when a city department requested help, they wanted the sheriff's criminalist to do all the work at the scene, in the lab, and then in court.

The layout of the market was identical to other 7-Elevens I had been in. As you entered the front door you faced a row of floor-to-ceiling glassed-in refrigerators on the back wall. There were four long rows of merchandise shelves on the left. If you took three normal steps and turned right, you were facing the checkout stand. The checkout was boxed in by an array of dispensers, the 7-Eleven trademark Slurpee machine, coffee, candy, and cigarettes, leaving only about four feet of open counter space. I noticed some loose items, junk food, on the counter, most likely foreplay by the killers to get the clerk to open the cash drawer. Fingerprints were possibly on these items, but not likely due to the type of plastic wrapping material. (This case occurred before the availability of Super Glue and the laser.) The cash register was still open and the money drawer had been removed and was on the counter, empty.

If you stood at the counter from the customer's side with the entrance to your right, you faced a wall with more dispensers and racks. About ten feet to your left was a door in the wall leading to a storage room. I had been told what to expect in the storage room.

The body was still in there. Paramedics from the nearby trauma center had pronounced death without disturbing the scene. Visible evidence that had been located and protected by the first officers on the scene and by Carl was pointed out. The most significant was a series of tracks leading away from the rear storage room toward the front door. Each track appeared to be a "right" shoe print impression made of a reddish material that looked like dried blood. (See bottom photo, insert page 8.)

"We think they must have chased him into the back room but he got there in time to get the door shut," Carl told me. "It looks like they forced the door open and then one of them shot him in the head, close range, pop, like that." He was holding his right index finger out like a kid playing guns, even recreating a kick.

The storage room door, hinged to swing from right to left into the room, was open about fifteen inches, making it possible to look in without disturbing any obvious evidence. The door could open no farther, as it was blocked by the victim's body. The floor was flooded with blood. The victim was positioned facedown at about a 45 degree angle to the wall housing the door, head and shoulder to the left, with his feet toward the right rear of the room. There was the appearance of a gunshot wound to the head, the exact nature of which would be unknown until the autopsy.

From the point of view of crime scene reconstruction, the blood on the storage room floor was critical. The source was most likely the victim since there was no indication that anyone else was wounded. Dry smears on the floor indicated the presence of a lot of blood prior to the head shot. If the head shot was as close as Carl had suggested, it could explain the placement of the bloody shoe prints. To get very close to the victim, the shooter would have had to place one foot into the room. It would take some effort *not* to step into the blood. (We would learn later, at the autopsy, that some of the blood on the floor in this area could have come from a wound in the victim's thigh.) One question would have to be answered: Did anyone else step into the room?

Eliminating the police and paramedic's shoes as the source of the tracks was simple enough. They were still on duty. A patrolman was dispatched to examine the shoes of both of the paramedics who responded to the scene. He returned later to assure us that there was no similarity to the pattern on the floor. Later that morning the shoes of everyone who had been at the scene were examined and eliminated as the source of the pattern. Nevertheless, everyone's soles and heels were photographed as a permanent record, in the event attorneys wanted to debate the origin of the scene prints at some future trial.

I had seen this type of impression before. It was consistent with a pattern of Vibram hiking and work boots. Carl began photographing the shoe prints. Three things were critical beyond the usual photographic requirements. One was to make absolutely sure that the camera's film plane was parallel to the surface of the floor. Even a slight angle distorts the photograph, making some details appear closer and others farther apart. To accomplish this, he attached his camera to a heavy-duty tripod. I watched him step back and eyeball the setup. As he reached into his gadget bag, he glanced at me, knowing I would be looking to see his next move. He placed a small carpenter's level on the top of the camera setup. The bubble settled neatly between the two scribes. He smiled, letting me know he understood the procedure.

Carl placed a six-inch plastic ruler on the floor next to the impression, making sure that it was lying parallel to the long axis of the print, heel to toe, while taking care not to cover any part of the print.

"I'm going to go three full stops with the close in half stops, then I'm going to repeat the series with the strobe light at an oblique angle," Carl said.

Carl was really getting into the swing of it. No screwups here! There were three separate shoe prints, each requiring the same disciplined photography. This would take a while. I took this opportunity to look around. Nothing else seemed to be disturbed or out of place.

"Carl, it would be a good idea to collect all these magazines," I said. "They may have been browsing, passing time. Could be prints here. You have ninhydrin, don't you?"

"Good idea and yes, in that order, but not with me," he replied.

Before I arrived, Carl had taken several overall photographs behind the counter and of the door. Thinking like the bad guys again, I considered what had taken place just a few hours earlier.

There was no indication of blood leading into the storeroom, but since it would only take two big steps to go from the rear of the counter to the door, there wasn't a lot of time for bleeding, assuming the victim was hit by the first shot.

There was a dark smudge, a two-dimensional transfer on the door frame fourteen inches above the floor. The door frame was painted white, so this foreign material stood out. The material was a blackish-gray, similar to stuff I had seen on other occasions. Those occasions, classroom demonstrations, involved holding a clean cloth at the side of a revolver against the cylinder as the weapon was fired. The appearance of the resulting marks, caused by escaping gases, vary depending on the specific revolver and the distance between it and the cloth. If the cloth is held tightly against the cylinder, the mark is sharp and distinct, usually in the shape of an L. At greater distances the marks become more diffused. Although this mark was not sharp, it had the characteristics of a cylinder spray. It meant a gun was wedged between the door and the door frame when a round was fired.

Carl took a series of photographs of the mark and removed a portion of it by swabbing with a moist cotton swab. The transfer material would be analyzed later to determine if it was, in fact, gunshot (powder and primer) residue (GSR). Next he dusted all the surfaces for latent prints, but found none of any value.

I walked out the front door to where I'd been told the surviving clerk had been parked. Standing in the parking space, I had a good view of the storefront. The alley was to the left of the store. While looking toward the alley, I noticed for the first time a potential source of evidence—a flower garden!

People in a hurry generally take the shortest route between two points, a straight line. If these guys ran out the front door and took the most direct path to their car, they would have run through the flower garden, a ten-by-twelve-foot patch, more garden than flowers. I had walked right past it on my way in and out and hadn't given it a thought.

I walked back near the front door and, like a golfer planning a putt, knelt and drew an imaginary line where I expected them to have run. About three feet in on my line, there was a deep impression in the soil. It looked good. Even in the poor light, I could see details of the sole impression. It looked like the same type of pattern, Vibram, that we had seen inside.

"Carl, how is your plaster of Paris supply?" I asked.

The moment Carl completed his work inside, he began the process of photographing the impression in the soil. I didn't have to tell him the routine. He had plenty of experience making casts at other scenes, burglaries and so on.

Carl was on his last two exposures when we heard a vehicle entering the parking lot. It was the first call service. There were no more excuses to avoid the next task. The plaster cast would have to wait. It was time to examine the body.

The store owner had arrived earlier and was being interviewed by detectives. At Carl's request he unlocked an outside rear door to the storage room, simplifying our access to the room. Once inside, this closer look at the body and the view from inside the room looking back provided some immediate answers to what had taken place.

Without moving the victim, I could see two apparent gunshot wounds, one in the left rear of the head and the other midway to the exterior side of the left thigh.

The back of the door was covered with blood patterns that resembled a monochromatic finger-painting reminiscent of what kids bring home from kindergarten, but in this case far too big to fit on a refrigerator door. There were several rounded areas of heavy compact spray, bursts of blood, three to four inches in diameter, that resembled the results one gets with a defective or clogged paint spray can held too close to the target. These marks were relatively high on the door, four to five feet above the floor, and each burst had long "legs"—trails of blood running down the door. Surrounding and occasionally running through these bursts and legs were numerous handprints, smears, and wipes that created the finger-painting effect. These smears extended down, almost to the floor. I would have to wait until the autopsy to fully understand just how this "painting" was created.

The smears in the blood on the floor provided an immediate explanation of some of the events leading to the killing. Most of the blood was dry. But a small amount, still a congealed liquid, was under the victim's head. The source of this blood was apparently a wound to the left rear side of the head. Most of the remaining blood on the floor consisted of two pattern types: overlapping quarter-size drops and long, wide smears that radiated out from the location of the victim's body, extending two to three feet toward the back of the room. (Blood patterns are discussed in Chapter 6.) These smears appeared to have been made by the victim's shoes.

I could visualize what had happened. Apparently, betrayed by his own blood, he lost his footing again and again as he fought for his life, eventually slipping and sliding farther back into the room each time he tried to regain his position. At some point in this deadly battle for the door, the killers prevailed, at least long enough to wedge one of their weapons between the door and the door frame to fire one shot into the victim's thigh. One more push and one of the two killers had a foot in the room. It was only a half step, but enough to place a weapon so close to the victim's head that there was no missing.

There was too much blood on the floor to see exactly where the shooter had stepped, but considering the total picture—that is, the bloody shoe prints, the black impression on the door frame that resembled a cylinder transfer, and the conditions in the storage room—it was apparent how the bloody shoe prints were created. All the more reason to find those shoes!

Carl completed the photography in the room, and we removed the door from its hinges. As the host for all the blood patterns, the door could become an important item of evidence if a trial was ever necessary. Also, other photographs could be taken looking into the room with the door out of the way. This done, the body was placed in a body bag, the bag was sealed with a coroner's security seal, and it was removed from the store.

The autopsy would be scheduled as soon as possible. Investigative leads were more critical than the last two hours of the pathologist's nightly sleep.

A few jobs remained. We had to remember to make the plaster cast out in the flower garden. Carl was dusting the cash register and the drawer for latent prints, not really expecting to find anything. There were smudges, partial prints that can be matched if you have a suspect but otherwise of little value. We would have to get elimination prints from all the employees. If any partial print was unidentified after they were compared to the employees, it would be a prize.

"Bingo! Look at this," Carl yelled. "It's as good as any latent I've ever seen."

Carl had the money drawer upside down and was pointing to the bottom of the drawer, where your fingers would touch if you lifted it out of the register. I looked at the print and agreed, it was a good one. You cannot date a latent print, that is, state that it was applied recently, but a lot of latent print experts will tell you that fresh prints stand out, appearing to absorb the carbon dust more than older prints. Right or wrong, this print stood out. We would have to wait for the elimination prints from all the folks with a legitimate reason for their prints to be on the money drawer to know for sure.

Carl took a photo of the latent before applying a strip of lifting tape over the area of interest. He pulled the tape off the drawer and transferred it to a lift card, a three-by-five piece of special white paper designed for latents' preservation. It was a good lift.

We didn't forget to make the plaster cast, but we should have done it sooner. Now we had to wait another twenty minutes for the plaster to set.

The autopsy was attended by the police investigators assigned to the case: Carl, me, and a photographer from the sheriff's department. The D.A. insisted that all autopsies of questioned deaths be covered by a sheriff's photographer, guaranteeing consistency in the product if the case went to trial. The pathologist, Dr. Richards, also had an autopsy assistant with him, whom he had picked up on his way from his home.

Once the coroner's seal was broken and the body bag opened, Carl and the sheriff's photographer took turns taking overall photographs, front and back, and the close-ups of everything that appeared significant, which included a wound on the left thigh and a wound that no one had seen until now, in the back of the left shoulder. The wound on the back of the head would be dealt with later.

The body was now on its back. A close-up photo of the face, as is, was taken by both guys. Richards began to examine the face by slowly dabbing at the blood, thinking ahead to the necessity for a clear photo of the face for identification purposes.

"Something here," he said.

With some of the blood removed, tiny red defects became visible and did not move or disappear when the doctor rubbed his gloved thumb over them. There were several of these tiny permanent marks above and below the victim's lips. The pathologist hooked his thumb and forefinger into the corners of the upper lip and forced a smile on the victim's face.

"Check this out."

Both front teeth, the two upper incisors, were shattered.

"Christ, they shot him in the mouth," someone from behind me said.

The tiny specks were most likely powder burns, called tattooing, that occur when a weapon is fired close to living flesh. If any partially burned gunpowder is still very hot, it will burn the flesh and often will still be lodged in the defect. The weapon has to be within inches of the skin for this to occur. More photos were taken before Dr. Richards forced open the victim's jaw, which was beginning to set with rigor.

"Don't put your cameras away boys, I'll need some pictures of this," he said.

The tongue was split down the middle like a hot dog that had been left on the barbecue too long. At the end of the split, about two inches into the tongue, something metal was visible.

After the photos had been taken, Dr. Richards worked the metal object loose with his fingers. It looked like a .22 caliber bullet.

This wound offered an explanation for the entire event, from the scene the surviving clerk observed to the patterns and amount of blood in the storage room. The victim had been shot in the mouth soon after he had opened the cash register. He ran to the storage room before he began spitting up blood. As he blockaded the door with his body, the volume of blood in his mouth increased rapidly, forcing him to spit it out, forming the bursts each time his mouth filled. It was just a matter of time until his blood covered the floor, causing him to lose his footing and eventually the battle.

Richards's attention now turned to the head shot that most certainly was the kill shot.

There was too much blood matted in the victim's hair for any powder burns or residue to be recognizable. Dr. Richards, or possibly I, would be asked about muzzle to first surface distance. A contact or near contact wound tends to emphasize the execution nature of this crime, that is, the intent to eliminate this human being and any possibility of his ever testifying against the attackers. In California there are varying degrees of murder. If it can be established that during the commission of certain felonies—robbery, rape, burglary, and so forth—the perpetrator killed the victim for the purpose of eliminating him or her as a witness, the crime becomes a capital offense and the D.A. may ask for the death penalty. California also has the accomplice law, which meant in this case that both robbers could be sentenced to death if found guilty, even if only one was the aggressor.

Dr. Richards held up an X ray that had been taken of the victim's head prior to the autopsy. I moved into position to get a peek for myself.

"There are at least two foreign objects here," he said. "This one is the one we already got." He pointed to the area of the tongue.

There were several opaque objects in the area of the teeth, one much larger than the rest. The larger one had to be the .22 caliber bullet, and the smaller ones were either fillings or, more likely, lead shrapnel caused when the bullet hit the teeth.

"If that one is the .22, then the mass higher up in the right posterior cerebral hemisphere has to be a larger caliber. Too big for a .22," he said.

"Do you mean the big chunk of metal inside the top part of his head is from a different weapon?" I said.

"You got it."

Before we would know for sure, there was other work to do. The hair surrounding the head wound was shaved and saved as evidence to be checked for powder residue. Photos were taken of the wound. It was clearly an entrance wound—there was no exit wound—but there was no evidence of tattooing to indicate proximity because the hair and blood masked the evidence.

Once Dr. Richards removed the skull cap, he followed the path of tissue damage and removed a metal object. It appeared to be a .38 caliber bullet.

The next day, I received some very good news. Earlier that morning an alert Santa Ana police officer had noticed a Chrysler vehicle bearing out-of-state license plates decorated with a mountain range, driving from a surface street onto the northbound I-5 freeway. The officer followed it onto the freeway, radioed for backup, and stopped the car. The vehicle contained two men, the brothers Hugh and Charlie Bean, and all their worldly possessions. It seems the Bean brothers were headed home, or at least out of Southern California.

The Santa Ana officers, who were aware of the felony want for such a vehicle, impounded the car. A subsequent search produced a pair of boots, one stained with apparent blood, a .22 caliber revolver, a .38 caliber revolver, and a cash bag containing the amount of money taken in the 7-Eleven robbery just the night before.

## Epilogue

I selected this case for this chapter because of the bloody shoe sole impression, but the entire case is a classic example of the value of physical evidence. The shoe impression is particularly significant since the wearer was the one who administered the fatal shot. All the physical evidence would be used in an attempt to answer the key questions:

- Could the two suspects arrested the next morning be placed at the scene during the time of the murder or at any other time?

- Were the weapons removed from the vehicle used to fire the bullets collected at the autopsy?

- Were the boots removed from the vehicle the source of the impressions found at the scene, the bloody shoe prints, and the impression in the dirt outside the front door of the store?

- Was the material on the boots human blood, and did it match the blood characteristic of the victim?

- What was the sooty smudge on the storage room door frame?

Here is how I processed the evidence. I examined the boots, and after photographs were taken of the blood and it was removed by the serologist assigned to the case, I began the comparison process. Ink was applied to the right boot, as described below, and a number of test impressions were prepared on white paper and on clear cellulose acetate. Our darkroom photographer made a life-size enlargement of the bloody impression from the crime scene. This was possible because a ruler was included in all the close-up photos. One impression, the first one out of the storage room, included both the sole and the heel. The test patterns and the photos were clearly the same. By laying the cellulose transparent test pattern directly over the photo of the bloody print, I could find the position of more than 150 cuts and tears in each that superimposed. The right boot had made the impressions.

The serology results established that the blood on the boot was the same as the victim's. I compared the right boot to the plaster cast, and it matched. The firearms examiner identified both weapons as firing bullets recovered from the victim. The smudge on the door frame was consistent with gunshot residue that escapes from the side of the cylinder of a revolver, and it contained the elements barium, copper, antimony, and lead. These elements are typically found in the primer residue of center core primers such as those used in .38 caliber ammunition, but not in most .22 caliber ammunition, which have rim-fire primers. This indicated that the .38 caliber weapon had been fired at that location and matched the wounds in the victim's thigh.

The fingerprint was identified as belonging to Charlie Bean, the younger of the two brothers. The money bag was identified by the store manager as the type they used to store cash before a deposit, and it could have been in the store at the time of the robbery.

The brothers asked for and got separate trials. Both denied wearing the boots, so I was asked to prove which one had them on at the time of the shooting. That could be easy if the size of the boot, 9D, precluded one of the brothers from fitting into it. Charlie was considerably taller than Hugh, so it was a possibility that their shoe sizes were different. I called the jail to check their records. The jail clothing records indicated Hugh requested a size nine jail-issue shoe and Charlie requested a size nine jail-issue shoe. Who said this would be easy?

I recalled the work of Reginald Abbott, an evidence examiner for the Royal Canadian Mounted Police. During the 1940s he wrote a book, *Footwear Evidence*, describing his work with footwear and referring to inner sole impressions. At my request the D.A. obtained a court order allowing me to examine the brothers' feet and make a replica of each one's right foot, if I felt it necessary. I also got permission to cut the top off the boot for the purpose of examining any foot impressions in the material of the inner sole.

I decided I would look at the inner sole before I checked out the brothers' feet. If I saw evidence of anything unusual, like a deformed toe, it would be easy to spot the brother, and I would know how to better spend my time. There was a definite impression in the inner sole, but it wasn't unusual.

I took all the materials needed to make the replicas of their feet with me to the jail: a hot plate, a set of double boilers, two big bags of moulage, and several chunks of molding wax. I worked with each brother separately. Both were very cooperative. After a few hours I had two precisely formed replicas of their right feet. Back in the lab with the exposed boot in front of me, I placed the replica of Charlie Bean's right foot in the impression. It fit perfectly! Then I placed the replica of Hugh Bean's right foot in the impression. It fit perfectly! Gee, that was easy. Either one of them could be the cold-blooded killer.

Both brothers were convicted of first-degree murder. The jury accepted the testimony of the clerk who had been in the parking lot. He testified that he saw the first shot fired, and it was by the taller of the two, who was wearing a black and white shirt. The first shot was a .22 caliber for sure, the one in the mouth. Charlie was the taller of the two and still had on the black and white shirt at the time of his arrest. That left Hugh holding the .38 caliber revolver and the bag, so to speak.

Hugh was sentenced to die for being the shooter, and Charlie was given life. Hugh hanged himself, however, before he could be executed.

## IMPRESSION AND IMPRINT EVIDENCE

Impressions or imprints are produced when two objects come in contact and their surface characteristics are transferred from one surface to the other. There are three types of impression evidence:

1. Two-dimensional impressions, sometimes called rubber stamp evidence, are flat images produced when one surface, coated with a visible substance, comes in contact with another surface. A perfect example is an ink-covered fingertip being pressed onto a fingerprint card. Other examples are impressions made when the skin on any part of the body comes in contact with a receptive surface. This includes lips, ears, and skin from other body parts. When inanimate objects such as shoes, their soles and heels, tire treads, or typewriter keys come in contact with receptive surfaces, they may leave a two-dimensional impression.

2. Three-dimensional impressions, sometimes called compression marks, are indentations produced when a solid object comes in contact with a softer object, such as a tire track in mud. Other examples of indented evidence are tool marks, for example, the marks made by the face of a sledgehammer used to break into a safe, and the dent in the primer of a round of ammunition made by the firing pin of a weapon.

   Teeth, depending on the pressure applied, may make bite marks in any number of soft materials. In violent crimes, humans may be the target of indented evidence. Teeth; fingernails; weapons such as hammers, clubs, and bats; and the ornaments or trim on automobiles, can make identifiable indentations in human flesh or bone.

3. Striation marks, or rows of parallel scratches, are produced when a moving surface comes in contact with another surface with some degree of force, for example, a bullet fired through a gun's barrel is usually marked with striations, called rifling marks. The harder of the two surfaces digs into the softer as one moves against the other.

   Other examples of striation evidence are pry marks

made by many types of tools, and heel marks when someone wearing shoes kicks in a door. Identifiable striations may be found in the abrasions made as a fast-moving weapon or any irregular surface scrapes across the skin. For example, scratches made by fingernails may include identifiable striations.

As tools and weapons are flailed about during violent criminal activity, the injuries to victims or damage to property may be made of a combination of impressions. Targets can be round rather than flat—a victim's head, for instance. During a struggle, the resultant tool mark—a wound in this example—may begin with striations and end with a deep compression mark. The scratch marks are made by the weapon scraping through tissue just before it makes a solid impact and comes to a stop.

The process of identification of any of the types of impression on an inanimate object or on a body (called a "defect") begins with the investigators, scientists, or pathologists recognizing that marks or patterns are present. This may sound simple enough, but there is no guarantee that anyone on the team will notice all the evidence. Contusions of any type—particularly bite marks made by the perpetrator of a sex crime, as opposed to deeper defense bites made by a victim—may be too faint to see soon after they are made. As time passes, bruising makes the damage more visible. In Orange County death investigations, our policy was to hold the body for at least forty-eight hours after embalming and reexamine the skin to see if any trauma had been overlooked. Embalming accelerates the darkening of blood that has leaked from damaged capillaries, pinpointing tissue damage.

Locating an impression may not be difficult, but proving what type of weapon made the mark can be. During the commission of a violent crime, such as an assault or murder, or a physical crime, a breaking and entering, any number of available objects may end up being used as a weapon or tool. Whatever is available to the perpetrator at the moment may be the assault weapon. An unusual murder weapon left at the crime scene, although in plain sight, could go unnoticed until the marks are studied and their cause identified. This means that there is no simple method of teaching investigators how to recognize the type of object used to make the wound. It requires a lot of imagination, reasoning, and thought.

Keeping an open mind while viewing wounds, combined with a constant "what if" dialogue at the autopsy between investigators, forensic scientists, and the pathologist, will often result in the recognition of the unusual defect. Marks made by unusual objects—spike heels, Phillips screwdrivers, hunting arrows, and protruding automobile trim, etc.—can be identified and assist in explaining the manner of death. Also, information about what could make the patterns will guide investigators in locating the unusual weapon should they return to the crime scene. If a search warrant for a suspect's home or office is sought, it can include a list of possible weapons capable of making such marks.

Some marks scream out to be scrutinized. Almost everybody is familiar with impressions such as tire tracks, shoe prints, and fingerprints. The presence of surface information seen in two- and three-dimensional impressions is often very obvious because of recognizable tread patterns and/or designs such as logos or symbols like those found on the soles of shoes.

Whenever possible, all forms of physical evidence must be successfully collected and transported to a proper place of examination, a crime lab, to be of maximum value. Obviously, impressions on portable objects can be collected along with the object, but not all objects with impressions are portable. In either case, the documentation of impression evidence begins with photographs showing the location of the evidence, followed by proper close-up photographs, with a ruler, showing the detail of the markings. Since most shoe impression evidence is not portable—for example, a bloody shoe print on a concrete floor—it may not be possible to collect the actual impression. The bloody boot prints located on the floor of the 7-Eleven in the case just discussed were documented by photography, and then some of the blood was collected for ABO typing.

Some two-dimensional impressions are made of loosely

compacted particles, such as dust. Methods, similar to lifting fingerprints, are available to lift this type of impression. Wide acetate tape, adhesive rubber lifters, and electrostatic dust print lifters are available to use at crime scenes to lift two-dimensional dust impressions from immovable objects or items that can't be transported to the laboratory.

Three-dimensional impressions that can't be transported are documented by one of several methods of casting. Prints in dry soil, mud, or snow are reproduced using plaster of Paris or a similar type of fast-setting plaster. Tool marks are documented using a silicon rubber material. As always, the process begins with a series of photographs and measurements in case the casts don't turn out.

Regarding three-dimensional impressions in dry dust or soil, a spray is applied to the impression to prevent the surface particles from moving during the pouring process. Hair spray, clear fast-drying acrylic paint, or a similar material can be used as long as it is not applied too close to the surface. Spray cans, in particular, are under great pressure and could blow away the detail if held too close to the surface while spraying.

Impressions in snow must be pretreated with special material before the plaster of Paris is poured. If not, the moisture and warmth of the plaster melts the snow and washes out any fine detail. The best pretreatment material that I have seen and used is a product called Snow Print Wax, developed in Sweden. It is a red-colored spray wax that is used to coat the entire inner surface of the impression prior to pouring the plaster. I conducted a controlled test applying the wax to half of a boot print in snow while leaving the other half unprotected. The detail in the waxed area was very good, but there was absolutely no detail captured in the untreated area.

Impressions in mud don't require any pretreatment unless the indentations contain standing water. If so, dry plaster powder can be sieved into the impression, adding just enough to absorb the free water. An ordinary kitchen flour duster works best, allowing the plaster powder to drop gently into the impression. The remaining plaster mix should be ready to pour as soon as this step is completed.

When mixing the plaster, the proportion of powder to water is seven to four for most types of plasters. The total volume needed depends on the size and depth of the impression. As a guide, a quart container of plaster and a pint of water will be adequate for a small- to medium-size impression. For larger or deeper ones, I suggest preparing a half gallon of plaster and a quart of water. The raw materials should be measured out before mixing begins.

The water is placed in the mixing vessel first, and then the powder is added gradually while stirring, until a thick, creamy consistency is reached and there are no lumps. This must not take more than five minutes. Plaster of Paris solidifies by chemical reaction, not by drying. Soon after five minutes, it will start to set. If you feel the liquid thickening as you stir, too much time has passed. Don't attempt to pour this liquid. Discard it and start again, this time moving a little more quickly.

The plaster must not be poured directly into the impression without breaking its fall. The weight of the material most likely would move things around, particularly in the drier soil. Any flat object can be held just above the impression and used as a target to pour the plaster onto while breaking its fall. A second person is needed for this step. Thin pieces of wood or wire can be added for lateral strength to impressions longer than seven or eight inches.

Related information—date, time, location, and so forth—can be scratched into the semihardened plaster after about ten minutes. To ensure that the cast won't break apart during removal, more time is needed. The total time to solidify before removing may vary from twenty minutes to one hour, depending on the material used and conditions. The plaster in the snow took longer to harden, about an hour. I could tell it had hardened when I could no longer scratch it easily with my fingernail. Another test to assure that enough hardening has occurred is to examine it for warmth. The chemical reaction is exothermic, and the plaster will get very warm as it hardens. After it starts to cool again, it can be removed. This touch method, however, didn't work in the snow.

Some tool marks are found on large or permanent items that can't be collected. These are documented at the scene by photography and by casting using a silicon rubber type of material. Several variations of casting material are available. The product I use is called Mikrosil. It is a viscous fluid that solidifies in about two to three minutes after being mixed with a catalyst. All the products on the market do an excellent job of capturing very fine detail. They can be used on a body to pick up defects in the skin such as bite marks, and a recently published study suggests using them for reproducing indented writing.

Casts of three-dimensional impressions are positive replicas of the original object. For example, the indentation in soil is, in effect, a mold. When you fill the mold, you produce a replica. Logos, figures, and letters will be readable, not mirror images. Casts can be compared directly to the suspect object; for example, the cast to the shoe. The two can be placed side by side to facilitate the search for matching marks (see Photo 3).

Class characteristics can be found on most items, as can individual marks on items that have been in use for a period of time. Class characteristics of tools, shoes, tires, and so forth are most often factory marks that tend to wear away with use as individual wear and tear marks are added. Occasionally, factory marks give the appearance of individual marks. Photographs 3b and 4a (see bottom photo, insert page 3; top photo, insert page 4, respectively) dramatically demonstrate how a factory mark can appear as an individual characteristic. The photos depict the same shoe, enough proof to convict the suspect; Photo 4b (see bottom photo, insert page 4) is of a brand-new heel. Many observers jump to the conclusion that it is as worn as the other heel. Take a close look at Photo 4b and decide for yourself.

Unfortunately, it is not possible to look at a shoe impression, measure it, and make any accurate statement about the size of the shoe or the size of the wearer's foot. Sole designs vary greatly, and the actual length of the sole is determined by many factors, as well as the labeled size.

Investigators who want to know the size of a shoe impression must first determine the brand of shoe. Then they must make impressions on a similar surface with various sizes of the specific model of sole pattern. Each size will vary somewhere between one-eighth to one-quarter inch. If the crime scene impression is complete, its size should match one of the test measurements.

***Shoeprint Image Capture and Retrieval (SICAR).*** The computer database of more than two hundred brands and three thousand known patterns is updated as new shoes are manufactured. Examiners can add to the database in three ways. Entries can be made using a standard flatbed scanner or digital camera:

- Reference file: All the known brands and patterns plus new patterns can be added from a local source if they are not already in the system.

- Suspect file: Prints from suspects can be entered into the reference database and compared to unsolved crimes.

- Unknown file: Prints collected at crime scenes can be entered and the brand and model identified, and they are automatically compared to prints from the suspect file and to other unknown prints.

Unlike the cast made from three-dimensional impressions, two-dimensional impressions are negatives or mirror images of the original and are not as easily compared directly to the suspect source. I prefer to make a known impression, reproducing the circumstances of the event while using the suspect object; for example, a shoe. By reenacting the crime scene events while wearing the suspect's shoes, you can produce an impression that is directly comparable to the crime scene evidence, such as stepping on a piece of broken window glass while wearing the shoe.

The surface information transferred will reflect to some extent the class characteristics and, if they exist, perhaps some individual characteristics.

The nature of crime scene impressions are unpredictable, however. They can be made on a soiled surface by a clean object or left on a clean surface by a soiled object. Therefore, there is no one way to predict what material to use to reproduce an impression for the purpose of comparison. I always begin by trying to use the same material that made the questioned mark, if I can tell what it is. If it is a dust impression made by a shoe, there may still be some of the original dust remaining on the shoe. I also try to use the same matrix to host the impression. For example, if the mark was made on white paper at the crime scene, then I would use white paper to reproduce the mark. In the case cited above, Photo 3b is a photograph of a heel impression made in dust on a piece of glass found at the scene of a burglary. Photo 4a is an impression I made by using the suspect's shoe to step on a piece of glass I had in the laboratory. They match. Had I tried some other material (like ink) on the shoe, I might have covered some of the detail and missed the match.

It would be a bad idea to put any real blood on a suspect's shoe if a victim's blood was already on it. To avoid any such problem, in the case of the 7-Eleven killers, I used regular fingerprint ink. My problem was that I didn't know how much ink to use, so I mimicked the action of the suspect. Before I cut the shoe apart, I placed far more ink on the shoe initially than I expected would be necessary. A criminalist with a size 9 foot helped. His first step was nothing more than a smudge, but with each step there was less ink left to transfer, and more detail was revealed. By the third or fourth step, the image was perfect. We repeated the process, this time substituting the cellulose acetate at the third and fourth steps.

Today I use ink made for silk-screening patterns on cloth. Not only does it come in different colors, it dries when applied to the cellulose. Fingerprint ink dries on paper, but years later it will still smudge on cellulose acetate.

## Two Other Forms of Impression Evidence

**Bite Marks.** Teeth have unique character, both as a set and taken individually. Given the proper target material, bite marks possess as much individuality as fingerprints. Bites into wax or in the rim of soft cups or just about any other pliable material except skin can be individualized to the biter. Unfortunately, most evidential bite marks are in flesh, and flesh is about as bad a matrix for retaining fine detail as one could imagine. On rare occasions, a bite in flesh is deep enough or extremely unusual, so that an absolute match can be determined, but far more often only class characteristics are recognized.

The comparison of a suspect's teeth to a bite mark always requires a dentist's participation, and unless the dentist is trained in forensic applications, he or she should not attempt the comparison without the direct supervision of a trained forensic scientist. A firearms and tool mark examiner or criminalist who is aware of the difference between class and individual characteristics must be able to recognize the points of identity and agree to their significance. Qualified forensic odontologists work alone, but they should always seek a second opinion, of any comparison, whether a match or an elimination. A case that should be made but isn't can cause as many problems as a case of mistaken identity.

During the act of biting, some amount of saliva containing the biter's DNA will be transferred within the boundaries of the wound. Any wound that appears to be a bite mark should be swabbed as soon as possible, before any other type of examination, regardless of the condition of the victim. Control swabs of nearby uninjured skin must also be collected (see Chapters 6 and 7).

*Handwriting*, typing, and electronically formed text are also potential forms of impression evidence. Handwriting is taught in two forms: cursive writing in which the letters are connected in a flowing continuous form, and printing, in which each letter is blocked out separately. Few people retain the stylized manner they were taught in school, and soon develop habits that make their writing unique. Individuality is difficult to disguise. Even when a person is forging another person's name, personal little flourishes may be recorded in the phony signature.

## PHYSICAL MATCHES

A physical match is perhaps the simplest form of comparative analysis, yet it offers the highest likelihood of individuality. When two (or more) pieces of material fit together, as in a jigsaw puzzle, it is indisputable evidence that, at some time in the past, the pieces had been one. Another way of describing the fit is to say the pieces have a common border. When the common borders exactly fit together, a single source is established for both or all the pieces. For example, when a fragment of metal found wedged in a door frame at the point of entry of a burglary fits into the broken tip of a pry tool found in the possession of a suspect, the certainty that the tool was used at the scene is seldom challenged. Of course, the judge or jury must now decide who actually used the tool to pry the door open.

Anything found at the crime scene that has been torn or broken is a candidate for physical match analysis. By their nature, violent activities produce an abundance of broken evidence. In the case of "The Key to the Crime," two types of physical match evidence connected the suspects to the crime. First, the small piece of black electrician's tape that Jim White matched to the tape wrapped around the tire iron he found in the suspects' vehicle established their tire iron as the tool used in attempting to open the victim's trunk.

The second physical match, bone to bone, placed the victim in the garage at the time his head was blown to pieces. The small piece of skull mixed in with the charred papers found in the footlocker fit precisely into the reconstructed skull of the victim (see Photo 1).

Physical matches of human parts are far less common than those of inanimate objects, simply because most things break apart more easily than a body, other than the teeth and fingernails. The edges of inanimate things are usually more defined than the edges of tissue. Fortunately for the investigators, with the exception of the investigation of disasters such as airplane crashes, there is seldom more than one possible source for the origin of the severed part.

Hit-and-run scenes almost always have some debris that broke away from some part of the suspect auto. An examination of a scene often results in locating broken pieces of car parts, chips of paint, and pieces of glass, plastic, and metal. During an investigation of one fatal hit-and-run, large pieces of undercoating were left at the scene, along with paint chips and broken glass. Undercoating, used for weather and soundproofing, is usually sprayed inside the fender wells and other parts of the underside of the frame. It is often very thick. These pieces fit back into bare areas on the inside of the heavily damaged fender.

Someone has to take the time to collect *all* the pieces of the broken material, the questioned evidence at the crime scene. Then it is necessary to collect *all* the pieces available from the suspect's source, the known or standard material. Taking shortcuts at either phase of the investigation could result in overlooking the key piece possessing the matching edge. Unfortunately, some investigators have been trained to collect only representative samples, that is, samples that will be sufficient to determine class characteristics such as chemical and physical composition.

The landmark Lorena/John Wayne Bobbit case epitomizes the need to collect all the evidence. Notwithstanding the outcome of the case and the irresistible impulse defense, consider the consequence to Mr. Bobbit if someone had not collected *all* the evidence.

A physical match examination is simple, requiring more patience than scientific skill. Other than a camera, no special equipment is needed for most cases. All the pieces must be kept separated until they are photographed and marked in a manner such that their source will never be confused. All the questioned evidence can then be placed on one side of the examination table, and all the known material can be placed on the other side. Patterns within the material, for example, ridges in headlight glass or polish scratches in paint, can be used to arrange all the pieces. From this point on it is very similar to putting together a jigsaw puzzle.

## The Bottom Line

The value of impression evidence and physical matches as associative evidence cannot be overstated. More often than not, a single quality photograph of a match, when shown to the defense, is enough evidence to save the time and expense of an otherwise costly trial.

## chapter five

---

# Firearms Evidence

## Introduction

When someone pulls the trigger on a loaded firearm, what follows is a contained explosion calculated to kill. The gun has no brain. It cannot stop in the middle of its work. In a flash, one action instantly leads to another in a chain reaction.

From the viewpoint of a forensic scientist, each reaction produces a wide array of physical evidence consisting of either chemical debris (all class characteristics) or tool mark striations (usually individual characteristics). An amazing number of critical questions can be answered by examining firearms evidence.

From the weapon:

- What is the make, caliber, model, and condition?

- Is there a serial number that identifies the registered owner?

- Who has handled it?

- How or where has it been carried or concealed?

- Is it contaminated with any foreign material?

From a recovered bullet of undocumented origin:

- What is the caliber?

- What make, model, or type of weapon fired the bullet?

- Is it contaminated with any foreign material?

- Do the land and groove marks match a bullet fired from a known weapon?

- Do the land and groove marks match any bullets from other investigations?

- Are there any indented patterns on any part of the bullet?

From a recovered shell casing:

- What is the caliber, brand, and model?

- What is the type of ammunition, and was it fired by a revolver or an automatic?

- Do marks made by a firing pin, breech block face, extractor, or ejector match marks made by a known weapon?

- Do these marks match the marks on casings from other investigations?

- Who has touched or handled the casing?

- Is there any residue of gunpowder or primer remaining in the shell casing?

From the debris created by the detonation of the round:

- How close was the weapon when it was fired?

- Who fired the weapon?

From the victim:

- What was the direction of travel, the entrance, and the exit?

- If no exit wound exists, where is the bullet?

- How close was the weapon to the victim when detonated?

- What are the size, shape, and color of any intact or partial powder particles around the wound?

- Did the victim fire a weapon?

- Did the wound contribute to or cause the death of the victim?

Although firearms evidence played a significant role in the cases I have described in Chapters 1, 2, and 4, other physical evidence was involved. In the following case it was the only physical evidence linking the suspect to the killing.

## CRIME SCENE:

### JOHN DOE SNORT

My high beams stretched out into the dark void of Santiago Canyon Road as I wondered if I'd somehow missed the crime scene. The watch commander had described the location as a place near where the new road crossed the old road and they ran almost parallel for a while. About the time I figured I had missed the turn, I picked up something off to the side of the road, maybe two hundred yards ahead of me. Before I could lift my foot off the accelerator, I recognized the reflection of the six-pointed star on the side of the ID van.

As I pulled in next to the van, my lights revealed at least five people kneeling over a large lumpy-looking thing. One of them moved his arm abruptly upward. The lump gave off a deafening roar. The two lamps of a portable generator lit up the scene. We wouldn't be able to hear each other, but at least we could see the evidence. I could recognize Sergeant Bob Reid, Willie Stansbury, and Bernie Esposito, who, by the manner in which he turned and walked toward my car, must have been expecting me and no one else.

"This one looks simple enough. Took it in the belly, at least twice. Really big holes!" Esposito shouted over the noise of the portable light generator.

The road at this point ran close to north and south. I had been traveling south moments earlier. With the light on, I could see the body just off the pavement a few feet to the east. He was on his back, feet toward the road. From this distance it looked as if most of his belly was gone. The soil around the body appeared undisturbed. The roadwork had left pieces of rock and gravel, with very little soft soil. Other than the body, there didn't seem to be any obvious evidence. As I moved in closer, I was able to see the details of the wounds.

There was no single opening. The shots, however many, had overlapped one another, resulting in one gaping hole. Enough bare skin around the perimeter was visible through the rips in his shirt to see the characteristic scalloping in the flesh around the wounds. The size of the scallops, in this case large, indicated buckshot, 0 or 00. There was a large amount of what looked like unburned gunpowder visible inside the openings of the wounds, more than I had ever seen. I glanced at the rest of his clothing—blue jeans, wide belt with a large buckle, heavy boots of the biker type. No damage to anything else. There were letters on his belt buckle. "What do those say?" I asked.

"It says Snort. Mr. Ragle, meet Mr. John Doe Snort," Stansbury said.

That meant at least two things. One, they didn't know who this guy was, and two, someone, most likely the beat officer who found him, had approached the body and searched for identification to no avail. I was almost next to the body now and could see no indications of shoe prints.

"Did someone pick up any casings? I don't see any."

"No one we know about. What you see is what you get," Stansbury answered.

A lack of casings at the scene could mean either that the shooting took place elsewhere, the weapon didn't eject the spent shells—like a double-barrel shotgun, for instance—or the shooter took the time to clean up the scene. It didn't appear that this guy was shot somewhere else and dumped here. There was no blood trail; the boots he had on were heavy, yet there were no drag marks in the area just off the pavement; and there were no tire tracks to indicate that his body was pushed from a truck or van.

The tight pattern of the entrance wounds, at least two, could be consistent with two blasts from a double-barrel shotgun. We would have to wait for the autopsy to determine if there were more than two shots.

The third possibility would indicate a calm, collected killer or one who had some understanding of physical evidence, enough to know that spent shell casings could be matched back to the gun that fired them while shot of any size couldn't. It would be cheaper to dispose of the casings than to get rid of the shotgun. A smart killer? They are hard to catch.

Assuming that it was a shotgun, and it sure looked like it was, the barrel was close, within feet, maybe inches. If the shells were ejected, they would be off to the shooter's right. There were no casings anywhere around.

It could be that the killer stood directly over the victim and fired downward. All that black powder in the wounds would make sense then, but powder is heavy enough to travel several inches horizontally, too. Once the body was moved, there might be some indication in the soil underneath. In any event, to establish the distance between the muzzle and the victim, the gun would have to be examined and test fired to determine just how long the barrel was and how big the shot spread would be at extremely close range. Unless the killer was eight feet tall or was using a sawed-off barrel, it was unlikely that he was standing over a supine victim. We could only speculate until the killer's gun was located. And it was time to move the body to the autopsy site.

The pathologist, Dr. Walter Fischer, should have done this autopsy for half price. The killer had done all the preliminary work to open up John Doe Snort's belly. With the standard preparations out of the way, I could focus on the black stuff that was so apparent at the scene. It was less visible now, after all the gyrations the body goes through just to get it from the scene to the autopsy. Putting a body in a body bag, picking it up, transporting it to the morgue, and then taking it out of the bag can wreak havoc with trace evidence. I made a mental note to myself: If you see something of interest on or in a body at the scene, collect it there, not later. You may never be able to find it again.

By using the tip of a small spatula, I was able to pick out an adequate sample of the powder. It was heavy black grains, not the usual-looking small specks of unburned gunpowder that is typical of handguns. I wasn't that familiar with shotgun evidence so it didn't occur to me that I could be looking at something different. It would take three years for me to find out I was wrong when I labeled the evidence container "Unburned gunpowder, from inside body cavity."

Dr. Fischer, holding an X ray up to a light box mounted on the wall, said, "Don't get this guy near water, he is so full of lead, he'd sink. Large pellets . . . looks like double aught buck."

I moved into position for a peek, and looking over Dr. Fischer's shoulder, I was close enough to hear him counting softly. When he got to thirty-one I realized there had to be more than two blasts. There are nine pellets in a regular twelve-gauge 00 buck, twelve in the long version and fifteen in the magnum load. That meant the shooter or the shooter's helpers cleaned up the scene of any spent shell casings. Calm, cool, and collected is not the usual mind-set for murderers. They seldom think to pick up items that can be used to associate them with the scene.

I didn't have to say anything to Esposito or Stansbury, who were watching Dr. Fischer from the side of the small autopsy suite. They knew they would be looking for a pro, and that meant it wouldn't be easy. Pros have a way of covering their tracks. Indeed, John Doe Snort could be just that, a track to be covered, someone who knew a little too much to stay alive. It would be a while before we found out.

The rest of the autopsy was uneventful.

John Doe Snort was later identified by his fingerprints. His true name was Harold Reinhart. Harold had led a troubled life. Stansbury, the principal investigator, would soon learn why Reinhart was murdered. Reinhart was connected to a group of thieves who had scored big after one of the group got in tight with a Portland, Oregon, man who had a fear of banks. It took a while, but the group eventually learned that the man hid all of his money, close to $100,000, in small wrapped packages, meant to look like meat, in his freezer. They stole everything the man had except the freezer.

The camaraderie faded quickly when Reinhart told the group, who had expected an even split, that he was due the largest share. His greed was perceived as a warning of things to come, so after a brief ad hoc committee meeting held without Reinhart's input, a decision was made to, in effect, rename him John Doe Snort. Besides, it meant a larger share for everyone else.

Stansbury learned that since none of the group wanted to go nose-to-nose with Reinhart, they had contacted a gun for hire who operated out of Las Vegas. Once they agreed on terms, the guy came down from Vegas, snapped up Reinhart, escorted him to that spot on Santiago Canyon Road, and gave him his new identity.

What allegedly happened next is ironic or at least a case of the group getting just what they deserved. The story goes, the hired gun from Vegas was ten times the miscreant his victim was. The ease with which he dealt with Reinhart, whom the group all feared, made that quite clear. So before he left town, he convinced the group to pay him his fee plus Reinhart's share, and eventually most of their share of the loot.

Stansbury knew the killer's name, John Tidwell, and where he could be found, but no one in the group was willing to testify against him. Three years passed, and Stansbury announced his retirement, turning the case over to Esposito. By this time Tidwell was in the Ohio state prison, serving time for a double killing. The break came when Esposito learned that Tidwell was bragging to his cellmate how he offed a dude for big bucks three years earlier in Orange County, California.

The cellmate agreed to testify, and Esposito started the process of bringing Tidwell back to California.

All the evidence had been stored in the property room since the day of the autopsy. There had been no reason to look at it until a suspect was identified. As it was, there wasn't much to look at. Since we never recovered the shotgun, it would not be possible to determine the distance from the muzzle to Snort. An estimate of four or five feet based on the size of the wounds would be as close as one could get. The actual weapon could have been a shotgun with a barrel sawed off, a standard length, or one equipped with a choke. The choke is designed to keep the group of shot from spreading for as long as possible, and a shortened barrel would result in quicker spread. The estimate fell somewhere between the extremes.

It would be important to analyze the black powder. It was possible that the unusual shape I had seen would turn out to be gunpowder that was used exclusively by one company. It wouldn't mean a hell of a lot without the gun or ammunition, but it was all I had.

The package was delivered from the property room and I began to remove the contents. The black powder was as I remembered, larger than normal for gunpowder. My first task would be to prove that it was indeed nitrocellulose. There are two tests. One involves determining the infrared absorption spectrum. That may sound complex, but it is fairly simple. Squeezing some of the particles into a flat sheet allows them to be placed directly in the light path of an IR spectrophotometer. The result is an ink profile, a chart that plots organic rotation and vibration. Many organic chemicals have unique patterns, called chemical fingerprints, that establish absolute identity. That's what I wanted.

The second test was very straightforward but not nearly as controllable or specific: nitrocellulose burns. By placing a particle on a slide under a microscope and applying measured heat, you can watch the particle soften, melt, and then burn. I opted for the definitive IR spectrum.

I began by selecting a few particles and placing them between two smooth metal plates. I put the plate inside a holder and then put the entire setup in a laboratory hydraulic press. The device looks a little like a larger version of a juice press. A few pumps of the handle created enough pressure to flatten almost anything.

I released the compressed air and removed the holder. I opened it and took out the metal plates. They looked odd because they were not tight against each other. When I lifted the top plate, I understood why. The black particles were unchanged. Something had gone wrong. No pressure, I was guessing. So I repeated the process, making sure that the holder was being compacted as planned. It was. I could see it squeezing together. I added one more little pump for good luck.

But the particles were still the same shape. Something was not right. I decided the flame test wasn't such a bad idea after all. To hell with the specificity, I just wanted to see if this stuff would burn. I took the temperature up fast but nothing happened, even when I exposed the particle on the glass slide to an open flame. I poked the piece with a probe and it was softer, so I held it over a burning match. Nitrocellulose would have flared up instantly, leaving no doubt of its flammability. Nada! At best it looked as if it might melt if I really cooked it. At least I knew it certainly wasn't gunpowder.

I wasn't too far out on a limb. I hadn't actually reported to anyone that this was gunpowder. Unless they had read my evidence tag, and that's not meant to be conclusive, no one was misinformed. But I had to know. What was the stuff? How did it get into Snort's body? Why was there so much of it?

My first move was to take a look at our collection of ammunition. The only 00 buck I could find was from a box of Western twelve-gauge, the ammo the department used in their shotguns. The casing is made of a red plastic with a brass base that houses the gunpowder and primer. The only safe passage into that area required cutting away the plastic. As I did that, the blade of the knife, once through the plastic, cut into a layer of matted paper fibers, a wadding that compacts the gunpowder in its place.

When I removed the entire plastic casing from the brass base, all the heavy round pellets fell to the tabletop and started rolling all over the place. Instinctively, I tried to stop them. Then I stopped grabbing at the shot. I didn't care what was happening to it. Something else I found drew all my attention. A large amount of white particles was falling out of the opened end of the casing, particles exactly the same size as the black ones. The powder looked like chopped-up plastic, the same kind that Tupperware is made of, polyethylene.

I placed a call to a local gun dealer hoping to find out the significance of the plastic.

"I was looking at the contents of a Western twelve-gauge 00 buck and found a bunch of plastic inside it. Is this a problem?"

"No, where ya been hiding?" the dealer said. "They've been using that stuff for a few years. Keeps the shot from banging into each other. Acts like little pillows."

"Little pillows?"

"Keeps 'em from getting dented. 'Least that's what they claim."

"Do all twelve-gauges use the same stuff?"

"Remington, far as I know, is the only other one."

"Do you stock the Remington twelve-gauge 00 buck?"

"Does a bear dump in the woods?" he answered.

"I'll be there before you can answer that question."

The only obvious difference was that the Remington plastic casing was a dark green. It didn't seem that my knife would ever cut through the plastic, but it did. I was careful to hold the casing base up as the last bit of plastic gave way. All I saw in the opened end was black. Black lead shot and lots of black plastic, like little pillows, packed tightly between the pellets. I let Esposito in on what I had found out. He was far more excited than I expected.

"Remington?" he asked. "You're going to love this. Yesterday I got some paperwork from the Las Vegas PD. They know this dude. He flew from Las Vegas to Orange County on the day before the murder. On his way to the airport he stopped at a gun shop, and guess what he bought . . . Don't bother, I'll tell you. A box of Remington twelve-gauge 00 buck. He had to sign for the purchase, Nevada law. I got a copy of the paperwork."

This case was starting to come together.

## Epilogue

Tidwell was convicted of first-degree murder. The identification of the brand and gauge of ammunition was meaningful information to the jury.

## FIREARMS

The potential for physical evidence begins the moment someone touches a gun, even before it is fired. For instance, handling and loading a weapon may result in the transfer of friction ridge patterns to the weapon or to the shells. Further, when a weapon is carried in a pocket or purse, there is the potential for a transfer of traces of debris. If located, this debris can be compared to residue that remains in the suspect's pocket or purse. Debris of this type—tobacco, cosmetics, and so forth—taken individually, are not a conclusive link. When several different types of debris are matched up, particularly if the debris includes materials unique to the suspect's employment or hobbies, a direct association can be considered.

### Firearms Nomenclature

To provide a better understanding of firearms in general, and to ascertain the answers to the questions posed at the beginning of the chapter, we will begin by naming the different types of firearms, their components, and how they work.

The term "gun" includes devices that have a barrel used to fire a projectile at a high velocity. Cannons, rifles, and pistols are all guns. Their common factor, the barrel, is a thick-walled tube. The diameter and the inside surface is called the bore. The bore can be smooth or grooved. The grooves, spiraling from one end of the barrel to the other, are called riflings. Cannons are big, usually larger than .60 caliber.

Other factors common to most guns are their firing mechanisms, that is, the trigger, the hammer, and the firing pin. The trigger is designed to release the hammer, allowing it to strike the firing pin, which is housed in the breech block. Enough force is needed to drive the pin into the primer of a cartridge. There are some variations to this mechanism. In older weapons, the hammer and the firing pin are all one piece. In some newer weapons, revolvers and semiautomatics, the hammer is enclosed and cannot be cocked by direct finger action. Center- and rim-striking firing pins have to match up to the type of primer. The action of the primer is described on the following pages.

Pistols are considered handguns, designed to be held in one hand, two if you are a movie detective, and sighted by holding the weapon with the hand and arm extended at shoulder height. Early pistols had smooth-bore barrels and fired round balls. Crimes committed with this type of pistol are extremely rare, usually limited to emotional or spontaneous crimes when no other weapon was convenient.

Modern pistol barrels are rifled to improve accuracy, but are distinguished from rifles by the short barrels and the manner they are held and sighted. Different types of pistols include single shot, revolvers, semiautomatics, and automatics. The last two types are sometimes called self-loading. This is a misnomer. No pistol can actually load itself. Someone has to load the weapon. Once fired, the pistol self-chambers the next round, called autoloading.

Single-shot handguns are almost always designed for target shooting. There is only room for one round of ammunition in the weapon. Target pistols are often unique in appearance. The barrel is longer than usual, it may be heavier, and the sights are often elaborate. Although impractical in the hands of an assailant, this gun's one shot can be just as deadly as any other pistol's.

Revolvers differ from other pistols in the manner they are loaded and advance the ammunition during firing. The revolver gets its name from the revolving cylinder that holds the rounds' chambers. The cylinder rotates, either right or left, and aligns the chamber with both the barrel to the front and the firing pin to the back, ready for firing. Most cylinders hold six rounds, some hold five, while others—.22 caliber, for example—may hold as many as eleven. Weapons designed for movies may hold at least thirty, even fifty rounds. Who counts?

Cylinder rotation is delivered in two ways: single action and double action. Single action requires the shooter to pull the hammer back manually, cocking it, usually with the thumb of the same hand used to hold the weapon. Each time, as the hammer is cocked, the cylinder rotates one position. When the trigger is activated, if loaded properly, the weapon fires. To fire again, the hammer must be pulled back again in the same manner.

Western sharpshooters were known to fan the hammer with the palm of their free hand. By keeping pressure on the trigger, the rapid fanning back of the hammer effectively created an automatic weapon.

Double-action weapons can be fired two ways: when the hammer is cocked like a single-action gun or uncocked by direct trigger pull. As pressure is applied to the trigger, the cylinder will rotate, the hammer moves back from the rest position to full cock and is then released, firing the round if properly loaded.

There are three types of cylinder loading orientations: gate-loading models, break-open or top-open models, and side-open models. The cylinder on gate-loading revolvers, such as the six-shooter used to win the West, turns in its place in the frame. To load and unload rounds, a small hinged gate on the rear of the stationary cylinder enclosure is opened to gain access to the chamber. With the gate open, one round can be inserted into the exposed chamber. The cylinder is rotated and the process is repeated. This may explain why, in the early Westerns, the movie version of the sheriff and the villains conveniently never ran out of ammunition during a running gunfight. It would have taken too long to stop and reload.

On break-open or top-open models, the cylinder is attached to the barrel assembly. Both are hinged to the frame just in front of the trigger housing. A latch, found on the top of the frame in front of the hammer, can be lifted, releasing the cylinder. When opened, the barrel drops down, exposing the chambers in the cylinder. With the same motion, all the shell casings in the cylinder are extracted. Routine reloading is fairly easy. Nevertheless, this type of weapon was soon found to be ill-advised for police work since it could be rendered unusable with a quick or lucky grab of the latch during a struggle.

Modern revolvers are designed to avoid most of the problems of the gate-loader and the break-open models. The cylinder assembly is hinged to the frame above the trigger. When released, the weight of the cylinder causes it to drop to an open position, usually to the left side of the frame. This is for the convenience of right-handed people, who then hold the weapon in their left hand and load the cylinder with their right. Models for left-handed people are also available.

The rounds are loaded by hand, one at a time. Once fired, the empty shell casings remain in the cylinder until they are all simultaneously ejected by use of a push-out extractor. The police use a device called a speed loader, making it possible to reload the cylinder in a single action. A clip positions the rounds in the proper alignment so all six rounds slip into the cylinder in one quick move.

Revolvers are still favored by some police departments and individual officers, but with recent advances in technology, and the resulting increase in dependability, many agencies are switching to semiautomatic handguns.

Often called automatics, the modern semiautomatic has one significant advantage over the standard revolver—firepower. They autochamber, have a capacity to fire up to eighteen rounds in rapid fire, and can be manually reloaded quickly with preloaded clips, each containing seventeen rounds. The one additional round can be chambered in advance, manually. Besides increasing the firepower, a chambered round decreases the time needed to get the first round off.

The ammunition is preloaded into a magazine or clip by feeding each round into it against the pressure of a spring. The clip, in almost all semiautomatic pistols, slides up into the grip assembly. When the clip is inserted, the uppermost round is held in waiting by the underhousing of the slide. Rapid fire in this case requires the shooter to pull the trigger repeatedly to fire each round.

Mechanically, all automatics and semiautomatics work the same way, relying on the principle of an action-reaction that automatically prepares the weapon to fire again. The dynamic component of autos and semiautos is called the slide—a spring-loaded, movable housing that fits over the barrel. Expanding gases not only propel the bullet out the front of the weapon, they also provide the energy to move the slide backward against a powerful enclosed spring; the slide can also be operated manually. The backward and subsequent forward movement of the slide is designed to clear the chamber or breech of any round, fired or not, to recock the weapon, and to remove a round from the clip and place it in the chamber (see top photo, insert page 5).

As the slide moves backward, a small hook called the extractor catches the rim of the shell casing and pulls it out of the breech. As the slide movement continues, the casing strikes another device, called the ejector, and the brass is flipped out of the weapon through an opening on the side of the weapon, the ejection port. The back of the slide moves against the hammer, pushing it back into a locked, full-cock position. As the slide reaches maximum extension, any excess gas is allowed to escape out the ejection port. With the gas pressure removed, the compressed spring can expand back to its regular shape, forcing the slide forward. For a moment an opening in the underhousing of the slide lines up with the clip, allowing the uppermost round to be pushed up into the slide. As the slide moves forward, the live round is carried with it and is forced into the breech.

Pressure on the trigger may release the hammer block, the shear pin, causing the hammer to fall, driving the firing pin into the primer. Detonation of the primer ignites the gunpowder. Gases created force the bullet out the barrel and act on the slide to repeat the process. When the last live round is fired, emptying the clip, a latch that had been depressed by the rounds catches the slide in its rear position and locks it open.

The classic models of semiautomatics are the Colt .45, the original Browning 9mm, the 9mm German Luger, the early Italian Beretta series, and the German P-38.

Unlike pistols, rifles are designed to be held by two hands, aimed and fired by bracing the butt against one's shoulder. Operationally, the major difference is the length of the barrel, usually twenty inches or more. The longer barrel serves two purposes.

First, it contains the bullet for a slightly longer period of time than a handgun does. Additionally, most rifle cartridges hold more gunpowder that can be manufactured to burn faster than the types used in handguns. A faster burn creates more gas pressure in a given time. When you combine that extra time in the barrel with the extra pressure, the result is a bullet that escapes the barrel with greater velocity. More velocity translates to greater range or distance.

Second, a longer barrel allows for more twisting in the riflings. More twists mean the bullet is rotating more than a bullet fired from a handgun. A rotating missile tends to travel a truer or more predictable course, increasing the potential for accuracy far beyond that of any handgun. Rifles offer deadly accuracy at extraordinarily long distances. Most people can't even see as far as some rifles will shoot straight, so someone invented telescopic sights for rifles. Rifles have been made in just about every loading style as handguns, even with revolving cylinders. The styles that are still manufactured for modern use are single-shot target models: pump action, where the rounds are held in a tubular magazine or in a clip until they are manually pumped into the chamber; bolt action, where a sliding bolt, moved manually, effects the loading process; and autoloading, which are powered by gunpowder gases. Many of the parts of a rifle have the same names and functions as those found on a pistol, although their shapes may be different.

A shotgun is designed to shoot a lot of small balls of

metal, lead, or steel at things you really want to kill. Although the name implies that it always shoots shot, a shotgun has a smooth bore barrel that can also be used to shoot a bullet—sometimes called a slug—on special occasions. This slug does not rotate, but if it hits you, you won't know the difference. The special occasions include, but are not limited to, knocking a doorknob off a door or ripping a huge hole through an automobile radiator.

Shot, the round balls, are graded by their diameter. The largest is double 00 buckshot, 0.33 inch in diameter, while the smallest is birdshot, #12 is 0.05 inch in diameter. As an example of the deadly firepower of a double 00 buckshot, a single load can contain nine, twelve, or fifteen pellets, all essentially the size of a .32 caliber bullet.

Gauge is expressed as the number of lead balls that can be made from a pound of lead, equal in size to the diameter of the barrel. The diameter of twelve lead balls that equal one pound is the same diameter as the inside of the barrel of a twelve-gauge shotgun. A sixteen-gauge shotgun barrel size would equate to sixteen lead balls weighing one pound, and so on. Bigger number, smaller balls.

Given the qualities that generate accuracy and distance, shotguns don't offer much range with their smooth barrels, and in their simplest form they don't offer much accuracy, either. Shotguns are designed to blow the hell out of anything in front of them. Their inaccuracy is their best merit. If you shoot a rifle into the dark, you would have to be a very good shot or lucky to hit anything. Shotguns are designed not to miss. Just inches away from the barrel, the flying shot starts to spread out of control. Imagine, just a few feet down a dark alley, fifteen bullets the size of a .32 caliber spreading out as they zip along their way. And there can be more shells fired as fast as the flick of an arm.

## Tool Marks or Impression Evidence Related to Firearms

Lands and grooves are called *rifling*. During manufacturing, grooves are cut into the hard steel of pistol and rifle barrels, coiling from the chamber to the muzzle. The number, width, and depth of grooves, and the angle and direction—right or left—of their twist are determined by the manufacturer's specifications. Rifling marks, transferred to the bullet as it is forced through the barrel, are both class and individual characteristics, the so-called signature of the weapon. When these marks on a questioned bullet match the marks on a known bullet fired under controlled conditions, a qualified firearms examiner can usually testify that both bullets were fired through the same barrel or from the same weapon.

Most manufacturers, other than Colt, use a right twist. The number of lands (or grooves) ranges from four to seven and their width varies considerably, depending on the number and the caliber. The degree of twist is measured by the distance traveled to effect one complete rotation and is expressed as a fraction; for example, $1/12$ requires a twelve-inch barrel to cause one complete rotation of the bullet. A typical Colt handgun can be described as a left twist, six lands, $1/12$. Most handguns have barrels much shorter than twelve inches. Consequently, the energy transferred to spinning the bullet is not as great as with a rifle. These bullets may lose their spin after traveling a short distance and start to wobble, then tumble, depending on the weapon. The bullet is still deadly but the eventual target may be more by chance than intent. Accordingly, handguns are designed for close combat, within feet not yards.

Properly planned, a bullet intended to be fired by a particular caliber will not easily fit through the appropriate barrel. It should be snug. Energy is required to force the bullet through the barrel. The expanding gases of burning nitrocellulose provide the energy. Additionally, sufficient heat is generated by the burning gases to cause some expansion of the bullet and possibly some surface softening of the bullet, particularly if it is made of lead. The bullet is initially blown out of the shell casing and forced into the barrel. Since the barrel is somewhat smaller, the bullet must conform to its dimensions. If the bullet can't exit the barrel, the whole weapon blows apart.

If it all holds together, the lands slice into the moving bullet and the outermost edge is squeezed into the grooves, transferring all the higher points of barrel information as scratches in the bullet. As a group, the scratches are called striation evidence—a single scratch, stria; two or more, striae. There are materials, other than lead, used in bullet construction that pick up striae to differing degrees. They are discussed below.

Recall the case of "Now I Love Her, Now I Don't" in Chapter 2. The killer loaded a .380 Webley with .38 caliber ammunition. The .38 caliber bullet actually measures .357 inch, while the .380 barrel measures .380 inch, a difference of .023 inch. That is not a big space, but you should now understand why the bullet wobbled down the barrel. A loss of power resulted because the gases could escape around the bullet rather than push the bullet. Consequently, the shot to the body didn't exit even though it only passed through soft tissue. Furthermore, several test shots were required to find one bullet that contacted the barrel in the same places as the scene bullet.

Some factors can limit the certainty that two bullets were fired by the same firearm. The first, and perhaps the one of most concern, is the degree of similarity between two barrels manufactured one after the other. The grooves are cut by dragging a tool with an even number of hardened steel blades through the barrel, creating the riflings. More than one barrel may be cut before the tool requires sharpening. The predominant marks on the blade's cutting edges, intentional or defective, that were the result of the latest sharpening can be cut into each barrel. This leaves the differences found in each sequentially manufactured barrel attributable to the subtleties left on the lands from the original drilling out of the barrel, and then to the fine changes that occurred to the cutting surface of the tool during each drag.

Barrels A and B, cut in sequence and used only to fire test bullets, will always have some differences, but it takes an alert examiner to recognize them. Realistically, it is highly unlikely that any two barrels cut in sequence would end up involved in the same investigation. That is, the coincidence of someone using weapon A to commit a crime and the owner of weapon B becoming a suspect is unlikely. But it would make a good story. Certainly, aware defense attorneys might ask such questions during their cross examination of firearms witnesses.

An injustice could occur if this coincidence actually happened, and a would-be expert conducted an incomplete examination, or a qualified examiner was pressured to make a quick identification. There is a much greater likelihood of running into a self-trained pseudo expert, isolated from any supervision or peer review, who might make incriminating blunders, than there is of encountering the barrel A and B coincidence.

Another factor that can alter the characteristics of the rifling is how frequently the weapon was used between the incident and the test firing. As barrels A and B are used to different extents, variations in the details of the lands and grooves will increase. Use will also alter the details transferred by the same barrel to bullets fired at intervals during its lifetime. Although the steel used to make barrels is very strong, the lands are susceptible to wear from frequent firing, cleaning, intentional damage, or corrosion.

Criminals often attempt to destroy their weapons by incineration or dumping them in the ocean, river, or lake. They may even try to alter the weapon by scoring the insides of the barrel with a sharp instrument or chemicals. One homicide suspect used a cutting torch to slice his semiautomatic pistol into pieces before throwing it off a pier into the Pacific Ocean. A tip resulted in divers recovering most of the pieces. Firearms examiner Bob Waganer took what was left of the barrel, removed any slag or frayed edges from the ends, and then pushed a soft lead plug through the riflings. The product was compared to the murder bullet and was matched successfully.

Rust or corrosion will alter fine detail inside the barrel. Weapons recovered from water should be dried and immediately examined for friction ridge information by using Super Glue, staining, or a laser or alternate light source. Photos should be used to document any prints that might be found.

Then, without delay, the weapon should be sprayed with a rust inhibitor such as WD-40 or coated in oil so that no details on transfer surfaces are eroded.

Remember that some firearms, notably semi- and full automatics, can be disassembled and have interchangeable parts. Their barrels can be switched easily.

Once the bullet has exited the barrel and is free flying, the quality of the land and groove marks are at the mercy of the materials hit or passed through. Bone, glass, metal, and hard plastics can damage the markings, drastically limiting their usefulness. Combining a worn barrel with ammunition that doesn't mark well and a destructive first surface may result in few or no identifiable characteristics.

A sizable section of the circumference of a bullet can be shaved away when it is fired from a chamber that has not aligned properly with the bore of the barrel. A badly worn weapon or one of poor quality can have play in movement of the cylinder. If the alignment is not exact, the outer edge of the bullet strikes the face of the barrel and sections of lead are shaved off. The net effect is the rifling marks are difficult and dangerous to reproduce during test firing.

Small fragments of metal can be forced out of the barrel and may become embedded in a close target. Pieces can also spray out to either side of the weapon—from the front opening of the cylinder—and wound the shooter's hand. Any fresh defects on the hands of a suspected shooter should be X-rayed, looking for opaque metal particles. If located, they should be removed and processed as evidence.

The shell casing is the recipient of additional tool marks. The first tool mark to occur, the one that initiates the entire process, is the result of the firing pin slamming into the primer. All firearms have some form of firing pin that can have unique surface characteristics. Usually their three-dimensional impression characteristics are reproducible by test firing the weapon using ammunition with similar primers (see bottom photo, insert page 5).

A firearms expert who is concerned that a weapon is unsafe or defective or fears further altering the barrel by firing bullets doesn't have to test a live round to examine the firing pin impression. The expert can open a round and remove all the gunpowder, leaving only the primer in place. For that matter, even the primer can be a dummy and the firing pin mark will still occur. The two shell casings—the crime scene unknown and the standard with indented primers—are examined side by side, using a comparison microscope.

As the expanding gases are blasting the bullet out the barrel and transferring striae characteristics, the shell casing simultaneously gets its share of the back pressure, forcing it to expand in all directions. In all weapons there is a moment when the back pressure slams the casing hard against the firing pin housing, the breech face. Made of very hard steel, the breech face may have marks or defects that transfer into the softer metal of the primer, and sometimes the casing. Depending on the manufacturer, these marks may represent signature defects or, in quality weapons, the hand finishing unique to each weapon made.

Breech face marks are compared in the same manner as firing pin marks, but a live round is needed to reproduce the standard marks on another casing during a controlled firing. Experts have two approaches to collecting marks from weapons that may be unsafe. First, a round can be prepared with a reduced load by removing part of the gunpowder. The bullet must be reset in the shell casing but may fail to pick up all the marks if adequate back pressure isn't generated. The second and certainly safer approach is to make an impression of the breech face using silicon rubber. The exact same material described in Chapter 4 when collecting tool marks at crime scenes will capture all the marks on the breech face. *Remember, the examiner compares impressions to impressions and replicas of items to the actual item*. Do we have to make a replica from the silicon cast to compare to the casing? No. The casting material is acting as the metal in the shell casing. The breech face information is impressed into the silicon rubber, so the cast is an impression and can be compared directly to the casing.

Shell casings are ejected instantly from semiautomatic and most fully automatic weapons very close to the exact place of firing. Although some full automatics—machine

guns, for example—use ammunition held in place by a belt,
I have never seen or heard of one used in a crime in California. That doesn't mean it hasn't happened or won't happen.
Revolvers retain the shell casings in their individual chambers in the cylinder until they are intentionally ejected. Most
often, they are carried away from the crime scene along with
the weapon.

If they are discarded at the scene, revolver casings are
readily distinguishable from casings designed for semi- and
full automatics. The difference is in the base. Revolver
rounds have a wider base, a lip, extending out beyond the diameter of the body of the shell casing (see Figure 9). This lip
keeps the rounds from sliding out the front of the cylinder
when their chamber is not aligned with the barrel or frame.
The lip on ammunition designed for semis and autos is the
same size as the body of the casing. The round when chambered is held in place by the breech's surfaces and the opening to the barrel.

Tool marks can be transferred to the shell casing by the
extractor and the ejector of semi- and automatic weapons.
These marks are indentations and scratches (striations) and
can reflect the individual characteristics of their source. Of
the two, the ejector is more likely to gouge distinct marks
into the casing. The extractor pulls the casing from the
breech at the beginning of the slide's movement. By the time

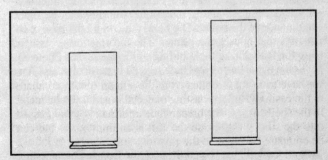

**Figure 9. A. Semiautomatic—no lip   B. Revolver—lip
Design of shell casings, base, and lip.**

the shell casing hits the ejector, the slide and the casing are at their top speed. The resulting collision can make a deep mark reflecting the individuality and factory characteristics of the working edge of the ejector. It's up to the firearms examiner to recognize the class and individual characteristics when they occur. It is important to note that the force of an exploding cartridge is not necessary for the ejector to gouge into the casing.

## AMMUNITION

Ammunition for handguns, rifles, and shotguns have several characteristics in common. They are all contained devices consisting of an outer casing or shell, some type of primer device to act as an igniting agent, a fast-burning material (nitrocellulose in one form or another), and, with the exception of blanks, a projectile designed to be propelled out a barrel.

The class characteristics of ammunition vary depending on caliber, load, material used to make the projectiles (bullet or shot), the bullet's weight, the impact behavior of the bullet, material used to make the shell casing, and factory marks or identification stamped into the bullet and shell casing.

Ammunition manufacturers mark their product intentionally and unintentionally. Intentional imprints can be found on the face of the bullet. The face is the round flat base of the casings that houses the primer. The information is stamped into the face during the molding of the shells (see Photo 8).

Some metal casing and bullets, lead in particular, also have an indented ring or rings around their circumference called a canellure. During assembly, the canellures on the bullet are smeared with grease or wax as the bullet is inserted into the casing. The material acts as a sealer, making the bullet at least water resistant, and it provides some degree of lubrication as the bullet is forced through the barrel. The canellures on the casing are imprinted within one-quarter inch from the top just after the bullet is inserted. This crimp acts to further seal the round and hold the bullet in the casing. Canellures may contain imprint characteristics unique to the manufacturer and even to a particular crimping device.

Other factory marks may be unintended, such as repeated scratches, dings, or indentations created by a temporary problem. Factory records and maintenance and sales records may be available to pinpoint the time frame when the problem was occurring, as well as the numbers made and distributions of the product.

Identical imperfections in the imprints found in more than one shell casing may establish that the casings were made by the same company at about the same time. Matching batch characteristics indicating that the two items were made by the same company may be significant during both an investigation and a trial, if shell casings and live rounds are the only evidence located.

Types of ammunition are distinguished first by their size. All handguns and their ammunition are designated by caliber, in either inches or millimeters. Measurements are expressed in hundredths of an inch. For example, a .22-caliber ($^{22}/_{100}$) is slightly smaller than one-quarter inch ($^{25}/_{100}$).

The length of the shell can vary to increase the gunpowder capacity. A .22 caliber has three sizes: short, long, and long rifle, plus a magnum load. All magnum loads contain more gunpowder and may propel a heavier bullet. Because they create more energy, magnum weapons are always designed to be heavier to contain the force. A magnum weapon can chamber a regular load, but a regular weapon cannot chamber a magnum round.

Some .22 handguns and rifles can chamber only the short, some can chamber the short and the long, and others can handle all three. The .22 short and long have the same weight bullet, while the long has more powder. The long rifle has even more powder and a heavier bullet, but it still is not considered a magnum load. All .22 caliber rounds of these types are rim-fire primers rather than center-core primers. Some high-powered rifles can propel .22 caliber bullets with center-core primers, but their shell casings are huge relative to this group.

The .25 caliber pistol purse gun was made popular in the early detective movies. The female villain always carried one, chrome with a pearl handle. It is small enough to fit inside a boot top and is used as a backup weapon.

There are .32 caliber revolvers and semiautomatics. The .32 caliber rim-fire primers were used in early revolvers, but all modern rounds are center-core primers.

The two types of ammunition for .38 caliber (.357) revolvers are .38 Smith & Wesson and .38 Special. The .38 S&W, a shorter shell with a smaller load, was made obsolete by the more powerful .38 Special, designed after law enforcement expressed a need for more stopping power.

The maximum stopping power for the .38 caliber became available when the .357 magnum was marketed, a weapon that fires a heavier bullet, with a longer casing that contains additional gunpowder. However, the power of the .357 magnum, when firing a solid lead bullet, soon proved to be a hazard to unintended secondary targets, like someone eating dinner inside his house downrange from the intended target. The penetrating power was too great, forcing many police agencies to ban magnum loads in populated areas. The heavier-framed .357 was relegated to using only .38 Special ammo in many cities.

Bullet designers thus began the search for a combination of stopping power and safety for others. Several rounds, in .38 caliber and larger, claim to impact only the first target struck without losing stopping power. All the kinetic energy of the bullet is transferred to the first surface. Hollow point bullets were designed for this purpose. A hollow point is a soft lead bullet encased in a thin metal jacket. The point of the bullet is actually an opening with thin lead walls. On impact, the walls flare out. The final shape of the bullet, in the side view, is similar to a mushroom, hence the term "mushrooming" is applied to the fate of this type of projectile. Hollow points don't necessarily mushroom every time and can still be harmful to secondary targets. For instance, they may pass through the soft tissue of the target and injure someone behind the target.

A few years ago "Glasser" bullets were marketed, hoping

to solve the problem of the errant bullet. The early Glasser bullets, the first of the prefragmented rounds, were constructed of a thin metal skin packed with very small lead particles suspended in a liquid Teflon. The weight of the bullet was equal to that of a solid lead bullet, resulting in an equivalent kinetic energy. When the Glasser hits any resisting surface, the thin walls flatten out, distributing the tiny lead particles over a wide area. A bullet hitting a human or animal penetrates and opens up, transferring all its energy to the inside of the target, having an elephant gun effect.

The Glasser offered an unprecedented level of safety since all the kinetic energy was expended when the bullet hit anything. An errant shot striking the pavement would not ricochet, and a bullet hitting the outside of a house would not penetrate the walls. There have been a few changes in the Glasser, primarily in the way the nose of the bullet is constructed and the manner in which the lead fragments are contained. Recently, other manufacturers began offering a line of ammunition with prefragmented bullets.

The Black Talon is described by the manufacturer, Winchester Ammunition, as a "truly revolutionary bullet design." It is a hollow-tip bullet designed to open up like all hollow tips. They are coated with a black plastic called Lubalox. The Black Talon bullets I have seen open up and the tip fans out to form what looks like a miniature buzz saw blade.

If a police officer shouts, "Stop or I'll shoot you with a Black Talon," freeze by all means. Law enforcement officers are always interested in a round that will drop suspects in their tracks. Speer, another ammunition manufacturer, is offering a new hollow-tip bullet called a Gold Dot. A small gold-colored dot is in the center of the core of the mushroomed bullet.

The typical shotgun shell is quite different from handgun and rifle ammunition. Although solid metal casings have been used, they are now more likely collectors' items and have been replaced by a casing that combines a metal face and base connected to a plastic or waxed cardboard cylinder. Shotgun shells are available in gauges 10, 12, 14, 16, 20, and

410. Instead of a visible bullet, the cylinder is crimped shut, sealing in the projectiles, the shot and other materials, and the gunpowder. The face contains manufacturer's information and marking, and houses a center-core primer. The projectiles vary in many ways. The shot, traditionally lead, is gradually being replaced by steel balls. Evidence indicating lead contamination of waterways frequented by game hunters has been offered by environmentalists hoping for the total ban of lead in ammunition.

The shot kills or wounds the target, but the other components of the shell often help the crime scene investigator to reconstruct the events of the crime. In cross section starting in the base, all shells have primers and all shells have nitrocellulose gunpowder. All this is contained within the metal portion of the casing. At the end of the metal casing, a layer called the wad separates the gunpowder and the shot. The wad can be constructed of plastic or thick paper fibers. A plastic wad is shaped like a nickel and is about one-eighth inch thick. It is usually made of a milky-colored plastic like polyethylene. Paper wadding may be very thick, a half-inch or more. There may be more than one layer of wadding, depending on the shell and its other contents.

In most shells with smaller-size shot, the pellets are packed tightly in a plastic sleeve inserted into the shell. Sometimes called a power sleeve, it serves as an escort once the round is fired, keeping all the shot in a tight wad as it travels out the barrel. Remember, shotguns have smooth bore barrels. There is no twist. The sleeve, the same diameter as the barrel, is actually a plastic cup resembling a tulip with long overlapping petals. The barrel restricts the sleeve just enough to keep it closed. Once it is out of the barrel, the sides of the sleeve open out like a parachute, allowing the shot to start to spread.

These pieces of stuff often travel reproducible distances that can be established by test firing the shotgun using similar ammunition under like conditions. Combining the crime scene information with test measurements, one can place the shooter in a specific place at the scene. The plastic disk, on the other hand, does not follow a predictable flight. Because of their design, they can get caught in the air and become aerodynamic, like a Frisbee, and take off for a long distance. Since this behavior is random, their locations may be of no value. The exception is a shooting at very close range. The plastic disk, along with all the material, the power sleeve, and the wadding and packing material, can end up inside the victim's body.

## Crime Scene Examinations

The timely examination of firearms evidence, initially at the scene, can provide vital investigative information, and during trial, provide convincing testimony connecting a weapon to a crime or even a person to a weapon. In the case of "Now I Love Her, Now I Don't," the bullet examination provided the make and model and caliber information, enabling investigators to recognize the key suspect once they located the hospital report describing the suspect's injuries. This information, combined with autopsy observations, explained much of the unusual aspects of the victim's wounds. For example, gunshot/firearms debris in the area of the wounds indicated that the weapon was very close when the victim was shot. Investigators knew all this before the suspect and the weapon were located.

When a weapon is recovered at the crime scene or elsewhere, a proper sequence of the examinations should be followed. During the early stages of the investigation and even into the trial, investigators do not know which issues will eventually become important. An overeager examiner who attempts to answer one question before considering all the questions in order, can forever destroy critical evidence. Following a logical order of examinations provides the best assurance of answering all the possible questions anyone may have.

The most obvious questions are:

- Is any foreign material adhering to the weapon, such as blood, hairs, tissue, or fibers?

- Are fingerprints on the weapon?

- Is the weapon loaded, and if so, what is the order or arrangement of the rounds?

- Once unloaded, what is the description of the rounds—type and brand, for example?

- Are fingerprints on the rounds?

- What is the mechanical and functional condition of the weapon—for example, the trigger pull, wear, and safety features? Is it safe to test-fire? (We'll get to this shortly.)

- What is the description of the weapon, such as make, model, and serial number?

- Do the marks created by the weapon during controlled test firing match questioned marks on crime scene evidence?

- How close was the weapon to the target when it was fired?

Ideally, any firearm evidence will be transported to the laboratory for most, if not all, of the examinations. Only a visual examination should begin at the crime scene, ideally by a firearms expert, if one is available to respond to the scene. Before the weapon is moved or anything else is done to it, a qualified crime scene examiner should conduct a visual inspection of every recovered weapon. Preliminary answers to certain questions must be sought before the weapon is handled. For example, is the weapon contaminated with blow back? Blow back occurs when a firearm is held in very close proximity to a living body. Skin, fat, hairs, blood, or other body tissue or even clothing fibers may be blown back onto the leading edges of the weapon.

A qualified examiner will also be familiar with how the weapon is to be packaged and transported to the laboratory. The firearms examiners in Orange County are typical of the many experts who want to see the weapon transported to the laboratory as it is found. They document all the observable conditions as they go about their examinations. Unfortunately, many investigative agencies don't have a firearms examiner, requiring them to deal with the weapon at the scene and eventually ship the weapon to a state or federal laboratory. Some agencies prefer or may even require that the weapon be unloaded before they will accept it as evidence.

Unfortunately, some movie and television versions of crime scene investigations show the *cops* picking up weapons with their handkerchiefs and putting them into their pockets, or perhaps they stick a pencil up the barrel to lift weapons off the floor. Neither method has ever been taught to legitimate crime scene investigators. In the movie *See No Evil, Hear No Evil*, a police officer enters the crime scene and immediately pulls out his handkerchief, uses it to pick up the handgun, and puts the package in his pocket. Who knows what DNA lurks on that handkerchief? Unfortunately, the movies are the only crime scene training some police officers receive.

Ideally, after complete photographic documentation, the weapon should be lifted using only the fingertips of one's latex rubber-gloved hand, lifting it in an area least likely to contain evidence, such as the engraved portion of the wooden or plastic grips or the narrow sides of the trigger guard.

A thin but stiff sheet of plastic, three-sixteenths of an inch thick, can be placed flat next to the weapon and slid under it while it is held in place with gloved fingertips. When the sheet is held from both ends, like a tray, it can be moved carefully into an open flat box, similar to a pizza box.

## Laboratory Examinations

Low-powered stereoscopic binocular microscopes and high-energy illumination combine to make the most effective visual examination. The laser and/or alternative light sources (ALS) reveal many types of trace evidence that otherwise might go unnoticed. Fibers and even fingerprints may glow in the dark when irradiated with high-energy light.

A firearm may also have blow-back material—blood, fat, tissue, or fibers—on it if it was in contact with a body at the time it was fired. If they are present, after close-up photos have been taken a serologist should remove the evidence and prepare it for the appropriate analysis. If a serologist is not available in person, one should be consulted by phone to assure that an effective method of removing the evidence is used.

The method of choice for examining firearms evidence, guns, and ammunition for fingerprints is the Super Glue method described earlier.

When a revolver is fired, the shell casings remain in the cylinder and the shell casing last fired remains under the hammer. So care must be taken to document exactly all the positions within the cylinder, whether they are filled or unfilled with live or expended rounds, and the relative placement of each shell. Many examiners use Wite-Out or other correction paint to place a small spot on the cylinder and on each shell. A corresponding number, say 1 to 6, starting with the position under the hammer, can be written on the spot at each position and on the shell when it is removed. The Wite-Out is nondestructive and can be removed if what it covers needs to be examined.

In addition, if for no other reason than the safety of the firearms examiners who will continue to work with the weapon, the overall condition of the weapon must be determined. Evidential issues may arise, such as: Does the weapon work at all? What is the trigger pull—the pressure required to pull the trigger?

Classically, trigger pull is determined by hanging weights onto a device hooked over the trigger of a fully cocked weapon that is clamped into a position pointing straight up. Weights are added until the downward pull moves the sear, releasing the hammer. The sear is the catch that holds the hammer either in half cock or full cock. Some examiners hang a fish scale on the trigger and pull down slowly until the hammer falls. Most weapons require a few pounds of pressure. The term "hair trigger" describes a weapon that fires with the slightest touch.

Semiautomatic weapons can be modified, drastically changing the manufacturer's specifications. An *experienced* firearm examiner was killed while test firing an apparent semiautomatic assault-type handgun. However, the mechanism had been altered, to fire full auto. Once the trigger was pulled, there was a burst of rounds, causing the weapon to spin around on the examiner's trigger finger as it fired.

Some would call this a freak accident, and others a vicious booby-trap. It could have been both. In any event, it should not have happened. Safety is always first. A California inventor has manufactured a device specifically because of this death, which should assure that it won't happen again. The device is capable of clamping any type of firearm into firing position, and it provides for a remote trigger pull device.

Booby-trapped weapons have been responsible for other deaths and serious injuries. Some actually contain small explosive devices that detonate the next time the weapon is fired. Altered weapons have been found that allow part of the chamber pressure to blast out on the hand or face of the next person to fire the weapon.

Other significant information gathered in the lab includes the condition of the barrel—for example, worn, rusted, or altered—and the presence of identifying information, such as a manufacturer's name and logos, and serial numbers. Obliterated serial numbers that were stamped into the metal can be restored by a variety of etching processes.

The scratches made on the bullet by the lands and grooves, and on the shell casing by the extractor and ejector of semiautomatic weapons, as well as indentations made by the firing pin and the breech face, can be compared using specially designed microscopes. A comparison microscope actually consists of two microscopes attached to a common optical bridge, allowing the examiner to study two separate surfaces as if they were side by side. The samples are placed on movable stages that can rotate while moving in an east-west-north-south direction, if need be. Two surfaces containing striations that line up are considered matches. The process of firearms manufacturing is sufficiently handmade that the source of the marks is considered unique and distinguishes a specific weapon as the origin of the mark. Aware firearms examiners know the types of factory marks that untrained examiners can confuse as individual marks.

**National Data Base**

In the 1990s the FBI initiated a nationwide program called Drug Fire aimed at identifying and linking firearms evidence found on shell casings recovered at otherwise unrelated crime scenes. The initial target was the so-called drive-by shootings where shell casings are often the only intact evidence. The concept of identification and linkage is based on the fact that firing pin and breech face indentations are unique to each weapon.

Firearms examiners, after studying the shell casings collected at one crime scene, have always been able to define the number of different weapons involved and compare them to other shell casings from other sources—if an investigator submitted casings from other crimes and requested a comparison. Until that happened, firearms evidence from one jurisdiction was seldom compared to evidence from another. Even two cases within a large city or from cities within a county using the same laboratory could escape comparison lacking an investigative hunch, a tip or plain old luck.

Drug Fire, the trademark for a proprietary database system, established a network of computers located in more than forty forensic laboratories that exchange breech face, firing pin, and ejector mark information. Each member agency is responsible for classifying all its cases, a process similar to how one fingerprint is distinguished from another. Once individualized, the classification is encoded into the memory of the computer and compared to all previous entries. From that moment on, any member agency on line can compare evidence from its next shooting to all cases in the system.

A second proprietary system, Bulletproof and Brass Catcher, was established by the Bureau of Alcohol, Tobacco and Firearms (ATF). Bulletproof scans and digitizes the nature of striations (lands and grooves) on bullets, while Brass Catcher records the marks on the shell casing, the breach face, firing pin, and ejector marks in a similar way as Drug Fire.

By 1993, ATF's program had also established networks connecting forensic laboratories in various states and coun-

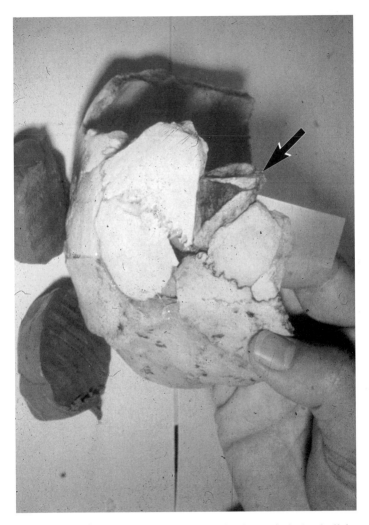

A physical match—fragment (dancer) fits into victim's skull in "The Key to the Crime."

An inked fingerprint (a loop pattern). Note the numerous minutiae points: ridge endings, bifurcations, and pore openings (white spots).

*Courtesy of the Orange County Sheriff-Coroner's Department, California*

A three-dimensional impression cast with plaster of Paris compared to suspect boot.

*Courtesy of the author*

A two-dimensional latent heel transfer: in dust on a piece of broken window glass inside the point of entry at a burglary scene.

*Courtesy of the Orange County Sheriff-Coroner's Department, California*

A dust print made on glass using the suspect's shoes. A match of thirty-one minutiae points, not counting the apparent worn letters.

*Courtesy of the Orange County Sheriff-Coroner's Department, California*

The letters appear to be worn as in photos 4 and 5, but this isn't so. This is an ink impression of a brand-new heel.

*Courtesy of the Orange County Sheriff-Coroner's Department, California*

The breech face, firing pin, and extractor of the Smith & Wesson 9 mm semiautomatic.

*Courtesy of the Orange County Sheriff-Coroner's Department, California*

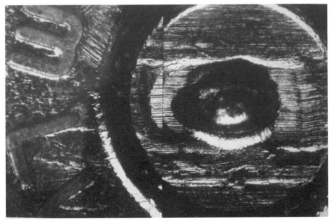

Fired Evidence Casing          Fired Test Casing

Markings on the shell case/primer made by the 9 mm Glock.

*Courtesy of the Orange County Sheriff-Coroner's Department, California*

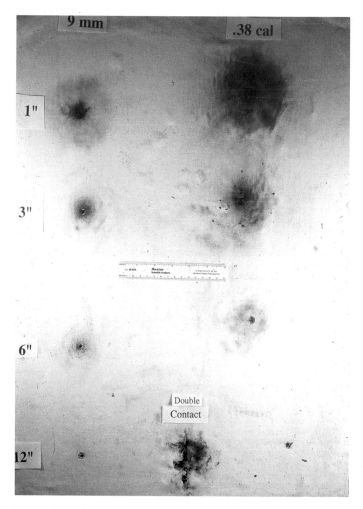

A muzzle to first surface comparison of two weapons, a 9 mm on the left and a .38 caliber on the right, at the same distances (one inch, three inches, six inches, and twelve inches). Note the grease wipe around the entrance hole on both twelve-inch shots.

*Courtesy of the author*

The crime scene for "Spanish 101 Would Have Helped." Note the broken blade on the floor.

*Courtesy of the Orange County Sheriff-Coroner's Department, California*

A blood spatter pattern on bucket near the victim's head in "The Key to the Crime."

*Courtesy of the author*

A bloody shoe impression found "The 7-Eleven Killers."

*Courtesy of the author*

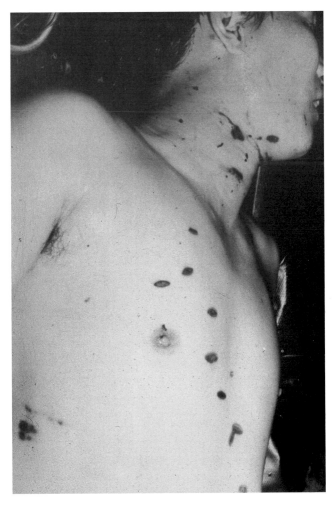

Multiple stab wounds.

*Courtesy of the Washoe Sheriff's Department, Nevada*

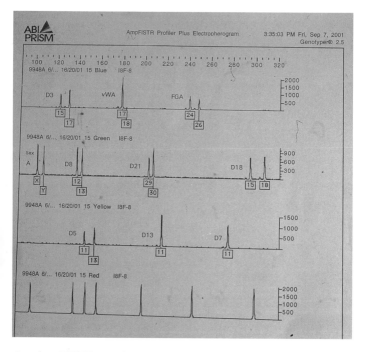

An AmpFISTR Profiler plus Electopherogram showing DNA types of nine STR loci and Amelogenin, x4, in the top three rows. Each locus, except vWA, has two obvious alleles. The bottom row is the allelic ladder used to size the results for comparison.

*Courtesy of the author*

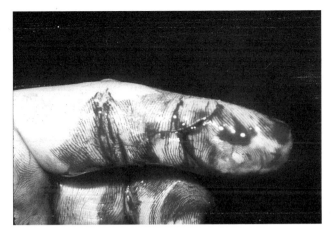

A slicing knife wound, classified as a defense wound.

*Courtesy of the Orange County Sheriff-Coroner's Department, California*

A sexual assault case related RFLP autorad. The two outside lanes contain the allelic ladder. Lanes 1, 2, and 3 are suspects.

*Courtesy of the Orange County Sheriff-Coroner's Department, California*

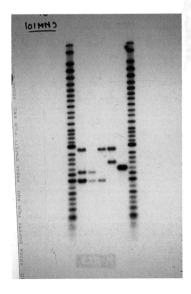

RFLP autorad of eight samples of unrelated individuals and three allelic ladders. Subject one appears to be a homozygote, same size allele.

*Courtesy of the author*

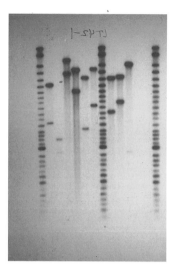

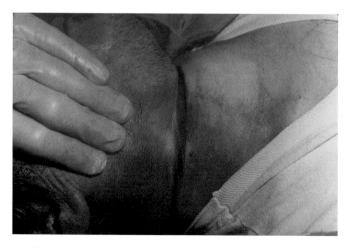

Narrow ligature mark. Notice the pattern.

*Courtesy of the author*

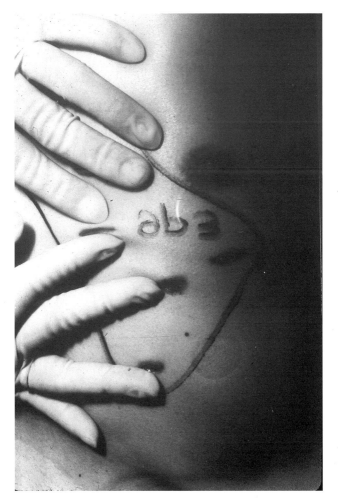

A close-up of some of the wounds on a victim: both ends of these cuts have fine edges, indicating a double-edged blade.

*Courtesy of the Washoe Sheriff's Department, Nevada*

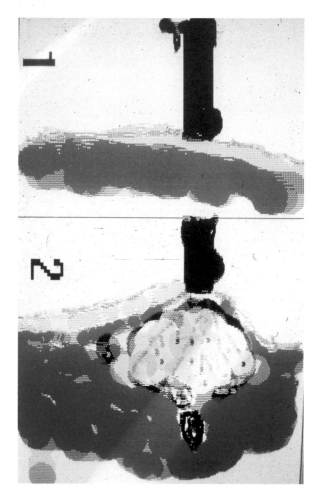

A computer-generated drawing in cross-section of a muzzle in full contact with the skin.

*Courtesy of the author*

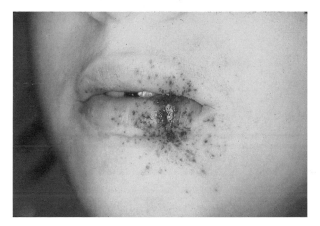

Tattooing, muzzle first to surface—2" to 4".

*Courtesy of the author*

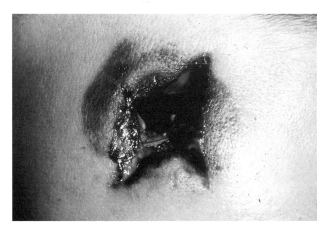

A semicontact firearms wound demonstrating three tears and sooting where the fourth tear could be expected. The sooting indicates escaping gas as when the weapon is held in contact with the target, but at a slight angle, allowing some gas to escape.

*Courtesy of the Orange County Sheriff-Coroner's Department, California*

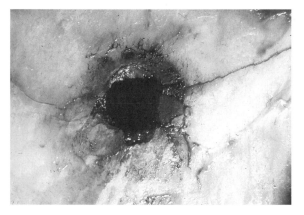

The same wound showing the defect (entrance hole) in the skull. Note the soot on the bone and the fractures.

*Courtesy of the Orange County Sheriff-Coroner's Department, California*

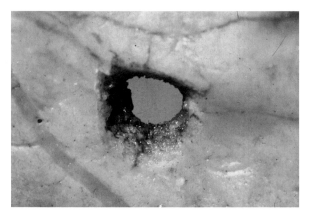

A view of the same defect as seen from inside the skull looking back in the direction of the weapon. This view demonstrates the coning out of the bone in the direction of the bullet's flight.

*Courtesy of the Orange County Sheriff-Coroner's Department, California*

ties to a central database. For a variety of reasons, local and/or state agencies installed one or the other system. Unfortunately, the two proprietary systems could not exchange data. Meanwhile, Bulletproof and Brass Catcher were combined and became the Integrated Ballistic Information System (IBIS).

In 1997 the National Integrated Ballistic Information Network (NIBIN) was formed expressly to find a way to exchange data between the two systems. When no direct solution was found, the executive board proposed integrating the best aspects of the two national systems, which was enacted in 1999. ATF's IBIS program was chosen over Drug Fire based on the recommendation of the forensic community. The elaborate communication network established by the FBI was selected to link all present and future NIBIN users.

The system digitizes the patterns of striations (lands and groove markings) on bullets and firing pin/breech face indentations (see bottom photo, insert page 5), and ejector marks found on shell casings. Data from crime scene evidence and from confiscated weapons are digitized and converted to minutiae overlays similar to an AFIS fingerprint pattern. Once recorded, items collected at local scenes can be compared to all known weapons or to items from crime scenes already in NIBIN. All new entries, knowns or unknowns, are compared to the existing files. Weapons can be matched to scenes and scenes can be connected to other scenes. As with AFIS, the computer generates a list of possible matches but an examiner makes the actual identification.

If you ask a representative of the companies that developed these systems how they sort and arrange the data to make these complex comparisons, the answer always involves the word *algorithm*. An algorithm is defined as step by step problem solving. That translates as "I don't know" or "It's a secret," a proprietary secret, actually.

As of 2001 there are 121 IBIS installations (twenty-two hubs-centralized database) in the NIBIN system and twenty-seven IBIS installations in twenty-two countries around the world.

*Virtual Serial Number (VSR).* The latest project, in its infancy, is a program to "fingerprint" all new weapons. The IBIS manufacturer, Forensic Technology, Inc., is working with Glock, the manufacturer of high quality semiautomatic weapons. Before it leaves the factory, each weapon is test-fired and the shell case markings are digitized and scanned into a database.

## Distance Determination

The proximity of the firearm to the target, called the muzzle-to-first-surface distance (MFSD), should be established in every case involving a shooting. Within limits, the distance can be accurately established. The science of distance determination is based on comparing patterns of the waste products sprayed out of the muzzle that can be found at the scene or autopsy to patterns created under controlled conditions.

Recently introduced terminology—Zone I, II, III, IV and V—has been suggested to describe MFSD, where Zone I describes a contact wound. In this system, Zones II to V relate to distances out to about four feet. In my opinion, only contact wounds may be identified accurately by their visual appearance. All other distance determinations require test firing as described below.

If the same weapon (same model, same condition) is used to fire the same type of ammunition at the same type of target from the same distance, the patterns produced will be comparable. In contrast, significantly different patterns can result by changing any one of the elements mentioned. For example, using the same weapon and distance while firing different brands of ammunition with different gunpowders and loads will produce markedly different-looking waste products and patterns (see Photo 9).

Distance determinations cannot be made without exact information about the weapon, caliber, make and model, and ammunition used. Merely looking at the pattern and guessing based on past experiences can lead to serious errors. Many well-meaning investigators or pathologists have estimated how close the weapon was to the target by comparing the pattern in front of them to their memory of prior cases and observations. It is not possible to make the MFSD by comparing information from past investigations alone.

During discharge, the flash, hot gases, and waste products (muzzle debris) will leave distinct distance-related information if held in close proximity to the target, from full contact up to thirty-six inches and more. It makes no difference if the first surface is bare skin, clothing, or other material. Although the term is not quite technically correct, the composite patterns are called powder burns by some authorities. The flames and hot particles created when a round is fired can indeed cause burns to any susceptible surface within a few inches of the muzzle, but the pattern is primarily debris. With other things equal, each time the distance between the target and the weapon is varied, the pattern changes. The soot—partially burned and unburned gunpowder—will leave a different yet reproducible pattern at each distance fired, which can be compared to the questioned pattern to establish its distance. With most ammunition there is some debris detectable as far out as thirty-six to forty-eight inches. One configuration of gunpowder, called ball powder, is made of tiny spheres. Since not all the gunpowder burns, these unburned aerodynamic particles can travel 120 inches or more.

One factor that may alter the appearance of the pattern is weather conditions, winds, for example, that can change the flight of particles. And the angle at which the weapon is held, pointing up or down, may alter the pattern if the distance is more than six to twelve inches. Gravity acts on the powder particles and their residue. The pattern created if a hand-held weapon is pointed at the ground when fired may appear denser than when fired horizontally because all the debris can fall onto the target. A third factor is an intervening surface—a glass pane or curtain, for instance—that can intercept the material that forms the pattern of debris. The pattern, wherever it is located, still has value since it can be used to place the weapon at a particular location at the time it was fired. Perhaps the most obvious factor is the presence of blood from the wound, since it may obscure the visibility of the pattern. Bleeding due to blood pressure stops at death, but oozing blood acted on by external pressures and gravity could obscure the pattern as the body is lifted and moved. Clothing on the body that retains visible evidence of firearms debris must be removed and collected at the crime scene before the body is moved or placed in a body bag for transportation.

Patterns can be reproduced by duplicating the conditions of the shooting event. Any limiting conditions, if known, can be included in the experiment, but four conditions must always be followed closely:

1. The same weapon (or, if it is not available, one of the exact same caliber and model) must be used. If a substitute weapon is all there is, ideally one would be available that has a similar history of use. The barrel length must be the same, since it is a key factor in the resulting pattern.

2. The same type of ammunition, load, and powder shape must be used, without exception. Ideally, the suspect's ammunition would be recovered along with the weapon, but if it was not, identical types of rounds have to be located. Some agencies maintain large collections of ammunition, while others rely on vendors for rare or unusual samples.

3. If the first surface was covered or clothed, the same type of material must be used. Some materials will tear apart or melt at very close distances, and at greater distances will retain more or less debris.

4. If it is believed the weapon was held in contact with the victim when discharged, a backing similar to human must be used. I recommend an animal product called fatback, that is, pigskin with the layer of fat still attached. It can be ordered from a wholesaler or perhaps from a butcher that serves Hispanic clientele. It is used to prepare *chicharone*, a deep-fried pigskin treat.

If a weapon is held tightly against fatback and fired, the resulting ballooning and blow back is similar to what occurs with a contact wound on a human.

Additional information, critical to most investigations, can be developed during the experimental shooting process. Typical questions are: Is the wound an exit or entry? Will the shooter have gunshot residue on his hands? Would the weapon leave any identifiable patterns if parts other than the muzzle were in contact with objects such as the victim's clothing? The direction of fire or the position of the victim can be challenged, even at witnessed shootings, and if left unresolved can confuse the issues of the investigation. Close observations at the scene and autopsy by a good firearms expert always reveal useful information.

Entrance wounds are documented by the effect of the muzzle flash, burning powder, and waste products, and the damage caused by the projectile. Full-contact entrance wounds can cause a tearing of the flesh that is sometimes confused with exit wounds by naive examiners. A close examination will reveal a predictable pattern of the tearing, which proves it is an entrance, not an exit. Also, soot and other debris will be inside the entrance wound when the weapon is held in contact simply because the expanding gases have nowhere else to go except inside the body.

If the weapon is fired within thirty-six inches, entrance direction is established by the other waste products sprayed out of the muzzle. Beyond thirty-six inches, some unburned gunpowder may be located on the victim, but regardless of distance, an entrance defect is almost always identified by a dark ring around the hole, called a grease wipe. Most bullets, where they are crimped into the shell casing, are coated with a thin layer of grease or wax. The heat of detonation softens the material, but some of it remains clinging to the bullet as it speeds out the barrel. During that brief time some waste products are absorbed into the soft lubricant. A grease wipe results when the projectile passes through the first surface it strikes, independent of distance (see photo, insert page 6).

The absence of a grease wipe does not indicate the wound

must be an exit. During the shooting experiment—same weapon, same ammo—shots into identical surfaces should be made to document the presence or lack of a grease wipe. Some types of material, a soft velour, for example, have failed to pick up the grease wipe.

A fast-moving projectile creates a predictable defect when it strikes hardened or brittle surfaces. Trauma to bone, particularly the skull, is similar to the defect created when a pellet strikes plate glass. A cone-shaped opening is chipped out as the kinetic energy of the projectile is distributed to the target material. The small opening points back at the source, and the large one opens in the direction of travel.

The question of who fired the weapon may be the most significant issue of all. Tests to establish the presence of gunshot waste products transferred to the hands of the shooter are available, although not always conclusive. The residue is chemically identical to the material that exits the muzzle, but its physical size is much smaller, allowing it to be forced through small openings along the sides of the firearm. It consists of the ash and oxides from two sources.

The burned nitrocellulose forms carbon and the oxides of nitrate and nitrite. The other components, for the most part residues of the primer chemicals, may contain the oxides or salts of barium, antimony, copper, and lead. Ammunition manufacturers vary the component of the primer. Center-core primers, found on most ammunition, have traditionally contained all four chemicals, but concerns about lead in the environment have resulted in its removal from some primers. Rim-fire primers, almost exclusively .22 caliber ammunition, often contain no barium or antimony.

Gunshot residue, or GSR, can contaminate the shooter because of the pressure generated inside the chambers of a firearm during the brief time the bullet is moving down the barrel. Firearms are constructed in such a way that excessive back pressure of gases and the debris they carry can leak through openings other than the muzzle, rather than blow up. In most cases these openings are intended to leak small amounts of the gases, but in well-worn weapons and weapons of poor quality the amount of GSR can be sizable.

The degree of back pressure is a product of the amount of gunpowder burned, and increases the longer the barrel. Therefore, the amount of GSR contamination depends on the design and condition of the weapon, the load of the ammunition, and the length of the barrel. A long barrel of a worn-out weapon combines with a heavy load to produce the greatest potential GSR.

By design, revolvers can leak from the gap between the front of the cylinder and the barrel, and at the rear gap, between the cylinder and the breech face. Semiautomatics may leak from the area of the ejection port or around the base of the slide mechanism. Rifles, depending on their construction and wear, can also leak. There is only one way to determine the leakage capacity of any weapon and that is to collect samples from the hands or face of the person firing the weapon under controlled conditions while using the corresponding ammunition.

The manner in which the weapon is held and sighted, and the placement of the hands of the shooter, contribute to the likelihood of contamination. For example, a shooter using a two-handed grip while firing a worn-out .357 magnum with a six-inch barrel would be a likely candidate for the GSR test.

Even the most modern GSR tests can be inconclusive. First, some guns don't leak or they don't leak enough for GSR to be detected. Well-made semiautomatics and new short-barreled revolvers are examples of weapons that don't produce detectable residue, even under tightly controlled conditions.

Second, in a case situation, elapsed time is critical. The residue is only clinging to the skin. Incidental contact will eventually knock off most of the particles. Merely putting the hands in and taking them out of one's pockets removes some of the residue. Also, most salts and oxides are readily soluble in water. Time allows shooters to wash their hands, even if they don't realize they're destroying valuable evidence against them.

Time and washing are not usually issues with self-inflicted fatal shots. Moisture can accumulate on the hands from rain, snow, dew, or condensation that can occur after a body has been refrigerated and then removed for examination. Regardless of the condition of the suspect, GSR samples must be collected at the earliest moment, ideally, at the scene.

Third, the method by which GSR is collected and analyzed is critical. The method can affect the chemist's ability to locate the particles.

The most effective method of collection is the *lift* method, followed by visual and chemical analysis using the scanning electron microscope (SEM). The examiner dabs the hand with an aluminum disk coated with a very sticky substance. These lifts can be collected anywhere other than in the area of the shooting. The examiner can be any trained individual who was not involved in the shooting and hasn't handled a weapon or ammunition. In any event, examiners must wash their hands before collecting the samples.

If particles are present, they will transfer from the suspected shooter's hand to the disk. The disk can be placed directly into the SEM and searched manually, as with a standard microscope, or automatically, using the most advanced equipment. Once a particle is located, a powerful electron beam can be focused on it, resulting in reflected X rays. Almost all chemical elements will reflect X rays, and so a specific wavelength will be detected for each element present.

*History*

The earliest method of detecting GSR was called the dermal nitrate test by some and the paraffin test by others. The test was intended to detect the residue of nitrates or nitrites that resulted from the burning of smokeless gunpowder, nitrocellulose. The examiner paints melted paraffin on the back of the suspect's hand and on the skin between the thumb and the index finger. It doesn't burn unless it is overheated. The examiner should test a dab on his or her own hand to be sure. After a few minutes the paraffin cools down and can be peeled off the hand in one piece. After it is removed to a safe place, the examiner sprays the paraffin with a solution of sulfuric acid and diphenylamine. Each tiny speck of nitrate or nitrite turns blue, and often a pattern develops that reflects the actual distribution of GSR. (On rare occasions an investigator told the suspect that any sign of pain when the paraffin was applied would indicate that the suspect was lying. The paraffin was never hot enough to burn, but even a tiny scratch in the skin would trigger at least a flinch of the hand, and maybe even a confession.)

By the early 1950s many aware forensic scientists considered this test unreliable. Nitrates and nitrites were commonly found as a food preservative, in fertilizer, and in cigarette ash. The blue specks could be found on the hands of ordinary folks who had never even held a gun, much less fired one. Unfortunately, the test was used by police agencies well into the 1960s.

In the mid-1960s, NASA fulfilled a commitment to share space age technology with other segments of the scientific community. A group of forensic scientists were invited to the facility of the General Dynamic Corporation in San Diego to witness a demonstration of a powerful atomic reactor, the ultimate tool for solving all manner of crimes.

Almost all elements—lead is a major exception—can be irradiated by a powerful radioactive source, converting the affected element into one or more radioactive isotopes of its former self. Radioactive isotopes lose their new energy, called decay, within a predictable period of time. The term "half-life" is a description of the time required for the element to lose half its radioactive energy. Each isotope has a different half-life, and the gamma rays for each isotope are emitted at a different wavelength.

Neutron Activation Analysis, or NAA, is a process that combines an atomic reactor that radiates the sample with a receiver that can record the frequency and measure the wavelengths of all the signals emitted from the sample. This information translates into the specific elements that were in or on the sample in the first place.

NAA never became a practical method for detecting GSR or any other forensic analysis for some obvious reasons.

First, no local crime labs could afford $500,000-plus for a full-blown nuclear reactor complete with complex licensing requirements, not to mention the inherent dangers. Second, the cost of sending the sample to private laboratories was prohibitive. Third, federal labs with access to a reactor, the FBI and ATF, were overwhelmed with requests for examination and were backlogged for months. But perhaps the most damning deficiency was that the process was simply *too* sensitive. You could break a sample of almost anything in half and find differences in the two pieces. Lack of absolute homogeneity, or more likely the handling of the two halves after the fact, left the impression that the two objects came from different sources even though you personally broke the two pieces apart. The difference was due to variations in the trace elements detected.

History repeats itself on occasion. After several methods of collecting the GSR from the hands of suspects for NAA were discarded, the historical method of painting heated paraffin on the hands of the suspect shooter was selected as the method of choice. It was efficient and allowed the whole ball of wax to be inserted into a sample holder and fed into the reactor. A paraffin blank was always submitted to be used as a control to detect trace elements inherent in the paraffin. Some attorneys in court attempted unsuccessfully to discredit NAA by referring to it as the paraffin test. Later they would ask their expert, "Isn't the paraffin test considered unreliable?" Tricky. You can't leave them alone for a moment!

The availability of a moderately priced Atomic Absorption Spectrophotometer, or AA ($15,000), in the 1970s introduced a new process for measuring small amounts of some of the elements. Barium and antimony, residue from the burning primer, could be identified, but the other components, lead and copper, were usually below the limits of detection. Nevertheless, the advantages—affordability, speed, and ease of operation—outweighed the lack of sensitivity. But there was one major problem.

Most rim-fire .22 caliber ammo contained no barium or antimony. All samples test negative for GSR even if the shooter fired several shots from a leaky revolver and the samples were collected immediately. This poses the biggest problem when the weapon is missing and the investigators have no idea what weapon and ammo were involved in the shooting.

The method of choice for removing GSR for AA is the use of cotton swabs wet with a 5 percent solution of nitric acid. The salts and oxides are readily soluble and are absorbed onto the cotton. The examiner rubs moist cotton swabs against the skin in areas of interest, usually the back side of the web of the hand between the thumb and the index finger, and in some cases the palms. A control sample of the liquid on the swab is also collected. This test is sensitive enough to give a false positive if the examiner's hands are contaminated with residue. A gun-carrying police officer is not a good candidate to collect any GSR samples, since it can always be implied that the samples were contaminated.

The AA instrument consists of a light source, a sample platform, and a detector. The residue is extracted from the cotton and inserted into the sample platform. The residue is burned while aligned in a finely measured beam of light emitted from the filament of a lamp made of the same element. For example, to test for antimony, a lamp using the light emitted from heated antimony is used. (The filaments of the lightbulbs we all use are made of tungsten.)

If the measured energy passing through the burning sample encounters any new energy of exactly the same atomic level, the energies combine, that is, the source energy absorbs the sample energy and the detector measures the higher level. If no antimony is present, no change occurs in the light measurement.

AA-GSR is still in use, although the SEM is far more informative. Many labs don't have an SEM, and even the ones that do may use the AA to perform a quick check for antimony before dedicating the time to the longer SEM procedure.

**The Bottom Line**

The science of firearms examination has evolved in the past ten years, meeting new challenges. Just when it appeared everything was under control, firearms and ammunition manufacturers have introduced some new products that defy analysis. For example, land and groove marks don't transfer as well, if at all, to some of the Teflon-coated bullets.

That is problem enough, but now a company has introduced a caseless bullet. No shell casing remains after the bullet is fired. The product that fires this bullet is an electronic .223 caliber rifle, called Lightning Fire, made by Jager Sport. The shell exists but is constructed of nothing but propellant. When the trigger is pulled, an electric charge, not a firing pin, detonates the propellant. The entire casing burns up! If ever this self-eliminating shell case is matched with a Teflon bullet, we are in big trouble.

## chapter six

# Blood and Other Physiological Fluids

## Introduction

Violent crimes often leave victims unable to assist investigators, and lacking other witnesses, the only verbal explanation of what occurred must come from the suspects. Their stories may be true, partially true, or completely fabricated. However, the proper interpretation of blood typing information and blood spatter analysis goes a long way toward providing an understanding of what happened at a crime scene. Because blood, semen, and saliva are fluids, their nature is to splash, to absorb into, to blot onto, or to flow from one surface to another. The location and distribution of blood, its patterns, shapes, and direction of travel, can be used immediately by a trained observer to substantiate or challenge the suspect's version of what took place. In some situations the patterns are so informative that they're as convincing as if someone had made a videotape of the crime as it was committed. The laboratory analysis of whose blood was cast about at the scene completes the reconstruction of the crime. The following case exemplifies the value of blood as physical evidence.

CRIME SCENE:

## SPANISH 101 WOULD HAVE HELPED

Newport Beach is a unique place. Eclectic in the broadest
sense, it has one common factor that ties the community together: wealth. A drive down Pacific Coast Highway illus-
trates the nature of the city. While traveling southeast along
the Mariner Mile, one passes a row of automobile dealers
who stock cars most of us see only in movies. A showroom
full of Aston Martins and Lotus Elans is connected to an
open lot with at least fifteen Ferraris on display. Right next
door is a Jaguar dealer so popular that an upscale hamburger
joint, Ruby's, operates in the showroom. Even rich people
have to eat.

On the other side of the road, along the water you can't
see, a dozen trendy restaurants are scattered between dry
dock facilities, yacht sales rooms, and open-air display areas
filled, gunnel to gunnel, with forty- and fifty-foot power
cruisers one can buy for $350,000 to $1 million. More than
nine thousand such yachts are docked or anchored in Newport Harbor.

William Bartholomae was one of the megarich. He lived
in what most people consider the ultimate district within
Newport Beach, near the tip of the Balboa peninsula, a narrow four-mile ribbon of land that parallels the Pacific Coast
and encloses Newport Bay. The Bartholomae house, at 2100
East Balboa, was an imposing two-story brick structure,
built on three lots giving him six hundred feet of waterfront.
A smaller attached house, an obvious addition, served as
guest quarters and housed the servants. The main house, although elegant, was small for a mansion, having only two
guest bedrooms and one master bedroom. One of the bedrooms had been converted to a closet for at least one hundred tailored suits and sport jackets.

How did I know that?

William Bartholomae had been stabbed to death on a
windy Sunday morning in January. Hot Santa Ana winds,
sometimes called the devil winds, were blowing offshore.

When I got the call at eight A.M., it was already 70 degrees. A radio weatherman said the temperature was headed into the high nineties, 30 degrees higher than normal. He was warning the drivers of trucks and campers to stay off the freeways and certain highways, describing the dangers of the forty- to fifty-mile-per-hour winds.

When I arrived at the Bartholomae mansion, the first thing I noticed was the sheriff's ID van parked at the curb. That was good. Some departments insisted on using their own technicians, but our ID people were by far the best trained crime scene investigators in the country. I was led into the main house by a uniformed officer. Detective Al Epstein and Sergeant Ken Thompson were waiting for me in the front room.

The house looked small from the street side, but this room was huge, like the lobby of an exclusive athletic club, and filled with expensive furnishings. The room was two stories high with an open-beam ceiling and portholes for windows near the ceiling. A staircase climbed one wall to a balcony leading to what I later found to be two bedrooms. As I entered the room I passed an elaborate dining table that could seat fourteen people. The detectives stood on a huge bearskin rug beneath a giant wall-mounted marlin, posed like models promoting a fine scotch. Epstein broke that mood by sucking on the cold stub of a cigar. He may have owned only one cigar. I could smell the stale wetness of it.

As my eyes completed the trip around the rest of the room, everything seemed in place. There was no indication of any criminal activity.

"You guys look very natural," I said.

"It happened in the kitchen," Thompson said. "Fath is in there now taking pictures." Thompson usually put on an abrupt front. He spoke in a sarcastic tone, but it was more a style than an attitude.

"What happened?"

"You tell me. All we know right now is we got three people at Hoag, one very pale man in their cooler who can't tell us a thing even if he wanted to and two who don't speak a word of English," Thompson retorted.

"I'll show you what we got," Epstein said, waving me to follow him. "The dead guy who owns . . . owned this place is William Bartholomae. If you look out the window, you'll see his yacht, the *Sea Diamond*. He had planned a cruise to Catalina Island this morning but the wind forced a cancellation."

I looked out the window and saw the biggest sailboat I had ever seen.

"Three other people live here," Thompson said. "The dead guy's brother, Charles; Charlie's wife, Carmen; and her sister. The women only speak Spanish. Charles speaks Spanish a little, the dead guy, *nada*." He added, "All we know is the sister has been cut. We don't know how, where, or why. Name's Minola. You'll get a chance to meet her."

The two of them led me back the way I had entered, past the dining area, but then into the kitchen. Walt Fath, the sheriff's ID investigator, was lighting up the scene with his strobe light. Each flash of bright light emphasized the size of the room—big, at least by my standards, for a kitchen. There were two refrigerators, a large commercial-style stove, a sink with three sections, lots of counter space, and a fairly large table near the middle of the room. Other than the refrigerators, nothing looked very new. The table was chrome and the chairs had plastic seats. Even I had a better table set than that. Eventually I realized it was a kitchen for servants, not for members of the household. There was more than enough room in the rest of the house for proper socializing.

The quantity of liquid blood on the floor, a one-piece, brick-red composition material, was not as much as I had expected. There certainly wasn't any one place where it appeared someone had bled to death. Most of the blood appeared to be from large drops that fell straight down to the floor. There were some marks in this blood, smears and smudges, indicating activity, but not much cast-about blood to indicate a struggle. The only blood on the cabinet fronts were fairly large downward drops with no indication of action other than gravity.

The most significant item on the floor was the seven-inch blade of a broken knife without a handle, and with a consid-

erable amount of smeared blood on it. There were drops of
blood around it but no drops on it that I could distinguish.
The handle was missing (see photo, insert page 7).

"They had planned a trip to Catalina with a picnic on
board," Epstein said. "When the captain called it off, it really
pissed off Bartholomae. That boat was his one love, and this
trip had been planned for weeks."

"Charles—that's Bartholomae's kid brother—maybe his
wife, Carmen, who just had a baby, and Minola were going,"
Thompson said. "I'm not sure about that. There was some
question about the wife going. She had just been to the doctor
Friday complaining of dizziness, blacking out, morning sick-
ness or whatever. Someone had to watch the baby as well as
Carmen. Anyway, they were almost out the door when the
captain announced that the wind velocity was too high, even
for the *Sea Diamond*. Bill went bonkers, according to Charles,
screaming and yelling and stomping around the house, like it
was their fault that the Santa Ana was blowing. Everyone tried
to stay out of his way but he was on a rampage."

As I worked my way around to look at the heaviest area of
blood, one pattern appeared different. There was some direction to it. Most of the others were large round blood
spots, all larger than a quarter, indicating someone was
bleeding profusely but not moving about. In this pattern the
roundness and the distance between the spots indicated that
the movement was somewhere near a normal gait, no flailing
about, anyway. All the spots were dry.

What started out as a somewhat random pattern eventually straightened out and directed my eye to a second door
on the east wall of the kitchen. This door led into a party
room with a beautiful wooden bar. Another door on the opposite wall opened to the outside and the dock. Based on the
shape of the drops, the blood trail headed in that direction. I
followed the trail out to a wide concrete sidewalk in the direction of the bay.

I started to head that way when I heard Walt Fath's voice.
He sounded excited.

"You may want to check this out before you do anything
else."

I saw him pointing into one of the sinks.

"I was using the ground glass viewfinder, focusing on the bottom of the sink," he explained. "When I dropped the depth of field a little I realized I was looking at the butt end of the wooden handle."

The screen in the drain was very deep, allowing the entire four-and-a-half-inch knife handle to drop down almost out of sight. We could have easily overlooked it.

Walt said it would take him a while to complete all the exposures. He was bracketing every shot—taking exposures over and under the optimum f-stop as determined by a light meter. A photo of a pure white sink bottom is a little tricky since the amount of light reflected from the strobe is hard to predict. I took the opportunity to go back to following the blood trail.

After a few feet down the sidewalk the drops started to show more movement. They were farther apart and more oval-shaped. The bleeder was moving faster. I looked up across seventy feet of perfectly manicured lawn that was crisscrossed by wide walks and got my first close view of the *Sea Diamond*. She was a ketch rig motor sailer, ninety-eight feet of pure luxury and power built by master designer Phillip Rhodes. She was ideal for the long haul through the Newport Bay out to sea. This was how a yacht was supposed to look, bright white with chrome fixtures, mahogany trim, and a sixteen-foot power skiff moored on the aft. And the blood trail led straight to it.

The sidewalk angled across the lawn and led to the gangplank. The trail stopped abruptly, although the bleeding didn't, in front of but not on the gangplank. It was as if the bleeder dared not go any farther, no matter the height of concern. That should have told me that Bartholomae couldn't have been the bleeder. To go on board would get blood on what was surely an immaculate deck. A dying Bartholomae wouldn't have cared. Someone who lived in fear would stop in his or her tracks. I stood looking down at the blood patterns when I heard someone say, "You can come aboard."

The voice belonged to the boat's captain. I stepped around the blood and climbed up the steps to the deck. It was immaculate. I explained what I was doing, and the captain explained what he had been doing. He had readied the *Sea Diamond* for an early departure. This required starting the engines and all the navigational controls. It was relatively simple to shut down the power, except for the gyroscopic compass, an essential part of the navigation system.

"Once you start this hummer turning it can take four hours for it to stop spinning. Anything happens to it during those four hours and it's $25,000 down the tubes."

He explained that after he informed Mr. Bartholomae that it was unsafe to leave the harbor, he headed back to the boat. He said Charles joined him to help shut down the equipment. Within a half hour they saw Minola, the sister-in-law's sister, standing at the foot of the gangplank screaming, *"Ayuda! Ayuda!"* Spanish for "Help." She was holding her hands tightly but was unable to stop them from bleeding. The two of them couldn't communicate further so she ran back to the house. He used the ship-to-shore phone to call the police.

The sun was starting to bear down on the blood on the sidewalk, telling me I had better collect some of it before the typing characteristics got fried.

I verified that Fath had already taken some pictures of the trail. He was planning to photograph the entire trail later. In fact, senior criminalist Bob Stettler came to the scene and worked with Fath to photograph almost every drop of dry blood. In the event the identity of the bleeder or the word of the captain became a serious issue, it was important to collect some of the blood before the heat denatured its typing characteristics. My evidence kit held all the things needed to scrape up some of the blood, at least under normal conditions. I was about to be reminded that these conditions were far from normal. I placed a small piece of weighing paper, used to package trace evidence, next to one of the spots and picked at the dry blood with the tip of a scalpel blade. The blood broke loose and disappeared into the lawn, propelled by the strong winds. I tried again, this time holding the paper upright, hoping it would catch the particles of blood. It didn't. This was not going to be easy. "I need a box," I said to Thompson, who was standing next to the house and out of the wind. In a few minutes he returned with the top half of a cardboard orange crate.

I cut a large opening in the top of the lid, leaving the sides intact. I placed the open box top over another blood spot and was able to scrape the blood onto the paper without difficulty. I repeated that process on several spots picked at random. That was enough to identify the bleeder if it ever became an issue.

Thompson was interviewing the brother, Charles, when I reentered the house. After seeing his brother's reaction to the canceled trip, Charles had gone to the yacht. His wife remained in the kitchen, cleaning up. His sister-in-law, Minola Gallardo, who had only recently moved there from her native Spain to help with the baby, was doing just that. She was staying in the servants' quarters, for that is what William considered the women.

Actually, before coming to America, both ladies were professional flamenco dancers. Of the two, Minola was the better known, with a degree of fame in Spain. She didn't take to the role of servant. Despite being warned in advance about William, she had come to help her sister, who had not been reacting well to her early stages of pregnancy or to motherhood or to William. Charles described Minola as the stereotypical Spanish flamenco dancer—high-spirited, fiery, with a low flash point. Both women were kept in line by William's overt brashness. Since neither sister spoke any English, Charles tried, in his best Spanish, to explain to both of them that William was putting on a front and wasn't as mean as he acted. But they apparently did not buy that line and lived in constant fear of his actions. Today their fear had become justified.

I wanted to look at Bartholomae's body before I spent any more time at the scene. If there was an explanation to all the blood patterns and trails, it could well be found in the manner of his death. There apparently would be no chance to talk to the sisters even though a translator had been summoned. Charles had already contacted an attorney, and the sisters had been advised not to talk to anyone for the time being.

The house could wait at that point. The investigators drove me to Hoag, leaving Fath, who was still working, and several uniformed officers to guard the scene. Bartholomae's clothing, a yellow bathrobe, had not been removed. The coroner's investigator, Jim Beisner, was at the hospital making arrangements for the autopsy.

William Bartholomae had cuts on his left hand, typical of defense wounds. One was superficial, a diagonal cut across the palm at the base of the index finger, too shallow to tell direction. The second cut was deeper and was located on the thumb across the inside fold of the first phalanges. The cut appeared to have been made with the sharp edge of the blade cutting toward the tip of the thumb and may have occurred when he received one of the puncture wounds.

There were two punctures in the upper abdomen. Both were about four inches above his navel and were no more than four inches apart. The sharp edge of the knife appeared to have been elevated to about 45 degrees toward the right shoulder. One stab had gone in and out and the other had made a four- to five-inch slice as it exited. The former wound was slightly to the right of mid-line, the latter to the left.

It was his face, chin, and neck that got my interest. There were gouges on both sides. Skin was missing. A deep one-inch-long gouge on his right cheek started in the area parallel with the tip of his nose about one inch from the right nostril. The mark moved upward from front to back. A projection of this scratch extended between his right eye and over his right ear. There were several marks under his right chin in a tight pattern. Two were similar in shape, arcs with the convex side pointing down and to the front. The same type of marks were on the left side of his chin, and a long scratch originated under the left side of his chin and moved up toward his lips.

Could I be looking at anything other than deep fingernail indentations? The marks clearly were made by someone attacking from the rear, digging fingernails in deep.

"I need to look at the sister's hands, the sooner the better!" I said.

Fortunately, both sisters had been at the same hospital without interruption since they left the house to come to Hoag for treatment. One sister was in the bed, her left hand bandaged. She was hooked up to IVs but was awake and alert, talking in a soft voice to Charles Bartholomae, who was seated on the edge of the bed. The other sister sat next to the bed. I didn't know who was who, and didn't know enough Spanish to ask.

Charles, seeing the confused look on my face, introduced his wife. She was the one seated next to the bed.

My inability to communicate made me feel helpless. I explained to Charles that although I couldn't ask them questions per their attorney's request, I did have the authority to examine their hands. I didn't need a search warrant to collect transitory evidence. To wait would allow time for fragile evidence to be destroyed, intentionally or not. He explained to the women what I was about to do. I wanted to look at their fingernails and remove anything that might be lodged there. He informed me that although the hospital had given her two pints of blood, Minola was still weak from loss of blood. He hoped that what I had to do would not be harmful.

Oh great, she's had a blood transfusion, I said to myself as I assured him out loud that I would not harm either of the sisters. Although the ABO blood types are matched donor to recipient prior to transfusion, whole blood (cells and serum) contain many other forms of genetic information. These other factors do not harm the recipient, but they can show up in forensic typing procedures as "false" information. I looked at Thompson and Epstein to see if either had picked up on the transfusion information. They gave no indication of concern.

Minola, because of her injured hand, was the most logical participant of the two, or at least was involved to some extent. I moved to the side of her bed and looked at her right hand. She didn't seem to mind my touching her fingers. Her fingernails were long. Not the nails of a servant. The undersides were encrusted with dried blood. That's not unusual for a person with cuts on her hand, but was it all from her cuts?

The blood on each nail was scraped onto a piece of filter paper using an ordinary nail cleaner. The left hand was bandaged but the nails were accessible. After folding and packaging the pieces of paper, I washed my scraper in the room's sink and approached Carmen. Although her hands were not injured, they bore a few small crusts of blood. The undersides of her nails were free of visible debris. I went through the motions anyway after collecting the blood crusts.

The attending physician had described the wounds on Minola's hand as incisions. Most likely these were defense wounds, that is, cuts due to grabbing the blade of a knife when it is in motion. The cuts on William's hands had looked the same. That both had cuts on their palms indicated both may have had a knife or, more likely, that they were fighting for possession of the same knife. I hadn't seen any other knife.

In English, I thanked the ladies for their cooperation, and we walked out to the hall. When we were far enough away from the room not to be heard, I said, "We'll need their clothes and blood samples for typing. If Minola has had a transfusion, we'll need the typing sample the hospital took before the transfusion. The blood in her veins at the moment could confuse our serologist. Now I'd like to go back to the scene."

There wasn't anything else apparent at the scene, but the patterns now made more sense. Although there were other very sharp knives in the drawers, only one had been bloody. Certainly there was time to have washed a weapon after the incident. Further, there was blood in the sink next to the one that contained the handle of the broken knife. Nevertheless, based on the amount of blood in the sink, the bleeding was heavy enough that if the wounded person was washing blood off a knife, once done, the person couldn't put the knife away without getting more blood on it.

I looked over the blood patterns closely. An intruder could have been responsible for wounding both of them, but since they had never mentioned that possibility to the police, that seemed unlikely. A mutual combat fit their injuries and the scene, but at what point did the mutual part start? Was William attacked and stabbed first, and did he then manage to get possession and fight back until he dropped, or did he start the fight, attacking Minola while in a rage?

For that matter, Charles could not be excluded as a suspect, nor could the captain or Carmen. Charles as the killer didn't seem right. Minola may have been too doped up to react normally, but she seemed absolutely comfortable with Charles at the hospital. Not too likely if he had cut her up earlier that morning. The captain as the killer also seemed unlikely since after Minola was injured, she ran to the *Sea Diamond* asking for help, or at least someone had laid a blood trail down.

Carmen had been working in the kitchen yet was not visibly injured. That didn't exclude her as the one attacking Bartholomae. Perhaps the origin of the blood on her hands would help sort out that part of the story. If she wasn't the killer, she must have at least witnessed the incident. But at this point, why would she tell what she saw if it implicated her or her sister? I collected samples of many of the stains from around the kitchen, figuring typing would become a critical issue.

I made a quick tour of the house. William's bedroom was unremarkable, for a millionaire. Then I checked the second bedroom, the one converted into a closet. I looked in all the other closets, dirty clothes hampers, bathrooms, and the laundry room. No bloody clothes anywhere and no partially washed anything.

The autopsy was conducted that afternoon. One of the puncture wounds in the abdomen was a direct hit into the liver, resulting in internal bleeding and death. The extensive internal bleeding, with very little blood at the scene or on his bathrobe, indicated that he was on his back at the time or sometime after he was stabbed.

I collected tissue samples from both cheeks along the perimeter of the torn skin. William hadn't shaved, and a stubble of his beard was protruding along the edge of torn skin. Other than the cause of death, there were no clear answers here. After a long day I still had to take all this stuff into Santa Ana and store it in the laboratory refrigerator.

Once in the lab, I decided to look at the fingernail scrapings. There was nothing in Carmen's scrapings, as I'd suspected. But the material I had collected from Minola's nails offered something quite revealing. Whiskers! In fact, there were small rolls of skin that included white whiskers.

Facial hair in cross section looks different than you might expect. The hairs are not round. They are square or triangular, at least in older men. He was missing skin and whiskers, and she had skin and whiskers under her fingernails. In my experience before and since this case, it is unusual to make this finding. In fact, it is rare to find any identifiable associative evidence under a victim's or suspect's fingernails. I called the Newport Beach PD and talked to Sergeant Thompson. He was there and very pleased to hear about my finding the whiskers.

As I went back home, I mulled over why Minola would attack him or he her. And, if she did it, when did she stab him? The position of the scratches and the shape of the gouges on his cheek and chin indicated she came at him from behind. When she scratched him, both of her hands were empty, since she most likely made all the marks at the same time. The E.R. people hadn't washed him up. There was some blood dribble on his face but no smears of blood on his cheeks, so when she scratched him, it had to be before she was bleeding so heavily from the cuts on her hand. Since she had to come up behind him to do the scratching, the upward motion away from his chin and up to his ears was very significant. He wasn't tall, but she was shorter than he was. He had to be lower than she was or have his head back over his shoulders at the time of the scratching. Why did they both have cuts on their hands? Were there two knives? Did I have the only knife? How and when did it get broken?

If everyone was telling the truth about the sister's fear of William, it would take something very traumatic for her to attack him in the first place. Minola had done the smart thing, according to Charles. She went to the baby's room when the ranting and raving started. If Carmen was in the kitchen cleaning up the dishes, why didn't she run to Charles or the captain for help when trouble started? But what if Carmen was unable to run for help?

That had to be the answer. Then everything else would make sense. For some reason, she couldn't run for help.

I called the detective division of the NBPD again. Thompson was still there, and I laid out my theory.

"Try this on. Carmen is in the kitchen washing the last of the dishes. She has just dried them and finished putting them away, except maybe the big knife. Her postpartum problem doubles her over and she goes down and passes out on the floor with the big knife next to her or nearby. William is close by and sees her drop or hears the noise and enters the kitchen. He sees Carmen on the floor. He kneels down next to her. Maybe even to help her. He can't be all bad. But at that moment Minola walks in on the scene. Maybe William doesn't even see Minola enter the room or maybe he does. But she sees him down over her flat-out sister with a knife next to him, or maybe he had even picked it up to move it. In any case, the knife had to be close by because one of them gets it real soon.

"He could be yelling out anything, like please get help or help her. But she doesn't have any idea what he's saying. She may be screaming like hell by now but he can't understand a thing she says. There's no communication. She thinks he has hurt, maybe even killed, her sister. Her fear is now rage. Before he can move, she comes from behind him while he's still kneeling down, grabs his face, and rips him away from her sister, scratching the crap out of his face. He's confused. Her attack doesn't stop. The knife is there. He gets it. She tries to get it away from him and maybe that's when her hand is cut.

"There wasn't much struggling after either is cut or he would have more blood on the front of his robe and there would have been some splash patterns on the walls, the table, or the fixtures. There aren't. I think everything happened down low. They may have been on the floor rather than standing. She is not stabbed, other than the cut on her hand, so if he ever had the knife, he must not be trying to kill her, just trying to keep her away, trying to get her to stop coming at him. She still thinks her sister is dead or dying. She wants to help her sister but thinks she can't do a thing as long as he has the knife. Somehow she gets the knife away from him.

"No matter what he says, she doesn't understand a word of it. He's dead meat as long as she has the knife. This is when he gets the cuts on his hands. Then it happens. She nails him. Two thrusts and he's down. The elongated cut is probably the second of the two wounds. The handle breaks off as he turns away or as she pulls it over at an angle. Snap! There is no blood on the blade near the handle end to indicate she cut her hand as she stabbed him or as the blade broke.

"Anyway, Carmen is still down and out. She is unaware of anything at this point. If she was okay she could have gone for help. She couldn't. Minola tries to aid Carmen, but when she doesn't respond, Minola runs to the boat to call for help. The blood patterns in the kitchen and the blood trails all over match this explanation. What do you think?"

"What has the postpartum stuff got to do with it?" Thompson asked. "You lost me at that point." He wasn't buying it. He would later. Both sisters were arrested for murder, but only Minola was charged.


## Epilogue

When I completed the comparison of the debris from Minola's fingernails to Bartholomae's whiskers, I was satisfied of the similarity. I could not say they had to be his hairs to the exclusion of all the men with white facial hair, but under the circumstances I felt pretty good about it. The defense pleaded their case to the jury, stating almost to the word what I had told Thompson. Either the defense attorney hit upon this explanation or had our phones bugged or my theory was right. The jury found her not guilty. In the legal sense, the killing of Bartholomae was considered excusable because of the situation and their inability to communicate.

The perception is that wealthy people die because someone wants their money. None of the people in the house at the time of the killing were in line to get much, if any, of Bartholomae's money. At the time of the incident, William was engaged in a divorce battle with his wife, with most of his holdings in jeopardy. Upon his death, his wife and their daughter became the major beneficiaries of the estate. Shortly after the trial, Minola returned to Spain.

## BLOOD AND OTHER PHYSIOLOGICAL FLUIDS

The human body at any given moment is either producing, altering, destroying or eliminating chemical compounds. The precise architecture of many of the compounds varies slightly based on inherited factors. The chemical components of value to a forensic serologist—DNA, carbohydrates, enzymes, or proteins, or their combinations—are transported by physiological fluids. After death or if spilled from a living body, many of these compounds have an astonishing durability. This durability facilitates their use as traceable genetic evidence, in some cases years after the crime was committed. Controlled studies have identified the blood groups that remain stable after death or out of the body and those that don't. Although time can alter the usefulness of the best of the materials, in the hands of knowledgeable crime scene investigators and serologists using quality control procedures, there should be no confusing intermediate products.

Four basic questions must be asked about PF stains associated with a crime scene:

1. Are the stains blood, semen, saliva, or some other substance?

2. Are the stains from a human or other animal?

3. Who or what is the source of the stain?

4. How, why, and when did they get deposited on items associated with the scene?

The answers to these questions solve crimes, implicate those involved, and exonerate the innocent.

## Blood

Almost everyone has witnessed bleeding—if not their own, that of someone they know. Bleeding can occur externally or internally, due to an inflicted trauma or natural disease or disorder. The bleeding we experience following an injury is due almost entirely to blood pressure, with some contribution from gravity. If a cut is deep enough, arterial bleeding may occur, producing spurts of blood each time the heart beats. In any event, the blood runs freely until it is stopped by compressing the area around or near the wound or, if it is only a slight break, until the blood clots, stopping the flow. If bleeding is allowed to continue unchecked, the heart will continue to pump until almost all the blood supply is gone from the circulatory system and death occurs due to ensanguination. Therefore, a large amount of pooled blood indicates the victim was alive for some time after the wound was inflicted.

The distribution of the unrestrained blood at the crime scene depends on the location of the wound, the position of the victim when the damage is done, and the victim's ability to react. For example, a victim of a gunshot wound to the chest who is already on his or her back or immediately falls faceup may bleed to death internally without a drop of blood exiting the wound. If there is no exit wound and the victim remains in that position, the scene may remain bloodless as long as the body isn't moved. Turn the body over and the scene may soon be deep with blood. A relatively blood-free scene where an open wound is on the underside of the body could mean either (or both) of two things: Death was quick and the blood is primarily the result of gravity, or the person bled elsewhere and was moved to the present crime scene after death.

Categorizing the nature of a bloodstain begins with a visual examination. During the initial search of the crime scene for stains, the most important requirement, other than good eyesight, is a good source of white light—light that contains all the colors of the spectrum—because stains can be completely overlooked if a white light source is not used to make the examination. Natural sunlight offers by far the best source of white light. A tungsten lightbulb is adequate. After the initial search, special types of lights—UV, lasers, and other light sources—may be used to locate otherwise invisible stains.

The reddish color we rely on to attract the eye to a blood spot is a result of reflected red light. So if a fluorescent, mercury vapor, or sodium vapor light is used to search for blood spots, any blood will not look red to the examiner, since these lamps have little or no red in the visible energy they radiate; thus, there is no red light to reflect. A red blood drop may look gray and be overlooked. To see this fact firsthand, take any red item you own and find a parking lot with mercury vapor lamps. They emit a light rich in blue and almost void of red. The normally red item won't look red under that light.

Once bloodstains are discovered, investigators try to determine how and why they got there and from where they came. Blood dripping from a wound will behave as any free-falling liquid—that is, the volume of each drop of normal blood will be the same. With gravity the only force, the drop striking a flat surface at 90 degrees will form a nearly perfect circle. The diameter of the blood spot will depend on the volume of blood in the drop, the height of the fall, and the nature of the flat surface. In theory, the volume of everyone's free-falling drop will be equal, based on the average density and surface tension of the blood. At heights greater than thirty-six inches, blood drops will all attain the same velocity, and beyond that all the spots will be the same size.

If a person is walking, running, or otherwise active while bleeding, the shape of the blood spots on a flat surface, such as a sidewalk, will change from round to oblong. Because of the motion, the blood is now falling at some angle instead of straight down. Momentum is added to the drops also, and their volumes vary accordingly, but for determining direction it makes no difference if the amount of blood in the

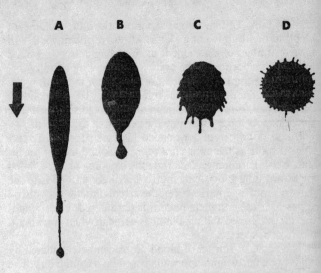

Figure 10. Four different shaped spots, their
measurements and angle calculations.
A = 12 degrees, B = 28, C = 55 and D = 90.

Direction

| A | B | C |
| Normal Walk | Fast Walk | Running |

Figure 11. The Shape of Blood Spots.

drops varies. Unlike height determination, the volume of blood in the drop is not a factor. All the resultant spots will have a similar oblong shape if the bleeding is from a wound located on a portion of the body that is moving steadily forward; for example, a bloody nose. The faster the motion, the more elongated the spots (see Figure 10). Secondary droplets can form after the main drop hits the sidewalk. The smaller spots break away in the direction of the movement.

Blood falling from a wounded hand can form different-shaped spots as the arms are swung back and forth—for instance, while running. Each time the bleeding hand is flailed backward, that blood will indicate a direction opposite the person's movement. However, the actual direction should be apparent if the complete pattern is considered. Understanding the nature of falling blood is critical when tracking a bleeding suspect.

The angle of impact of blood drops can be calculated by applying a fairly simple formula based on trigonometry. The distance the blood has traveled is not important. Instead, the ratio of the width of the spot to its length must be considered.

$$\frac{\text{Width of the spot}}{\text{Length of the spot}} = \text{Impact angle (expressed as a sine function)}$$

For example, a blood spot is 3mm wide and 11mm long.

$$^3/_{11} = .2727 = 15.8 \text{ degrees}$$

And the more oblong the spot, the greater the angle of impact (see Figure 11).

This description of free-falling blood drops does not explain patterns that occur when momentum is also considered. Movement breaks up the surface tension of the drops, so the more energy there is, the greater the drops' velocity and the smaller the drops become. The Orange County Sheriff's Crime Lab uses the following definitions for drop size. Note that the drops get smaller as more force or velocity is applied.

- *Large*: greater than 6mm. Most likely due to gravity—dripping.

- *Medium*: 2mm to 6mm. Typical of the splashing of blood near the victim of a beating. For example, the head is injured within a few inches of a wall. Depending on the surface and angles involved, beatings will also produce drops that indicate direction and angle. These drops may appear smaller overall. If the victim is able to move during the incident, a trained investigator can relocate each different place the beating occurred. There can be smaller drops associated with a beating due to secondary splashing and cast off, described below.

- *Fine*: 0.1mm to 2mm. High energy is involved when the spray is consistently this small. This level of energy is applied to blood that is coughed up by the victim of a mouth wound. In the case of "The 7-Eleven Killers," the victim, while barricaded behind the storage room door, was coughing up blood, producing in part a pattern of spray this size. Cast off blood can also appear as fine spots if the activity producing them is violent enough.

- *Mist*: less than 0.1mm. Mist occurs with high-velocity trauma such as a high-powered rifle projectile passing through a victim's head or the explosive force of a firearm held close to a human's head, as in a suicide or execution. The fine spray from the exit wounds can travel many inches, depending on the energy of the round, but is visible only when a surface is close enough to retain the pattern. With contact wounds that produce a blow back, a few drops of a fine mist of blood may be transferred to the weapon or other objects within an inch or so of the contact wound, but no farther.

Cast off occurs when a weapon is used to inflict repeated blows, strikes, or stabs. The weapon can be anything, even a fist, as long as it retains blood for a moment and then is used to inflict at least one more blow. Once the victim's

skin is broken by the initial impact and bleeding begins, subsequent contact in the areas of bleeding will contaminate the
weapon with liquid blood. As the bloody weapon is withdrawn and raised to deliver another blow, at some point
when the maximum extension of the attacker's arm is
reached there is a stop and a change of direction, back toward the victim. Depending on the speed of the withdrawal
and the abruptness of the momentary stop, some quantity of
blood will fly off the weapon. A narrow directional spray
may be found on nearby objects, and each cast off can be
used to determine the participants' positions. Even the hand
used to hold the weapon, right or left, may be determined if
the victim's body remains in place or its position was documented before it was moved or can be ascertained by other
evidence.

Cast off may be found on any nearby object regardless of
the nature of the crime scene. To locate cast off if it is not
obvious, look up and behind the likely position of the attacker. Indoors, the patterns may appear on the ceiling,
walls, or furniture. Outdoors, the pattern may be found on
the underside of overhanging foliage, on tree trunks, or on
nearby vehicles or walls. The clothing of the attacker, if
available, is a likely source for cast off blood. The back of an
attacker's shirt may be contaminated with a fine spray of
blood, matching the blood group of the victim.

During the examination of blood spatter on a wall or furniture near the victim, it is not unusual to find areas within
the stains that are relatively void of blood. This lack may be
the result of shadowing, which occurs when the attacker or
another object is between the victim and the stained area
during the attack. The blood lands on the attacker or object,
leaving the shadowed area with no spatter or far less than on
the surrounding areas. (See top photo, insert page 8.)

The distribution of blood surrounding the shadowing
gives the crime scene investigator a solid clue that blood
will be found on the attacker's clothing or some other object that was moved after the attack. If the clothing or item
is located before the evidence is altered, the pattern and distribution contained on it will be consistent with its relative

location at the crime scene when compared to the nonshadowed areas.

Perhaps the best-known bloodstain pattern is rarely found. The Hollywood special effect that shows blood exploding out of an entrance wound totally misrepresents firearms trauma. Blow back occurs when the weapon is held tight against the body, as in the wounds described in Chapter 5. One exception occurred in Orange County years ago. Jack Cadman, the first criminalist in the county, tells of a case of murder where a husband shot his wife in the back at ten-inch range with a twelve-gauge shotgun. The woman was at least two hundred pounds overweight. The bundle of shot pushed a load of fat in and then out, spraying fat back onto the husband's clothing.

## Using Bloodstains to Determine the Order of Events

I recently examined a series of crime scene photographs and associated documents where the victim had been shot in the head three times with a .32 caliber weapon, each close to full contact. There were blood patterns on the floor and on top of furniture, blood drops straight down, indicating that the victim moved about the scene a distance of a few feet before he fell to the floor. There was a large area of blood spatter above the victim on a bookshelf, on the sides and bottom of a flower planter (fifty-four inches above the floor), and on drapes up to seventy-two inches above the floor. The spatter was of medium velocity, to the sides, upward and downward. A forensic pathologist agreed that two of the shots would have disabled the victim instantly due to brain damage. The other shot entered near the ear but traveled downward without any central nervous system trauma.

Can you explain how all this happened, which happened first, second, etc., and how the spattered blood got on the items described?

The downward shot was first. By the time the second shot took place, a few seconds later, the first wound had produced the blood trail and blood on the victim's face and hair. The second shot, also near the ear, had to occur while the victim was still on his feet but going down. The energy of the muzzle blast impacting the now bloody head accelerated the blood already on the victim's head, resulting in the spray on the planter, walls, drapes, and the nearby bookshelf. The shooter would have a similar spatter pattern on clothing worn. The third shot occurred after the victim was on the floor.

A similar pattern could have resulted if the victim had been struck with any high-energy blunt force, but no such trauma was located on the victim at autopsy.

The order of events can also be determined by studying the presence of disturbed blood, swipes and wipes—terms, along with spatter, used by the International Association of Blood Pattern Analysts (IABPA).

Activities that occur after bleeding can result in overlapping evidence. For example, one activity involving subject A could cause that subject's blood to be splashed across a wall. After that, a second activity causes large drops of blood from subject B to hit the same wall and then run down and through subject A's blood. Typing the blood will clarify the sequence of events.

A swipe means "to apply" and is generally considered an event where an object such as a bloody hand or bloody clothing is moved across a surface. The surface can be clear of other blood or the swipe can move through existing blood patterns. A bloody swipe will always have a visible point of origin. If a swipe passes through an existing pattern, it then alters the pattern, establishing which occurred first. A swipe doesn't necessarily destroy any value of the evidence; in fact, it may add value to the interpretation of the scene. I use the term "smudge" to indicate activity that has obliterated what could have been fine detail such as a bloody or latent fingerprint.

When blood is already on the object or surface and the pattern is disturbed by an otherwise bloodless object moving through it, this is called a wipe. A wipe has no obvious point of origin until the bloodless object moves through the existing blood. At the end of a wipe there is usually an accumulation of blood and the pattern is heavier, a halo. An outline of the wiping object may even be apparent. A wipe can be a conscious attempt to alter or clean up blood pattern or it may be a coincidence, as when a garment, sheet, or towel is dragged over liquid blood. In either event, wipes help investigators understand what occurred after the bleeding.

When a bloody object comes in contact with a clear area on another object, the pattern of the wet blood can be transferred. It can be an unrecognizable outline, a plain transfer, but it may help to explain the sequence of events. A transfer can occur on a single object when one bloody part is pressed against a bloodless area, or folded, producing an inkblot pattern. If this occurrence is not recognized, it can mislead the investigators.

The location of bloody transfers—such as bloody fingerprints, even if they are only smudges, on a doorknob or a light switch—and the existence of a trail of blood, clearly explain some of the events that occurred during or after the bleeding.

Objects containing patterns, moved about during or after a violent crime, that come in contact with liquid blood can behave like a rubber stamp and transfer their contaminated surface characteristics to receptive items—a pattern transfer. Bloody fingerprints were discussed in Chapter 3. The bloody boot print described in the case of "The 7-Eleven Killers" is another good example (see bottom photo, insert page 8). Its location explained the events leading up to and after the final shot, and its fine detail was used to identify the specific boot after the suspect's arrest.

An impression in blood can appear as a negative; that is, a blood-free item such as a shoe or a finger can disturb moist blood and displace it. Acting like a squeegee, the fine detail of the object forces the blood aside and its pattern appears as a void in the blood. It is likely that some blood will transfer to the object during this action. Now, when the object next contacts a clear surface, for example, as a person moves about the scene, there may be impression transfers. All this information is beneficial in sequencing the events.

Even the makeup of the missing murder weapon can be understood when the bloody article is momentarily laid down on a receptive surface, such as a bedsheet or tabletop.

Although carried away from the crime scene, the object can leave its markings behind, thereby assisting the crime scene investigator in recognizing the type of weapon.

## Presumptive Tests

Sometimes an investigator may not be sure a stain is the result of blood. A presumptive test is then conducted by placing a small part of the stain in a chemical solution. The appearance of a characteristic color indicates a positive test. By definition, any positive presumptive test is nonspecific for blood and not meant to be an absolute identification. It is an indication that something is present that will require laboratory confirmation to establish its identity. A negative result, no reaction at all, is considered an elimination. But if a test has no reaction, it could also mean the chemicals have gone bad. It happens. A control sample, a known material that will always trigger a reaction, should be added to the same negative test solution to verify its activity before the investigator concludes that the sample is not blood.

A presumptive test should only be conducted when there is an immediate need to be assured that a stain may be blood. This process destroys that part of the sample being tested. So unless it is critical to the investigation—for instance, an investigative turning point and not merely curiosity—this level of testing should be postponed. One turning point could be that there may be no crime if the stain in question is not blood. In any event, only a tiny portion of the sample should be sacrificed, leaving as much as possible for the laboratory examination.

In some jurisdictions a positive test, combined with other evidence, could be considered probable cause to confiscate the contaminated evidence or even to detain or arrest the suspect. Regardless of the perceived importance, a presumptive test must never be run directly on the stained surface, or run at all if the sample size is small. Typing or profiling is far more important.

Almost all the presumptive tests for blood induce reactions with the iron part of the red blood cells, that is, the heme or hematin found in hemoglobin. Iron-containing materials similar to heme can be found in naturally occurring plant products. Additionally, some common household condiments contain peroxidase, which will trigger a positive reaction. For example, horseradish and orange juice and some chemicals that are classified as oxidizers will trip a chemical reaction. The positive reaction of these materials with presumptive test chemicals is the reason the tests are nonspecific for blood.

### Benzidine Test

Until the 1970s the benzidine test was the favored presumptive test for blood. During that time benzidine was identified as a carcinogenic compound producing cancers after prolonged exposure. Its positive attribute was a quick vivid blue color. The original reagent consisted of benzidine and sodium perborate mixed in glacial acetic acid. During the 1960s it was noted that many of the false positive reactions could be eliminated by delaying the addition of the perborate. A small fragment of the stain was placed in the acidic solution of benzidine. If an oxidizing agent or peroxidase was present, the blue color would appear with no further testing. This clearly indicated the sample was not suitable for the presumptive test even if blood was present. If no color appeared to this point, a solution containing the perborate or peroxide was added. The immediate appearance of a blue color was a valid positive test.

### Leuco Malachite Green Test

This reaction yields a bright green color under the same conditions as the benzidine test. Its advantage is that the chemicals, leuco malachite and sodium perborate, can be stored in a dry form and mixed with acetic acid at the crime scene. Since some of the same interference will occur with products that contain heme, peroxidase, or other oxidizing agents, the addition of the perborate or hydrogen peroxide should be delayed until after the suspect material is mixed with the leuco malachite and acetic acid. If a green color appears before the perborate is added, the sample is not suitable for presumptive testing.

## Phenolphthalein Test

This procedure is one of the more sensitive presumptive tests. Even blood that has been diluted with water—for example, the water in the sink trap after someone has washed blood off hands—will test positive.

The stock reagent is prepared by treating phenolphthalein with potassium hydroxide and zinc. The stock solution is made ready for testing by adding perborate. The number of false positives is far less with this test than with benzidine, but a few do occur. They can be recognized, in part, by adding the perborate after the stock solution has shown no reaction to the suspect sample. A red to pink color will indicate a positive test.

## Luminol Test

Blood that is so dilute that it is not noticeable to the eye is called "occult," which means hidden from view or requiring a chemical test to detect. Luminol is the method of choice for occult blood at crime scenes that has been cleaned up or has escaped detection for extended time periods, even several years. But luminol should never be used as an overall spray if the stain is visible and typing or profiling the blood is desired. A spot test—phenolphthalein is suggested—is adequate to justify the collection of evidence.

The chemicals, 3-aminophthalhydrazide and sodium carbonate, are mixed in water with sodium perborate and sprayed in a fine mist over the questioned area. This could be an entire room, but the area must be in the dark, and the darker the better. Luminol, in the presence of blood—and yes, some interfering substances—glows in the dark. Older samples are said to glow brighter than fresh ones.

All presumptive tests are hazardous to the examiner and should be avoided if adequate ventilation is unavailable. Further, the acidic tests destroy the evidence treated by the chemicals. Once, some bloodstained bedding on which a field investigator had sprayed an acetic acid-based presumptive chemical was submitted to the lab. He received his positive field test, but the blood and the bedding were effectively destroyed by the acid.

### False Negatives

Critical evidence could be overlooked if a false presumptive test fools the examiner. A 1999 study indicates that there can be false negatives, even when the test solution reacts as expected with a known sample. This can occur if the stain is in the presence of certain chemicals (reducing agents) found in common household items, medicines, and foods. The presence of these interfering chemicals may be impossible to detect at a crime scene. My advice—if it looks like blood, collect it.

### Collection of Blood at the Crime Scene

Prior to DNA profiling (circa 1990), if fluid blood was located at a scene, every attempt was made to collect the liquid intact to protect any remaining whole red blood cells. Direct typing (ABO), agglutination by anti sera using the Lattes slide method, is quick and highly accurate when conducted by a trained serologist. The sample was collected by pipette or eyedropper and added to a vial containing an appropriate amount of saline solution, a saltwater mixture equal to a body fluid's salt content (isotonic). Red cells in a nonisotonic solution are affected by osmosis, and either rupture or are crushed. In either case, the cell walls, the site of the ABO substance, are in disarray and useless for the direct agglutination process.

From 1971 to 1990 modern forensic laboratories typed or profiled blood using both ABO (H) methods and electrophoresis (see "The Value of Blood as Evidence—History," to come). Intact red cells were still used in ABO (H) methods. For electrophoretic methods, wet blood cells were soaked onto cotton thread and dried before packaging. Sections of the thread were placed directly in gels for the electrophoretic separations. Between 1990 and 1994 most modern laboratories abandoned all "conventional" typing methods, converting to DNA techniques. Since there is no chromosomal DNA in human red cells, collecting them intact is no longer necessary.

Currently, biological evidence is analyzed by a technique of amplifying the DNA as described in Chapter 7. Every precaution must be taken to avoid contaminating the evidence, to assure the integrity of the sample. Protective clothing—such as hair nets, dust masks, and rubber gloves—must be worn. Sneezing, sweating, or even bare hands on the evidence will introduce foreign DNA to the sample. Gloves must be changed after collecting or handling each piece of evidence. Scraping, as described below, requires a new blade for each spot of suspected blood. Every sample must be packaged separately, assuring no cross contamination.

All laboratory DNA analyses are now conducted in a clean room environment. The analyst must also wear protective clothing and must never examine more than one sample at a time. Surface covering, paper, must be changed between each item examined. Standard samples must never be handled before questioned items without a complete change of protective materials. Ideally, they are examined in a totally separate location.

At the scene, all stains, wet or dry, should be photographed in place, with and without a scale, and examined for any pattern evidence before it is disturbed.

**Wet Stains.** Wet or moist stains can be absorbed directly onto cotton. The cotton must be dried before it is wrapped or placed in a container. *Never use any airtight container— plastic bags, glass vials, etc*. There is always some moisture in our atmosphere to aid bacterial formation, damaging the evidence.

*Dry Stains.* Historically, the method of collecting dry stains remains unchanged. Stains on portable surfaces should be collected and transported undisturbed. Crusts of dry stains on nonportable surfaces should be scraped off and packaged dry. Any remaining stain or stains which could not be scraped can be transferred to moist cotton swabs or swatches (small pieces of cotton cloth). Since adding moisture to scene stain introduces the potential of bacterial activity, the cotton must be dried before it is wrapped, or placed in a non-airtight container. Use distilled or deionized water for swabbing. Anytime moist material (cotton) is used to sop up a stain, a control swab must also be collected. Using the same source of moisture, dampen a new swab and rub the same surface but in an area where there is no obvious foreign material. Package the control with the same level of care as the unknown.

All samples for DNA analysis should be protected from sunlight and heat and should be frozen while stored.

DNA collection kits containing cotton swabs pretreated with an antibacterial substance are now available.

## Semen

A field search for semen on clothing, bedding, or other potential surfaces is more difficult than a search for blood since fresh semen stains normally have no color. Older semen stains may yellow slightly, and those mixed with blood or urine may be visible due to the natural color of the other liquid. If a darkened room is available, an inexpensive short wavelength ultraviolet lamp, a mineral light, may help locate stains on some surfaces. Semen reflects a bluish-white light under ideal conditions. Surface characteristics of some materials and contaminants—detergent residue, for example—can interfere with the absorption-reflection activity, producing their own intense fluorescence. In the laboratory a trained examiner may use the touch test. Semen stains have a stiff feel similar to a starched garment. Use gloves.

Most law enforcement agencies provide sexual assault evidence collection kits that can be used by a trained nurse or a physician to collect all the possible transfer evidence from the victims of any type of sexual contact crime. The kit includes:

- Cotton swabs for collecting fluids from the victim's vagina, or other body cavities, as required

- Microscope slides for preparing fresh smears of the vaginal contents

- A comb for collecting loose pubic hairs

- A container for standard pubic hair (to be pulled)

- A vial for a whole blood typing sample

- A vial for a saliva sample to determine secretor status (described below), and for DNA-STR profiling

- An assortment of containers for the victim's clothing

- Container for the fluid from a vaginal lavage (collected by some agencies)

In aware communities, select officers or civilians are trained in crisis counseling to assist the victim through this evidence-collecting process. The sooner the samples are collected, the better the chances of locating useful evidence.

Some agencies provide kits for the collection of evidence from sexual assault suspects. The kit should include cotton swabs for removing vagina residues from the penis; combs for collecting loose pubic hairs; and containers for the hairs, blood, saliva, clothing, and other samples as described in the victim's kit.

Crime laboratories, criminalists, or forensic serologists—not the attending physician or the hospital laboratories—should analyze these kits.

## Saliva

There are no presumptive field tests for saliva. Laboratory tests include looking for the enzyme amylase, and a microscopic search for the presence of nucleated epithelial cells—tiny flakes of mucous membrane that contain a small dot, the nucleus, that is visible at 200x magnification.

## THE VALUE OF BLOOD TYPES AS EVIDENCE— HISTORY

Between 1992 and 2002 conventional typing methods, ABO, and the enzyme/protein have been replaced, first by high molecular weight DNA profiling (RFLP-VNTR) and then by PCR-STR (short tandem repeat profiling). Some of the following terms and descriptions are now primarily of historical significance.

These terms apply to blood grouping systems. However, for the purpose of simplicity, only the ABO (H) system is used as an example. Other systems associated with red cells are MN and Rh. They have little forensic value and will not be discussed in any detail.

### Definitions and Descriptions of Key Words

*Blood.* A complex fluid made up of red blood cells, white blood cells, platelets, and plasma. At any moment in time, the plasma also contains sugars; proteins, including enzymes; fats; and minerals. The red cells transport gases, oxygen, and carbon dioxide under normal conditions. Blood also transports many forms of chemicals, beneficial or harmful—alcohol, for example—that have entered the body.

The red blood cells are coated with materials—carbohydrates—called ABO. The liquid portion contains many polymorphic materials, including antibodies. Type A blood contains anti-b antibody, type B blood contains anti-a antibody, type O contains both anti-a and anti-b antibodies, and type AB has no antibodies. An antibody to type O, lectin H, is made from plant material. Since the discovery of lectin H, the ABO system is also referred to as the ABO (H) or ABH system.

*Blood Typing.* A system or a method of classifying by observing reactions—the clumping of cells or agglutinations, for example. The letters or names used to describe the groups, like ABO, are sometimes arbitrary, while other types are named for the person who discovered the material or for the material itself. We inherit two genes or types, one from each parent: with the ABO system, either an A, B, or what is referred to as O. Each variation of the gene is called an allele. The resulting combination of the two alleles is called their genotype. The possible combinations are AA, BB, AB, AO, BO, or OO. The inheritance is random, as in most gene transfer. That means it is possible for a mating of the same two people to produce offspring with different ABO combinations.

*Plasma.* The liquid portion of blood after the solids have been intentionally separated, usually by centrifuge.

*Serum.* The liquid portion of blood after the cells have clotted.

*Gene.* Inherited material that determines the nature or characteristics of organisms. The offspring inherits genetic information, half from the mother, half from the father.

*Polymorphic Markers.* Identifiable variations of a specific genetic material. For example, a substance called an agglutinogen is associated on the surface of the red blood cells. Three primary types called A, B, and O (H) have been identified. Functionally, they are not different, but their presence and character in whole or dry blood and other body fluids can be distinguished by various blood-grouping procedures.

*Agglutinogen.* Usually referred to as an *antigen*. Antigens of the ABO (H) system are carbohydrates (sugars) and therefore are stable for long periods of time even when dry, if they are stored properly. The red blood cells are coated with either A antigen or B antigen or both, AB, or neither in the case of type O. In the presence of a specific antibody called an agglutinin, the type A or AB red cells will clump together, a reaction called agglutination. Type O blood cells are coated with an antigen substance referred to as H, which is the simplest form of the sugar from which the A and B antigen evolved. By the 1970s forensic serologists recognized that there was H antigen on all blood cells in varying amounts by type. Confusing at first, the differences in the amounts of H on otherwise similar A cells was used to distinguish two forms of group A—$A_1$ and $A_2$—with $A_1$ demonstrating the most H reactivity.

*Secretor.* A person whose other body fluids contain identifiable quantities of ABO (H) antigen. Approximately eighty percent of the general population are secretors. Saliva, semen, and vaginal fluid from secretors can be treated in the same manner as dry blood in some of the procedures described below in this section.

*Agglutinin.* Also referred to as an antibody. In reference to blood, a substance found in the liquid portion, the serum, that has two forms, anti-a or anti-b. The antibody to O (H) is extracted from plant proteins.

*Antiserum.* Any serum, naturally occurring or man-made, that contains antibodies that will react with a specific antigen. For example, most human serum naturally contains either anti-a or anti-b or both. Antiserum can be manufactured by injecting laboratory animals with a known antigen. The animal's immune system reacts to the foreign substance and produces an antibody to fight it. Blood containing the antibody is drawn from the animal, and the serum is isolated containing the antibody. Anti (any species of animal) is created by this process. For example, a rabbit can be injected with a small amount of bear blood and will produce antibear serum. The antibear serum can then be used to test for bear blood in cases of poaching, hunting out of season, or posses-

sion of an endangered or protected species. Mixing a suspected serum with an antiserum is called a precipitin test
and is described in this section.

*Agglutination.* Any clumping of red blood cells, ideally reacting to a specific antibody. The clumping occurs when one
unit of a specific antibody links between its complementary
antigen on two red cells holding them together. It appears as
if one antibody is between two cells, holding their hands. A
second antibody can link to one of these cells with one hand,
but link to a third cell with the other hand. Now three cells
are linked. Eventually, depending on the strength of the antigens and agglutinins, most of the cells will clump. Auto agglutination is a phenomenon that can occur independent of an
antibody. Without the proper parallel control samples needed
to detect auto agglutination, false positive tests can result.

*Genotype.* A description of the inherited gene types, that is,
the two actual alleles, AA, BB, and so forth.

*Phenotype.* A description of observable allele or antigenic activity. Although two alleles are always present, the $A_1$ allele is
the most dominant, the $A_2$ allele almost as dominant, the B allele next, while the O allele is recessive. A person who inherits either A from one parent and an O from the other will type
as an A. The antiserum to detect the presence of O is called
lectin H or anti-H lectin. The cells of type O blood clump
when mixed in the presence of the lectin. There was hope it
could be used to distinguish between an AA and an AO or a
BB and a BO, but that did not prove to be the case because of
cross reaction with other blood types. But once forensic serologists recognized that there were varying amounts of the H
substance on all red cells and in dry blood, they realized this
would not be possible. Nevertheless, the lectin H could be
used to distinguish subgroups of type A: $A_1$ and $A_2$.

*Homozygote.* A person who has matching alleles, AA, BB,
and OO.

*Heterozygote.* A person with different alleles, AB, BO, and AO.

Although a substance may be determined to be blood, perhaps as a result of a positive presumptive test, or even the visual appearance of stains to an experienced serologist, this is not proof that the sample is blood from a human source. The precipitin test determines whether it is.

Antiserum can be prepared for almost any substance that is foreign to our bodies or to the bodies of other animals (the preparation was described previously). However, any antiserum to be used in a forensic capacity must be specific for only one antigen. The precipitin test for human blood relies on the specificity of antihuman serum. If the blood of another animal common to the area of the crime scene also reacted to the test, the test would have little value.

The test procedure involves the formation of a cloudy precipitate at the common boundary of two solutions: the questioned blood and the antihuman serum. Larger stains can be extracted and run in small test tubes. The questioned materials are added to test tubes in various dilutions, and the antiserum is injected into the bottom of each tube slowly, so as not to disrupt the layer between the liquids. After time, if there is human blood in the stain, the cloudy precipitate will appear at the interface of the two layers.

Most serologists prefer a procedure run in a petri dish containing a layer of agar gel. A cutter is used to create wells (small one-eighth-inch holes) in the gel in a circle surrounding a central well. A drop of a solution containing the questioned stain is placed in the central well and a different antiserum is placed in each of the outer wells. As time passes, all the materials migrate out through the gel in the shape of a ring. If an antiserum specific to the questioned material is present in any of the outer wells, the cloudy precipitate will form only where the two migrating rings intersect.

When multiple stains of questioned blood have been located at a crime scene, the same process can be run, with a slight variation. In this case the human antiserum is placed in the central well and extracts of each questioned stain are placed in the outer wells. A cloudy precipitate will appear between every interface if all the stains are human.

Controls should be run to eliminate any concern of false positives. For example, a similar size area on a garment where there is no visible stain should be extracted in the same manner as the questioned stain and treated with the antiserum.

### Direct Method

Finally, once blood is shown to be human, there are many methods for typing it. The Lattes slide method is the simplest of all the tests.

If whole blood is available, the ABO antigens can be identified by direct agglutination techniques. A drop of liquid blood is placed in a microscope slide next to a drop of anti-A serum. The two drops are connected by moving the tip of a toothpick or other fine probe from one drop to the other. The slide is observed under a conventional microscope at 100x. Clumping indicates the sample is type A or AB. No clumping means the sample could be type B or O. The process is repeated with anti-b serum. Clumping indicates the presence of B antigen, identifying the blood as type AB. No clumping identifies this sample as type A. In a sample where neither anti-a nor anti-b caused clumping, type O blood is present since it contains neither A nor B antigens. It could also mean that the serum is no good, so control samples of known blood types must be run and observed in parallel and must react appropriately. Once lectin H became available, it was included as a direct approach to clumping O cells.

Since the ABO agglutinogen (antigens) is normally found on the outer skin of the cells, once lysis—the rupturing of the cell walls as blood ages or dries—has occurred and there are no longer any cells to clump, direct agglutination typing techniques cannot be used. Nevertheless, the antigens and agglutinins are still available to link to their complementary counterpart. Several more indirect methods of typing take advantage of this attraction.

*Slide Method*

The simplest of indirect methods is also conducted on a microscope slide and works only if relatively large chips or stains of freshly dried blood are available. Cells from known blood types—called "indicator cells"—are separated from the serum, washed, and suspended in a bovine albumin/saline solution. A drop of indicator A-cells is placed on the slide and a chip or a section of blood-soaked thread is pushed into the solution. If there are any anti-a antibodies in the questioned sample, the type A-cells will start clumping around the margins of the sample. Since both type B and O contain anti-a, the unknown can be either type B or type O. It cannot be type A or AB since neither contains anti-a. The process is repeated using another sample of the questioned blood, with a suspension of indicator B-cells. If there is clumping, the questioned sample contains anti-b. Only type O blood contains both anti-a and anti-b. Therefore, the questioned sample is type O blood. If there was no clumping, the sample would be type B blood.

This method, popular in the 1930s, sounds simple but in fact is susceptible to many false results. For that reason it is seldom if ever relied on in modern laboratories.

*Absorption Inhibition*

By the 1940s a superior method was introduced that relied on the inhibition power of the antigens. A section of the questioned sample and appropriate control materials is prepared by bathing them separately in a solution of antiserum that has been titered (diluted) to various strengths. The object is to add slightly less antibody than there is antigen in the stain. For example, if the right amount of anti-a serum is added to a small extract of the stain, any A antigens from the stain will combine with all the antiserum, inhibiting its capacity to clump A type blood. When indicator A cells (antigens) are added to the solution, there is no anti-A free to react so there is no clumping. No reaction means A antigen was present in the questioned sample and inhibited all the anti-a antibody. At this point the questioned blood could be A or AB. If clumping occurred, it indicates there was no A antigen in the sample to inhibit the anti-A, so the sample must be type B or O.

The process is repeated with anti-B serum. When indicator B-cells are added, no reaction indicates the inhibition of the anti-b antibodies by type B antigens. Type B antigen had to be present in the sample, so the blood type of this sample is AB.

The clumping of B cells, combined with the clumping of A cells in the previous test, means neither A nor B antigen was present, indicating the questioned sample is type O. You may have noticed that this method, where nothing means something, is a little confusing.

The lectin H is used to confirm the presence of type O (H). If present, the H antigen will combine with the titered down amount of lectin H. If this has occurred, when indicator O-cells are added there will be no clumping.

The control samples—a section of material of whatever stuff the stain was on—should always agglutinate since there should be nothing present to inhibit the expected reaction. If there is inhibition, it must be explained before any results are considered meaningful. Known samples of dry blood are also used as controls. Known types should inhibit the agglutination as predicted.

*Absorption Elution*

About the time I almost figured out the logic of absorption inhibition, the absorption elution method was introduced to forensic serology by S. S. Kind, a foremost forensic scientist who became the director of the British national laboratory system.

A section of a stain is dissolved onto three pieces of thread. Controls are treated in the same manner. One of each of the three threads is soaked in anti-a, anti-b, or anti-h lectin for a period of time, no less than four hours and as long as overnight. As described above, if the appropriate antigen is in the stain, the antibody will be absorbed and bind to the thread. If the unknown blood has A antigen—type A or AB—the anti-a will bind to the thread. At this point the samples are rinsed several times with a chilled saline solution, removing any unbound antibodies. Each sample is then treated with the complementary indicator cells, A-cell to the thread where anti-a was added, for example. All the samples are then warmed to 50 degrees Celsius for fifteen minutes. Any bound antibodies are eluted and free to agglutinate the indicator cell if they are right. Our sample contained A antigens, so the anti-a antibody bound to the thread. When it was heated, the bond was broken and it clumped the indicator A-cells. In this test a positive reaction means a positive result. If the thread treated with anti-B serum also showed clumping, the unknown blood is type AB.

The only definite statement that can be made once ABO (H) information is available is an exclusion when the sample's types don't match. When questioned blood does match a known source, it does not mean they have a common origin, although that is one possibility. The likelihood that two people selected randomly would have either type A or type O is quite high, since about 45 percent of the general population has type O and 40 percent has type A. This means that if type O blood was found at a crime scene in such a manner that it indicated the suspect had bled, forty-five of the next one hundred people that you happen to come in contact with who had a fresh injury could be suspects. That's almost one out of every two people!

When the crime scene is in a controlled habitat such as a jail, matching ABO (H) types may be all that is necessary to identify the source. Even though more than one inmate may be type O, if only one is injured, the evidence speaks for itself.

In criminal and civil litigation it is not uncommon for a survivor of a fatal automobile collision to claim that the deceased person was the driver at fault and that the survivor was the passenger and therefore not responsible for the collision. When the only two people in the vehicle involved have different ABO (H) types, that information may resolve the issue. The location of blood becomes critical and can place both the driver and the passenger in their correct orientation. When both have matching ABO (H) types, the forensic scientist has other methods available to identify several other polymorphic genetic markers.

Bryan Culliford's *The Examination and Typing of Blood Stains in the Crime Laboratory*, published in 1971, describing the separation of polymorphic alleles of proteins and enzymes by electrophoretic techniques, was a major breakthrough in the quest to individualize bloodstains. When all his systems gave results, the probability of two randomly selected individuals possessing the same genetic types went from the one out of two with type O alone to better than one out of fifty thousand using the product rule (discussed in Chapter 1). This was not individualization but it provided juries with much more confidence in making their decision.

By 1980 many refinements in the techniques had occurred and more systems and markers were identified. Further, the frequencies of the distribution of the alleles in question were defined after thousands of blood donors were studied. Unfortunately, many of the markers are not considered reliable when the sample is a crime scene stain because crime scene conditions and passing time are enemies to most markers. ABO marks are primarily carbohydrates and are reasonably stable. The markers outlined by Culliford are proteins and enzymes. Carbohydrates can be stored dry for long periods, but proteins must be frozen, and even then they go bad. So aware serologists analyze protein evidence as soon as possible.

## Semen

Seminal fluid is a mixture of many components. The forensic scientist is interested in many of them, in particular: the spermatozoa (sperm), which is the male gamete (seed); acid phosphatase; the specific ABO (H) antigen present if the donor is a secretor; the alleles of phosphoglucomutase (PGM); and, after 1986, the DNA information.

The identification of one or more sperm is considered

proof of the presence of seminal fluid. If sperm cannot be located, a positive test for acid phosphatase is also considered proof by itself. Seminal fluid may lack sperm, aspermia or aspermatic, for several reasons. If the male has had a vasectomy—the blocking or cutting of the vas deferens—sperm cannot be transported from the testicle at ejaculation. Congenital and glandular disorders also may prevent the formation of sperm.

Identifying sperm or seminal fluid in samples does not prove any crime has been committed in most situations involving adults. A crime is established when there are positive findings in children below the age of consent, usually eighteen or sixteen years old, depending on the state. If the victim is mentally retarded or drunk or drugged, regardless of age, the semen may be the key evidence in proving the crime. Unfortunately, traditional genetic typing is limited to ABO (H) antigen with secretors and PGM. At best the two factors produce only a 90 percent elimination, meaning one out of ten men could produce the same results. DNA has changed this dramatically, offering discrimination such as one in 100,000, and up to one in several million in some cases.

Semen ejaculated directly onto an otherwise clean surface such as bedding or clothing is called a neat sample. Almost every other completed sexual act creates a mixture of the semen and the victim's body fluid, either vaginal discharge, blood, or saliva. Standard blood and saliva must be tested for all persons involved—the victim, the victim's consensual partners, and all suspects. Each person's secretor status and ABO (H) and PGM types must be determined before any sense can be made of the evidential samples. Meaningful information is still possible that could exclude or include a suspect. Unfortunately, coincidental matching of victim or friend to the suspect could negate any interpretations.

Anal intercourse presents another problem—a mixture of semen and fecal material. Unpleasant as it is, semen can be isolated if the sample is examined before bacterial action destroys the sperm and other genetic material. Decomposing bodies are another unpleasant task. Bacteria will destroy most genetic information, host or foreign, if decomposition proceeds too long.

The presence of the victim's blood when mixed with semen is a solvable procedural problem whether the blood is from trauma or menstruation, however, the flushing action of heavy vaginal bleeding can eliminate the semen evidence. In a case recently under investigation in Orange County, the victim was savagely beaten and raped with some foreign object, causing internal vaginal bleeding. Then she was strangled to death. If semen was present, the blood flow may prevent its identification. Fortunately, this crime was captured almost entirely by a parking lot security video camera. After the killing the suspect is seen in the videotape leaning against a painted wall in the position usually assumed during an arrest and search. The crime scene investigators checked that location and found the suspect's fingerprints.

*Saliva*

Saliva is located by expectation and logical guesswork rather than by visual methods. Investigators should expect to find saliva within bite marks on the genitalia, nipples, buttocks, and faces of female or male victims of sexual murderers. Nonsexual bites—defensive bites, for example— cigarette butts, stamps and envelopes, chewing gum, and obvious spots on the floor, ground, clothing, or bedding are also likely locations for saliva. Prior to DNA profiling ABO (H) typing was often successful although of little discriminating power. It could exclude an innocent person, and that always justified the time and effort to conduct the tests. The DNA in saliva has all the same genetic information found in blood or semen, offering the same discrimination power at several thousands of times that of the ABO (H) system.

The same problems with mixtures are solvable with proper logic and control samples. One new problem is encountered with bite mark samples swabbed from the victim's skin. A secretor's perspiration can contain detectable amounts of ABO (H) antigen and DNA, so swabbing saliva from a bite mark will likely pick up some of the victim's perspiration and cellular material. Control samples must be collected from an area of skin close to the bite but free of teeth marks. The victim's blood will be used to determine type, and the victim's saliva sample will be used to determine secretor status. Perspiration on a wearer's clothing left at the scene may be sufficient to be typed for ABO (H) antigens or DNA profiling.

## The Bottom Line

Although the pattern of blood as it appears at crime scenes remains one of the most powerful tools for the reconstruction of the events, the traditional blood typing techniques described in this chapter have been replaced by one or more DNA procedures.

## chapter seven

# DNA

## Introduction

A typical profile of DNA—deoxyribonucleic acid—can be as individual as one's fingerprints, but like fingerprints, DNA profiling is circumstantial evidence. A defendant, however, has a much better chance of explaining why his fingerprints were found on the victim's car than he does explaining why his semen was found in her vagina. A suspect may be able to explain why her fingerprint was on a child's toy but may never be able to explain how the child's blood got on her clothing. DNA profiling is powerful, compelling evidence. Although it is keeping innocent suspects out of jail, it is scaring the hell out of defense lawyers, some judges, civil libertarians, and, on occasion, defendants.

Why? Because DNA information is the first form of physical evidence in felony or capital cases that truly challenges who will make the determination of what the law terms the ultimate fact, that is, guilt or innocence. An expert witness testifying to the results of DNA profiling has the potential to identify the defendant as the only possible source of the genetic information, beyond any doubt. Juries can hardly ignore that level of certainty. As that potential increases—and it has already—there may be nothing else left to decide. If there is no innocent explanation why their DNA is present, the only possible escape for the defendants is a successful challenge to the admissibility of the evidence, in the hopes of preventing the jury from ever hearing it.

In the following case, the defense made every attempt to exclude the DNA results. When that failed, they tried to blend it into their case. Did it work?

## CRIME SCENE:

### ONE SON, ONE HONEY TOO MANY

Jennifer Ji and her infant son, Kevin, lived a lonely life in the midst of one of Orange County's hubs of activity, Rancho Santa Margarita. She was a Chinese national living in the USA for only one reason—to be near the father of her son.

Sometime on August 16, 1993, someone came to her front door. Ji was wary of strangers, according to the few people who knew her. Describing her as cautious, Kevin's baby-sitter said Jennifer always looked out a window next to the door before she would think of opening it. She would never open the door unless she recognized the person. That's what is unusual about that occasion—it appears she opened the door and allowed the person to enter. The person may have had a key, but there was no evidence of a forced entry. If she let her guard down, it was a catastrophic mistake.

All the details of what followed may only be known to Ji's killer, but the physical evidence collected by Orange County Sheriff's senior criminalist Dennis Fuller and forensic specialists Vicki Enlow and Linda Ratze grotesquely demonstrated what may have occurred. They spent countless hours detailing each bit of evidence to reconstruct the crime scenario.

The attack could have been an explosion of rage ignited the moment Ji opened the door, or perhaps the visitor struck first while preparing to leave. Whenever it started, the attack progressed rapidly. Her blood patterns suggested that in the time it took Ji to take a few steps back from the door in the direction of her sofa, she was stabbed at least eighteen times. Ji's body came to rest as if she were seated on the floor, with one leg under her, and her torso, chest, and head resting on the seat of the sofa. Her left side faced away from the front door. When Ji fell, the killer still wasn't finished. Fuller found that several stabs missed Ji altogether, landing instead in the lifeless sofa. Ji was fully dressed but her panties were pulled down around her knees. The scene had the look of a rape or attempted rape gone to the worst conclusion. Even before Fuller arrived at the scene, the investigators had already begun contacting neighbors in the hopes of developing some information on potential assailants. As the team made their preliminary survey of the crime scene, one thing was not found. There was no murder weapon in sight.

When Fuller first arrived at the crime scene, he was met by sheriff's homicide investigator Ron White and deputy coroner Kurt Murine. White explained that the integrity of the scene could be in doubt. The father of Ji's child, Jim Peng, said he had come to the apartment for a visit. He saw Jennifer's body the moment he walked into the living room. For reasons of his own, he didn't call for help for an hour and a half. White knew the scene was altered to some extent. For one thing, Peng picked up a button from a woman's garment that he had found and gave it to the first officer who arrived at the crime scene.

Paramedics were also at the scene before the deputies. They searched the apartment for Jennifer's son. They found him in his crib under several layers of blankets with an item of clothing stuffed in his mouth. The paramedics cleared the baby's airway, but he was dead. Murine told Fuller he estimated the time of death for Jennifer and her baby at one to one and a half days earlier. He couldn't call it any closer.

Fuller inspected the rest of the apartment and the outside area for evidence of blood. Other than a small amount of a transfer in the baby's bed, he found no bloodstains inside or outside the apartment. There was no reason to believe the killer was cut during the attack.

When all the crime scene team members agreed that the position of and evidence on Jennifer's body was fully documented, Fuller and Murine moved her onto a plastic sheet away from the sofa. The knife or other evidence might be under Jennifer, or behind or under the sofa. It wasn't. As they moved the body, their attention was drawn to Jennifer's left arm, now exposed. A circular-shaped wound was high on her left arm. It wasn't another stab wound. It looked like a bite mark.

Generally, the impression details of a bite mark in skin are too vague to identify the biter. Fuller was aware of that, but he knew from time to time a forensic odontologist was able to match the marks to a suspect. If nothing else, an innocent suspect could be eliminated as the biter. He also expected some saliva would be left in the bite mark. Until recently, the only way to characterize saliva was to determine the ABO type, but now, a modern serology laboratory can analyze saliva for DNA, a far more discriminating indicator of the biter.

Fuller carefully cleaned the area inside the mark with moist cotton swabs to remove any material that might be present. He noted he could actually see some substance on the skin inside the margin of the bite. He followed the same procedure a few inches away. The second swab would be used as a background control to test for the presence of any other DNA material, such as the victim's skin cells or any contaminating substance.

During the following week the few leads the investigators had found during the neighborhood check failed to produce anything useful. Jim Peng, a suspect from the beginning if for no other reason than the fact that he had been there, was coming across as clean. The sexual assault connection wasn't materializing. The swabs collected from Jennifer's vagina were negative for seminal fluid. That didn't rule out a rape or an attempted rape. It just meant, if it was a sex crime, there was no ejaculate. That's not unusual when accompanied by this much violence.

One week after the murder the sheriff's investigators received information that Peng's wife had been visiting him at the time and was still in town. Remembering the button from a woman's garment, the team wasn't about to overlook any female suspect. They made an appointment to talk to the couple. Peng's English was very good, but his wife spoke little or no English. The investigators knew that chief criminalist Margaret Kuo spoke several dialects of Chinese and so invited her to go along. The Pengs' house in Rancho Santa Margarita was not far from Jennifer's apartment.

When the team arrived, the mood was cordial. Eventually the investigators asked about the button Mr. Peng had found in Jennifer's apartment. Mrs. Peng denied any knowledge of the button or the incident but offered to help in any way. At that point the couple gave their permission to the team to look through the house for a garment with a missing button. Although no such garment was found among Mrs. Peng's clothing, the curiosity of the team was piqued when two bags of woman's apparel were found in a guest bedroom. As each item was pulled from the container, their amazement grew. Nothing matching the button was found, but each item had been mutilated, sliced into ribbons. It had to have been done with a very sharp blade. There were dresses, blouses, pants, lingerie, even shoes. Before the inventory could be completed, Mr. Peng offered an explanation for the shredded clothing.

In 1992 his wife had made an unannounced trip to California. When she arrived at the house, nobody was home. She went in and looked around and found a woman's clothing. The items all belonged to Jennifer Ji, who was living with him at the house. Sometime later he and Jennifer returned home. By then Jennifer's clothing had been shredded and thrown into a pile. There was a verbal confrontation between Mr. Peng and his wife, and he elected to take Jennifer to a motel. When he returned, his wife had calmed down. He made some promises and that was that. He stored the damaged clothing, planning to replace each item with an exact copy. He just hadn't had the time to do it.

The pile of mutilated apparel delivered a strong testament to the rage of a woman who had just discovered her husband had a mistress. Thus, the investigators had a likely suspect, Lisa Peng, age forty-four, Jim Peng's wife and the mother of his first two sons. She had the motive to kill, one of the oldest motives known to us, and she had the ways, means, and opportunity to commit the crime. On that day in 1992, she hadn't known that Jennifer Ji was pregnant with Jim Peng's third son.

But this was still not enough to make an arrest for murder. Dr. Bob Kelly, DDS and board-certified forensic odontologist, was called in. A dentist by day, the leader of the sheriff's volunteer aerosquadron as needed, and a scientific sleuth by night, Dr. Kelly performed all the dental identification for the coroner or police departments. If Lisa Peng's teeth matched the bite mark, it would place her at the scene, a fact she denied. If her teeth could not have made the marks, she would no longer be the sole suspect.

Dr. Kelly first had Mrs. Peng bite into a piece of dental wax, a thin slab of pliable material that captures a detailed impression of both the top and bottom teeth simultaneously. This is done to determine the degree of over- or underbite. Then he made a three-dimensional impression by placing a wad of soft dental goop—clinging, top and bottom, to a small metal container—into Mrs. Peng's mouth as she bit down. After the goop set, it was removed from her mouth, and later Dr. Kelly filled the impressions with a dental grade of plaster. Once the replica was complete, he mounted it on the metal hinge device that reproduced the articulation of Mrs. Peng's jaw. He used the wax bite to verify the alignment.

Dr. Kelly was provided with life-size photographs of the bite mark. He compared marks he could make with Peng's replica to the photographs. The two sets of marks were not an absolute match although they lined up in size and shape. This comparison didn't identify Lisa Peng as the biter or provide sufficient information to arrest her, but it failed to eliminate her as the prime suspect.

During the next few days all thoughts focused on the swabs Fuller had removed from within the bite mark. It was the only remaining evidence that could be used to place Lisa Peng at the crime scene. Saliva contains epithelial cells from the buccal lining of the mouth, a source of genetic information. If the saliva came from a secretor, ABO typing could absolutely eliminate Peng as the source, but matching ABO types wouldn't be very helpful. However, the PCR process is a method of amplifying small amounts of DNA—typically the case with saliva—that would likely provide more discriminating information regardless of secretor status.

At the time of this investigation, it was thought that only PCR/DQ-α (DQ alpha) was ideally suited as a quick analysis to exclude possible suspects or include others as possible donors of saliva. The likelihood of two individuals having the same DQ-α types ranged from one in twenty to one in one hundred, depending on the markers identified. The markers are called "alleles," and we inherit two, one from each parent. If the evidence had been blood, the process of choice in 1993 was Restriction Fragment Length Polymorphism–Variable Number Tandem Repeats (RFLP-VNTR), which examines five or six locations (loci) of DNA and produces the "one in a billion" likelihood for a single source of the questioned blood. PCR can produce some information on very small samples and damaged or old samples, whereas RFLP needs high molecular weight DNA.

The case had a new twist, however. Lisa Peng had returned to Taiwan without giving a blood sample needed to compare to any DNA found in the saliva. With no standard of Peng's DNA, there could be no test, at least not until Margaret Kuo gave the problem some thought. She had not forgotten her innovative work in another case, in which menstrual blood from the victim's panties was used as a secondary standard. The chances of getting Peng's soiled panties seemed remote, but then Kuo remembered Peng's wax dental impression taken by Dr. Kelly. She confirmed that he had isolated and stored it and it had not been cleaned or treated with any chemical. Her plan was to rinse off and collect any of Peng's saliva left in the wax.

As senior criminalist John Hartman prepared the bite mark sample for analysis, his first step was to assay the total DNA present. He was astonished by the quality and quantity of high molecular weight DNA. Fuller had observed a lot of material as he swabbed the site, but no one expected this much DNA to be present. Hartman did the same assay on the wax impression. Kuo's idea was working; there was some

DNA on the wax, at least enough to amplify. Then Hartman analyzed some of both samples, from the bite and the wax for a DNA-DQ-$\alpha$. When the results of the two were compared, Peng was not eliminated. But the samples fell in the most common group. Out of every one hundred people, you could expect twenty would have the same DNA-DQ-$\alpha$. This added to the evidence against Peng but was not enough to book a flight to Taiwan.

At the time, the laboratory staff had just completed its validation study on another process using PCR amplification. This test identified DNA information at a chromosome location called D1 S80. Its discrimination power is considerably higher than DQ-$\alpha$. There are thirty-six possible D1 S80 types, with 666 possible combinations of two alleles, compared to twenty-one DQ-$\alpha$ combinations. The samples were compared, and again Mrs. Peng was not eliminated. The D1 S80 types matched, placing Peng in a one out of two hundred group. It is generally accepted that the two locations are independent of each other, which means the product rule can be applied $20/100 \times 1/200 = 20/20,000$, or one out of one thousand. This could change everything.

Perhaps even more important than the results of the two tests was the realization that the saliva sample from the bite mark was loaded with high molecular weight DNA in excellent condition. Kuo and the team of scientists working with her were convinced there was more than enough DNA to do the highly discriminating RFLP procedure. The *wax* saliva sample, a secondary standard, was now the problem. It was too weak to be counted on to yield enough DNA for all the probing. Kuo wanted a primary standard for this test, a blood sample from Lisa Peng.

Coincidentally, Jim Peng had been in contact with the investigators, asking how he could clear his wife and his name at the same time. The Chinese community newspaper regularly printed accounts of the event and had obtained information from more people than the police had. Peng was told that his wife would have to give a blood sample. That was the only way she could absolutely be eliminated. He agreed to have her return to Orange County. She arrived on New Year's Day, 1994.

Kuo and her team of scientists, Mary Hong and Ed Buse, were already at the laboratory preparing all the equipment needed for the RFLP analysis. It would take several days to complete the first of five probings—the term used to describe each identification step. New Year's Day or not, there was no time to waste. There was nothing to keep Lisa Peng from immediately returning to Taiwan except her confidence that the blood test would exonerate her—an innocent person could be confident that his or her DNA would not be found at the scene—or, knowing that she had not bled, she might have been confident that DNA would not be found in the blood at the scene. If the latter explained why Lisa Peng stayed in Orange County, she was apparently unaware that saliva contains DNA.

As expected, the first test took almost a week to complete. Peng's DNA in the first probing matched the DNA in the bite mark saliva. This was more than enough for the D.A., considering she held an open-return ticket to Taiwan. A criminal complaint was filed and an arrest warrant issued for Lisa Peng, charging her with the murders of Jennifer Ji and her son, Kevin. Peng was taken into custody on January 7, 1994. She pleaded innocent to all charges.

Within the next few weeks the four other probings were completed. Peng's DNA and the DNA in the bite mark matched on all four runs.

The next step in the case against Lisa Peng came during the preliminary hearing. The municipal court judge first had to rule on a challenge to the DNA results. If the challenge succeeded, the DNA information could not be considered as evidence placing Peng at the scene, and the remaining evidence might prove inadequate to send the case to the superior court for trial. The judge, however, denied the motion to suppress the DNA. There would be three superior court trials and an appellate court decision before this legal tale would stop wagging.

During the 1994 trial, the DNA data results from the bite

mark were introduced, as was supporting information that
Peng had learned of the affair with Ji and discovered Kevin's
existence during her visit to Orange County and Rancho
Santa Margarita in 1993. That visit placed her in the area at
the time of the murders. Also introduced was information
from two interviews made prior to her arrest. The first was
videotape of investigators asking questions, during which
Peng said on three occasions, "I need an attorney." She was
arrested after the third request.

At that time, the Pengs were placed in a small room
with the door open. Unknown to them, their conversation
was recorded. This incriminating tape recording included
statements made, in Chinese, by Peng to her husband. She
admitted to him that she was at Ji's apartment late on the
night of the murders and that there had been an argument.
She said Ji had a knife and attacked her. She admitted biting
Ji and said that during the struggle Ji fell on the knife. When
the trial began, the admissibility of the tapes was challenged
by the defense; however, the conversations were allowed
into evidence based on the premise that there is no guarantee
of privacy of any conversation inside a police interview
room.

After weeks of testimony, the jury announced that it could
not agree on a verdict. The vote was ten to two for guilty.
The D.A. immediately filed new charges, and the second
trial was scheduled.

The second trial was much the same as the first. The major difference was that Peng admitted biting Ji but nothing
else. The defense was that the bite had occurred hours before Ji and Kevin were murdered. Ji's sister testified that
Jennifer's hygiene habits included a bath once or twice a
day.

This time, Peng was found guilty of two counts of first-
degree murder, and she was sentenced to prison for life.
Peng hired a new attorney, John Barnett, and he filed an ap-
peal, based primarily on the secret tapes. In 1999 the appellate court agreed with Barnett and ruled in Peng's favor,
granting her a new trial.

During the third trial, the defense again admitted to Peng

biting Ji, accounting for the DNA, but admitted nothing else. Again the biting incident was said to have occurred some-time earlier, and that Ji was alive when Peng left the apart-ment. The jury could not agree, and the trial ended the same way as the first trial, with the same inconclusive ten-to-two vote.

On June 29, 2001, Lisa Peng pled guilty to two counts of voluntary manslaughter, eight years after the bodies of Jen-nifer Ji and her five-month-old son Kevin were discovered in Ji's apartment on August 13, 1993. Based on her admission, she was sentenced to eleven years, but was given credit for the seven years served and time off for good behavior. She was immediately placed on probation. It was reported that she would be deported back to her homeland, Taiwan.

On July 24, 2001, Peng returned to Taipei, Taiwan, and was immediately detained by the local police. She was re-leased after two hours of questioning. However, under Tai-wanese law, any national can be held accountable for crimes committed elsewhere regardless of the outcome; whether they were found innocent or were convicted and served time. The local authorities would not comment on their plans for Peng. This case may never be over.

## DNA

In 1953, James Watson and Francis Crick, working in England, announced their discovery of the elaborate physi-cal configuration of the DNA molecule, for which they re-ceived the Nobel Prize. With a model of DNA before them, researchers could begin to understand the millions of possi-ble functions performed by the molecule. The molecule, however, was massive, by molecular standards, and nearly thirty years passed before Alec Jeffreys, an English molecu-lar biologist at the University at Leicester, discovered a method of rendering it into small but predictable strands. His procedure separated the strands by size into neat rows. He realized the value of his process of forensic investigation as he repeated the exact analysis on more and more individuals. Each individual's DNA produced a slightly different pattern, with the exception of identical twins. As early as 1984 he predicted his method could be used to individualize blood samples, and in 1985 he coauthored a technical paper, *Forensic Application of DNA Fingerprints*. The same year, he directed his efforts toward showing family connections, establishing a means of proving or disproving an immigrant's claims of direct relationship to a citizen of Great Britain.

In 1986, Jeffreys was presented with evidence samples collected from the body of a murder victim and a blood sample from the suspect. This case and the investigation that followed is documented in Joseph Wambaugh's *The Blooding*. What seems to have been forgotten by those who oppose the use of DNA in criminal investigations is that Jeffreys's discovery, called the DNA fingerprint, and the testimony he presented were used to free a young man falsely accused of a rape-murder. The same DNA procedure was then used to identify the true rapist-killer and also connect him to an earlier killing.

By now, the science of DNA has become a multifaceted bazillion-dollar business of unlimited potential. All manners of businesses, large and small, are benefiting from the race to map the human genome and from lesser research projects. However, corporate competition is clothed in secrecy and their discoveries are proprietary. One pays for the opportunity to use them.

Relying on secret ingredients to evaluate evidence is a relatively new experience for forensic scientists. The scientist must testify when subpoenaed and must explain the process he or she uses. When the answer is, "I don't know, it's a proprietary secret," a potential legal issue is raised. Our justice system does not allow for secrets. The defendant has the right to question any witness, and if he can't, critical evidence can be excluded.

Historically, forensic scientists developed their own methods and procedures to suit their needs, and then shared their discoveries with other scientists, either by word of mouth, publishing a paper, or presenting a paper at a technical meeting. Fellow scientists experimented with the method, and if it worked for them, the word spread and the method became common practice. The raw materials or instruments required were generally generic and could be used for any number of other procedures. This is rarely the case anymore. Today, almost every procedure is developed by outside interests and requires dedicated instruments, designer grade reagents, and a lot of money.

In 1990 the FBI formed the Working Group for DNA Analytical Methods—the TWIGDAM committee—consisting of state and local laboratory analysis, to work out basic standards for profiling DNA. Fourteen laboratories, state and local, were selected to participate in a pilot program to determine the practicality of a national database, to be named the Combined DNA Index System (CODIS). This index would be based on marker size, the molecular weight of fragments of DNA alleles, determined by RFLP-VNTR. The process produces highly discriminating information that is essentially a biological "fingerprint." The only individuals who could not be singled out by this process were identical twins who have duplicate DNA. By 1994 CODIS was operational and became the core of the National DNA Index System (NDIS).

During the decade 1990–2000, driven by corporate research, major advances in forensic DNA analysis were almost exponential. However, the rewards of each new technology—higher discrimination in far less time—had a price. It wreaked havoc with the effort to establish a standardized national database and with courtroom presentations. By 1997 many forensic laboratories had converted to the Polymerase Chain Reaction process (PCR) that produced Short Tandem Repeats (STR), which are relatively small fragments of DNA. To be useful, the existing database samples, VNTR, had to be reanalyzed by the newest method. Forensic scientists had to validate each new method, determine the population frequency of the STRs, and then gain the acceptance of the methods in the courts.

Also in 1997, the FBI's TWIGDAM committee resolved the problem by selecting a single approach, PCR-STR, relying on a combination of thirteen loci of DNA. This process had several advantages over the original database method, RFLP-VNTR.

1. Thirteen STR genetic markers produce a likelihood of a match greater than four or five RFLP-VNTR markers.

2. The complete analysis of forensic samples can be accomplished in days rather than weeks.

3. Degraded or contaminated samples, common in evidence collected from crime scenes, can be amplified and profiled.

4. Extremely small samples can be amplified and profiled, such as saliva on a cigarette butt or flakes of dried skin on garments. There is enough DNA in fingerprint residue (amino acids) to make an otherwise useless smudge traceable in CODIS.

5. Ancient samples and case samples years old, even when improperly stored, can be amplified and profiled. This process has exonerated hundreds of innocent prisoners, and more will be.

Two private companies, Promega and Applied Biosystems, are producing the kits and chemicals that identify the STRs. Though their methods differ, both identify the same thirteen markers that can be entered into CODIS.

## Terminology and Definitions

The two methods still in use in forensic laboratories, RFLP-VNTR and PCR-STR, are based on the same phenomenon: the incredible uniqueness of selected locations (loci) within the DNA genome.

*DNA Genome.* The complete molecular structure and location of all the chromosomes and genes.

***Chromosomes.*** Each cell's nucleus contains forty-six chromosomes—twenty-two exact pairs and two sex determine chromosomes. The forty-six chromosomes are made up of DNA containing several thousand different genes that are the source of each person's genetic information, half maternal, half paternal. Each chromosome has genes that are coded for a specific function that controls the production of new cells and growth, such as producing proteins or polypeptides. Under normal circumstances the chromosomes are identical throughout the life of the host, plant or animal.

***Gene.*** A gene is a group of nucleotides along a stretch of the DNA molecule that contains a code; specific genetic information needed to perform a function. Some genes contain the hereditary information that governs our physical characteristics at birth; for example, eye color. Genes of known functions are located throughout the DNA molecule, but in all take up less than 10 percent of DNA's total length. The area between determinant genes has no known function and is referred to as *junk* DNA. However, the areas of junk DNA contain the arrays of tandem repeats used to individualize forensic samples.

***Homozygote.*** Many of the genes we inherit may be exactly alike and determine class characteristics. Ideally, all humans have exactly the same genes that govern the basic geometry of our bodies—two eyes, two ears, etc. All of the members of a subgroup who share racial characteristics have many identical genes. An individual can inherit two identical genes, by coincidence, when the two parents donate the same gene. When there are two identical genes or two that are so similar in size they can't be separated, the genes are homozygous.

***Heterozygote.*** All other genes are *heterozygous*, which means that we inherited two different forms of the gene, one from our mother and one from our father. Either gene is capable of determining a characteristic, but if one form is dominant, that is what you get. If you inherited two blue eye genes, your eyes will be blue, but if you inherited one blue gene and one brown gene—a dominant gene—your eyes will be brown. Even areas of junk DNA are heterozygous, and more often than not we inherit two distinct variations within a chromosome.

*Sex.* The gender chromosomes, X and Y, can be identified by the PCR-STR process by amelogenin.

*Twins.* Identical twins develop when a single sperm fertilizes a single egg. At the time the fertile egg completes the first cellular division, the two cells separate and form individually in different parts of the uterus, sharing a common placenta. But since a single fertilized egg had divided, creating two individuals, the two offspring share the identical DNA.

Fraternal twins are formed when two sperms fertilize two eggs. Each fetus has its own placenta while sharing the same uterus. Their DNA follows the random mix rule, and no siblings, other than identical twins, have ever been found to have completely matching DNA profiles.

*Chromosomal DNA (nuDNA).* Deoxyribonucleic acid provides the blueprint for each nucleated cell to precisely reproduce itself. DNA is a nucleic acid consisting of two chains, or strands, of nucleotides twisted into a double helix.

Pictorially, the double helix can be compared to a twisted rope ladder. The two side pieces, the strands of rope, are made up of alternating phosphate (P) molecules bonded to deoxyribose sugar (S) molecules. This continuous chain—P-S-P-S-P—with the dashes between each representing one chemical bond, is a polymer. Phosphates only bond to sugars, but each sugar bonds to one of the four purine bases—adenine (A), thymine (T), guanine (G), or cytosine (C). This combination of the phosphate, sugar, and base is a nucleotide. Each rung of the ladder is hooked together when the nucleotide's base on one side of the helix bonds, with the base on the other side linking the two nucleotides of the helix.

Watson and Crick's observation of the spatial relationship between the bases has led to the practical understanding of DNA. In this nucleotide geometry, adenine can only bond with thymine, and guanine can only bond with cytosine. The four possible rungs of the ladder, with the equal sign representing two open chemical bonds, can be =S-A-T-S=, or =S-T-A-S=, or =S-G-C-S=, or =S-C-G-S=, with no exceptions. In the complete polymer, phosphate (P) is linked to each open bond (-) on the sugars (S). The upper and lower phosphates are bonded to the next sugar, and so forth (see Figure 12).

The DNA polymer ladder has three billion of these rungs.

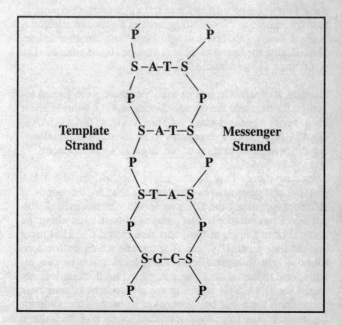

**Figure 12. The AATG tetranucleotide.**

***Mitochondrial DNA (mtDNA).*** Said to be 16,569 base pairs long, containing only thirteen genes (coded for polypeptides), mtDNA has great forensic potential because it is found in large concentrations in most cells, the hair shaft in particular. The FBI is analyzing hair samples for mtDNA when there is no tissue likely to contain nuDNA. In any case, when the quantity or quality of nuDNA is lacking—for example, from decayed bone and teeth—mtDNA can be extracted. Additionally, it is maternally inherited and can be used to trace lineage. The FBI has established an mtDNA missing person data bank and is incorporating mtDNA in the National DNA Index System, NDIS/CODIS. A notable use for mtDNA is to identify the missing in action (MIA) when remains are recovered.

***Base Pair (s).*** The difference in the number of base pairs in tandem repeats allows one fragment of a gene, an allele, described below, to be distinguished from another allele. Specifically, the union of either cytosine (C) to guanine (G), or thymine (T) to adenine (A).

***Tandem Repeats.*** Groups of matching base pairs linked together, for example the tetranucleotide AATG, would appear in a seven repeat locus: AATGAATGAATGAATGAAT-GAATGAATG. Length equates to molecular weight, allowing the precise separation of the target DNA components.

***Locus or Loci.*** This is the exact location on the DNA genome of a gene or area of interest. There are thousands of different loci along the DNA molecule. One locus is distinguished from another by the patterns of base pairs along the chain. For example, at the locus designated CSF1PO there are tandem repeats of AGAT, repeated seven to fourteen times—eight discrete alleles. Each locus contains two alleles, one maternal and one paternal. The thirteen loci selected for DNA-STR profiling are all tandems of four base pairs. Each locus has between seven to twenty-seven identified repeats. The frequency of repeats for each of the thirteen loci have been determined by profiling thousand of samples from all races and is used to calculate the uniqueness of a sample.

*Alleles.* Describes any variant of a genetic marker. Each locus has two alleles of forensic interest, one maternal, one paternal. Discrete alleles form the basis of individualization. Ideally, if it is to have discrimination power, a particular gene must have numerous dissimilar alleles—heterozygosity—each capable of being isolated, separated, and identified. Forensic laboratories rely on two methods to detect the variation in the length of alleles: Restriction Fragment Length Polymorphism–Variable Number Tandem Repeats (RFLP-VNTR) and Polymerase Chain Reaction–Short Tandem Repeat process (PCR-STR).

*Variable Number Tandem Repeats (VNTR).* The differences in the size of the VNTR allows one allele to be separated from another, thus distinguishing one person's DNA from another. Intact DNA's (high molecular weight) alleles are in the hundreds to thousands of base pairs and are expressed as kilobase pairs, or kb. A particular locus may contain kilobase pairs that run between three kb to twenty kb. This means that for the smaller, three kb allele there are three thousand pairs or a thousand repeats using C-A-T as the simplified model, and twenty thousand base pair or 6,667 repeats for the larger allele.

*Short Tandem Repeats (STR).* These are much smaller fragments of DNA, containing repeats of three to seven base pairs in a range of only one hundred to four hundred total base pairs.

*Restriction Enzymes.* These enzymes have a unique quality. Enzymes, in general, are biological catalysts, but a restriction enzyme will only cut a strand of DNA between a specific sequence of base pairs. Restriction enzymes technically are called "restriction endonuclease" but are referred to commonly as *biological scissors*. They are very smart scissors. They know exactly where to cut the chain and will not make any other cuts if conditions are controlled. The enzyme used for RFLP-VNTR by the FBI and most local crime labs is a microorganism, *Haemophilus aegyptius*, conveniently referred to as Hae III (sounds like *hay three*). Hae III finds and cuts all strands at GG-CC.

For example, it will cut the following strand of twenty-nine base pairs as shown,

```
-C-A-T-G-G-C-C-C-A-T-C-A-T-C-A-T-C-A-T-C-A-T-G-G-C-C-C-A-T-
-G-T-A-C-C-G-G-G-T-A-G-T-A-G-T-A-G-T-A-G-T-A-C-C-G-G-G-T-A-
```

leaving this allele, a restriction fragment.

```
-C-C-C-A-T-C-A-T-C-A-T-C-A-T-C-A-T-G-G-
-G-G-G-T-A-G-T-A-G-T-A-G-T-A-G-T-A-C-C-
```

**Recombinant.** Saying DNA is recombinant means the entire helix can be easily opened up like a zipper by breaking the bonds between the base pairs. All the original bases can bond together again or they can recombine with another strand of bases as long as the sequence is exactly the same. Forensic techniques take advantage of the recombinant nature of DNA. Fragments of DNA created by the scissor action of restriction enzymes can also recombine. The recombining is called *hybridization*.

**Hybridization.** In molecular biology, hybridizing is the creation of a new material by combining a restriction fragment of DNA with a chemical that contains the exact complementary bases. DNA hybridizing only takes place under controlled conditions when each base lines up with its complementary base. The match-up is similar to a lock-and-key alignment.

**Probe/RFLP-VNTR.** This is a single strand of a nucleic acid, much like RNA, that has been manufactured in such a way that its base sequence lines up to hybridize with areas on an allele of interest, and nowhere else. The probe can be labeled, providing a method of visualizing or locating and evaluating the DNA hybrid. Most probes used in forensic analyses are labeled with a radioactive material or fluorescing dyes.

Two types of probes are used: multilocus probes and single locus probes. Jeffreys's original method used a multilocus probe identifying twenty or more alleles in a single run.

Single locus probes are available for a variety of DNA loci. They result in just two alleles per person hybridizing per probing. This is the approach most laboratories have used. They have one main advantage. Forensic samples can be mixtures. A mixture of the DNA from two suspects in a gang rape, for example, would be impossible to separate using a multilocus probe. A single locus probe could mark six bands per sample, two for each rapist and two from the victim. That is workable, but sixty bands would appear as one long smear.

There are probes used to locate monomorphic alleles— that is, an allele common to all people at the same location— and can be added to any probing. This probe is used to compare the migration of all the samples being compared on a single run. It can confirm equal movement in the test gel or identify a condition called *band shift*.

***Primers/PCR.*** There is a forward primer and a reverse primer: short strands of tagged nucleic acids in sequence complementary with an allele's specific sequences of base pairs, and nowhere else. In the PCR procedure, the DNA in the sample, regardless of its condition, is unzipped, allowing one primer to bond to a complementary sequence. The sample DNA is not digested—cut into short pieces. The tag, usually a fluorescent dye, provides a means of detecting the new fragment. (See *gel electrophoresis*.)

***DNA Template.*** The sequence of bases that binds to the complementary sequence. In PCR, it is the tagged primer that links to the template DNA.

*Amelogenin.* A sex specific gene, expressed as AMGY and AMGX. It is not an STR but is compatible with the simultaneous PCR amplification process for the CODIS loci. There is one study that reported a problem. For reasons unknown, out of a few hundred test samples, three known phenotypic (XY) male samples failed to yield the Y product. Since the male carries the XY chromosome, the results were read as just X, female.

*Gel Electrophoresis.* A method of separating components. The gel—for example, acrylamide—can be spread over a glass plate or can be the coating of a tiny (capillary) tube. Using the plate, all the samples—unknowns, standards, and controls—are placed in the gel, submerged in a buffer, and placed in an electric field. As the current flows across the plate, the charged samples are attracted toward the opposite charge (+/-). In the case of DNA alleles, the shorter the length of the base pairs, the farther it moves, while the longer alleles lag behind. In capillary gel systems the separation principle is similar, but the samples are injected sequentially into the capillary tube and a laser detects each tagged allele as it exits the system.

*CODIS.* Databases of DNA profiles of individuals convicted of sex crimes and other violent crimes, unsolved casework profiles, and missing persons. All state and federal jurisdictions have enacted laws that require convicted offenders of sex and other violent crimes to give blood and saliva samples. Currently, thirty-four states are actively using CODIS. The samples collected are analyzed for the thirteen CODIS alleles (see Figure 13), and the DNA profile data is entered into a computer system. Crime scene samples with no suspect, and/or cold cases, are analyzed by the same procedure. The DNA data, a series of numbers corresponding to the sizing of two alleles from each of thirteen alleles, can then be compared to existing data by a computer search.

If a match is found, the law enforcement agency treats it as an investigative lead and can focus on the individual as soon as they locate him or her. Theoretically, the whereabouts of released offenders are known at all times. Sex offenders are required to register with local officials, indicating their home address and place of employment. Violent criminals are almost always on some form of parole with supervision for several years after their release.

## Methods for Profiling Chromosomal DNA

Whether to choose RFLP or PCR to analyze crime scene DNA depended at one time on the size and condition of the sample. Now, advances in PCR-STR technology have all but eliminated the need for RFLP-VNTR. Profiling the samples from one case by RFLP-VNTR could take four or five weeks to complete, while the same set of samples can be analyzed in a twenty-four hour period using PCR-STR. Further, RFLP-VNTR requires almost perfect unknown samples, while PCR-STR is successful with almost any sample. In fact, it is almost too sensitive.

PCR is the invention of Kary Mullis, who developed the process in 1985. In 1993, Mullis was awarded the Nobel Prize in Chemistry for his discovery. Mullis's find could be equated to Benjamin Franklin's discovery of electricity—there weren't many ways to use it at the time. The procedure was developed to determine compatibility for tissue transplant, not finding criminals. However, like electricity, availability was this mother of invention. Today, PCR is the chemist's magic wand and the molecular biologist's key to the future and the past.

PCR is a method of copying specific alleles, making millions of replicas from trace quantities of DNA, intact or fragmented. Crime scene stains are often small, old, improperly collected, or poorly preserved. Environmental conditions can cause DNA in any size stain to degrade from high molecular weight (MW) strands to short, low MW strands.

PCR solves the problem of small or damaged samples by a process of gene amplification. In effect, PCR is a replicating process that can begin with a tiny amount of DNA of low MW fragments and build a million or more exact copies.

| Locus | D3S1358 | D8S1179 | D21S11 | D18S51 | D13S317 | D5S818 | D7S820 |
|---|---|---|---|---|---|---|---|
| Repeats | 8 | 11 | 26 | 21 | 8 | 9 | 8 |
| Locus | vWA | FGA | THO1 | TPOX | CSF1PO | D16S539 | Amelogenin |
| Repeats | 12 | 27 | 9 | 7 | 9 | 8 | X or X, Y |

Figure 13. The Thirteen CODIS Loci and Amelogenin.

The process takes advantage of DNA's *in vivo* ability to re-produce itself. The original process was so simple the entire reaction could be done in a test tube—in the beginning, that is.

## The PCR Process, circa 1985

Mullis's original PCR method involved three steps, repeated manually, over and over in a single piece of laboratory equipment called a thermal cycler. The sample DNA does not have to be restriction digested (cut into short pieces).

**Step 1.** All the DNA in the sample is denatured by heating it to 95 degrees centigrade, splitting the bonds between the two complementary strands, regardless of length.

**Step 2.** The heat is reduced and DNA primers and a supply of the nucleotides, cytosine (C), guanine (G), thymine (T), and adenine (A) are added. The primers, forward and reverse, are like a short probe. They hybridize (anneal) to any available locus-specific sequence of complementary bases within or near a target allele. Since we inherit two alleles at each locus, regardless of their tandem repeat numbers, both alleles are amplified in the same reaction. The two primers are now attached to the sample DNA templates, blocking the original complementary strand from recombining.

**Step 3.** DNA polymerase is added to the cooled mixture. A polymerase is an enzyme that performs similarly to the ones in our body that replicate our own DNA. Remember the four bases only pair up (C) to (G) and (T) to (A) and nothing else. The polymerase binds to the primer and then it attaches complementary bases to the primer, building a strand of bases complementary to the original template. The product is an exact replica of the original allele. Because there was a primer on both original strands, there are now two new copies, one of each strand of the sample DNA base pair sequence.

The three steps are repeated over and over. During the second cycle, the two new PCR product strands split off the original template and, by the same process, becomes four. In the third cycle they divide to make eight, and the eight become sixteen on the fourth cycle. Each time the cycle is completed, the DNA doubles. By twenty cycles, for each original fragment in the sample there are more than a million copies, and by thirty cycles more than a billion.

This was a slow process, since the temperature of step one destroyed the polymerase and new enzymes had to be added at each third step. The first automated thermal cycler system was introduced when a temperature-resistant polymerase, Taq, was added at step one. Taq polymerase is from an organism, Thermus aquaticus, that survives the over 90 degrees centigrade temperature of natural hot springs.

### The Products of PCR: Forensic Applications, Then and Now

**Circa 1985.** The first useful locus with discriminating power was HLA-DQ-α (DQ alpha). DQ-α is found in all the body cells except red blood cells, and it has been found in good shape in the most disgusting of samples—old bones, teeth, and even rotting human tissue. There are seven recognized alleles, with twenty-eight possible combinations or types. The reaction is measured on a treated paper, a dot blot card. Depending on the rarity of the type, one in twenty to one in a hundred people would have matching DQ-α results. If the types don't match, it is an absolute exclusion. However, a DQ-α inclusion is not individualization.

**Circa 1990.** The size of D1S80—the second target locus of PCR—allowed PCR amplification. D1S80's alleles are repeats of 16 bp repeats and range from 350 to 1,000 bps, too long to be considered a short tandem repeat. The PCR product was separated and visualized by gel electrophoresis. The modified process was named Amplified Fragment Lengths Polymorphism—AmpFLPs (sounds like *amp flips*). The D1S80 referred to in the case of "One Son, One Honey Too Many" is an example of the usefulness of AmpFLP technology at the time.

*Circa 1993.* CCT was the first multiplex system that profiled a triplex of three loci—CCTCSF1PO, TPOX, and TH01. The simultaneous amplification of several loci together in a single tube is called "multiplexing." After amplification and gel electrophoresis (plate), the products can be located in the gel by silver staining. The average discrimination power of this system is one in four hundred. CCT-A, the amelogenin gene, was incorporated with this multiplex system.

*Circa 1994.* Another multiplex system, the Polymarker System (PM), combined DQ-α plus five other loci in one process, offering expanded discrimination. The loci are LDLR, GYPA, HBGG, D7S8, and GC. The combined discrimination was considered to be one in a thousand. These markers were demonstrated on dot blot cards.

*Circa 1995.* John Hartman, a pioneer in forensic DNA casework, describes the major development in PCR-STR technology that led to the demise of RFLP analysis.

> *A commercial method enabling the simultaneous amplification of three triplexes—nine loci—was developed. Each triplex was tagged with a different fluorescent dye. This allowed for all the triplexes to be analyzed in the same gel. A sophisticated system of lasers and other optics could separate and detect each product within the gel. Together, the discriminating power of the system equaled that of the much less sensitive and time-consuming RFLP technology.*

*Circa 1997.* The FBI and a few public DNA laboratories began evaluating two commercial semiautomatic systems while creating a massive national population database to establish the utility of the system and to identify the rarity of the profiles. Since the discrimination factor of just nine alleles described by Hartman was approaching that of RFLP, the FBI's TWIGDAM committee recommended abandoning RFLP in favor of PCR-STR. However, in order to surpass the discrimination power of the RFLPs, the committee recommended using the thirteen loci listed in Figure 13. The FBI laboratory began reanalyzing the entire CODIS database.

*Circa 2002.* Two commercial systems are in use, both offering similar approaches to amplifying—now call megaplexing. Various "kits" are on the market for the process. Currently, one kit is available that contains everything needed to tag all thirteen CODIS alleles plus amelogenin plus two pentanucleotide alleles, repeats of five base pairs. A single test tube contains everything needed for the simultaneous amplification, and eventually identification, of the sixteen genetic markers. As many as ninety-six samples can be analyzed simultaneously.

## The Current PCR Process—A Cursory View

### Step One: Evaluation

The known history of the sample and its visual appearance and condition—such as fresh blood or rotten tissue—is considered. This can determine the amount of the sample used. Of the ninety-six spaces available, one case may require as little as two spaces. For example, in a sexual assault case with one victim and no suspect, there will be a victim standard and the vaginal swab. If a suspect exists, his or her standard would require one space. If the victim identifies any consensual partner, their standard is required to evaluate the results. In a complete investigation there may also be samples from clothing, bedding, automobile seats, etc. Samples collected by swabbing surfaces require control swabs that must also be analyzed—to determine possible interference with the reactions. The blank of the swabbing liquid on an unused swab should be analyzed, too. Furthermore, quality control samples require several of the ninety-six spaces, depending on the laboratory's written procedure. QC samples include blanks—that is, all of the reagents used lacking any source of nucleotides, and the same mix with a known amount of nucleotides. It is possible that one bloody crime scene could fill out all ninety-six spaces.

## Step Two: Purification

Since bacteria and fungi are to be expected in crime scene samples, the DNA must be isolated from all contaminates that would otherwise interfere with quantitation. When necessary, purification is achieved using proprietary kits.

## Step Three: Quantitation

The optimum amplification of STRs is quantity dependent. Too much DNA template can cause more problems than too little. Since each cycle doubles the amount of product, the analyst must have an idea of the quantity and quality of the DNA templates before amplification. If there is a question, quantitation can be achieved using proprietary kits.

## Step Four: Amplification

Each tube now contains the sample, a mix of all necessary tagged primers, the Taq polymerase, a supply of the four nucleotides to be incorporated into the product strands, and appropriate buffers. After the amplification, the samples are reheated to denature the untagged PCR product prior to analysis.

## Step Five: Fragment Analysis

There are two methods of separating the specific alleles in each tube: cross-linked acrylamide gel (plate) electrophoresis—for example, the ABI Prism 377 DNA Sequencer, and linear acrylamide polymer (capillary) electrophoresis—for example, the ABI Prism 310 Genetic Analyzer. In both cases an internal lane size standard is used to size the alleles. Also, allelic standards are run by themselves in the plate method. When twenty-four samples are applied in lanes, four of the twenty-four lanes would contain the allelic standard only. In the capillary method, the allelic standards are injected as often as the analyst thinks necessary. A sizing ladder, internal molecular markers, or internal lane standard (ILS) are mixes of known base pairs ranging from 60 bp to 500 bp used for fragment analysis or profiling.

The first step to determine the size of the PCR product fragment is by comparing its position to the internal molecular weight markers. A different color fluorescent tag is used to distinguish the sizing marker from the PCR product. Using the plate method, the migration is compared. Since each individual has two alleles at each locus, there are two numbers assigned. If the location of one allele aligns with a marker of ten repeats, and the second aligns with the eight marker, the locus is described as 8, 10. Should only one allele be observed, lacking any other explanation, the locus is described as 10, 10. In the capillary method the comparison of standard to product is based on elusion time—the time between injection and detection. In either system, when all thirteen loci are sized there are twenty-six alleles identified. Directly comparing profiles of a crime scene sample to a suspect, or searching CODIS, all twenty-six alleles must be consistent. (See photo, insert page 10.)

## Step Six: Evaluation

At this point, computer programs are used to evaluate the data collected by either of the above methods. Where the suspect's sample was in the run, a direct comparison is made. In no suspect cases, the results are entered into the CODIS database for comparison, with other case evidence profiles and with profiles of felons convicted of certain crimes.

## Exclusion Factors

The fifteen markers plus the gender identification yields a probability of two people having the same profile as roughly one in $4 \times 10^{17}$, or roughly one in a quintillion.

## Disadvantages

Contamination is a principal concern. Whether the crime scene sample is a situational mixture or is tainted during handling, all of the DNA present will be amplified. Mixtures and contamination before the scene is protected cannot be avoided, but afterward it must be. Crime scene investigators have to be trained in methods to avoid any contamination or damage to the evidence once it is under their control, and laboratories must be meticulous in their efforts to protect the integrity of each item of evidence (see Chapter 6).

There are some idiosyncrasies noted in the PCR-STR process: one stutter peaks or bands, sometimes called "shadow bands," and variant peaks. Stutter can be expected and in general are understood. Any extra peaks can cause concern in mixed samples, as in a gang rape.

## The RFLP Process

The Restriction Fragment Length Polymorphism process is rarely used now, following advances in PCR-STR technology. For one thing, it is far more time-consuming. What follows are the steps in the RFLP process, beginning with the evaluation of the biological evidence, unknown and known.

### Step One: Visual Evaluation and Preparation of the Unknown Sample

The nature of the questioned material—bloodstain, semen, saliva or tissue, skin or hair root—is evaluated for size and condition. The dry stains or tissue samples contain intact DNA, which is protected within the cell. The sample must be treated and the DNA extracted from the cellular host. This is done by soaking the stain in salt solutions, detergents, and proteinase K. They combine to free up most DNA. Sperm, if present, are resistant to proteinase K and remain intact. Because of their size they can be isolated by centrifuge and then treated with another chemical that frees up the DNA.

### Step Two: Assay

The DNA is subjected to a quick electrophoretic separation by loading a small portion of it into a gel containing a dye—ethidium bromide—that makes the stain visible. A single heavy tight band in the gel perpendicular to the electric field indicates intact high molecular weight DNA or at least DNA all the same size. A streak of color indicates there are many fragments of something, perhaps DNA. This means the DNA has been broken up and RFLP analysis will probably not be successful.

### Step Three: Digestion

The DNA is digested by the restriction enzyme, Hae III.

### Step Four: Test Gel

A small portion of the digest is examined by electrophoresis in a similar manner to step two.

If the digestion was successful, a long stretch will run with the flow of the current. A single band or several heavy areas indicate incomplete digestion, in which case the process of digestion must be repeated.

### Step Five: Known Sample Preparation

Blood is usually the source of the known DNA if the principals are available to examine. If any of the victims cannot supply fresh blood, but the true parents can, their blood would be one way to connect an unknown sample to a victim. Each known sample is prepared exactly like the unknown, as described in the first four steps.

### Step Six: Analytical Electrophoresis

Several samples, up to fourteen, are placed at one end of the gel, equally spaced along a *start* line. The flow of electricity will move the sample from one pole (−) toward the other (+) in a straight line called a *lane*. These samples include three lanes of a standard mix of DNA fragments. These fragments are selected to create a molecular size marker called a *ladder* in each of three lanes, usually the two outside lanes and the middle lane. The ladder will be used to calculate the size of the fragments in the other samples of DNA.

Known samples from the victim and suspect(s), and the unknown sample(s) collected at the crime scene, are loaded on the gel. Once all the samples are in place, the gel is positioned in the apparatus and exposed to a flow of electric current for sixteen hours. During this time all the alleles produced by the Hae III biological scissors are in the same lane and are attracted to the opposite end of the gel. The gel acts as a molecular sieve, allowing the smaller molecules to move farther due to less interference.

## Step Seven: Southern Blot

The blot technique transfers the entire DNA from the gel to a convenient thin membrane. The gel is soaked with a solution of sodium hydroxide. This frees up the DNA from the gel and breaks all the base-base bonds that have been holding the DNA fragment together, exposing all the nucleotide's base sites along the fragment. The gel and the membrane are pressed together for about six hours. The DNA is now on the membrane and ready to hybridize.

## Step Eight: First Probe/Hybridizing

The membrane is soaked overnight in a solution containing an allele-specific probe that will recombine to alleles of a known locus on the DNA and no others. The probe is labeled with a radioactive material. To assure complete exposure, the container and its contents may be rotated gently on a mixing platform that moves just enough to keep the liquid from standing still.

The membrane is removed and washed in a chemical solution. This strips off any partially linked areas along noncomplementary alleles that hybridized despite the stringent conditions. If the probe is not removed, it could produce false bands. It also removes the free probes in the solution that did not hybridize at all. The membranes are washed repeatedly to remove any residue.

## Step Nine: Autoradiography

This process must be done in a dark room. The membrane containing the radio-labeled hybridized DNA alleles is placed in direct contact with a sheet of X-ray film for an extended period of time. X rays will eventually expose the film, and an image of all the bands will appear when the film is developed. This piece of film is referred to as an *autoradiograph*, or *autorad for* short. (See bottom photo, insert page 11; top photo, insert page 12.)

The exposure time is, at best, guesswork since the amount of radioactivity is a function of the amount of DNA present. If there was an abundance of DNA apparent in the original assay, step two, twenty-four hours may be enough exposure time, but when the sample size is questionable to begin with, the time may be extended to as much as three weeks. If the film is developed too soon, the results may be too faint to see and the exposure must be repeated for an even longer time. The ideal results are bands that are narrow, compact bars that have not spread out and are optically dense, meaning they exposed the X-ray film.

## Step Ten: Imagining

The location of the visible alleles on the autorad is compared. Computer programs are used to *size* the bands. Sizing assigns a number, the molecular weight of the band, that can be used to compare the bands to frequency distribution statistics and can be used by forensic scientists to compare DNA information electronically to DNA data banks (see earlier discussion of CODIS).

## Step Eleven: Stripping

The membrane is soaked and heated for twenty minutes at 95 degrees Celsius in a sodium citrate solution. This action breaks the hybridized bond, putting the probe back in solution. In that state the membrane is washed repeatedly until all of the probe is removed.

*Step Twelve: More Probing*

A different probe, specific to a second locus, is applied and all the steps from step eight down are repeated. After step eleven, a third probe is applied and the process repeated, followed by a fourth probe. A fifth probe may be used if there was sufficient DNA at the start. Step eleven does remove some of the DNA as the probe is stripped away.

## The Future

*DNA Warrants.* Arrest warrants are being issued using the CODIS profile to identify the suspect when no name is known before the statute of limitation runs out. There is a statute of limitation for most crimes other than murder. California has removed the statute for some sexual assault crimes committed after January 1, 2001. However, all prior cases will run out after six years if no suspect is named. Some thought that a "CODIS profile" was as descriptive as a name. Warrants were issued in the weeks before the time expired. The profiles are assigned to the unknown suspect file. In early 2001 a new entry matched one of the DNA warrant's CODIS profile. An arrest was made using the DNA warrant six months after the statute expired, and the case was filed. The defense appealed, and the state supreme court refused a hearing in August 2001. This means the trial of the defendant can proceed.

*Sequencing.* Eventually, sequencing large areas along the intact DNA molecule will have forensic value. A reasonably tight range of characteristics, sex, eye color, etc., could be predicted. A few years ago I predicted there would be a day, twenty to thirty years from now, when a speck of blood semen, or other cellular material could be sequenced and the data used to compute something akin to today's composite drawing of a suspect. Some DNA scientists doubt that it is even a remote possibility. What do they know? Consider the progress all science has made in the past twenty to thirty years, or with DNA in just ten years! If I'm wrong, I'll be happy to admit it at the public entrance to the Orange County Crime Lab on January 1, 2025.

## The Bottom Line

The FBI started accepting cases for DNA analysis in 1988. They had to limit the types of cases accepted. Approaching trials were given a high priority. Sexual assault cases were a statistical cross section of pending trials between 1988 and 1990. Before a rape case was accepted by the FBI, a suspect had to be identified by the victim—a lineup—the traditional ABO and PGM typing had to be completed and, of course, match the suspects to the crime scene evidence. At that time, lacking a miracle, prison was a certainty for these defendants. After examining the evidence from the first several hundred rape cases, 25 percent of the suspects were excluded as the source of the seminal fluid, apparently victims of mistaken identity.

If one-fourth of those accused during the window between conventional and DNA testing were eliminated by the DNA testing and were spared a trial and perhaps conviction, does that mean a similar percentage of defendants convicted before DNA were innocent? That would equate to hundreds of inmates. Certainly anyone whose conviction was based on a lineup-type ID and ABO-PGM typing and who requests a DNA test should be given one. The state of California has established an innocence program where inmates can request DNA testing. There are at least thirty-four privately funded programs. The original, the Innocence Project, founded by Barry Scheck and Peter Neufeld in 1992, and other worthy efforts have freed dozens of death row inmates.

## chapter eight

# Trace Evidence, Hairs, and Fibers

## Introduction

Trace evidence describes crime scene material that, if you *can* see it, could be considered by some as useless debris. In fact, it usually is debris, but debris that may tell a story of what happened at the crime scene and, perhaps, who did what to whom. But first you have to find and collect it. When you can't see it, that can be a problem. Knowing where to look is a blend of experience and intuition. Crime scene investigators do have their tricks: vacuuming, tape lifts, picking, combing or scraping, anything to collect the right stuff. However, they won't know what they found until a criminalist evaluates the debris.

Compared to all the other types of evidence described in the previous chapters, trace evidence is the least likely to be individualized. The only obvious exception is hair. Advances in DNA, chromosomal and mitochondrial, as described in Chapter 7, make it possible to associate a crime scene hair to its source with a high degree of certainty. Trace evidence, most often, is debris made up of materials that are mass produced or occur in abundance in nature, where the probative value of trace evidence is limited to class characteristics. Regardless, the circumstances of the crime may elevate the value of trace evidence significantly.

In the following case it was as compelling as fingerprint identification.

## CRIME SCENE:

### To Hair Is Human

I was the only one in the lab to answer the phone. The voice on the other end was the watch commander's.

"Sorry to screw up your lunch but we got a hot one for you," he said. "South Patrol is headed your way from San Juan with a sexual assault suspect. It's so fresh they say the guy still has a smile on his face."

"What am I supposed to do with a suspect?" I asked.

"Use your imagination. There are no witnesses, and they need proof that this creep stuck his dingus where it ought not to have been. Proof! That's what you lab guys do, isn't it? Good-bye."

That wasn't a question, it was a challenge. That's why he was the watch commander. He had good ideas. I should be able to prove something, like sexual contact, if it really was a fresh case. But why no witnesses? Did I miss the part about a murder?

I looked at my watch and realized I had at least a half hour before the patrolmen would arrive. It was unusual, at the time, to examine a man suspected of a sexual assault, particularly at the crime lab. The victim was more likely the one who would be examined, but at a hospital. But there was the watch commander's challenge. I would have to plan the examination by myself. It was lunchtime, and everyone else who worked in the lab was out.

The obvious evidence would be semen, the victim's pubic hairs, or even some blood from the victim. All were possibilities. Maybe there would be some vaginal fluid or menstrual blood. And if the victim struggled, the clothing could contain fiber transfers, assuming the victim was dressed at the time of the attack.

Remember to collect his underwear, I thought.

The time passed quickly. The doorbell rang, jarring me out of my thoughts. I opened the door and saw the two deputies, each holding one arm of the suspect, as if to lift him off his feet. He wasn't smiling anymore. But they were.

"Larry, meet Ralph. Ralph here swears he has nothing to hide," the deputy said. "In fact he got real excited when we told him he was going to get to see the inside of a real crime lab. Seems he's always wanted to work in one."

"Take Ralph to the back room," I said. "Our receptionist will be back from lunch in a minute or two. I don't think she'd be too happy to see your friend with his pants off. Has he gone to the bathroom?"

Now I think of that! That could screw up the sample, or at least wash some of it away. I should have told the watch commander to radio the no bathroom advice to their patrol car while they were driving in.

"We kept him like you see him," the deputy said. "The WC told us you had advised no potty stops."

"Good job!" I was saying it to them, but I meant it for the WC. He had covered my butt.

I told Ralph to remove his pants and underwear. I had him drop the shorts into a new brown paper bag. I had on rubber gloves—three pairs, in fact. No use touching anything unless you have to.

Now he was standing in front of me, his penis in his hand. I didn't remember telling him to do that. Perhaps it was his habit. The good news was he had a foreskin. That was good, evidencewise, because the foreskin could trap vaginal fluids as well as semen. The bad news was that I was preparing for the worst, to swab this guy's pecker with a cotton swab. Semen under the foreskin wouldn't mean a hell of a lot, but maybe our serologist—who was still out to lunch--could dream up some new test for vaginal fluid.

"Pull your foreskin back," I said in my most commanding voice, imitating one of those medics at boot camp, except they always added, "like you really like it." The last thing I wanted to do was to get this guy excited, so I kept the command in the short version. As he followed my order, with the deputies chuckling in the background, he revealed the upper surface of the head of his penis, the glans.

It wasn't what I expected to see. Two hairs were revealed, clinging to the tip of his penis, glued there by some kind of mucus conglomerate. I used the cotton swabs to tease the hairs loose, and transferred them to a microscope slide. When I looked up, he was smiling again.

"Watch him," I said as I left the room, headed for the microscope room. If either of the hairs were the victim's pubic hairs, it could be something the D.A. could hang his hat on.

A quick focus of the stereoscopic binocular microscope and I was looking at two hairs, side by side, that were entirely different than I had anticipated. First, they didn't look like any pubic hairs I had ever seen. They were both as straight as an arrow, not curly like most pubic hairs. Further, I couldn't believe they were human, because I had never seen a human hair that had three layers of colors. This was before the days of punk rockers. These hairs were each about one inch long. They were dark brown at the root for about a third of the length, then white for a third, then a reddish-brown out to a very fine-pointed tip. Animal hairs! Someone was pulling my leg! I returned to the examination room, where the three sat in silence.

"Okay, I need to talk to one of you kind deputies," I said. "Let's go out on the roof."

They looked at each other for a moment, then one of them said, "There are some things you might need to know."

The roof of the jail was the backyard of the crime lab. It was strewn with an array of crates, old equipment, and storage bins. Someone before me had attached a six-foot deepwater tank to the side of the building, where we could fire bullets and recover them undamaged. And there were a half-dozen marijuana plants that had been confiscated. I watered them daily, in the event the case went to trial.

"I was told that you have no witness to this crime, yet no one has mentioned the demise of the victim," I said. "The hairs you saw me remove are not human, leaving an animal as the best source. What was it that you wanted to tell me?"

"Actually, the victim is alive and kicking, as they say," the deputy said. "And you could say that Ralphie was just horsing around, but it really is a crime. Bestiality. Look it up, it's in the penal code."

"I got your penal code," I said. "Let's get serious here."

The deputy laid out exactly what they knew had happened and what they believed had happened before their arrest of Ralph.

"A horse, you say."

A rancher had found this guy in his stable with a horse, his best mare. But it wasn't a case of catching him in the act. That's why the WC said they needed proof. The deputy wasn't all that excited when I informed him of the next assignment.

"I could have saved you a lot of time if they had been straight from the beginning. I need some things from the horse. I think I can prove your case. It's up to you guys. I'll need standards, just like you would do under normal circumstances." I handed the deputy some small bags and cotton swabs, "You know what the cotton swabs are for? In a case like this, semen in the horse is going to prove a lot more than semen on the guy's dingus. But if I can match these hairs, you may have your case today. The semen could take days to analyze, so get a bunch of hair."

As we walked back, I said, "And don't leave that guy here. And pull me a wad of Ralph's pubic hairs. I need them for standards."

Standards are samples from a known source. Evidence is meaningless unless you have examples of the things believed to be involved in the case. I would have to be able to say the hairs weren't Ralph's before I could say where they did come from. I knew they couldn't be his but I would have to demonstrate it if this case went to a trial.

Ralph, it turns out, had been released at eight A.M. from a hospital where he had been detained on a seventy-two-hour hold. You have to be a total wacko, or found guilty of some crime, to be held involuntarily for any longer than that in California. The detention facility was in San Juan Capistrano, one of the last bastions of cowboyland in Orange County. It is the site of the famous mission, and the annual target of thousands of swallows each year. It's also the site of a lot of small farms and stables.

I'm guessing, in retrospect, that Ralph dreamed of being a cowpoke. He had concocted an experiment, his own version of animal husbandry, and found a suitable barn just a short walk from the hospital. He wasted no time.

The owner of the horse was a cowboy, and cowboys do have that sixth sense. They always know, one way or the other, what is happening to their hat, dog, pickup, horse, girlfriend, and wife, in that order, at all times. Even sleeping off a night at the Swallows, a local hangout where beer and tequila are served in the same glass whether you want it or not, wasn't enough to dull our rancher's sixth sense. "Somethin' was a callin' him." He entered his barn in time to see this young researcher, who was now looking rather horsish, pants unzipped, and standing next to an orange crate that was still positioned at the rump of Daisy, a three-year-old mare. The owner was not an understanding man. Daisy was his prize animal. The young man was, nevertheless, still alive when the deputies arrived.

I learned two lessons that day. First, be specific, in fact very specific, when you request samples. Second, I learned that human nature being what it is, the deputies weren't all that brave. They would run into a burning building to save a life, I'm sure, or they might shoot it out face-to-face with a felon, but they were not going to get too close to that damn horse. I should have given them the rubber gloves.

When the deputies returned to the lab, they presented me with five packages of hairs, from the mane, the chest, the back, and both sides. Great! I did give them the courtesy of examining each sample before I asked the first embarrassing question since none of the hairs resembled the "penis" hairs.

"Did I get this story wrong?" I asked. "Did this Ralphie boy try to stick his pecker through the side of the horse?" I explained more carefully this time. "I need hairs from the point of attack, I mean, as close as you can get without committing a felony yourself." I half expected them to tell me to go get my own damn hairs. Rubber gloves in hand, they began their third trip to the barn.

The deputies returned the second time with a packet labeled, "Pubic." It contained hairs that visually matched, exactly, the hairs removed from the guy's penis—same length, same shape, and the same color distribution out to the fine tip. Content that they had done an excellent job, which they had, the deputies headed off to the D.A.'s office to file a complaint.

Several weeks passed before I heard anything about the case. A defense attorney hired by the family called to complain a little. "No way," he said, "can you prove those were horse hairs."

"Before you decide what I can prove or not prove," I told him, "I suggest that you pay me a visit. I'll be happy to let you view the evidence. Then you'll be in a much better position to decide whether I should have the swabs examined for human semen."

He accepted my invitation to come to the lab. I placed the "penis" hairs on one side of a comparison microscope and the "vaginal" hairs on the other. He looked for about twenty seconds, thanked me, and left. I never heard from him again on that case. I learned later that the young man pled guilty, went back to the hospital, and eventually recovered. The last I heard, he had enrolled in a veterinarian college. Just kidding about the college thing.

## CRIME SCENE:

### A LUCKY CUP OF COFFEE

At about three A.M., a night watchman making his usual rounds of businesses stopped to check out a large nightclub on Harbor Boulevard about two miles south of Disneyland. He was anticipating a cup of coffee because the staff always left some warm in the urns as they locked up. Using his pass key to unlock the rear door, he was startled by a flash of bright light seconds before he was knocked aside by a group of men as they ran past him. One of the men stopped abruptly and turned back. He was less than six feet away and was pointing a pistol at the guard's face. Both subjects froze in their positions as the gunman said, "What the hell." Then he lowered the pistol, turned, and ran in the direction of a car that was now ready to make a quick exit from the scene.

When the police arrived moments after the guard called for help, they found the source of the bright light. The gang of burglars had been at work for some time trying to burn a hole in the door of the club's huge safe with an acetylene/oxygen-cutting torch. They had managed to make a small hole in the door, and used a water hose they found in the club's kitchen to fill the safe with water. The water was meant to keep any paper money inside from burning up. In their haste to leave, they abandoned all their equipment. The torch consisted of a two-wheeled cart; two large metal cylinders, one acetylene and the other oxygen; and hoses attached to the tanks by brass fittings, with the cutting nozzle at the other end. Everything was collected as evidence, including a quantity of metal beads found on the floor. These beads, slag, were the product of the extreme heat generated by the torch as it liquefied the metal of the safe's door.

In less than an hour a vehicle matching the description of the one used by the burglars was spotted, parked at the rear of another restaurant a few blocks to the north. The scene was surrounded before officers approached a rear door. It was unlocked. A team of four officers worked their way past the storage area and the kitchen. No one was in sight. They were well into the darkened dining area before they saw the first sign of activity. A beam of light and the sound of muffled voices was coming from the direction of the bar. At the bar's entry the officer in charge said loudly, "Gentlemen, don't move! Don't even think about it."

Five men were seated at a table with a whiskey bottle centerpiece. All five had drinks in front of them. One of the officers asked, "Does this place ever close?"

They were all arrested. Their clothing and the suspected vehicle were seized as evidence. My job was to examine these items for evidence of the burglary. I began by taking a look at the debris that was loose on the floor of the car's trunk. There seemed to be a considerable amount of paint chips of various colors. After sorting out the material, I also found some brass-colored metal shavings and a few tiny fragments of a blue and silver decal material. Later I visually compared these items to the cutting equipment. The brass-colored metal shavings visually matched the brass fitting on the gas hoses. The fittings were scored, typically, as when tightened down with a wrench. The decal material matched the company label, a blue and silver decal on the cylinders, which were still on the cylinders and chipped along the edges. The remaining material, all paint, matched a source from either the cart or one of the cylinders. The soles of shoes from two of the burglars were covered with small round burn marks, and beads of slag were stuck in some of these holes. The pants of one of these two men had dozens of tiny pinholes burned through the area between his knees and the cuff of the pants. They were the same size as the slag collected from the floor in front of the safe.

I didn't have to do any other work on this case, though there was a preliminary court hearing. First, the facts of the initial encounter were presented by the night watchman, followed by the events of the arrest. Then their attorneys looked at my photographs of the paint, decal, and metal fragments side by side. At that point all four burglars entered a guilty plea. The fifth man was the owner of the second restaurant and their host at his bar. All were associates of a large organized crime ring. The four men had traveled from Las Vegas, their home base, to steal the weekend receipts from their friend's rival restaurant, hoping to put it out of business. On the way out of Vegas they burglarized a welding shop and stole the cutting torch equipment.

## Epilogue

There was a bit of irony to this case. There had been over $30,000 in the safe. The burglars weren't doing all this work purely out of friendship. Their plan was to split the money. Had the night watchman stopped elsewhere for his coffee and not interrupted their efforts, they, rather than the police, would have opened the safe. Their attempt at wetting the inside of the safe didn't work. The money had burned up.

## TRACE EVIDENCE, HAIRS, AND FIBERS

Trace evidence can be any small pieces of material, naturally occurring or man-made. The particles can be inherently small or they can be tiny fragments due to breaking. They may be microscopic or pieces too small to find matching edges. Whatever the material is, either plant or mineral or matter manufactured in bulk, it is often found in abundance and distributed over wide areas. That presents a problem for forensic scientists since this kind of evidence almost always lacks individuality.

There was a time when the world around us was a smaller place. The uniqueness of trace evidence was weighed by a different scale. Folks were born, lived their lives, and died within the same community. Everyday goods were either handmade or manufactured in small batches that filled the needs for a specific order. Quality control was not yet an issue, and the formula of the product could change from day to day, depending on which person was doing the mixing at the moment. If a forensic scientist found a chip of paint on a suspects' pry tool, and the paint matched the paint around a pry mark on a doorjamb, it was convincing evidence that the two paints had a common origin.

Today, mass production and tight quality control are standard operating procedures creating a world of homogeneous materials. Huge batches of material with identical characteristics reduce the uniqueness of many forms of trace evidence. Paint, for instance, is manufactured in one enormous batch and then sold to different companies that apply it to their products. The exact same paint can be found on thousands of different types of items. The problem is compounded by the potential mobility of the criminal population. Although small community life still exists, its isolation and sanctity is a thing of the past. Planned crime sprees—raids, so to speak—the freedom of movement, and the abundance of drifters have the effect of enlarging even small population bases, at least statistically, to that of the largest metropolis.

Often, the value of trace evidence, hairs, and fibers is the fact that they are at the crime scene and the suspect has no way of explaining why. This group of physical evidence typifies what is meant by circumstantial. When there is only one plausible circumstance, the evidence speaks for itself and is elevated to the value of a fingerprint.

Chinese officials figured out a use for trace evidence hundreds of years ago. They are credited with using trace material contamination to devise the first form of lie detector. A person who was suspected of committing a crime was told to go into a windowless room where he would find a donkey. The suspect was told he had to pull on the donkey's tail. If the donkey brayed, it meant the suspect was guilty and would be put to death. If the donkey made no noise, it meant he was innocent. The expectation was that no guilty man would pull on the tail unless he was sure no one was watching. Since there were no windows, the bad guys figured they could get away without touching the donkey. What they didn't know was that the man in charge had coated the donkey's tail with carbon dust. An innocent man with faith in the donkey was not afraid and pulled the tail. Donkey noise or no donkey noise had nothing to do with it. If he came out of the room with traces of carbon on his hands, he went free. Clean hands, and he was in big trouble.

Edmund Locard took the Chinese use of trace evidence one step further when he wrote about the transfer process. When two objects come in contact with each other, small amounts of materials from one surface may be transferred to the other and vice versa. The intensity and duration of the contact, and the nature of the surfaces, determines the extent of the contamination. Locard published the first scientific approach to understanding this process and is credited with pointing it out to investigators in 1934.

The value of Locard's observation had more to do with the power of deduction akin to the Sherlock Holmes approach to solving crime. For example, a few feathers clinging to the victim's clothing meant the dead man was attacked by a chicken farmer (or a chicken). Many feathers on a victim's clothing and/or compacted in the bottom of his pockets combined with a little chicken manure on his shoes meant he was the chicken farmer. If the victim's body was covered with feathers and the chicken manure was under his body, it meant he was the chicken.

The evidential value of transferred debris varies, however, depending on the uniqueness of the material. This uniqueness may be determined in three ways:

1. If there is only one source for the transfer material within a controlled environment where the contact took place

2. If there is contamination of *several* different materials from the surface one to surface two (a one-way transfer), or several materials from surface two to surface one, or both (a two-way transfer), that is, multiple cross-contamination

3. If there is a method available to characterize the material, such as applying DNA technology to profile blood transfers, that offers individualization of the source

Controlled environments such as the Chinese donkey test still exist, although the contamination is seldom as cleverly planned. Some uses of chemical tracers are nearly as clever. Dyes and stains are available to tag objects, such as petty cash, that are frequent targets of thieves. The dyes stain the skin of anyone who touches it. Some brands are only visible under a UV lamp. Some dyes intensify if the person attempts to wash the color away.

Some businesses place a package of what looks like a stack of twenty-dollar or higher denomination bills in their cash drawer. The package actually contains a device that can be detonated and will spray a red stain on the thief. Locally, an armed robber was caught recently after the package exploded in his pocket, where he had stuffed the "money" as he ran from the scene. He is suing the company, claiming the detonation affected his manhood.

In another case a police officer, while patrolling at three A.M. in a light manufacturing/business district in Orange County, spotted a man standing in an empty parking lot. No businesses were open in the area and the man failed to give a reasonable explanation for his presence or for the wet stains on the cuffs of his pants and his shoes. The officer didn't have to go far before he located several large containers stacked on the curb across the street. A search of the adjacent business—a computer circuit board manufacturer—revealed it had been broken into, and a subsequent inventory established that more than $80,000 of a liquid solution of gold chloride was missing. The containers on the curb contained the missing liquid. The police officer submitted the clothing to the crime lab, and the questioned stains were analyzed. Gold was identified in all the stains. The suspect, who had no explanation for the source of the gold in the stains, was charged with burglary.

Two-way transfers can be equally condemning. For example, the physical act of breaking window glass can create a cloud of trace evidence that can settle on the suspect, in hair and on clothing, or become embedded in the soles of shoes. A pane of glass may act like the skin of a drum until it reaches a critical point. Whenever it breaks, the edges of the cracks are compressed, propelling small particles of glass back in the direction of the force. If anyone is within five or six feet at that moment, the particles will catch in any receptive clothing surface. Even some of the larger pieces may spring back and fall outside the window frame. The transfers of glass to clothing can occur from the shower of small particles, from the act of entering through the window, or from walking on the broken pieces. A two-dimensional impression of the details of the shoe will most likely be made by anyone stepping on the glass (see photos, insert pages 3 and 4).

During violent activities—murder, sexual assault, assault in general, or any time two or more people come in contact during a struggle—a two-way transfer of clothing fibers is likely. Loosely woven garments are more likely to shed and retain fibers than slick fabrics. Slick materials, such as the type of nylon used to make windbreakers, don't shed many fibers readily but may retain transfer material. There may be a transfer or exchange of head, pubic, or body hairs. Fingernail scrapings may contain clothing fibers and pieces of skin, hairs, or blood, and pieces of broken fingernails may be entangled in the other person's clothing.

Materials already at the scene of a struggle, such as soil, plant material, pieces of glass, or other debris, may contaminate the clothing of all participants. The victim's and the suspect's clothing could contain the same trace evidence. If either bled, blood could be exchanged and found on the debris remaining at the scene. Before PCR amplification of DNA, samples of blood too small to type could be considered trace evidence.

Burglary achieved by breaking and entering through windows, doors, roofs, or walls will create small pieces of glass, paint, wood, metal, plaster, insulation material, and roofing material consisting of tar and/or small to tiny rocks. Any of the materials may be found adhering to the burglar's clothing. When the forced entry requires squeezing through a small opening, items or material from the suspect's clothing may be detected and found clinging to jagged edges. Loose buttons, pieces of torn cloth, or fibers are also likely evidence.

Finally, materials normally used by a business, inside the scene, may be found on the clothing of an intruder.

Hit-and-runs perhaps best illustrate the two-way transfer of evidentiary materials. When a painted surface of one car collides with another car, paint will invariably be transferred at all contact points regardless of the extent of the impact. If both surfaces at a point of contact are painted, there will likely be a two-way transfer. The greater the impact, the more likely it is that large amounts of paint and other materials will be exchanged, such as glass, metal, plastic, and even undercoating material. If evidence from the suspect's vehicle is not transferred to the victim's vehicle, it is likely to be on the ground near the point of impact. If the suspect's vehicle is located, someone familiar with the damage to the victim's vehicle should inspect it for two-way transfer evidence.

When a pedestrian is struck by a moving vehicle, several possible things can happen to the victim. What actually happened at a scene can be determined by looking at the victim's injuries and at the vehicle, if it is available. If the victim was standing, walking, or running, the body may follow one of at least four different paths. These are in part related to the vehicle's speed; the driver's attempts, if any, to avoid a collision; and the last second position of the victim, who may be trying to get out of the way. In general, the speed of the vehicle could be expected to be less with each subsequent behavior.

*Path One.* The victim's body makes one contact with the vehicle's surface, grillworks, headlight assembly, bumper, or any combination, and is propelled forward and up like a ball off the toe of a kicker. There is one point of contact on the vehicle, and major damage is common. Secondary injuries to the victim occur when the body collides with whatever is in its way.

Within the damaged area on the vehicle, pieces of clothing or fabric marks may be embedded in paint or plastic. If the victim's face was involved, there would likely be blood, hair, or tissue in the grillwork. There may not be any blood on the vehicle if it was a high-speed impact with just the torso of the victim. The amount of time in contact with the vehicle doesn't allow for much bleeding.

Regarding evidence on the victim, paint or matching plastic from the grillwork or bumper may be fused into the weave of the victim's clothing. The fusing is caused by the heat of the friction created by the impact. If a headlight was involved, glass may be embedded or plastic fused into the clothing or flesh.

*Path Two.* The victim's body makes the same initial contact, is lifted up, lands on the hood, and collides with the windshield or the top of the car and then tumbles off to the side or all the way over the back of the vehicle before landing on the ground. Major damage may occur to the vehicle at the initial point of contact—the hood may have scratch marks in the paint where the body slid, the windshield may be broken out or cracked, and there may be a concave dent somewhere on the top of the vehicle. This happens if the victim's head impacts the top. There are at least two points of contact, more likely three.

Because the body spends more time in contact with the vehicle in this scenario, there may be more evidence transfer. Blood may be found particularly at secondary points of impact. Fibers may be fused or torn and embedded in any number of contact points. If the head contacted the windshield and the glass broke, hair may be found in the cracks of the glass. In return, paint chips, broken plastic, or glass may adhere to the victim's clothing or skin.

*Path Three.* The victim is propelled downward and the body ends up on the pavement in front of the vehicle and is run over. Major damage may occur to the vehicle at the initial point of contact but there will likely be evidence that the body was under the vehicle's frame.

Material from the victim may be found on the grillwork or bumper. Parts of clothing, skin, or hair may be caught on exposed bolts or frame work. The hot muffler may have flesh cooked on it if there was contact with bare skin. On the body, there will likely be oil and/or grease, and other road debris on the clothing and skin. Body parts and large sections of skin and clothing may be missing, but can be found on the underside of the vehicle if it is located quickly.

*Path Four.* This scenario occurs when the victim is already down. The victim may be previously injured, drunk, playing around, acting on a dare, trying to prevent someone from driving any farther, suicidal, or a child. This often happens at a very slow speed, so the only evidence available is body parts and large sections of skin and clothing found on the underside of the vehicle.

Trace evidence can also resolve two other mysteries commonly surrounding accidents. Following a collision, particularly one involving a fatality, it is not uncommon for a survivor to deny driving the vehicle. One suspect claimed, "It was the dead guy who was doing the driving. I was the passenger." If proper standards are collected from the parties involved, the transfer of hairs, blood, and fibers to parts of the interior of the vehicle, such as the steering wheel and the windshield, can be used to identify the relative position of the individuals at the time of the accident. In this example, the injuries to the subjects were consistent with the damage, and the blood on the steering wheel matched only one of the subjects, while the hair was similar only to the other subject. The nature of the collision is a factor. If the subjects were tossed about before the moment of impact, who was driving could still be in question. This case involved a sudden impact.

Whether a broken seal beam tungsten filament headlight or taillight was on at the time of impact can be determined by studying the filaments. Three major changes occur if the vehicle's electrical system is heating the tungsten, unusually to more than 1,000 degrees Fahrenheit, at the moment of impact. All the events occur essentially at the same time, but consider them in this order: Oxygen enters the seal beam unit and is burned by the glowing tungsten, forming the white tungsten oxide seen on the terminals. The coiled tungsten is distorted by the abrupt deceleration and loses its original shape. While still white-hot, the tungsten is sprayed by tiny particles of the broken lens or glass housing and becomes liquid. When the current is broken or shut off, the liquid glass hardens and clings to the coils. None of these events occurs if the lamp is off.

## Collection of Trace Evidence, Hairs, and Fibers

Some evidence can be seen with the naked eye or made visible for the moment by a special light source, a laser, or an alternative light source. These items can be picked at or scraped off and packaged in paper bundles, vials, or pillboxes. When the circumstances at the crime scene suggest the likelihood that evidence is present but is too small to see or handle safely, the surface can be processed in various ways, assuring that everything adhering to it is collected.

Nonportable items must be processed at the scene by either a special vacuum cleaner or a tape lift. A special vacuum cleaner attachment, available to suck particles off surfaces and trap them on a piece of filter paper, works well in a house or business, where electricity is available and the decision has been made not to cut out suspected sections of a sofa or carpet.

At outdoor crime scenes where there is no source of electricity, tape lifts are used to remove evidence from nonportable surfaces. The tape used, 3M #355, is selected because the tacky material is the least reactive in laboratory tests that are likely to follow. Tape lifts should be taken of exposed areas of the skin. Clothing should be removed if possible and packaged separately.

Tape lifts should never be done on transportable items, with the exception of bodies that must be placed in body bags. If it is dark or the scene can be darkened, the body, clothing, and skin should be examined by one or both of the special evidence lights. Equipment, such as a tent, should be available to enclose a body and make it dark enough to use these lights, regardless of the time of day.

## Laboratory Examinations

Trace evidence, hairs, and fibers are distinguished from similar material by their class characteristics. Once it is determined what the material most likely is, a specific regimen of tests is applied for each type of material. The most obvious questions are:

- What is it?

- Is it man-made or natural?

- What is its source?

- How common is it?

- Can it be identified to a single source?

The identification process is based on evaluating the material's physical and chemical characteristics. All schematic approaches or flow chart regimens begin with some form of visual evaluation to classify any obvious physical characteristic, such as color. The equipment for visual examination should include:

1. A low-power stereoscopic, binocular microscope, 10x to 60x (times magnification). This is used for sorting by color, shape, and any other characteristic. A trained examiner can recognize most items and ascertain what the material is and if it is man-made or natural most of the time at this stage.

2. A compound microscope, 100x to 1,000x. This is used to resolve very fine detail in transparent subjects, such as hairs and fibers. Otherwise similar items can be sorted further at this point.

3. A phase contrast microscope, 100x to 1,000x, is designed to enhance detail by increasing the microscope's capacity to resolve fine points or lines. This microscope is otherwise a regular compound unit. When used as a phase contrast microscope, it separates light into two paths and delays one path very slightly before it passes through the object. The out-of-phase light increases the contrast of otherwise faint and closely aligned detail.

   The following microscopes provide both a visual examination and a level of analytical data, either physical or chemical characteristics, that identify the object or some of the object's chemical components.

4. A polarized light microscope is used to recognize a phenomenon called birefringence, which is specific to certain minerals found in soil. Sand is one of hundreds of birefringent substances encountered as evidence. All of them can be distinguished by their birefringent nature. Their crystalline structure can change the angle of the polarized light as the microscope's stage is rotated. If the crystalline structure is at the same degree of rotation as the polarized light, it

looks normal. As the stage is rotated—the light passing through sand, for example—that light's angle changes relative to the unchanged light around it and the grain appears colored. The process of making glass out of sand alters the crystalline structure, so glass is not birefringent. Small particles of glass can be sorted in this manner.

5. In a scanning electron microscope up to 100,000x (most forensic applications are magnified no more than 4,000x), electrons rather than light are used to image objects, and a computer transforms the image to recognizable shapes on a video monitor. The object, an SEM, is under vacuum during observation, limiting some applications. When the sample is not suitable, strange results will occur, as trapped gases or liquid expand and escape, a condition called degassing. The object appears to glow if it is degassing. Organic materials may not conduct the electrons, resulting in inadequate images. Surface conductivity is improved by coating the object in an ultrathin layer of gold.

When an electron strikes most elements, an X ray is given off. One element's X ray can be differentiated from those of other elements by an accessory attachment to the SEM called an energy dispersive X-ray unit (EDX). The combination, SEM-EDX, locates, sizes, documents and analyzes trace evidence, producing an exhibit that maps out elemental distribution. The particles of gunshot primer residue are mapped out in this manner. Layered paint that has matching colors in the same order can be examined, layer by layer, showing the inorganic elements distributed within the organic component of the paint.

6. A Fourier Transform Infra Red Spectrophotometer (FTIR). Infrared light is heat as we know it. A spectrophotometer, in general, is an instrument that directs a beam of monochromatic light (a single wavelength) onto or through a sample. It can be programmed to scan a sample, in series at each wavelength within a

selected region. Spectrophotometers that use visible and ultraviolet light are also available.

Most spectrophotometers provide only data but the FTIR can be combined with an optical microscope that is capable of visually focusing on very small areas. The beam of IR energy can then be focused on the same spot. The FTIR translates the absorption/transmission ratio or the reflection ratio of the IR light into a graph that can be used to identify the organic components of the sample. Layered paint can be characterized layer by layer. This approach is called step-down analysis. When the FTIR results are combined with the SEM-EDX results, it is likely that the source of the paint can be narrowed down to one location if more than four layers match in all respects.

A major advantage of all these visual methods, including SEM-EDX and FTIR microscopy, is that the sample is not destroyed. The same material can be reexamined if necessary.

Prior to the availability of the SEM-EDX during the 1970s, there were two methods of conducting elemental analysis of inorganic compounds:

1. Atomic absorption spectrophotometry (AA or AAS). This approach is still in use for specific tasks. It is much quicker than the SEM-EDX but far less versatile and destroys the sample. The AAS directs a beam of a specific wavelength of light generated by a lamp into a path above the sample. The amount of energy generated by the lamp is recorded by a detector at the other end of the optical path. The sample is vaporized, emitting energy at the wavelengths of all the elements in the sample. As the lamp's beam passes through the vapor—if it intercepts energy of the same wavelength—that new energy is absorbed into the beam. The detector at the other end of the optical path monitors all the incoming energy and records the increase if the sample matched the beam's wavelength. If the new energy did

not match the beam's light, the detector's readings do not change. The examiner must know in advance which element lamp to use or must check for elements one at a time, changing to a different lamp each time.

2. Spectrograph. Inorganic elements emit light when they get hot. The red light of hot iron and the white light of electrified tungsten are well-known. We see these lights as a single color, but in fact they consist of a wide range of wavelengths that include a multitude of colors. The spectrograph is an instrument that separates light into all its wavelengths. There are only four parts to a spectrograph.

- A power source needed to generate instant high energy, enough to vaporize solid metals.

- A carbon arc furnace consisting of a sample holder, a hollow carbon rod, and a contact carbon rod mounted above the sample. The positions of the rods are adjustable, allowing them to almost touch.

- A camera and film. This is a big camera, six feet long and two feet wide. The film is a twelve-inch-long strip of 35mm film.

- A prism or gradient with a narrow slit to separate the light into single wavelength spectral lines.

The sample is vaporized when high voltage arcs across the carbon rods. Iron is arced as a reference. I used two ordinary bolts for this purpose. Iron has several bright triplet bands and double bands at convenient wavelengths that are used to orient unknown samples. The samples are destroyed. The instrument was made obsolete by the SEM-EDX.

The following instruments are used to identify organic compounds:

- A gas chromatograph (GC). Mixtures of compounds as simple as ethyl alcohol or as complex as gasoline can be separated and characterized by a gas chromatograph. The sample is injected onto a column that is being flushed with an inert gas. The column may be straight or coiled or may be packed with a chemically impregnated mesh, or simply lined with a chemical. The inert gas pushes the sample along, while the chemical, called the stationary phase, selectively slows down individual chemicals in a mixture, usually based on molecular size or electric charge. Gasoline, for example, will separate into dozens of components, in part based on the number of carbon atoms in the components. Like samples are matched by comparing their retention time, that is, the time it takes for the compound to overcome the stationary phase and move from the injection site to a detector. Each component is recorded on a piece of chart paper, and the relative quantity of each component can be estimated by comparing peak heights. Some very complex GCs on the market are automated. They are programmed to do most of the work, and even calculate the area within the peak to give an accurate quantitative analysis of the sample.

- Pyrolysis gas chromatograph (GCP). The gas chromatograph is basically no different than the type described above. The pyrolysis unit acts as the injection port. A solid sample, such as paint, is vaporized by instant heat and the fumes are flushed into the column. The products of the pyrolysis are forced through the column and their retention times noted on a piece of chart paper. Two samples from the same source will produce the same results, class characteristics, but samples from other sources can have the same class characteristics and produce the same results.

- Gas chromatograph—mass spectrometer (GCMS). The GC separates the compound of interest, and then it flows into the MS. Organic molecules break apart reproducibly as they pass through a strong magnetic field. The total mass of the original compound is broken into many smaller particles of varying mass. Each particle's mass is measured, producing a mass fingerprint for many compounds.

## Some Materials of Special Interest as Physical Evidence

### Paints

Paint is a generic term that covers a wide variety of surface coatings. Types of paints include enamel and lacquer, which are either oil-based or water-based, and acrylic or latex (rubber).

In the lab, the first thing determined when comparing known to unknown samples of paint is: Are any individual characteristics common to both samples? A visual comparison of the color of each sample should always be the first test, followed by an evaluation of any possible physical matches of the broken edges. The presence of surface defects may indicate an unusual history common to both samples. For example, if there is some form of contamination on both samples, such as an overspray of one or more other paints or fragments, or something intentionally applied to the original painted surface, such as a decal, it may indicate a single source for both samples. If the paint was on a metal surface, the inner surface of the primer or paint may have retained an impression of the metal's surface characteristics. The primer can act as a casting material, capturing all the detailed striations; for instance, those left by a metal grinder. Marks of this type would be randomly applied. A match would indicate a common origin, even if there was missing paint between the two pieces.

The identical layers of paint *may* indicate an unusual history for both samples that suggests a common source. Five or more matching layers is considered significant, depending on the history of the surface. The location and history of ownership is very important to the determination of the uniqueness of layering. For example, all the doors and windows of several different business complexes owned by the same organization may be repainted periodically using the same paint source. Further, if a vehicle was owned by a business, it could be one of a fleet of vehicles that were all repainted on a regular maintenance schedule. There could be twenty identical layers common to one hundred trucks. If it can be verified that the vehicle was always privately owned, then it is a question of individual choice and random selection of the paints. It is an interesting question: What is the likelihood of the existence of two different automobiles that have similar damage consistent with the incident that also have a similar history?

Class characteristics—color, type, and chemical composition—of the paint are considered next. If the two samples match in every class characteristic, they still may be from different sources. Since paint is originally a liquid, if two otherwise common paints were mixed together to complete a job, the characteristics would be individualized if the paint was used on only one surface.

The FTIR and the SEM-EDX procedures combined with visual color comparisons and solubility tests is the method of choice to characterize paint. In a national proficiency test, laboratories that did not profile the sample completely with these combined procedures, comparisons, and tests misidentified one paint as matching another. The paints were visually identical in every way. The paints were made by the same company and contained all the same chemicals with one tiny exception: One sample contained a small amount of an inorganic material that was added as a rust inhibitor. This blend was sold in parts of North America where drivers encountered snow, ice, and salted roads.

Paints can also be classified by type, lacquer or enamel, acrylic, or otherwise by solubility tests. Small chips are exposed to various solvents while they can be observed under a stereoscopic binocular microscope.

## Glass

Glass is a supercooled liquid, that is, it remains clear after it cools down rather than recrystallizing. Locating individuality in glass calls for a process identical to the one used for paint, matching pieces and surface contamination. A few other types of intentional surface materials are found on glass: tinting films, labels on bottles, and painted writing or pictures on bottles, doors, and store windows. Any one of those qualities matching between a known and unknown sample could establish their common source.

The class characteristics of glass are its color in different lights, refractive index, density, and chemical composition. Color or tint must be considered carefully since a thin chip may appear as a lighter color than a thicker chip of the same source. It is examined in both natural light and the light of an ALS. Refractive index (RI) is an expression of the ratio of the speed of light as it passes through a transparent material relative to air (technically, to a vacuum). For example, light bends when it passes from air into glass.

Refractive index can be determined directly with a refractometer if both sides of a sample are flat. This is seldom the case with chips of glass. The RI of glass fragments is determined by comparing the behavior of light as it passes through a glass sample that has been submersed in liquids of known refractive indices. These liquids are called *immersion oils* and are available in a series of slightly different RIs.

The comparison is made under a microscope. The piece of glass is placed in the oil so it is fully submerged. Its edges can be seen in the oil because its RI is different than the RI of the oil, and the microscope's light is bent as it passes the interface. If by chance the RI of the oil selected is exactly the same as the glass, the glass cannot be seen at all. The next step is to determine whether the oil selected has a greater or lesser RI than the glass. To do this, the microscope is focused on an edge. What appears to be a halo or double image of the glass's edge can be seen near the actual edge. This is called the Becke line. If the objective of the microscope is moved up slightly away from the glass, the Becke line will appear to move. If it moves away from the glass, the liquid has a higher RI than the glass. If it moves toward the glass, the glass has the higher RI. Ideally, clearly different shapes of chips can be found, one from each source, their shapes sketched as a record, and the two submerged in the same liquid. This eliminates any variable such as a change in temperature or residual oils.

The RI of each of the glasses is eventually determined by bracketing the glass within the closest two liquids. By changing liquids until one in the series is higher and the next one in the series is lower, the closest possible range of RI can be considered. If the two sources always behave the same, it may be necessary to mix the two fluids in varying proportion to achieve indices in between. The exact RI of the mixed oils can be determined by a refractometer.

The tedious aspects of this procedure were somewhat eliminated with the introduction, in the 1970s, of a programmable hot stage capable of being mounted on a microscope. The RI of any liquid is temperature dependent, immersion oils included. This procedure relies on Becke line movement but needs only one oil of relatively high RI. As the temperature of the stage slowly increases, the apparent RI of the liquid decreases. The Becke line will progressively move in the direction of the glass. At a point where the two are identical, the edge disappears and the temperature is noted. When the Becke line reappears on the inside of the glass's edge, the program can be reversed. The Becke line will begin to move out and should disappear at the same temperature. The process can be repeated with other pieces of glass.

Even many ultramodern forensic laboratories are without the newest of RI devices, known as GRMS (pronounced *grimes*)—glass refraction measuring system. After the examiner loads the sample in the equipment, it is fully automatic. It does all the same measurements but without the human watching.

The density of glass is determined by comparing it to liquids of known specific gravity, which is defined as the material's relative mass to an equal volume of deionized water. The SG of liquids, like their RI, is temperature dependent. The idea is to find a liquid whose density is the same as the glass. At that SG, the glass will be suspended in the liquid. Density gradient tubes can be prepared to create a liquid that just matches the density in the glass. A long glass tube is filled halfway with bromoform, SG greater than four, and topped off with bromobenzene, SG around two. The tube is allowed to equilibrate overnight, and one piece of glass from each source is dropped into the tube (their shapes are sketched so they can be identified). The glass chips will descend until they arrive at a point that just matches their density. If they have the same density, they will be seen suspended at the same level.

## Gasoline

Hydrocarbon fuel is manufactured in mammoth single bulk quantities, and seldom has the qualities needed to be individualized, except under special circumstances. Each batch of gasoline is composed of a couple of hundred individual components, hydrocarbons and additives, that create a so-called fingerprint for each company's product. Each major company varies its product enough that a complete forensic laboratory examination of an unheated product could identify the refinery.

A forensic lab should be able to analyze a sample from an arson crime scene, identify a brand and grade, and possibly lead the investigator to a local dealer. That sounds good but it doesn't always work. First, it is almost guaranteed that most samples collected at crime scenes have been exposed to heat. The most volatile components, often the ones that are used to vary the formula, are evaporated, or topped off, making batch identity more difficult. It is like trying to solve a puzzle where the first ten to twenty parts are missing. One approach is to take small quantities of the known sources submitted for comparison, top them off progressively, and see if the residues produced match the crime scene sample.

Perhaps even a bigger mystery for arson investigators to unravel is the practice of one manufacturer selling surplus gasoline to other companies. Solving the puzzle can have its payoff. At any time, company A may sell one or more grades of its product to company B or even to company C. All the different stations on the same corner could be selling exactly the same product. I have even heard that one major company's pipeline through a small town was the only supply of gasoline to all the town's stations. They all sold one product and labeled them all three grades, depending on what was in the pipeline on a given day when they filled their tanks.

This is not all bad news. When one type or brand of gasoline is mixed with another, the hybrid produced may be unique. For a brief time the same unique mix of gasoline brands sold to an arsonist are available to the investigators if they get to the station soon enough. A couple of interesting cases worked by my boss at the time, Jack Cadman, involved mixtures.

One time, an arson fire was accelerated by gasoline found to be a mix of two brands. No container was found when a suspect was questioned, but someone matching his description had been seen buying a can of gasoline at a nearby station. Samples were obtained from the station and found to be mixtures of two different brands, and the mix matched the sample from the crime scene. The uniqueness of the fuel was assured when investigators learned that the station had only recently been reopened, but by a different company. The station had been closed for several months but the underground tanks contained quantities of the original brand.

Another time, following an arson fire, a suspect was apprehended and an empty one-gallon can was located in the trunk of his vehicle. As in any empty vessel, there was some residue in the bottom of the can. This residue was not a mixture of two gasolines. The vast majority of the liquid was gasoline but the remainder was paint thinner. The sample collected from the scene indicated a gasoline/paint thinner mix of the same proportions.

## Hairs

Hairs used for evidence can be from a human or an animal. Human hairs can be classified based on their origin: the head (scalp, eyebrows, eyelashes, whiskers) and the body (chest, pubic, arm, or leg). Head and pubic hair are more likely to be found as evidence, the former pulled out during a struggle and the latter exchanged during sexual acts. Animal hair can be directly from a living or recently killed animal, from a cured pelt, from a variety of animals, or from a garment, such as a wool sweater. It is not uncommon to find animal hairs on the clothing of a dumped body. The hair could be from the victim's own pet, or the transfer could have occurred at the death scene or from a vehicle used for transporting the body. In either of the latter situations, there is a possibility of some level of association.

Many species of animals have two major variations of

body hairs: guard hairs and down hairs. Guard hairs are coarse and down hairs are thin and soft. Guard hairs are flatter, sometimes as flat as a knife blade, and may be layered with color. They grow to a certain length and then stop. Eventually they fall out and are replaced by new hair. Some species, sheep and certain dogs—poodles and bichons frises, for example—have hair that grows continuously. Hairs from some animals are used as fibers to manufacture a variety of materials for clothing, carpets, and upholstery and may be found in large numbers at a crime scene although no animal is around.

All hairs, at one time in their existence, have the same general characteristics visible to the unaided eye—a root, a shaft, and a tip. Most human head hair has been cut, so the tips are missing. The same is true of certain dogs, as noted above. Other animal hair is very characteristic and can be distinguished by the layers of colors and the blade-shaped shaft. Without magnification, human hairs are not easy to distinguish from natural wool and the long hairs of certain dogs. With magnification, human pubic hair and other body hairs are similar in appearance and not easily confused with animal hair. Nevertheless, no conclusions should be offered based solely on a macroscopic examination.

If you study hairs under a microscope of at least 100x, you'll notice that the shaft of all hairs contain the same morphological characteristics. The outer surface is enclosed by overlapping scales and looks somewhat like the shingles on a roof. The internal body of all hairs is called the cortex and contains a central core, the medulla. The medulla is often no more than empty air sacs but may also be heavily pigmented. The cortex also contains granules of pigment, ranging in size from tiny to large. The arrangement and distribution of these characteristics allow the distinction of animal from human hair, the identification of animal species, and in some instances the ability to discriminate one person's hair from another.

Most animal hair can be recognized as such almost immediately under the microscope. With down hairs, scales dominate the outer structure. They look a lot like tall stacks of ice cream cones, one stuffed in another. The scales are huge relative to the diameter of the hair. Internally, the cortex is almost all medulla and is usually unpigmented. Down hairs are very similar regardless of species. Guard hairs have many more variations and can be used to tell one species from another. The scales are very heavy, particularly in the short blade-shaped hairs. The internal structure is dominated by the medulla, which can occupy most of the cortex and can be heavily pigmented.

All human head hair has the same morphological characteristics. The scales are far more discrete and sometimes require special techniques just to be seen and studied. Where an animal hair may have a dozen overlapping scales, a human hair may have close to one hundred. Internally, the medulla is consistently smaller in diameter than that of animal hair, if it is present at all. The human medulla is never larger than half the total width and is usually no more than one-third of the diameter. Determining sex from hairs alone is not possible. Determining race from hairs alone is chancy. There is such a wide range of variations in color, curl, and thickness within ethnic groups that crossovers of characteristics can occur.

One person's hairs, regardless of what part of the body they came from, can often be distinguished from another person's by a scale count. Scales are counted at numerous locations over a specific length of the shaft using a micrometer ruler inserted into the microscope's eyepiece. Dozens of counts should be done on several different hairs from the same individual. The counts per distances should be consistent for an individual. This approach may allow one person to be excluded as a source of a hair, but a matching count doesn't necessarily indicate a common source. Scales are counted more accurately if the hair has been cast by embedding it in a pliable material.

Comparing pigmentation in both the cortex and the medulla is another way to discriminate between hairs. The suspect and standard hairs are viewed simultaneously using a comparison microscope. The hairs must never be placed together on the same slide since they must look similar if this examination is needed. If they are similar, they could get mixed up.

Each hair is immersed in an organic solvent that has a similar RI to hair. The scales blend in and the internal characteristics, the pigment and medulla, stand out. The color and overall distribution of the pigment can vary from person to person. Two people who had indistinguishable scale counts may have quite different pigmentation distribution, allowing one or both to be eliminated if there is no match to the crime scene hair.

Two other ways to examine hair are worth mentioning. The ABO substance has been identified in human hair, but testing for it doesn't always provide reliable results. Mapping drugs embedded in hairs has been suggested for two reasons. One is to demonstrate use over an extended period, and the second is to compare to crime scene hairs. Drugs and poisons are absorbed into the hair at the root as the hair is formed. But drugs can also contaminate the hair surface. If the samples are not properly prepared, false conclusions could be drawn in either case.

## Fibers

The word "fiber" has many meanings. As evidence, fiber generally refers to small elongated pieces of material used to manufacture cloth, carpet, paper, cardboard, rope, cord, or string. The forensic classification of fibers begins with their origin: natural or man-made. Natural fibers occur as animal hairs (wool), excrement (silk), plant (cotton), and mineral (asbestos). Man-made fibers include many polymers and their variations, such as nylon, polyester, and other nonpolymers, like viscous rayon.

Fibers can be sorted by color, fluorescence, and thickness using a stereo binocular microscope. Color variations do not necessarily mean different sources. A single carpet, for example, may contain a dozen or more shades of color. The ALS or laser can be used to scan the standard fibers to determine if they fluoresce. The unknown sample can then be examined for this activity using the ALS. The same procedure should be used at the crime scene and autopsy to locate trace evidence and fibers.

Almost every type of fiber can be grouped into a general class by visual examination at 100x to 200x. Some fibers show birefringence in the polarizing microscope. The FTIR can be used to distinguish between variations of nylon and to study surface dye characteristics in general. When everything else is indistinguishable, as with cotton, the dyes used to color the fibers can be extracted with solvents and studied by various methods of chromatography.

Perhaps the most useful method of distinguishing the wide assortment of otherwise identical fibers manufactured for use in carpets is by studying the cross section. The polymer is extruded and the cross-section shapes are formed at that time.

## The Bottom Line

Many new investigators and prosecutors may be unaware of traditional trace, hair, and fiber evidence. In recent years it has become more difficult for the lab personnel to justify spending the time it takes to characterize trace evidence, hairs, and fibers, or even to train new scientists in the techniques. As has already happened in some major jurisdictions, crime scene investigators no longer spend the time to search for and collect the standards necessary for comparison should trace evidence be important as the investigation progresses. Either they know it is unlikely the crime lab will ever examine the material, so they don't want to waste their time, or, as with some new scene investigators, they have never been trained to anticipate its usefulness as circumstantial evidence. When investigators fail to collect *all* of the evidence, they risk overlooking incriminating or exculpatory information.

## chapter nine

# Forensic Toxicology

## Introduction

Poisonous materials and some drugs occur naturally in certain species of the animal, plant, and mineral kingdoms. People and lesser animals learned by observation, when one of their kind suffered the consequences of eating the wrong stuff or becoming too friendly with a rattling serpent. The animals, for the most part, learned to avoid these obstacles to live. People learned to put them to devious use.

Toxicology is the science of isolating, purifying, and identifying toxic chemicals, usually from biological materials. Forensic toxicology is an extension of this science to situations of legal consequence. Prior to the introduction of toxicology to the investigation of questioned deaths, murders, suicides, and accidental deaths due to poison escaped detection and were often considered natural deaths. Even if the events leading to the subject's death were suspicious, proper classification was unlikely without toxicology results.

There is no death where the proper classification is insignificant, but in some investigations the consequences of an incorrect classification can be devastating to the surviving parties. The role of forensic toxicology in establishing the cause of death is demonstrated in the following case.

## CRIME SCENE:

### ONCE IN A LIFETIME STRENGTH

San Clemente, California, is the southernmost city in Orange County, hugging a narrow strip of shoreline at the western edge of the Santa Margarita mountain range. The city is perhaps most famous as the location of the Western White House during President Nixon's term in office. It was once famous for its roofs. Because of the slope of the hillsides, from the I-5 freeway you can see most of Old San Clemente.

Late one afternoon in 1985 a young woman living alone in a quiet residential part of town heard a knock on her front door. She opened it to see a stranger standing on her porch, a man in his twenties staring at her with an odd, distant look on his face. Uninvited and mumbling something she didn't understand, he walked past her into her front room and began taking off his shirt. He paid little attention to the woman, allowing her to run out her front door and go to a neighbor's place, where she called the police.

Two patrolmen who were near the end of their shifts were dispatched to the scene, advised that a residential burglary was in progress. This meant they would approach the scene with their red lights on but not their sirens. As the first officer arrived, he observed the suspect on the sidewalk walking westbound away from the original location. The shirtless suspect wasn't carrying anything. When the suspect noticed the patrol unit dead ahead of him, he continued walking but changed directions. The first officer, now on foot, caught up with the suspect and told him to halt. The suspect stopped as told, but the officer said later that he acted incoherent at this first contact. His conversation made no sense. Then a backup officer arrived and the suspect attempted to leave. The two officers detained him for a moment but he started to resist. The suspect, smaller than either officer, picked up one of the officers, a 180-pound man, held him over his head, and threw him to the sidewalk.

Neighbors who had been watching the action called the

police station, and every officer in the city responded. The timing of the event, during a shift change, more than doubled the number of officers on duty in the city.

In less than a minute eight officers were at the scene, which had now moved farther west as the remaining uninjured officer attempted to control the suspect. As they surrounded him, he threw another officer to the pavement. The group eventually controlled him, holding tightly to his extremities and forcing him to the ground. For a moment the pile of men looked like two football teams fighting to regain a fumble. The thrashing and kicking suspect's strength seemed to increase as he rolled about on the pavement. Three officers now lay injured, cast aside like rag dolls and unable to assist in the struggle.

Then the suspect stopped moving. As suddenly as he had rebeled, he went limp. The officers slowly loosened their grips. One by one they sat up. One started to use his portable radio to call for medical aid but stopped when he saw the paramedic unit approaching from down the block. Another officer was able to get his handcuffs on the suspect without resistance. The injured officers were quickly examined by the paramedics and prepared for transport to the local hospital. A second paramedic unit arrived and attended to the suspect. He had remained noncombative next to the curb. The paramedics, warned of their patient's strength, approached him with great caution. He didn't resist. They began their treatment as they always do, checking for the vital signs. He had none. The suspect was dead.

The media accounts described the eight officers as ganging up on the lone suspect but said little about their injuries. In defense of the media, this looked like a case of police brutality. Only an autopsy and forensic toxicology could discover the truth.

The autopsy was held to establish a cause of death. Sheriff's investigators were called to investigate, and the D.A.'s office was called to witness the autopsy. The questions of particular interest were: Was there damage to the deep muscles surrounding the suspect's windpipe, his larynx? Had he been choked to death? Had his hyoid bone been fractured?

The hyoid bone is located at the base of the tongue, just where the chin meets the neck, and is usually fractured during manual strangulation.

The autopsy took several hours to complete as each area and organ of the body was examined and photographed. There was no damage to his breathing apparatus. There was no significant internal trauma to any part of his body, only a few external scrapes and scratches consistent with fighting and rolling around on pavement. The officers were injured far more than he was. But he was dead. And there was no cause of death.

Samples were submitted to Robert Cravey's toxicology section. Sudden unexplained adult deaths were handled as a general screen. That is, the samples were examined for just about every kind of possible toxic material. Each test was negative except one. Cocaine and its metabolite, benzoylecgonine (BE), were found in the blood and brain in levels indicating recent use. But the levels were not in what would be considered the fatal range.

As similar cases were investigated, a clear pattern developed. In the meantime the press was having great fun echoing the screams of police brutality voiced by those who had witnessed the officers relying on force to control the suspects. To the suspect's friends and those who don't appreciate the officers' responsibilities, using any force against an apparently intoxicated person is unjust.

I call them suspects because in each case someone had reported a person acting suspiciously. In each case the suspect became argumentative and then combative as the police officers attempted to control the situation. In each case the suspect demonstrated incredible strength, forcing the officers to respond accordingly. And the deceased in these cases all tested positive for cocaine and the cocaine metabolite, benzoylecgonine.

A few years after our experience, I attended a meeting of international forensic scientists and heard a presentation of nine cases that occurred in Florida during the mid-1980s. Each case related the identical situation: bizarre behavior, officers detain the suspect, a struggle, the suspect suddenly stops resisting and dies. The cause of death in these cases was most likely due to the cardio toxic effect of cocaine; that is, a jumbled stimulation of the nerves regulating the heartbeat. There is no anatomical damage caused by fibrillation. At death the heart muscle relaxes and appears normal. And the police had nothing to do with it.

# FORENSIC TOXICOLOGY

## POISONS, DRUGS, AND NARCOTICS

The definition of a poison is rather broad. Poisons are harmful. Their effect is universal; they make you feel bad or they kill you. If relatively small amounts of any substance adversely affects the life of an organism by chemical or physiological means, it is considered a poison. Drugs are generally considered a medicine, that is, something that cures or makes one feel better. Narcotics are drugs that dull the senses or induce sleep. There is a fine line between a drug and a poison. Many drugs, narcotics, and other chemicals are not poisonous by nature but can nevertheless cause death if used excessively or improperly. Even water is deadly if allowed to interfere with our breathing process or if consumed in extremely large quantities sufficient to create imbalances in blood chemistry.

Chemicals may cause death directly due to a single dose (acute toxicity), or as the result of continuous exposure or frequent single doses of otherwise nonlethal quantities (chronic toxicity). Some chemicals produce low levels of toxicity, that is, intoxication. Various animals, including humans, seek them out, particularly for their euphoric effect, a feeling of well-being.

The use of chemicals can also be a secondary cause of death. For example, intoxicated drivers may cause an auto collision, or persons hallucinating on drugs may believe they can safely fly off a tenth-floor balcony. The chemical didn't cause the death, but it led to behavior that did.

To be considered a drug or a poison, the substance must

have a measurable effect on some physiological activity. Drugs used for legitimate medicinal purposes are expected to provide a benefit. They cure an illness or provide relief from pain or anxiety. Nevertheless, many useful drugs become poisons if taken in excess or when mixed with another otherwise useful drug. That is, the chemicals will progressively inhibit or alter a behavioral or life-sustaining activity if exposure continues.

Pharmacodynamics is the study of what a compound does to the body. The physiological activity of a drug is a measurement of the magnitude of the effects on behavior, relative to the quantity of the dose administered. Other factors that affect the extent of the physiological activity are the weight of the person and the person's ability to eliminate or metabolize the toxicant.

A true poison, by its very nature, abruptly overcomes the body's defense to deal with it, and death occurs. However, other than the heavy metal poisons that continue to accumulate in the body, the body attempts to detoxify every poison. If the system survives the initial episode without severe liver or kidney damage, it will eventually rid itself of the toxin.

The term "parent" describes the unchanged invader. The term "metabolite" describes one or more compounds that are created, usually in the liver, by the body's defense mechanism. Many metabolites of particular drugs are known to be physiologically active. Some metabolites are even more active than the parent drug.

The duration of the drug's activity is defined by its half-life. This means that after a specific period the total amount of drug in the system, as measured by the blood level, has been reduced by half. With each half-life, 50 percent of the remaining drug is eliminated.

Some drugs administered by an anesthesiologist have a very short half-life, only seconds, and are used to block the autonomic nervous system during critical surgery. For example, the heart will be stopped just long enough—a few seconds—for the surgeon to complete a procedure that would be impossible during the normal contractions of the heart muscle. Some fentanyls, strong analgesics, are examples of such fast-acting drugs. Technically, the patient dies when the heart stops beating. The anesthesiologist then applies a stimulant to the system and the heart restarts.

Pharmacokinetics is the study of what the body does to the drug. Pharmacokinetians study the absorption, circulation and distribution, metabolism, and elimination of medications by monitoring the patient under controlled conditions. The health, body size, water-to-body-weight ratio, and many other conditions are all factors in achieving the ideal therapeutic level. Understanding each drug's half-life is critical for the successful treatment of most diseases. From the perspective of the forensic toxicologist, the information is critical when interpreting blood and tissue levels, explaining behavior at significant moments, and constructing hypothetical scenarios to explain when drugs were taken and in what quantity.

Drugs typically are used for their therapeutic effect. That is, an intended benefit is achieved from some ideal dose that produces a narrow range of blood levels for a specific period of time. This ideal range of blood levels is called the therapeutic window. There is also a threshold level that must be passed to reach the lower range of the window. If it is not reached, the drug provides little or no benefit. The physician's instructions—for instance, "Take one tablet every four hours"—is calculated to attain and keep the patient within the range of the therapeutic window. The toxic threshold is beyond the upper level of the therapeutic window. If a drug is overly prescribed, or taken without regard, in amounts that push the blood and tissue levels above the toxic threshold, the patient may suffer a variety of toxic symptoms.

## Classification of Toxic Materials

Every compound that is intended for use on humans or animals, and many chemicals, such as pesticides used where humans could be exposed to them accidentally, have been studied for their relative toxicity. Historically, the process involves the sacrifice of laboratory animals. A large group of test animals is exposed to the compound in question in the manner the chemical is most frequently used or in which accidental exposure might occur—ingestion, inhalation, skin absorption, or injection. A dose that kills any test animal would be considered the minimal lethal dose, and a dose that kills 50 percent of the test population is called the lethal dose-50 or LD-50. Doses are calculated based on the weight of the chemical and the body weight of the test subject.

Experiments on humans in concentration camps during World War II have been described in accounts by survivors. Recently, it has been alleged by United Nations investigators that tests of this nature were done by Iraqi scientists on large numbers of their own citizens to determine the toxicity of nerve gases they are developing. In this country, death row prisoners have volunteered to be tested to determine the effect, but not the LD-50, of certain drugs. This practice is no longer in effect.

Drugs may interact with one another, affecting the toxicity of the doses. If interaction occurs, the effects may be regarded as antagonistic, additive, or synergistic. Death investigators repeatedly encounter cases in which physicians prescribe drugs without properly admonishing the patient about potential drug interaction. Patients may see more than one physician and thus obtain interacting drugs. Drugs sold illegally on the street are often described as uppers (stimulants) or downers (depressants). Sellers and users seldom display any concern for the potential for drug interaction.

Aware pharmacists keep customer records to check for drug interaction before issuing a new drug. Obviously, some patients may use different pharmacies for any number of reasons. A pharmacist can't know what customers are buying at another store.

A notorious street mixture of two otherwise antagonistic drugs is the blending of cocaine and heroin. A dose (a hit) is called a speed ball. The concoction is injected directly into a vein, resulting in its rapid distribution to the brain. Cocaine is a powerful stimulant, while heroin is a powerful analgesic (downer). Both are fast-acting. Cocaine is said to provide a sudden euphoria, an exciting lift of emotions, while heroin in the vein provides what the users call a rush, a euphoric feeling of warmth and well-being. In this cocktail, the cocaine affects the brain seconds before the heroin. For a moment, the antagonists reverse their roles and become a great enhancer. The cocaine upsurge is in full swing just as the heroin's blast of warmth and well-being fills the body, producing the ultimate high. Sounds too good to be true? Ask John Belushi. Ask River Phoenix.

The additive effect occurs when the physiological activity of two drugs combine in direct proportions as if the user had taken more of one or the other drug. Fortunately, unless the user is approaching the toxic threshold with drug number one, drug number two will more than likely not cause any serious direct health problems.

Unfortunately, not understanding or anticipating any intoxication, the user may attempt to go on with everyday business, such as driving a motor vehicle, flying a commercial jet, or teaching children how to shoot a bow and arrow. The additive effect of two drugs can result in indirect catastrophes and yet never be recognized as the cause for the behavior of the user. Considered individually, the blood levels of the drugs can appear harmless to the uninformed investigator.

Synergism defines any event in which two components mix to create an overwhelming response. Drug synergism occurs when two drugs mix in the system, greatly magnifying one or more of the physiological activities of the drugs, propelling the user into the toxic level. Additive effects resemble simple addition. Two plus two equals four. Synergism resembles unchecked multiplication. Two times two may equal six, eleven, or twenty-seven.

Our laboratory in general, and in particular our chief forensic toxicologist, Robert Cravey, has enjoyed a worldwide reputation for excellence. In the late 1970s we were one of a few labs that had both the equipment and the experience to conduct comprehensive toxicology examinations of complex mixtures of drugs at therapeutic levels extracted from small samples of body tissue. Cravey walked into my office one morning and announced that he had been asked to examine tissue from Elvis Presley's autopsy. Cravey is a modest man. What he didn't tell me was the story behind why he and his staff were selected to work on this case. It took me a long time to get the whole story.

Vernon Presley, Elvis's father, did not believe the findings of Dr. Jerry Francisco, the medical examiner of Shelby County, Tennessee. Francisco, without conducting an autopsy, had signed out Elvis's death as due to cardiac arrhythmia. This is used to describe a lot of conditions of irregular heartbeats, but the only way to prove it is when the patient is alive and hooked up to an EKG. Arrhythmia certainly can kill a person, but with the exception of a timely EKG hookup, there is no way to establish that, even with an autopsy. Francisco was guessing.

Mr. Presley wanted to know what killed his son, so he called Dr. Eric Muirhead, the chief of pathology at Baptist Hospital, where Elvis had been taken after he was found collapsed. Mr. Presley requested and paid for an autopsy conducted by Dr. Muirhead. Muirhead was assisted by Dr. Harold Sexton and other staff pathologists, and the autopsy was witnessed by Dr. Francisco, who requested to be there.

They found no anatomical cause of death. No cause was what Dr. Francisco wanted to hear, that is, nothing to prove his guess was wrong. Since autopsy findings can't eliminate cardiac arrhythmia as a cause of death, he felt vindicated. In fact, so vindicated that he left the autopsy and met with the press, who were waiting outside the hospital for Dr. Muirhead. Francisco told the press the autopsy had confirmed his findings. Meanwhile, Muirhead and his team were collecting samples for toxicology in anticipation of finding the real cause of death. For some time, Mr. Presley had been concerned with his son's use of drugs and had tried to intervene. He had even hired two private detectives to check out if, how, and where Elvis was getting drugs.

Dr. Muirhead was reluctant to release the toxicology sample to Dr. Francisco's laboratory, an otherwise normal procedure. Instead he sent the samples to Dr. Norman Weissman at Bioscience, a private laboratory in Van Nuys, California. After Weissman completed his work and reported his finding to Dr. Muirhead, Vernon Presley asked that the finding be confirmed by other experts. Cravey and Bryan Finkle of the Center for Human Toxicology in Salt Lake City, Utah, were singled out as the foremost authorities in the country to confirm the tests.

Each toxicology report confirmed that Elvis had numerous drugs in his system at the time of his death. Individually, none of the drugs should have harmed Elvis. He had levels of codeine, methaqualone, and ethinamate, all downers, that were above the target therapeutic levels, but each was below fatal levels. The problem was that ten active drugs were in his system. There were therapeutic levels of six other drugs plus a substantial level of the physiologically active metabolite of diazepam. Elvis died—he is dead—from taking acceptable doses of too many types of similarly acting drugs, an incident forensic scientists classify as being due to polypharmacy.

## Classification of Drugs by Physiological Activity and Behavioral Effect

Perhaps the most useful information for purposes of general interest is to understand what the drug or poison is expected to do to the user. The following is a brief description of the categories of this classification method. There are thousands of drugs and poisons. I'll discuss some of the more common drugs. Some drugs may fit into more than one category, depending on the blood and tissue levels reached. For example, a drug may produce desirable stimulation at its ideal therapeutic level but cause hallucinations at a toxic level.

The 2001 Drug Enforcement Administration's report on the twenty-five most frequently seized and analyzed drugs is a good indication of street use or popularity or, perhaps, the drugs used the most by people who got caught. The notations DEA-15 and DEA-3 are the rankings of these two drugs. Cannabis compounds are DEA-1.

*Stimulants*

***The Amphetamines.*** Amphetamine (DEA-15) and methamphetamine (DEA-3) and other closely related compounds are called sympathomimetic amines.

Sympathomimetic amines are man-made, synthesized compounds that mimic the ability of adrenaline (epinephrine) to produce norepinephrine. Norepinephrine, in part, is meant to stimulate the sympathetic nervous system in moments of need, such as fear, stress, or exercise, to prepare the body to respond and be more alert. Amphetamines do the same but for much longer periods of time.

Amphetamine has two possible molecular orientations, called optical isomers; one right-hand view, dextro; and one left, levo. Dextroamphetamine is more physiologically active than levo. Unless it is specified as the dextro isomer, amphetamine is usually marketed as a mixture, called racemic amphetamine. Dexedrine is a trade name for dextroamphetamine.

Methamphetamine, based on a survey by the DEA is the most frequent street drug seized and analyzed in the western states and third over the entire country after cannabis compounds and cocaine. Street/slang names for methamphetamine are endless but the most common are still meth, crystal, crystal meth, crank, and speed.

Tolerance or reckless abandon leads to increased uses and larger single doses. The two most critical toxic effects are, first, hallucinations, then drug-induced psychosis. Drug-induced psychosis leads to all forms of aggressive antisocial behavior, including violence. High blood levels of amphetamine also result in elevated body temperature. Body temperature can rise well over 104 degrees. At 106 to 108 degrees, unless cooled down artificially, the subject will become comatose and die. The phrase "fried his brain" graphically describes the process.

Over-the-counter diet pills contain large quantities of phenylpropanolamine, an amphetamine-related drug. It is also found in many nonprescription cold medications. It is not an effective stimulant, but it does kill appetite for some people, and dries up your nose whether you want it to or not.

Deaths due to long-term use of diet pills, regardless of the sources, are often caused by loss of body fluids and chemical imbalance called electrolytic imbalance. Excessive elimination of water by urination can remove necessary electrolytes that control vital involuntary functions, and unless they are replaced, the resulting shock to the system can be fatal. Similarly, extreme weight loss that includes muscle over a period of time can produce ketones that alter the pH of the system, causing acidosis and, if unchecked, death.

*Cocaine.* (DEA-2) is extracted from the leaves of the coca plant, *Erythroxylon coca*. Seconds after it enters the blood, it acts as a powerful stimulant to the central nervous system. Applied topically, that is, directly on the skin, it is a simple local analgesic. It is related to a number of "caines," for example, lidocaine (Xylocaine) and procaine (Novocain). Until recently, cocaine was routinely used by physicians and dentists as a topical analgesic. It may still be in use in some areas, but since its availability is controlled, other chemicals have been substituted by most clinicians.

The classic method of ingesting cocaine is inhalation. The street term is "to snort." Cocaine is absorbed through the mucous membrane inside the nasal passages. Once it penetrates the outer membrane, it can enter the capillaries filled with moving blood and it is on its way to the brain. Heavy users and addicts have found that injection directly into the veins is more effective and efficient.

*Free Base.* Needles scare some people. They leave scars (tracks) and may transmit the AIDS virus. Additionally, heavy users can waste some of this stuff just putting it up their nose. Someone who knew a little chemistry realized that the ionic state, the free form or free base of cocaine, would burn slowly. While burning, all the fumes could then be sucked into the mouth and lungs, where they would be absorbed simultaneously for a flashlike high.

The process begins by dissolving the cocaine salt in mildly basic water. The salt form changes in the water to the ionic form, the free base. This free base becomes much more soluble in an organic solvent, if one is present, than in water. Ether, essentially insoluble in water, is often used for this purpose. The two solvents are mixed for a moment and then allowed to separate into two layers. Once it is isolated from the water, the ether contains the free base and will dry down quickly. The street name for the solid residue is rock cocaine.

This process can be extraordinarily dangerous. Ether is extremely volatile and highly flammable—explosive, in fact. An anxious and eager user who tries to smoke the free base while any ether is still around is in for a big surprise. Ask comedian Richard Pryor, who suffered serious facial injuries from burning ether.

A less dangerous but less sophisticated and hence less effective free-basing process is common today. No flammable solvent is required. The cocaine salt is dissolved in water and the water is saturated with bicarbonate—that is, plain old soda. The fluid is heated and then allowed to cool down. At first a scum appears on top of the liquid. As cooling continues, the scum solidifies into a flat disk of rock cocaine. The major difference between the two processes is that the second type of "rock" is about half bicarbonate, while the older process was capable of producing almost pure cocaine.

Rock cocaine is smoked by packing a chunk of it into a tube, usually glass, tight against a wad of brass wool of the type used to clean pots and pans. The tube is held in the mouth and the other end heated briefly. A flame from a butane cigarette lighter or a small propane torch vaporizes the chemical as the user sucks in abruptly. Street officers are finding bottles of 151-proof rum included in the paraphernalia of smokers. Since some of the coke condenses inside the tube, they use the rum to dissolve and collect the cocaine for later use.

Cocaine toxicity and death can occur unexpectedly and is not necessarily dose-related. A particular blood level is not necessary to produce marked symptoms. The individual and the individual's susceptibility to and experience with the drug seems to be more at fault than the dose. Reported side effects include hallucinations, delusions, and paranoia. These symptoms add up to psychotic behavior.

Death due directly to cocaine is attributed to the cardio toxic nature of the drug. Without warning, on the first use or after repeated uses, independent of the blood level, some users drop dead very soon after ingestion. Cocaine, in any event, is believed to interfere with neurological transmissions. The autonomic nervous system, by means of the sympathetic nervous system (SNS), regulates the body so we don't have to remember to perform vital functions like breathing. The rate of the heartbeat is regulated by the SNS. In cocaine deaths a garbled message may be what causes the heart muscle to rapidly twitch, called fibrillation, rather than maintaining its proper rhythmic pace. Blood does not move properly, if at all, during fibrillation, causing unconsciousness, and unless proper medical aid is available to restart the heart, death occurs.

Hypersensitivity, an allergic reaction resulting in anaphylactic shock, has also been blamed for cocaine deaths. The user, for an unknown reason, is sensitized to cocaine during an exposure, not necessarily the first one. The next time the drug is used, a fatal episode can occur.

## Depressants

**The Alcohols.** Numerous alcohols, all liquids, all toxic, are readily available. The least toxic alcohol, the only one recommended for human consumption, is ethyl alcohol or ethanol, usually referred to simply as alcohol. Alcohol is by all accounts a drug capable of providing a feeling of euphoria. In small amounts, it is a *miracle* drug of sorts, in that it fulfills a wide range of needs. People drink alcohol to cheer themselves up or to intensify their courage. Some drink hoping to forget or expecting to relax. If you have a need, alcohol has a way of making you think you have filled it. It is not a stimulant, though. It simply lowers one's inhibitions.

Alcohol is the product of the fermentation of grains or sugars. Wine and beer are fermented by naturally occurring yeast or by introducing yeast to the ingredients. Ethyl alcohol is fermented up to 14 percent in wine and 6 or 7 percent weight per volume in beer. Ethyl alcohol kills the yeast at the 14 percent range and fermentation is halted. Any beverage stronger than 14 percent is created by distillation to concentrate the alcohol, or by the direct addition of distilled pure ethyl alcohol to a beverage. Brandy is an example of a distilled beverage, and fortified wine is wine with alcohol added to it.

The amount of alcohol in beverages is expressed in different ways, by percent and by proof. The use of the word "proof" is based on the method used by early liquor merchants to validate the alcoholic strength of their product. Fearing that some vendors were diluting their booze below the standard 50 percent alcohol mix, containers would be randomly examined by sampling a small amount, dipping it in a wicklike apparatus, and lighting it with a flame. Mixtures below the standard would not burn. If it did burn, it was proof of the quantity of the alcohol. The 50 percent mixture was considered 100 proof. One percent is equal to 2 proof.

The alcohol in beer and wine is expressed in percent. Some liquors are labeled with the percent of the alcohol but most express the proof of the alcohol. Regardless of how it is described on the container, alcohol is alcohol. For purposes of further discussion, a *drink* is any mixture that contains a half ounce of 100 percent alcohol. For example, one twelve-ounce container of beer (as sold in California, 3.2 percent by weight or 4 percent by volume) contains about a half ounce of 100 percent alcohol, as does a four-ounce glass of 12.5 percent wine or a mixed drink containing one ounce of 100 proof alcohol.

Alcohol levels in the body can also be expressed by percentages or by describing the quantity of alcohol (by weight or volume) found in a quantity of blood (by volume). It may sound or look different, but it means exactly the same thing. California uses percentages. It is illegal to drive a motor vehicle with a blood alcohol level of 0.08 percent weight per volume (W/V), or greater; that is, the chemical weight of the alcohol found in a volume of blood. Other jurisdictions describe the weight of the alcohol in a volume of blood. Eighty milligrams per 100 milliliters describes the same level as 0.080 percent W/V (0.8 grams per liter).

The immediate toxic effect of alcohol is due only to the amount that reaches the brain, expressed as the blood alcohol level (BAL). Once consumed, alcohol enters the stomach and takes only moments to begin passing through the stomach lining and into the bloodstream. Once in the blood, the first molecules of alcohol need only seconds to reach the brain. As the concentration increases, the alcohol acts as a depressant to the central nervous system (CNS).

The absorption of a drink can be completed in twenty minutes if it is swallowed quickly and the stomach is nearly void of food, but can take forty to sixty minutes if the stomach is full. Following a brief drinking episode, the maximum depression to the CNS—that is, the highest blood alcohol level—will almost always peak during the first half of the absorption period.

Our circulatory system is a dynamic process taking only three to four minutes to complete one cycle. Alcohol in the stomach lining is swept up by the moving blood and carried and distributed to all water-containing tissue until an equal distribution occurs. If alcohol is consumed faster than it can be eliminated, the additional alcohol is added to that already distributed. As long as the BAL is increasing, the brain and tissue levels all increase proportionately.

While distribution is occurring, the liver recognizes the presence of alcohol and produces an enzyme, alcohol dehydrogenase, to detoxify the body by oxidizing alcohol. Once some alcohol is in the blood, it is being eliminated in an amount based on body weight. A 110-pound person will usually eliminate half the alcohol found in a drink in one hour. A 220-pound person can eliminate all the alcohol in one full drink in an hour.

Once the stomach and upper intestines are void of alcohol, the distribution process is reversed. During the blood's next pass through the body, the tissue levels are slightly higher than the blood and some amount of alcohol is reabsorbed from the tissue to bring the blood and tissue back into equilibrium. A healthy liver always has a lower alcohol level than the incoming blood, so it is accepting and destroying some alcohol as long as there is alcohol in the body. The kidneys and the expelled breath account for about 5 percent of the elimination figure.

Once consumption and absorption stop, there is a measurable reduction of 0.012 to 0.200 percent of the blood alcohol level per hour regardless of body weight. This means that a person with a 0.12 percent BAL will be alcohol-free in six to ten hours. It means that a driver booked into jail with a 0.24 percent BAL and released four hours later still has a BAL between 0.16 and 0.19 percent. Sleep does not change the elimination rate. Go to bed at midnight with a BAL of 0.16 percent and you will still have a BAL of 0.08 to 0.10 percent between six and seven A.M.

There is always someone, usually a defense attorney, who knows a person who "drinks like a fish and never gets drunk." Actually, it is possible for a person to drink large amounts of alcohol and never get drunk—for example, a fifth of booze a day and never get loaded. The drinker has to be very large and drink at a constant slow pace. A 250-pound man could consume 1.5 ounces of 84 proof every hour for the rest of his life. His failing liver would shorten his life, but it could be done. It is done, as a matter of fact. Heavy drinkers may start out fast, to get up to a blood level where they feel good, and then maintain that level by slowing their drinking pace. It would only take sixteen hours to drink the first fifth. But drink the fifth all at once and it could kill most people, even the heavy drinker. Fatalities due to CNS depression begin to occur at levels above 0.30 percent, and few people survive levels above 0.50 percent.

The long-range toxicity of alcohol is usually limited to heavy users and is often first apparent in disease to the liver. Continuous heavy use will cause a fatty liver (reversible if one stops drinking), and cirrhosis, an irreversible hardening of the tissue, making it ineffective. Since serious drinkers would rather drink than eat, an improper diet can accelerate the liver disease. A damaged liver that can't remove toxins leads to numerous other health problems.

**The Other Alcohols.** Other alcohols consumed accidentally or out of ignorance or desperation are highly toxic. Methyl alcohol (methanol) is metabolized to formic acid. Formic acid causes optical nerve damage often leading to permanent blindness. Isopropyl alcohol (Isopropanol), so-called rubbing alcohol, is less toxic than methanol but causes liver damage.

## Seductive-Hypnotics

**The Barbituric Acids.** Collectively called barbs for short, this group of drugs has fallen from favor of both users and abusers, for good reason. They are killers. Only the mildest of the group, phenobarbital, is routinely used to maintain and prevent epileptics from suffering seizures. Unaware of their addictive nature, physicians dispensed these compounds for years, placing many patients in jeopardy. Barbs gained popularity on the street, producing a calorie-free drunk. Their ultimate effect on the CNS mimicked that of alcohol.

Beginning with phenobarb, amyl, pento, and secobarb produce increased effects on the CNS. Their activity slows transmissions in the brain, in the case of phenobarb, nullifying the errant messages of the epileptic's brain. For emotionally stressed people using the stronger drugs, the effect was to curtail all thoughts, lulling them into sleep. But as with the other drugs discussed, users developed a tolerance to the drug, requiring larger and larger doses to reach the desired therapeutic threshold. In spite of tolerance, the toxic threshold was not significantly increased, placing heavy users in danger of toxic reaction.

Toxic symptoms included psychotic behavior. During the 1960s and 1970s incredibly violent crimes were committed by users under the influence of barbs. Hysteria, delusion, paranoia, and induced psychosis drove some people to kill, some to eat the flesh of their victims, and many to end their own lives by violent means.

Barbiturates, as a direct cause of death, kill the user by depressing the CNS to the point that breathing and the heartbeat are lowered below life-sustaining levels. Lack of oxygen to the brain, asphyxia, is the actual cause of death. Marilyn Monroe's death in 1963, after she ingested barbs, brought national attention to barb toxicity. Nevertheless, hundreds died from barbs after her death, many accidentally, many by suicidal intention, and some by the actions of intoxicated users.

Barbs, if consumed with alcohol in the system, produce a classic example of synergistic activity. Since some alcohol can still be in the system hours after drinking, the window of synergistic danger is elongated. Intoxicated drivers who for any reason mix barbs with alcohol may not have a clue to the degree of their impairment.

But perhaps the most unfortunate victims of alcohol/barb synergism were the folks who used barbs on a regular basis to go to sleep. Uninformed of the danger, these occasional drinkers came home from parties where they were served alcoholic drinks and took their regular dose of the pills to go to sleep, but never woke up.

*Chloral Hydrate.* Chloral hydrate, a sleep-inducing sedative, was the chemical in the notorious concoction called a Micky Finn, allegedly used to shanghai sailors, seduce women, and knock out private investigators in movies. Perhaps it was, but it would take a lot longer to put people to sleep than the fictional adaptation would imply. For the sake of screen time, directors instructed the actors to down the drink, look at the glass curiously, and instantly drop to their knees, taking one last "I wonder why I drank that drink" look at the villain before passing out. It would be boring to watch the actor for the several minutes required for the drug actually to take effect.

*Tranquilizers.* Early versions of this group of drugs weren't much safer than barbs. For example, a local dentist handed a patient, who was noticeably nervous, two capsules containing the tranquilizer meprobamate. She assumed that she was supposed to take them both right away. She did. Within a few minutes, after paying her bill and making another appointment, she left the office, loaded her two kids in her car, and prepared to drive away. She made a sweeping turn as she left her parking space, drove over the curb onto the sidewalk, then back onto the wrong side of the road as she hit several parked cars. She was never going more than five to ten miles per hour. A police officer spotted her and tried to get her to stop. She didn't until she struck his vehicle. She remembered none of her erratic driving.

The popularity of tranquilizers prompted a cornucopia of products:

Librium—chlordiazepoxide
Miltown and Equanil—meprobamates
Quaalude—methaqualone
Doriden—glutethimide
Valium—diazepam (DEA-10)
Klonopin or Rivotril—clonazepam (DEA-13)
Xanax—alprazolam (DEA-7)
Halcion—triazolam

When tranquilizers didn't solve all the problems, antidepressants helped:

Prozac—fluoxetine
Zoloft—sertraline
Paxil—paroxetine

Or antipsychotics:

Haldol—haloperdol
Risperdal—risperdone

Three of these drugs—alprazolam (DEA-7), diazepam (DEA-10), and clonazepam (DEA-13) are on the DEA's twenty-five most frequently identified drugs, as indicated.

*Analgesics*

Analgesics produce a narcotic effect, that is, they dull the senses and induce sleep. Opium, primarily from the poppy flower, *Papaver somniferum*, is the source of all the naturally occurring opiates—morphine, codeine, plus more than twenty other lesser known related alkaloids. The opiates, like most of the synthetic painkillers, prevent the sensation of pain by blocking the receptor sites in the brain that would otherwise receive the signal that something is hurting.

*Semi-Synthetics-Opoids*

**Heroin** (DEA-4), diacetyl morphine, thought to be the most addictive of the opiates, is synthesized from morphine. Just after World War I, heroin was believed to be a miracle drug because it cured recovering servicemen of the addiction to morphine. The patients no longer needed any painkillers other than heroin.

Toxicologists know now that heroin is metabolized by the body and converted back to morphine within moments of absorption into the blood. Users prefer heroin because they claim there is some heightened sensation of relief following the injection of heroin that is missing if morphine is used. Other than that, the two are the same.

Heroin, the parent drug, is never found in the body unless death occurs during the injection process. It may be found unchanged in the tissue at the injection site.

It is not unusual to find a user dead, with the needle still stuck in the arm. Usually the death is due to a so-called hot shot—an injection that may have three or four times, maybe more, the usual dose. Since the illicit production and distribution of heroin lacks quality control procedures, the user never really knows how much drug is about to be injected. Even when the user has experienced a dose from an identical source, the supply is not necessarily homogeneous, and the next injection may be grossly different.

The term "stepping on" means dilution, usually 100 percent. The supplier, to double profit, will step on the stuff one or more times. The intermediate dealer will undoubtedly step on it again, and then the street vendor will step on it before the product is sold to a user. It doesn't seem too likely that a hot shot would ever occur, but they do, possibly because of incomplete mixing. There is always the possibility that a hot shot is a planned homicide. Not too likely, but possible. If the dead user is a loner, the apparatus, needle, syringe, tourniquet, and spoon should be nearby.

*Oxycodone* (DEA-8) is synthesized from opium and was prescribed for years under the name Percodan, and others. Recently, a drug company developed a method of packaging oxycodone as a time-released tablet, Oxy Contin. One tablet contains a day's dosage, a true convenience for people in pain. However, crushing a tablet and injecting as much as 80 mgs in one shot creates a heroinlike rush. And like heroin, it kills on occasion, over two hundred at the time of this writing. The lust for the drug has motivated numerous crimes—armed robberies of pharmacies and burglaries of medical facilities. In August 2001 the manufacturer of Oxy Contin announced a solution for the reported abuse of their product. They will add coated pellets of Naltrexone, an antagonist to narcotics and alcohol. The coating will not dissolve in the digestive system if left intact. However, if the tablet is crushed, so will the pellets of Naltrexone. The ball is back in the court of the dopers.

*Hydrocodone* (DEA-9) is also synthesized from opium and was prescribed for years under the name Vicodin.

*Meperidine,* or Demerol, is a far stronger analgesic comparable to morphine. In fact, it is so much like morphine, it too is usually the target when a doctor's office is burglarized. If a physician or other health care employee becomes a drug addict, meperidine is usually the problem drug.

*Fentanyl,* and its related compounds, is a synthetic analgesic. It is, by weight, many more times physiologically active than its medicinal equivalent, morphine. Due to the nature of the basic molecule, it can be readily modified by reacting it with other chemicals to construct a series of similar compounds. Most of the series, all analogs of fentanyl, become progressively more active as the molecules become more complex.

*Other analgesics.* Aspirin is by far the most common analgesic in the Western world, followed by acetaminophen, the active ingredient contained in Tylenol, and ibuprofen. Of the three, aspirin has the greatest potential for acute toxicity in the event of an accidental or intentional overdose. Its chemical name is acetylsalicylic acid, a weak organic acid. Nevertheless, in high doses it is acidic enough to cause a chemical acidosis, resulting in death.

Acetaminophen (DEA-22) is used for patients who have problems with aspirin. In overdoses it can be fatal. Although it is seldom mentioned, the combination of alcohol consumption and acetaminophen use had been described as long ago as the 1950s as causing damage to the kidneys.

Ibuprofen acts as an anti-inflammatory chemical, reducing pain by reducing swelling or congestion in damaged tissues and muscles.

Propoxyphene, (DEA-21), sold under the name Darvon, was marketed as a nonaddicting painkiller comparable to codeine. This prescription drug was often combined with aspirin, and later acetaminophen. When used on occasion, following dental work, for example, it was considered safe and usually effective. When used on a regular basis—for example, treating addicts with the drug to get them off opiates—problems were reported, including patients becoming equally addicted to the cure. Some addicts died who were believed to have developed a cardio toxic sensitivity to the drug.

*Hallucinogens/Psychotomimetics*

*Lysergic Acid Diethylamide* (DEA-14). Although LSD was not known to the forensic scientific community at large until the early 1960s, its use is well-documented as an experimental drug since its discovery by Dr. A. Hoffman, working for Sandoz in Switzerland in 1938. Hoffman was working on derivatives of ergot, a fungus found on rye seeds and other grains. Extracts of ergot have been used as medicine for years, but little was known about the deadly effects of the fungus when it was consumed as a contaminant in breads and cereals.

The twenty-fifth derivative isolated by Hoffman was LSD. It was known as LSD-25 for a number of years. During the 1950s it was available, to some extent, to psychiatrists and psychologists for treating specific disorders. Some saw it as a mind-expanding chemical while others expressed great fears when some users developed deep psychoses. Eventually, in the early 1960s, Dr. Timothy Leary introduced LSD to the college campus, first as a mind-enhancing chemical and later as a party drug.

Until the mid-1960s all LSD was the legitimate form, a Sandoz product, and was relatively rare. It did not take long for entrepreneurial chemists to learn the process of synthesizing the drug to make it available for the street. We saw our first known case, submitted to the crime lab on sugar cubes, in 1966. Fortunately, our chief forensic toxicologist, Robert Cravey, was aware of the growing interest in the drug and had already acquired a pure sample from Sandoz as a standard. There was no published analytical data. We used the standard to create our own instrumental information, making it possible to identify the evidence.

There were no known blood or urine tests for LSD or, for that matter, many of the other hallucinogenic compounds, until the early 1970s. A laboratory in Riverside, California, developed a test, but it required large samples of body fluids, usually available only in death investigations. Further, the process was sensitive to many other chemicals that produced false positives. Today, and since the 1980s, there are reliable laboratory blood tests for LSD.

*Peyote, Lophorphora williamsii,* is an unattractive cactus, native to the southwestern United States and parts of Mexico. It contains alkaloids, mescaline by far the most active. Sections of the dried plant, called buttons, can be chewed directly or the mescaline can be extracted from the plant by brewing it in water. Mescaline is reported to produce wild colorful hallucinations as well as trancelike sleep, nausea, loss of appetite, and, of course, psychosis.

The plant is considered a ceremonial necessity in the religious practices of several Native American tribes who first inhabited the Southwest. During the 1970s, several tribes formed the Native Church of North America, challenged the restrictions on the use of mescaline in their church's services, and won their case.

William Emboden, in his book *Narcotic Plants*, reports that many other cacti contain mescaline in abundance and are used for similar purposes in the mountains of South America and elsewhere. Emboden tells many fascinating stories—mythical, ceremonial, and modern—focusing on people's quest to escape boredom through the use of narcotic plants.

Peyote and mescaline are controlled substances, illegal to everyone other than the priests of the Native Church of North America. As evidence, it is confiscated as living plants, dried, broken into buttons, or ground into powder. The ground material is most often packaged in large clear gelatin capsules.

I have never seen a street sample sold as synthetic or extracted pure mescaline that ever actually contained any mescaline. The active drug in these samples was always phencyclidine (PCP) or a mixture of PCP with a little LSD.

*Phencyclidine* (DEA-12). This chemical was introduced as a short-acting analgesic, so powerful that an awake patient would feel no pain during minor surgery. It was used widely until the reports of serious side effects accumulated, offering a warning to alert clinicians. The most dangerous reported side effect was concurrent hallucinations. There were some reports of delayed hallucinations, flashbacks days or even weeks later. The drug, for human use, was withdrawn from the market, but it continues to be used on animals as a sleep-inducing tranquilizer.

PCP was introduced as a recreational drug, reportedly by

a branch of the Hell's Angels. The drug's connection with this group was responsible for its nickname—angel dust.

PCP is a short-acting drug with the potential of producing hallucinations. Heavy doses intensify all the drug's symptoms, which include drug-induced paranoia, psychosis, and hyperthermia. Its painkilling effect adds a macabre dimension to its use as a party drug. It can also cause superhuman strength.

True and drug-induced psychotics have superhuman strength because their nervous system, at the extremities and in the joints, doesn't register pressure or pain. One of the most infamous cases, before all the facts were known about PCP toxicity, occurred when a Los Angeles city police officer responded to a field call and found the suspect nude and, by their description, freaking out. All attempts to subdue him failed. When he eventually charged the officer (with a baseball bat), he was shot several times and died. Witnesses claimed he was shot unnecessarily. The police officer said he had tried all he could to subdue the suspect and as he shot he feared for his life. Toxicology tests identified PCP in his autopsy samples.

Some years later, in the Rodney King case, the officers stated that they believed King to be under the influence of PCP based on his initial wild behavior, followed by his apparent indifference to the pain of their batons and their Taser gun. What they reported seeing was exactly what they were trained to expect, but they should have been trained to know that a person on PCP (or cocaine) is not going to respond to pain. Clearly, after the first few hits, with the number of officers present, they should have backed off and tried a different approach. In fact, lab tests failed to identify any PCP in King's blood.

The recurring hallucinations experienced days or weeks after the use of PCP can be explained as either a true neurological abnormality due to nerve damage or the release of the drug that has been stored in fatty tissues. PCP is absorbed and retained in body fat as the parent drug. At autopsy, fat is the best sample to establish long-term PCP use.

Unusual cases of death due to drowning are often attributed indirectly to the toxic effects of PCP, or methamphetamine. With predictable common factors, the victims' bodies, fully clothed or nude, are recovered from an unlikely watery location. The death scene is often a treacherous ice-cold surf, a muddy pond, or a shallow pool not considered suitable for recreational swimming. On some occasions the victims have been seen walking trancelike into the water and disappearing.

What might appear to be a suicide is frequently a hyperthermic PCP user who somehow instinctively realizes the need to cool off quickly and takes advantage of whatever cool place is available. The Orange County cases have always involved water, but in some locations snow or even refrigerators or freezers may be involved. Unfortunately, because of the other toxic effects, the victim doesn't anticipate any danger or feel any sensation of cooling down, and so doesn't make any attempt to escape. These cases should be classified as accidental deaths, and would be if aware investigators insisted on forensic toxicological analyses to determine the presence of PCP.

## Other Hallucinogens and Cannabis Compounds

**Ketamine.** Known as Special K or K, ketamine is a general anesthetic for veterinary use. It is said to create out-of-body visions and hallucinations similar to PCP, with the visual effects of LSD.

**Marijuana** (DEA-1). The hemp plant, *Cannabis sativa l.*, produces a resinous material that contains several related chemicals said to cause hallucinations, in particular delta-9 tetrahydrocannabinol (THC). William Emboden classifies the active ingredient as hallucinogenic. Nevertheless, most people who use marijuana say it does not produce visions or cause a bad trip. That's because the leafy material used in marijuana cigarettes seldom has enough THC to cause serious intoxication, much less hallucination. To solve this problem, marijuana devotees have developed growing programs that greatly increase the amount of resin on the plant.

They began their quest by studying the sex life of the marijuana plants.

Male and female marijuana plants are not born equal. The botanical term is dioecious, which means two plants with distinctly different flowers. The female plant is superior and much richer in the intoxicating resin, which it creates to attract and trap the male's pollen.

The immature female fruit—the seed or achene—is surrounded by a husk that is another type of modified leaf, called a bract. As the reproductive urge develops, two elongated organs called pistils emerge from the bract and reach out, like antennas, to collect pollen. The two pistils are oozing with the sticky intoxicating resin, ready to trap any pollen. The bract, working in unison, also produces resin, which would attract pollen. Once the female plant is pollinated, the secretion of resin subsides somewhat.

Thus, marijuana growers try to prevent the completion of the reproductive cycle. As soon as any plant develops the male characteristics—light yellow flowers—they remove the plant. What remains is a field full of young female plants with only one thing on their cellular minds. Sex. As the female matures, the pistils emerge from the bract. Both are covered with adequate resin, but nothing happens. The plant responds by producing more resin. Still nothing happens. In desperation, the frustrated flower oozes and oozes resin, to no avail. The entire plant becomes coated with resin, with the bract so gooey they stick to each other. The Spanish call this deprivation sinsemilla, from sin, "without," and semilla, "seed."

All the leafy parts of the plants are harvested. Sinsemilla is, of course, a premium product on the street. In Thailand these flowering stalks are entwined with thin thread before they are cut from the plant and then kept separate from the rest of the leaves. About six inches long, they are called Thai sticks. Smoking sinsemilla, Thai sticks, or hashish, the concentrated resin, depleted of much of the plant material, may indeed produce hallucinations.

*Hashish.* Heavy-duty users of marijuana prefer hashish. The story goes that the name hashish is derived in part from a gang of thirteenth-century Persian assassins who called themselves ashishins. They gained the courage needed for their deadly work by smoking the stuff. Many authors, including Emboden, associate the words "assassins" and "hashish" with a powerful Middle East warlord, al-Hasan, and the ashishin gang he employed to do his dirty work.

The classic method of producing hashish involves field workers who walk through the rows of sexually mature flowering plants while wearing jackets with sleeves made of suede. The suede is scraped periodically and the trappings are compressed into a brick-shaped bar.

*Hash Oil* is manufactured by dissolving pulverized marijuana or low-grade hashish in an organic solvent and filtering out the remaining cellular particles of plant material. The process serves the dealer more than the user since the oil is more difficult to use than the solid hashish. The dealer has the advantage of disguising large quantities of the oil as legitimate products. Additionally, most laboratories rely on the visual identification of marijuana related evidence by their botanical parts, the single cellular hairs and glandular hairs. When these components are missing, the oil may not be recognized unless chemical tests are conducted.

*Psilocybin* is a chemical contained in the *Psilocybe* mushroom and a few others from the same family. As a group, they earned the name magic mushrooms during the 1960s. The drug's effects include hallucinations similar to peyote but without as many distressing side effects. Magic mushrooms can get a user into trouble, particularly if the search for them includes sampling other varieties. Some mushrooms can be fatal.

*MDA* (DEA-18). Methylethylene dioxyamphetamine and MDMA (DEA-6), methylethylene dioxymethamphetamine, have been sold as the love drug and as Ecstasy. MDMA is said to act as a hallucinogen, a stimulant, and has aphrodisiac qualities, perhaps explaining its popularity at nightclubs and rare parties.

*DOM.* Called STP by the street people of the 1960s, this was a short-acting hallucinogen that quickly fell out of favor after a few users deep-fried their brains. It was billed as the lunch break trip since the effect lasted for only thirty minutes. Some of the users lasted less than that.

*CAT.* Methcathinone is an addictive stimulant that after frequent use is said to cause delusions and hallucinations. This drug has been known since 1957 but didn't make it to the street until 1989.

### Designer Drugs

This is a catchy name applied to controlled substances intentionally modified to evade the law. For example, amphetamine and methamphetamine are named as controlled substances. A clever chemist can hang a free radical here or there on some parent drug such as amphetamine and create a new compound. The new chemical may or may not have any physiological activity, but in any case, it is not listed as a controlled substance. MDA and MDMA, described above, are examples. They may be more dangerous in some ways than their parent drug, but they were sold openly by the owners of bars and other businesses for years until they made the controlled list.

*China White.* One of the most deadly episodes of designer drug uses began in Orange County in 1979. In all, nine people in the county and at least 120 nationally died. It took more than a year to find out why. In the beginning, the word on the street was that a new form of heroin was making the rounds. It was called China white. But it wasn't heroin, it was methyl fentanyl.

### Date Rape Drugs

The three drugs listed below have been associated with sexual assaults. All are considered modern day knockout drops. They have resulted in deaths.

*Clonazepam* (DEA-13)—Klonopin, Rivotril (Mexico)
*Flunitrazepam*—Rohypnol
**Gamma Hydrozybutyrate**, known as GHB

*New Fads*

How about smoking a cigarette that was dipped in formaldehyde? It's called a wet stick or fry, or just wet. How about crazy? In some cases the cigarette is also dipped in PCP. Smoking that wet stick, users claim, causes hallucinations, delusions, a feeling of invincibility, increased tolerance to pain, anger, paranoia, distaste for meat for six hours to three days, and an urge to take off one's clothes. Well, duh! Wet sticks go for about twenty dollars each. I don't know if that includes the PCP.

**The Bottom Line**

Toxicologists are a special breed. They work with an array of body parts and coroner's samples that under the best of circumstances are disgusting just to think about. Along these lines, a reporter asked one of our toxicologists to describe what makes his job different than other people's. He answered: "Toxicologists wash their hands before going to the bathroom."

## chapter ten

# Evidence From the Coroner

## Introduction

Every death is a mystery. Sometimes the mystery is solved based on the prognosis of an attending physician. However, a prognosis is a guess, nothing more. All deaths require a certificate stating the cause. When no physician is willing to offer a prognosis—and in some specific situations, a coroner must become involved. And the coroner must decide first whether to perform an autopsy.

An autopsy and the confirming lab work are the only means of actually determining the cause of death. Even then, on occasion the cause isn't always absolute and the death remains a mystery. Surprisingly, autopsies are not mandatory, even in suspicious deaths, but they are almost always conducted if the death was at the hands of another. If, however, the investigator's suspicions are not aroused, there may be no autopsy and an injustice might occur.

If there is a way to guarantee a fail-safe scene investigation of suspicious deaths, it is the team approach described in Chapter 2. The following case reveals the importance of the coroner investigator's opinion as a member of the team.

CRIME SCENE:

## Blood Suckers Loose in Newport Beach

When the police department dispatcher called me, her voice was full of excitement, saying things faster than I could write them down. One line I didn't even try to write down, maybe because I didn't believe what I was hearing: "Blood suckers are loose in Newport Beach! Hurry."

I turned off the Coast Highway and sped down the hill in the direction of the ocean. This area of coastal cliffs and beaches is collectively called the California Riviera, the most desirable section of the most desirable district in Newport Beach: Corona Del Mar. Every house was built low to the ground and closer than usual to the curbline, assuring each resident some view of the ocean and a big backyard. There was no need to check the house numbers. The one I was looking for was undoubtedly the one with a fleet of police cars parked in front of it. Any doubt that I had the wrong house was erased when I recognized one of our deputy coroners standing in a sunny spot at the front of the house. I drove past the long row of police units and parked half a block away.

Each step I took back to the house made it clearer that the deputy coroner was acting very strangely. He was smiling. Not a happy smile, but more of a sarcastic grin.

"What does it look like in there?" I asked.

"It's a godawful mess," he said. "Your friends Thompson and Epstein are in there already and will tell you what they think it is, you can count on that."

The first thing I noticed when I stepped into the entrance hall was a very pungent, very sour odor. The stink, I would learn, was one part stale cigarette smoke, one part stale booze, and the dominant part, the familiar acrid odor of drying blood. Blood on the edge of rotting has a sour, unpleasant smell.

Thompson was waiting for me just inside the front door. He got straight to the point: "I'll show you the body. She's in the back bedroom."

Despite what I'd been told about the crime scene, it was hard not to show shock as we walked through the house. It was a bizarre tour of a crime scene unlike any I had ever seen. That is no exaggeration. There was blood everywhere.

We walked quickly, first past the dining room. It was filled with an extra large table and surrounded by several chairs. The unusual part of this scene was the six or eight drinking glasses full of what had to be blood. They were arranged in a manner not unlike a morning after a party. If you are a vampire, that is. A uniformed officer was taking photographs of the glasses as we passed. Thompson led on, saying nothing, not stopping or looking back.

We approached the kitchen, on the right opposite the dining room. At the entrance to the kitchen, the tiled floor abutted the wall-to-wall carpet that covered the rest of the living areas. I could see that the tile was covered with blood patterns, trails, smears, and splatters. I could see over the top of a two-level breakfast bar/desk counter combination into the kitchen. There were more glasses filled with blood on the kitchen counter and the breakfast bar. The kitchen light was bright, and I could see the appearance of the blood much better. It looked older than it smelled. Its color was more brown than red, and for the first time I was close enough to notice that the blood in a glass on the desk next to the phone was frothy, like milk gets if you blow air into it through a straw.

We continued our swift pace. Three steps later I got a quick view of a bathroom. The floor, the sink, the toilet lid, and what I could see of the bathtub in that brief glance were covered with blood.

We reached the bedroom. I was prepared for almost anything except what I saw. I expected to see body parts strewn about or perhaps a mutilated corpse dangling from a makeshift meat hook and bloody graffiti warning of future crimes scrawled across the walls. None of that. The victim's body was spread-eagle, faceup on a king-size bed, in a resting position more like that of sleep than of a final death struggle. The only thing missing from the subtle stereotypic ritualistic movie scene were the hundred or so burning candles surrounding the body. She was fully clothed. There was no visible trauma. Thompson broke the deadly silence.

"You may have noticed, we are looking at a very weird situation. I remember a case you guys had. Was it last year? The Hurd guy, where he and his dope-crazed buddies ate the heart and the flesh of their victim. They're all in jail, aren't they?"

The shock treatment was over. Now it was down to the serious job of figuring out what the hell had happened there. Before I could say anything, Thompson added, "I got some problems. This lady lived alone. There are no witnesses. No neighbor saw any activity around here for the past few days. The media somehow found out about all the blood and they want to interview me. Even our own dispatcher is telling people unbelievable bullshit about the scene. But my biggest problem is Toe Tags out front there. Your deputy coroner is trying to kiss this off as a natural death. You've got to talk to that guy."

A natural death? The deputy must have been really sticking it to Thompson, trying to set him off. Talking to the deputy was a good idea anyway. Our deputy coroners were all trained in the changes of the body after death, and would at least be able to estimate a time of death. From what I could see of the blood, some of it dry and some of it still liquid, the scene was fairly fresh. The odor I had described was powerful but not putrid. Until that moment I hadn't thought about the temperature in the house. That would affect the drying of blood and the decomposition of the body to some extent. The house, if anything, was cool. No one had opened any of the windows for fresh air. These cops knew not to alter the scene in spite of the odor. I made a mental note to check the thermostat, something I should have done when I first entered. Always note the conditions before someone changes them, lights on or off, I reminded myself. Even things like the mail, the last food served, or the newspaper last picked up can help establish basic time-of-death information. That would have to wait now. I wanted to make a much closer study of the bedroom and the victim.

It turns out there was nothing remarkable about the rest of the bedroom other than the blood on the carpet. The staining was not as heavy as I had seen in the other rooms. The body lacked even subtle trauma. Her hands showed no cuts or scratches, although there was evidence of older injuries, bruises that were yellowing on the backs of her hands and on her forearms. She was a heavy smoker, indicated by the staining on her fingers, not to mention an ashtray full of cigarette butts on the bed stand.

There was what looked like traces of dried blood in the creases of her skin where the upper and lower lips meet. That's not unusual. Regardless of the reason a person is dying—natural, suicide, or homicide—near the time of death, purging of body fluids is common.

After viewing the body I looked at the bathroom I'd seen on the way to the bedroom. It would be difficult to estimate the amount of blood scattered about this room and the rest of the house. A controlled experiment measuring the area of free-flowing blood could help, but that would take time, perhaps days.

I looked into the toilet bowl. It was full of watered-down blood. The sink basin was covered with dry blood, but redder than what I had seen in the glasses. The tub had a lot more blood in it than I'd thought when I glanced in earlier. There was another ashtray filled with cigarette butts.

The eerie feeling about this scene intensified rapidly. The question raising its ugly head was: Could all this blood come from just one person? As I said, some of it looked old and some fresher. Maybe two or more victims were done in, with some time in between. Maybe there was another victim. Or maybe this victim was worked on, with days in between. No one had mentioned the possibility of other victims, but the thought had to be going through their minds, too. Collecting and typing representative samples of these numerous stains could establish if there was more than one bleeder, but that could take several days. Epstein was standing at the doorway to the bathroom, close enough that I could ask him without shouting out my concern.

"Thompson said this lady lived alone," I said.

"Has the rest of this place been checked out for other victims?"

"Hey, we looked everywhere, garage, car trunk, other rooms, backyard, you name it, we looked. Nada. We've been here for a while, you know, waiting for you. Would you believe the coroner guy got here almost as fast as we called his office? We never figured he'd get here before you, but it turns out he had just finished a call in Laguna and got here in less than five minutes. They're never around when you need them. Right away he started telling us we were full of shit."

Their deep-seated distrust of the coroner was still evident despite years of team-building meetings. Every city police department had agreed to comply with the law requiring immediate notification of questioned deaths to the coroner. Several always had. Newport had reluctantly agreed, and until now things had smoothed out pretty nicely. Whatever was going on between Thompson and the deputy coroner was reopening an old wound.

The amount of blood in the bathroom concerned me, and the extent of the blood in the kitchen convinced me that we would find another victim. More than just the glasses were filled with blood. Every possible container, except the liquor bottles, held the same frothy-looking blood I had noticed earlier. There were more bottles than I'd realized at first glance. All were unsealed and two were empty. Two ashtrays were full of cigarette butts. A lot of partying going on. I noticed fingerprint powder on the bottles. Someone was busy at work.

I hadn't looked closely at the phone until now. There was blood on the dial and on the headset, and an open personal phone book next to the phone. Coincidentally, I recognized one of the names on the page, a local doctor whom NBPD called when they needed to draw blood from suspected drunk drivers.

The blood patterns on the kitchen floor didn't indicate much motion. That was contrary to what you would expect during a violent confrontation. The lack of struggle by the victim could be explained easily enough. The number of glasses around the dining room table indicated not one, but a gang of attackers, who could easily contain the victim. That was a scary thought.

Throughout California—in Los Angeles, San Bernardino, and San Francisco, in particular—indications of increased satanic cult activities were on the rise. I had attended training programs where crime scene photographs were displayed documenting human and animal sacrifices where blood was consumed in a ritualistic induction ceremony conducted by a high priest of the cult. The only thing missing so far from this scene was the trademark of these cults, the pentagram, Satan's sign, a five-point star inside a circle. They are often found finger-painted around the scene using some of the sacrificial blood. The horrible consequences of the scene were getting more and more scary. I needed a breath of fresh air. On my way to the front door I looked around the entrance hall one more time. And there it was, right on the wall in plain sight: the thermostat. I just hadn't noticed it on my way in. It was set to Off. That's why it was so cool in the house.

Outside, the deputy coroner watched me take my first deep breath of fresh air. You learn to appreciate clean air in this line of work. He was still smiling, an incredible feat, I thought, considering he had been kept waiting for over an hour. He had a lot of work to do once the scene investigation was completed. He still had to arrange for the deceased to be transported to an autopsy site and then schedule an autopsy.

He beckoned me closer. I considered that unusual. Then he said two words I didn't understand. He was talking Greek.

"Esophageal varices. This woman died due to esophageal varices. There's no murder here. It is a natural death. It may be a scene, but it is not a crime scene."

"They told me you were talking natural, but I thought they were kidding or you were just stroking them. You really think so?"

"Not think, I know. Hey, I get the picture. It is bizarre in there, certainly the most unusual case of this type that I have ever seen, but that doesn't change the facts. I've seen these cases before. Enough anyway to recognize this as just another esophageal varices. Did you notice all the booze bottles? That's a big clue. Did you notice the old bruises on her hands and arms? That happens to a drunk. They fall and hurt themselves. Heavy drinkers are susceptible to esophageal varices. Did you notice her phone book? It was turned to a page with her doctor's number on it. She was calling for help. While you guys were screwing around in there I had our dispatcher call the doctor's exchange. The exchange received a call from the victim Friday night. The message said that she wanted the doctor to call her, that's all. We can't contact the employee who took the message, she's off until Monday. I'll try again to contact the doctor tonight before I go off duty, but he apparently never got the message."

"She was alive this Friday, yesterday?" I asked. "The blood looks a lot older than that."

"Some of it does look old, but you probably noticed some of it also looked fairly fresh. The dark color is due to stomach acids. The varices—you've heard of varicose veins—that's a swelling, happens in the blood vessels, in this case in the esophagus, not the legs. You will see them firsthand at the autopsy, count on it. Something like this uncontrolled bleeding happens if and when the vessels rupture. Just the heavy hacking cough typical of a smoker can bring on the rupture. The victim doesn't even know what's happening until they get nauseated from the blood they're swallowing. They start to cough or gag up the blood. The blood is mixed with stomach acids at first. That's why it looks off color. After a while, with so much spitting up, the blood never makes it to the stomach. This woman, at least in the beginning of this episode, was fastidious enough to spit up her blood into glasses. She bled to death through the mouth. You didn't see any visible wounds, did you? If there is any heart blood left, I'll bet she has a substantial B.A. level."

"Did you explain all this to these guys?"

"I tried. They weren't buying. But I understand. I really do. Admit it, Ragle, you fell right into it. Like you, those guys only get called to scenes of violence. A town like Newport may have a few questioned deaths to deal with, but they could go all year without a murder. We get called to all reportable deaths. I go to more death scenes in a week than most cops see in their entire career. If cops do come to our scenes, they don't stay long. Cops are usually not all that interested when some known alcoholic dies in bed, drowning on his own vomit and blood. It's not their job, it's mine."

I went back inside the house, alone. I called Thompson and Epstein aside and said that we should schedule an autopsy right away, at least before we spent any more time documenting the scene. Then I walked them around, explaining the probable cause of all the frothy darkened blood, the blood patterns on the floor, and the redder blood.

The more intense the bleeding, the more glasses she filled. The glasses on the table were a set and must have been kept there as a display. It was like she was saving the blood for some reason, maybe to prove to her doctor that she wasn't lying about the extent of her bleeding, or she just didn't want to mess up her house. It did look like a blood feast was in progress. The boys seemed to accept the explanation since it was coming from me.

The autopsy, held later that afternoon at the local mortuary, confirmed the deputy coroner's opinion. In this case, because the scene was so ghastly, it was assumed it had to be the result of a murder, and the deputy had been relegated to a secondary role, that of body removal.

### Epilogue

This particular deputy coroner gained the complete respect of the NBPD investigators that day, elevating their confidence in the entire coroner's office, something long overdue. Afterward, they no longer referred to him as Toe Tags.

From that day on he was Mr. Toe Tags.

## CRIME SCENE:

### How *Do* You Stomach This Job?

My favorite case that proves the worth of examining stomach contents at the autopsy involved the death of a young woman. She had left her home in Los Angeles and was driven by her brother to Oceanside, where she had a job interview. She had planned to go back home by bus later the same day but never returned as expected. Her body, without any identification, was located the next day, dumped along an isolated road near a construction site in the south end of the county. Her head had been bashed in. There was a three-inch piece of a two-by-four with hair imprints lying nearby.

During the autopsy, undigested food—assorted pieces of what we all agreed had once been a taco—were found in her stomach. Stomach contents are routinely examined and saved for toxicology. The condition of assorted ingredients indicated that she had eaten them less than an hour before her death. The crime scene was a half hour drive north of Oceanside.

When she failed to return, family members, fearing the worst, called the authorities and were told to contact the Orange County Sheriff's Department. They arrived, bringing with them a recent photograph of the victim and an account of her trip to Oceanside. One family member viewed the body and confirmed her identity. Our investigators, armed with her photo and the knowledge of her last meal, traveled to Oceanside and prepared to make inquiries at every taco outlet in town, and if necessary to retrace the route between there and the crime scene.

They had checked only a few places in the city when they located a waitress who recognized the victim's photo. She remembered that the victim had purchased some tacos, but when told they didn't sell beer, left with her tacos and went to a bar across the street. The bartender also recognized the victim's photo. He told the investigators the woman had been talking with a regular customer, a marine assigned to Camp Pendleton Marine Base. Once she finished her tacos and beer, the two were seen leaving together. The bartender knew the marine by name. The investigators contacted the base and were told his off-base address.

Next they called me, and I headed for Oceanside. It was around eight P.M. by the time we all knocked on the door of the marine's apartment. He was home with his wife. He admitted offering the victim a ride, but claimed he only walked her as far as the bar's parking lot, where two Mexicans offered to drive her all the way back to Los Angeles. He said he went directly home after the three drove out of the parking lot. He volunteered to let us examine his car; why, I'm not sure. When he opened the trunk, the victim's purse and some clothing were in plain view.

Later that night he told the investigators what had happened. She needed a ride to Los Angeles so he agreed to take her there. After traveling awhile he told her she would have to "put out" if she expected him to drive her all the way home. He said she agreed, so they got in the backseat and had sex, after which she started to cry. He told her to stop, but she didn't. They got out of the car and she continued to cry. He told the investigators her crying reminded him of a wounded animal. Since they had ended up in a construction site, there was the piece of a two-by-four on the ground next to his car. He picked it up and, in his words, "Put her out of her misery." That may be exactly what happened.

### Epilogue

This case was solved because of a limp piece of taco shell, some ground beef, a little shredded cheese, and a leaf of lettuce.

## THE CORONER/MEDICAL EXAMINER SYSTEM

The coroner and the medical examiner have the same primary responsibility, although their job descriptions vary. Both conduct a medical-legal investigation to:

1. Identify the deceased.

2. Establish the time and date of the death.

3. Determine a medical cause of death and classify the manner of death—natural, accidental, suicide, homicide, or undetermined. The coroner's classification

does not have to coincide with the police or prosecutor's opinion of criminal involvement, although it usually does.

4. Protect the estate of the deceased.

5. Notify the next-of-kin.

Although the coroner/medical examiner may determine that a death occurred at the hands of another (a homicide), it is the responsibility of the district attorney or state's attorney to determine if the killing is criminal or noncriminal.

A death certificate must be issued in all deaths, coroner's cases or not. There are no exceptions. A private physician may sign a death certificate if he or she believes their patient died due to natural causes directly related to a previously diagnosed life-endangering malady. The physician must be willing to sign the certificate, verify the cause of death, and assign the classification as natural. The coroner issues certificates in all other deaths. The certificates are recorded, in California, by each county health department and must be on file before a burial certificate can be issued. No autopsy is required.

The need for accurate information in all other deaths—the unattended, sudden and unexpected, unnatural, and obvious criminal cases—necessitates a medical-legal investigation in many deaths, but not necessarily an autopsy. All these death certificates must be signed by the coroner or medical examiner or one of their authorized deputies. The phrase "signed out" or "signed out as" is used to describe the final process. Since a medical-legal investigation can take months to complete, an interim certificate can be issued in order to obtain a burial certificate. The cause is listed as pending and is amended when the investigation is complete.

The coroner is elected, usually by popular vote. No medical training or special knowledge is required. The coroner can be of any profession. Many are physicians. Some hold the dual office of sheriff-coroner or are local businesspersons; for example, morticians. For a time during the 1960s in a rural Southern California county, the local butcher was also the coroner.

Unless they are physicians, coroners do not perform autopsies. Coroners employ staff physicians to do that. As an example, Orange County has a sheriff-coroner system. The sheriff performs the administrative functions of both offices. The day-to-day operations of the office are conducted by the employees of the coroner's division, managed by the chief deputy coroner. Orange County contracts with a private firm of pathologists who conduct all but a few of the autopsies, such as those in which a conflict of interest might be involved.

If any Orange County law enforcement office is involved in any way with any death, or an inmate dies under any circumstance in jail or within twenty-four hours of release, the Orange County district attorney takes charge of the investigation and contracts with a pathologist from an organization not affiliated with the county. Before the case is closed, the facts are presented to a panel of the county's grand jury for consideration.

The scene investigators have the title Deputy Coroner. In some agencies the deputies are full-time coroner's investigators. Some deputy coroners perform peace officer activities when not at death scenes. Some of the smaller sheriff-coroner office's investigators wear regular deputies' uniforms. Some agencies hire civilians who have some paramedical experience or are former peace officers.

The medical examiner is usually appointed by the governing body of the host city, county, or state. The M.E. is always a physician and is often a specialist, such as a certified pathologist. Medical examiners may actually perform autopsies. In state systems and in the larger cities, the office is more administrative and, with the exception of high-profile cases, autopsies are usually performed by staff physicians. The job title Chief Medical Examiner is used to distinguish the boss from the other staff physicians, who then carry the title Medical Examiner or Deputy Medical Examiner.

From this point on, unless there is a specific reason—for example, a particular case or example involving a medical examiner—I will use "coroner" as a generic term to cover all systems.

## Reportable Cases

California has established nineteen categories of death that must be reported to the coroner without delay. The government code directs the coroner to inquire into and determine, in all cases, the circumstances, manner, and causes of the following deaths:

1. Unattended deaths. Any death when a physician isn't present.

2. Where the deceased has not been attended by a physician in the twenty days prior to death.

3. All sudden, unexplained deaths when a physician is unable to state the cause of death.

4. Known or suspected homicides.

5. Known or suspected suicides.

6. Involving any criminal or suspected criminal act.

7. Related to or following known or suspected self-induced or criminal abortion.

8. Associated with an alleged rape or crime against nature.

9. Following an accident or injury, either old or new.

10. Drowning, fire, hanging, gunshot, stabbing, cutting, starvation, exposure, alcoholism, drug addiction, strangulation, or aspiration.

11. Accidental poisoning.

12. Occupational disease or occupational hazard.

13. Known or suspected contagious disease and constituting a public hazard.

14. All deaths in operating rooms and all deaths when a patient has not fully recovered from an anesthetic, whether in surgery, recovery room, or elsewhere.

15. In prison or while under sentence. Includes all in custody and police-involved deaths.

16. All deaths of unidentified persons.

17. All deaths of state hospital patients.

18. Suspected Sudden Infant Death Syndrome (SIDS).

19. All deaths when the patient is comatose throughout the period of the physician's attendance. This includes patients who are admitted unresponsive and expire without regaining consciousness.

## CORONER'S SCENE INVESTIGATION

An ideal approach to any death scene investigation taken by thoughtful deputy coroners is to momentarily assume the role of the deceased. They control the scene with the idea that the victims still have rights, their property still belongs to them until a next-of-kin can be located. If the death is really unexpected, why did it happen? Their primary focus is on the remains, but they are also concerned about the victim's surroundings, whether it is the home, auto, or place of employment. Everything within the scene that belongs to the deceased is under the control of the deputy coroner, even if it is obviously a death due to a criminal act. This is why a team approach that includes the police investigator, crime scene investigator, and a criminalist has to be a cooperative effort. By law, the coroner is in charge of the death scene and the autopsy, but by identifying with the deceased, the coroner wants every effort made to ascertain the person responsible for the death. Of the four primary duties, the most important during the first moments on the scene is to establish the time of death.

Coroners don't declare that a person is actually dead. Death is assumed, and that is why the coroner has arrived at the scene. A police officer, paramedic, doctor, nurse, or even a citizen are most likely the ones who reported the death. On occasion a deputy coroner has been known to declare a person alive!

Knowing exactly when a person died has some obvious advantages. The foremost is to relate that time of death to the activities of all possible suspects. If the death is due to an act of violence, eventually it must be established that it was physically possible for a suspect to have committed the crime.

Reliable witnesses are usually an excellent source of time-related information. They may have actually seen or heard the activity leading to the death. But their reference point must be accurate and verifiable. If all a witness can say is "Sometime after midnight," that may be helpful but lacks the specificity to challenge an alibi. On the other hand, if the witness had checked a watch, was watching a specific TV program and remembered what was on the screen at that moment, or called the police immediately, the information should be considered. The investigators must look at the overall picture to determine if the statements are credible.

Mechanical failures may also provide some information about the time of death. Clocks that stop at the moment of an impact or during a fire or explosion will provide a record, but it should be determined that the clocks had been working and were set properly prior to the incident, and that may not be easy to find out.

Without reliable firsthand information, the investigators must estimate the time of death relying on their observations of the scene in general and the appearance and condition of the deceased. Under ideal and known conditions, these estimates can be very accurate, but because of uncontrollable variations at most scenes, there is always a plus or minus factor to consider.

Evidence of normal activity at the scene is often helpful to establish the general time of day that the death occurred. Indications that some event was in progress—such as sleep, work, or a meal—can be compared to known schedules kept by the deceased. Even leftover food on plates, on the stove, or in the sink may have meaning. The type of food served and number of places set for the last meal can be helpful in setting the general time of day as well as indicating the number of people present who are potential sources of information. At autopsy, the stomach and intestinal contents should be examined and related to the kitchen scraps. If they don't match, it is a strong indicator that the victim's last meal was somewhere else. The nature of the meal and perhaps even the type of establishment might be indicated by the material recognizable in the victim's stomach.

The single most significant occurrence at the moment of death is that the heart stops beating. Ultimately, that occurrence will assist the death investigators in establishing a time of death. When the heart stops, the blood pressure drops to match the atmospheric pressure and the blood stops moving about inside the circulatory system. From that moment, only gravity and the orientation of the body have any action on blood movement within the circulatory system or anywhere else, internally or externally, as long as the body stays at rest.

Without blood pressure, injuries to body surfaces may still appear to be bleeding from wounds that happen to be at a low or inferior point. Regardless of appearances, any blood flow after death is drainage due entirely to body orientation and gravity or some external force. For example, heroics, CPR, and defibrillation may cause the heart muscle to contract and cause some movement of blood in the circulatory system and the organs it supplies. It would be unusual for that amount of movement to add to any noticeable internal or external drainage or bleeding if the heart fails to respond.

As time passes, changes to a dead body at rest are readily recognized by a trained investigator. Lacking other reliable information, these changes may be very useful in estimating time of death. The changes include postmortem lividity, rigor mortis, decomposition, and loss of body heat.

*Postmortem Lividity.* When blood pressure drops to ambient levels, the blood flow ceases and gravity takes over. Blood trapped in the vessels of the circulatory system slowly begins to settle to the lowest available space within the vessels. The smallest vessels, the capillaries, are also the closest to the outer surface of the skin. The reddish color of blood in those capillaries, in life or death, is usually visible. In life, it adds the pinkest tint to the existing pigmentation, and at times when the capillaries dilate, is called a blush. In death, as the blood settles and the external color intensifies, a similar blush is called postmortem lividity. Sometimes PML is referred to as livor mortis.

The settling begins immediately but the lividity may not become visible for some time, and not apparent at all in some situations. Ideally, it can be seen on a fair-skinned individual within thirty minutes, and should be obvious in almost all cases within one hour. There are exceptions. With very heavily pigmented skin, although lividity is present, it may never be apparent. If a victim has lost a large volume of blood, PML may never be obvious. It may not even occur.

As the blood settles in the capillaries, it begins to congeal. Lividity is starting to set, or solidify. Once any blood in the capillaries has completely congealed, it doesn't move. At some time, between four to eight hours after death, all the blood in the capillaries will set permanently. Throughout this time the lowest (inferior or dependent) surface will progressively change to a dark red to reddish-blue color and the upper (superior) surfaces look paler or washed out. The color is affected by activity just prior to death. Reduced respiration, for whatever reason, will make the color bluer, or cyanotic, as will cyanide poisoning. Carbon monoxide poisoning results in the blood turning a bright cherry-red color, which affects PML accordingly. If the body is lifted and examined, the color of PML will be visible everywhere on the underside except where the skin was compressed against the places of rest. Those areas will look pale because the compression kept the blood out of the surface capillaries.

During the first hour after death and for up to eight hours under normal conditions, visible PML can be affected by compression, such as finger pressure. Trained death investigators use their thumbs or index fingers to press hard for several seconds against the livid skin. When the finger is removed, the appearance of that compressed area reveals much about the time of death. If death has occurred within a few hours, a phenomenon known as blanching occurs. The blanched areas appear as light-colored marks in the shape of the investigator's fingertip. The compression momentarily forces all but the congealed blood out of the capillaries under the pressure point.

You can demonstrate blanching on your own arm. After pressing your fingers into the muscle of the underside of your forearm for a count of ten, remove your fingers, and you will see areas representing the size of your fingertips. You have momentarily excluded all the blood from your capillaries in those areas. The apparent color will be much lighter for a few seconds, but if you continue to count after the pressure is released, the color will be back to normal almost immediately, within two or three seconds. Blood pressure forces blood back into the capillaries, shortening the blanching time.

Soon after death, minimal finger pressure will cause blanching and it will disappear within seconds. As time passes and PML becomes more noticeable, the duration of the blanch time continues to increase to several seconds. During this time, as more blood settles, filling the capillaries with more and more congealed blood, extra time and pressure is required to achieve any blanching. There is a crossover eventually. As the time after death nears eight hours and the PML has set, blanching will not occur regardless of the pressure.

The intermediate surfaces—for example, under the armpit area, if the body is flat on the floor, faceup or facedown—will show a gradation of color, becoming gradually darker toward the dependent parts. Death investigators generally start the blanching process in these areas and work their way down to heavier areas. The experienced death investigator will use the overall appearance of PML and the duration of blanching activity in part to estimate time of death.

Since lividity is a function of the force of gravity acting on stationary blood, it is possible that antemortem lividity (AML) can occur in a living person when the heart rate and respiration is significantly impaired and the person is immobile. Inadequate blood pressure will slow the movement of blood to the point that it may begin to settle in dependent areas. A lingering death due to chronic respiratory failure could result in lividity confused as PML. In fact, the PML has had a head start. In some cases of lingering death—a result of an overdose of a sedative hypnotic drug or acute alcohol poisoning, for example—the exact time of death may not be all that critical, as it is in cases when death is at the hand of another.

The study of PML can provide other facts beyond establishing the time of death. Since its behavior is predictable, finding PML out of character alerts the scene investigators that the mise-en-scène—the arrangement of the scene—has been tampered with. It is a fact that settling blood is affected by gravity and will always move into the inferior capillaries, regardless of the orientation of the body. We know that very soon after death some of the settled blood congeals, and once it is set, it doesn't move much, if at all. This means that once a body has been in place for some time, even thirty minutes, some hint of fixed lividity may be apparent. If any fixed lividity shows up on any surface other than the inferior one, it is an indication that at some time thirty minutes or so after death the body was moved, either rolled over or completely repositioned. For example:

- A body exhibiting lividity only on the lower surfaces has not been moved after the first thirty to sixty minutes following death.

- A body found with light but fixed lividity on the upper surfaces and heavy lividity on the lower surfaces must have been repositioned sometime soon after death, within one hour, and then remained as found for three or more hours.

- A body found with heavy fixed lividity on the upper surfaces and light but fixed lividity on the lower surfaces was moved after three or so hours and has been in place for one or more hours.

- A body found with heavy fixed lividity on the upper surfaces and lividity on the lower surfaces that still blanches has been moved within a relatively short time.

This can happen for nonsinister reasons, for instance, if heroics have been attempted and the body was rolled over in the process. The degree of superior PML still can be used to estimate total time when added to the estimate of the inferior lividity.

- A body found with equal degrees of lividity on the upper and lower surfaces was repositioned or rolled over after two to four hours.

- A body that has been hanging by a rope for a few hours will have lividity in the neck and chin just above the ligature, in the hands, and in the lower legs and feet. If there is lividity spread out on other areas of the body—all across the back, for example—it's an indication that the person died by other means, lay around for a while, and was strung up later to appear as if hanged.

PML not only alerts the aware investigator that the victim's body has been rolled over, it also can indicate it has been moved to the place of discovery from an entirely different surface, or has had clothing items removed after PML has formed. Patterns, replicas of whatever is under a body at rest, will be visible in the skin. In fact, indentations can occur on skin, dead or alive, with or without PML. To observe this imprint phenomenon, press a coin tightly against your inner forearm for approximately two minutes. The resulting imprint will last for many minutes.

Three-dimensional compression marks in a dead body, with or without PML, may last as long as the body lasts. Objects that are wrapped tightly, like a rope or chain or even tight underwear, will leave permanent marks regardless of the body's position. But the dead weight of a body alone creates ample pressure to register patterns of the host surface and/or objects that are layered between the skin and the surface. The imprints will show the accentuated detail of the marks, if PML is present, as a reversal. The high points of the pattern will show as pale skin color because blood could not settle on those capillaries. The rest of the pattern will be the color of the PML. If the PML is fixed, the patterns, as with compression marks, will remain clearly visible both at the scene and at the autopsy and will last as long as the body lasts.

Bodies that have been transported in automobiles will register imprints of anything trapped underneath them, such as tools, the spare tire, the texture of a floor mat, or the weave of a cloth used to wrap the body. The body might as well be a piece of film recording a picture of objects on the floor of the car. If the suspect car is located before the items are removed, it is just a question of taking a photograph of the object and showing their matching class characteristics. An imprint of two or three objects in an identical random arrangement, or even just one unique object, could be enough to prove the body had at one time been in the vehicle.

***Rigor Mortis.*** The term "stiff" comes from the fact that bodies for a period of time pass through a state of rigidity. Rigor mortis is predictable in almost every situation, but there are some obvious exceptions to the rule and some more subtle exceptions. RM is the result of lactic acid, a chemical that is present to some extent in active living tissue.

RM is a process that covers approximately thirty-six hours. Lacking complications, the process begins in the shorter muscles of the face and extremities, the fingers and toes. The neck is involved next, and the stiffening moves down and out with the long muscles of the extremities and forearms, with the legs stiffening last. This first phase may take about twelve hours. The entire body remains rigid for twelve hours or so before the shorter muscles start to go limp. Over the next twelve hours the RM disappears in the same order as it appeared.

The following estimates during the first eight hours after death should be consistent with PML and blanching. PML can fine-tune these times if an experienced investigator is making the observations.

- The jaw and neck are rigid but the rest of the body is limp, indicating early rigor, one to four hours. Everything down to the legs is rigid, up to eight hours. Once the entire body is rigid there is no change for twelve hours or so.

- The jaw is limp but from the neck down is rigid, placing the time at twenty-four hours plus. Everything but the legs being rigid indicates thirty to thirty-two hours. No rigidity plus some early signs of decomposition indicates thirty-six hours or more.

Exceptional circumstances are almost always involved when RM behaves atypically. Starvation can affect the onset of RM, usually delaying it. Extreme temperatures delay the onset. Freezing cold weather could delay it until after the body is moved to a warmer location. Physical exertion just before death can accelerate the onset, as can ingestion of some poisons, such as strychnine, which causes rapid muscle contractions. Victims of drowning may go into RM rapidly if they were struggling for survival. Certainly, deaths due to intense fire that denature muscle tissue would mask any RM. What tissue survives is rigid from the heat.

*Decomposition.* We are constantly consuming live bacteria in the things we eat or drink. Many species are helpful and some are vital, for instance in aiding digestion, and they are always present, making their way through our intestinal tract. Others, called pathogens, such as salmonella and some strains of E. coli, are notorious toxins and can produce so-called food poisoning that can be fatal. Bacteria can make its way into the bloodstream and affect healthy body functions. Normally, the bacteria we consume fail to make their presence known, except perhaps when you find yourself in a crowded elevator.

At the time of death, as body functions come to rest, the bacteria in the blood—but primarily in the intestines—find themselves in an ideal environment and, with few exceptions, seize the opportunity to mass produce. Carbon dioxide, a gas, is one of their by-products. The death investigator sees this as abdominal swelling that begins to be noticeable hours after death.

One of the earliest visible signs of decomposition is the discoloration of blood veins close to the surface of the skin in the area of the upper abdomen. The darkened vessels give the appearance of marbling. The effect is due first to simple cellular lysis—the breakdown of the red blood cells—and second to bacterial action leading to a discoloration of the veins. I don't even like to think about it. Although gravity has drained most of the blood from superior vessels, there are always some residual fluids remaining. Their color shifts from the normal red color of blood to a darker red to purple to green as putrefaction progresses. Surface vessels appear as thin darkly colored lines on subjects with light-colored skin. The darker the natural pigment, the less noticeable these lines are.

No matter the pigmentation, the next stage of decomposition is unmistakable. Within two to three days the gases of decomposition, sometimes collectively referred to as putracine—vile-smelling, nauseating odors that defy accurate description—become unmistakably noticeable. When students ask what the odor is really like, I can never find the words to adequately describe it. I suggest they purchase about ten pounds of chicken entrails, place them in a metal garbage can, set the can in full sun for three or four days, then, with one hand on the handle of the lid, exhale completely, lift the lid, place their face into the garbage can as far down as possible, and breathe in. Don't take a deep breath.

**Rectal Temperature and Liver Temperature.** The loss of body temperature is used by many death investigators to estimate the time of death. Body temperature is maintained for most people at 98.6 degrees Fahrenheit (37 degrees Celsius), held in fine balance by the selective burning of calories and the cooling as needed over the surface of the skin. In life, thanks to a small section of our brain, the hypothalamus, we are unconsciously able to maintain a constant temperature, independent of air temperatures. Except in extreme highs and lows, the body adjusts with no effort on our part. We can consciously increase our body temperature by doing physical activity. If we start to feel the cold or if we are working out, the demand for energy increases, more calories are burned, and the body temperature increases temporarily. But very shortly the body will return to the ideal temperature. In death, the body will start to cool down, beginning with the moment of death when oxygen no longer is available for the metabolism of glucose.

Under ideal conditions the calculations can be very accurate. Consider a location where it is possible to measure rectal temperature (RT) and the room temperature is known to have been controlled at 70 degrees Fahrenheit. The experts say RT drops about 2 degrees per hour for the first six hours and 1.5 degrees for the next six hours. This is assuming that the body was at 98.6 degrees to begin with. Measured rectally, that would be 99 degrees. If death was five hours earlier, the rectal temperature should be 89 degrees; if eight hours earlier, 84 degrees.

The size (mass) of the body, the body's temperature at the time of death, and the range of temperatures during the time the body was believed to be at the scene are all factors that will affect temperature loss. Since temperature drop is going to follow some of the laws of physics, many facts have to be known before any rate of loss is applied. One fact, the size of the victim, can be established. The second, the scene temperature, can be measured at the time, but it is also necessary to know what it was earlier, at the moment of death. That's the first catch-22. We don't know when the person died. That is what we are attempting to estimate. But since the body's temperature will change to match the ambient temperature, we must know what it had been all along.

Outside temperatures can change dramatically in many locations. For example, a person killed at four A.M. in some places in California could cool down quickly when the air temperature is 40 degrees Fahrenheit and then could start to warm up after the sun heats the air and the ground. The outside air temperature could be 100 degrees by ten A.M. and the body could be back to normal temperatures soon after.

The other major limitation is knowing what to use for the starting temperature. Normal people vary a few degrees from 98.6 degrees Fahrenheit. Physical activity, like fighting for your life, can elevate the body temperature, and disease and some drugs can cause hyperthermia—elevated temperatures. Amphetamines can push the temperature up to 108 degrees. Death is expected at that level. Unattended, this body in a controlled environment would appear normal sometimes six to ten hours after death.

## THE AUTOPSY

A pathologist is a specially trained physician who studies the various aspects of disease—the causes, its process, its development, and its consequences. By far, most deaths are caused by disease. Most pathologists work more on very small tissue samples, biopsies, from living patients than they do performing autopsies.

The science of histology, the application of microscopy to determine cellular changes in the tissue, is a vital tool relied upon by almost all types of pathologists. Histology samples, small chunks of organs or tissue, are prepared by a histologist or the pathologist and are studied under the microscope. Changes due to disease, trauma, or natural anomalies can be observed and used to identify a disease, estimate the age of the trauma, or establish a cause of death. Iron staining is the classic method of aging trauma. Iron is contained in red blood cells. Trauma can cause some red cells to rupture, freeing the iron. The staining makes the iron visible, and the amount of dispersion of the stain indicates the age of the stain.

Pathologists perform two types of autopsies, which are sometimes referred to as postmortem examinations and occasionally called necropsies. The first is performed in hospitals on noncoroner cases and is usually quite different in purpose and scope than the typical coroner's autopsy. The hospital autopsy is more likely a process of confirmation, where the pathologist may be focused on a specific region or organ of the body. The patient was under the care of a physician and in the hospital for a specific purpose. More than likely a death certificate could have been issued without the autopsy results. Sometimes it is the family who wants the autopsy. Sometimes the attending physicians insist on it because they want to learn more about a particular disease. Only tissue samples needed to confirm a specific disease are collected.

On the other hand, a coroner's autopsy is an extremely intensive and invasive search for information. Of the many reasons a coroner conducts an autopsy, one purpose is common to all of them: to locate physical evidence to determine the cause of death. But the search does not stop there. If and when a case reaches the courts—and remember, that is the ultimate purpose of all forensic investigations, medical or otherwise—the pathologist must be prepared to offer physical evidence about why this person died.

Forensic testimony is not a prognostication based on the art of medicine. Forensic testimony is a conclusion based on the science of pathology. Because there is the autopsy, the pathologist can eliminate the guesswork of prognosis. There are no secrets left after a complete autopsy. The team can enter the body and probe every nook until they are aware of all possible reasons this person died. All other possible causes, natural and unnatural, must be eliminated. To provide this level of certainty, every organ and all tissues vital to life must be removed and examined. Because this is forensic evidence, small sections of all organs are retained for histology and toxicology in quantities sufficient for a defense team to reexamine the evidence and reach their own conclusions.

Although there are some emotional reasons not to conduct an autopsy when there are objections from the family, usually based on religious doctrine, most coroners look at the facts of the case and nothing else while deciding what to do. The objections may be legitimate or self-serving. They can be self-serving for noncriminal reasons. The family might just be in a big hurry to deal with the many obligations following the death of a loved one. It is not easy for people in this state of mind, or people who vehemently object, to understand why the coroner, who has a legal obligation to investigate the cause of death and related factors, proceeds against their wishes.

In many of the cases reported to the coroner, the identity and the time of death could be answered without an autopsy. Even the question of classification, in some cases, can be answered without an autopsy—for instance, a witnessed suicide when someone jumps from a height in front of a crowd.

In this case the identity has been established, the time is about as precise as can be, the cause is certainly due to acute massive trauma to the central nervous system due to sudden stopping, and the case is positively a suicide. Notwithstanding the obvious, the coroner must conduct an autopsy, seeking to answer questions beyond the cause—for example, the contributing factors that may establish the motive for the death. In a case such as this, a terminal disease, pregnancy, or intoxication due to alcohol or drugs may have contributed to the reason the person committed suicide. If the death was due to drugs, for instance, one of the many that cause hallucinations, the case could well be an accident and not a suicide.

Traffic deaths may appear straightforward, but all such deaths are autopsied to establish the cause and contributing factors. A disease may have caused blackouts or the driver might have had a heart attack, for instance, causing the vehicle to be out of control in the first place. California and most other state laws require the blood of all fatalities to be tested for alcohol and drugs of abuse.

Every death case that is handled as a forensic investigation should be autopsied by a board-certified forensic pathologist (BCFP). Unfortunately, in most areas of this country that is impossible. The total number of BCFPs in the entire United States is fewer than five hundred, and there is very little incentive to interest new candidates to enter the field. The pay is usually less than that earned by other types of specialists; more often than not, they must work in less than ideal situations, and often on bodies that are in advanced stages of decomposition; and when they go to court they become the target of an attorney whose aim in life is to make the witness look, act, and feel like a complete moron.

The BCFP is always a licensed physician, at the least. A certified pathologist, usually anatomical or clinical or both, has completed two years' internship working with a BCFP and has passed the examination given by the National Association of Medical Examiners. This means that all BCFPs are brilliant, but it doesn't mean they all are good at what they do.

Another frightening note: All other forensic autopsies are conducted by physicians with no special training. Experience maybe, but no special training. That is not to say that most of them don't do an adequate job.

The basic members of the forensic autopsy team are the pathologist, an assistant, the deputy coroner, a criminalist, a forensic photographer, and the police investigators. The members of the forensic team should meet with any other specialists who have been deemed necessary to be present at the autopsy—for example, depending on what is known about the case, a neural pathologist or a forensic toxicologist. The team determines what evidence-collecting activities remain to be done before the actual medical inspection begins.

The entire outer surface, clothing, and skin of the body are still very much a part of the original crime scene. The only thing that has changed is that part of the scene has now been moved to the morgue for closer study. Many of the tasks listed below should be completed at the scene if a criminalist is present. Fragile evidence is always in jeopardy of being altered or lost by moving the body to transport it and by placing it in a body bag.

Unfortunately, in many areas of the country there are no forensic scientists trained to collect evidence at crime scenes, or not enough to respond to all critical scenes. And, odd as it may sound, some coroners or medical examiners cling to the policy that the body must not be touched until it is examined at the morgue. In any case, everything that could not be completed at the scene must now be done before the body is altered any more. The following steps must be taken, and preferably in this order:

1. Preautopsy meeting of all the team members. The case is reviewed, primarily for the benefit of the pathologist, who is most likely totally unfamiliar

with the case. Ideally, as suggested in Chapter 2, the pathologist would go to as many crime scenes as possible and participate with the initial observation of the body and the mise-en-scène.

2. Photographs. Once the body is removed from the body bag, it should be photographed in full view to record any changes that may have occurred since the body was placed in the bag. The bag and any wrapping should be saved for examination.

   Note: Overall photography should be taken at almost every one of the following steps and, as noted close-up photos taken for specific reasons.

3. Reexamination. Before any clothing is removed from the body, the entire exposed surface of the victim's remains should be closely examined with a bright white light, a UV lamp, a diffused beam laser, and an alternative light source. Whenever possible, this should be done at the scene but also repeated at the morgue. The clothing and jewelry or other items can be removed once every team member has agreed that their work to this point is completed.

4. Collection of fragile evidence. If any potentially fragile evidence not already collected at the scene is located, it should be dealt with at this time, close-up photos taken, and the material collected. Any remaining loose material such as fibers, loose hairs, glass fragments, or other visible debris, should be photographed and collected at this time.

5. Collection of vulnerable evidence. Bite marks are one very good example of vulnerable evidence—not because of the bite, but because of the possibility of contaminating the potential saliva transfer. Any inappropriate handling can alter or destroy the small amount of saliva transferred to the victim's skin during a bite. The saliva is collected, using a cotton swab lightly moistened with deionized or distilled water, by rubbing the swab in the entire area within the

marks and over the marks. A control sample is collected in the same manner from the skin very near the bite mark. ABO secretor status is not an issue if DNA is to be used. Nevertheless, the control could prove vital if phantom DNA markers—ones in addition to those of the suspect and victim—are detected in the bite area. If the same phantom DNA is found on the control, along with the victim's but not the suspected biter's, it may help to clarify what happened.

Keep in mind that sexual activity often involves licking and sucking without visible bite marks. When crime scene circumstances suggest sexual assault as an element of the crime, swabbing target areas such as the genitalia, breasts, and buttocks of the victim is suggested even though nothing is visible. Circumstances that hint of sexual assault are those in which victims, regardless of sex or age, have been abducted, found nude or with their genitalia exposed, or are bound or tied in compromising positions.

6. Swabs. Vaginal or penile, oral, and anal swabs should be collected in all cases, but must be if there is any hint of sexual assault. Nasal swabs should be collected if drug use is suspected.

7. X rays. Full-body X rays should be taken in all cases of homicide. Obviously broken or fractured bones may be significant in violent deaths, but X rays also are a must for locating metallic objects such as bullets, bullet fragments, shot, and the tips of knife blades. Healed fractures can document prior violence, reported or unreported, in child or domestic abuse cases, and they have been used to confirm the identity of John Does when all else fails. To make this type of ID, someone must supply medical histories and X rays of the person believed to be the John Doe. Although dental X rays may eventually be needed to confirm questionable ID, to avoid contamination of potential evidence they must be delayed until the mouth is swabbed for semen or other materials

and the tongue and teeth are examined by the pathologist for trauma.

8. Gunshot residue. When appropriate, the hands should be examined and evidence collected by the method suggested by the local crime laboratory (see Chapter 5).

9. Fingernail scraping. The area under the fingernails should be examined for loose debris using a stereoscopic medical microscope. If anything is observed or if no microscope is available, the fingernails must be scraped.

10. Wounds. Any wounds should be examined, close-up photographs taken, and any trace evidence removed.

11. Pubic hair combing, when appropriate: in a possible sexual assault where there is a possibility of pubic hair transfer. This can occur when the two pubic areas are in close contact and, like the man-made material Velcro, the hairs hook onto one another and transfer if any are loose (see Chapter 8).

12. Collection of standard hairs. As described in Chapter 8, standard hairs must be pulled, *not cut*, from all anatomical areas. A minimum of fifty to one hundred hairs from each area is necessary.

13. Casts. Three-dimensional casts are critical in all suspected bite marks, after swabbing, and is suggested in other types of indentations or wounds. Entrance holes, cuts, punctures, firearms indentations, and entrance holes are all candidates for casts once swabbing and debris collection have been completed. The same material used to capture the detail of tool marks works well in these types of marks. A silicon rubber catalytic material is used. The only problem I ever had was a long wait for the chemical reaction to take place in a case when the body had been refrigerated and was very cold when the cast was made.

14. Identification photographs. Full face, front, and side views should be taken. If trauma is obscuring one side of the face, a photo should be taken at an angle, avoiding the trauma, so the photo can be shown in the least offensive manner. Close-ups of other possible identifying features should be taken, such as notable scars or tattoos.

15. Fingerprints. If all team members agree that all the potential evidence from the hand have been collected, complete friction ridge information should be obtained. This includes the standard rolled ten-print card, full palm prints, the wrists, and the rounded outer edges of the hand. These edges are the radial aspect (thumb) and ulnar aspect (little fingers). The ten-print card will be used to check against known files or missing persons. The other print information will be kept on file in the event they are needed to compare to crime scene lifts that don't belong to any suspects or to known people who had reason to be at the scene.

    This sounds a lot easier than it may be. Remember the discussion of rigor mortis. The hand and fingers can be in full rigor at the time of the autopsy. It is possible to break the rigor by forcefully manipulating the hands and fingers, but it can become incredibly hard work, and the product may be inadequate. It is best to return to the morgue after twelve hours or so and work with a relaxed hand.

At this point the pathologist begins the medical autopsy and becomes the main player, assisted by the team members. Although items of evidence may be located inside the body—bullets, for example—the focus will be on documenting trauma, establishing the medical cause of death, other possible causes of death, all contributing causes, while eliminating every other possible cause, natural and unnatural. Since there can be more than one apparent cause of death, the pathologist must also seek evidence to establish which cause preceded the other. Sometimes the difference is obvious, sometimes academic, but it can be critical in some cases.

Consider a victim of a knife attack who, in an attempt to escape the attacker, runs onto a highway where he is struck by a vehicle. Witnesses can establish that the attacks came before any vehicular trauma, but do we have the elements of murder? In most jurisdictions the criminal responsibility would remain with the person who did the cutting, regardless of the cause of death. Nevertheless, the pathologist must distinguish between the two possible sources of trauma and be specific as to a cause of death. The significant questions are:

- Was the victim cut or stabbed?

- Were the cuts, lacking any other trauma, sufficient to cause death?

- Was there trauma from being struck by a vehicle?

- Does the trauma suggest whether the victim was upright or on the pavement when struck?

- Would this trauma, lacking the knife wounds, have been fatal?

- Could the victim already have been dead when struck?

The answers provided by the pathologist will most likely impact any criminal charges against a suspect. For example, the total number and depth of the cuts or stabs would be used to show intent, as would the location of the wounds. Cuts on the palms of the hands could indicate defense wounds. The pathologist is the only person qualified to answer all the critical questions.

While performing the autopsy, the pathologist should never make any assumptions as to the nature of the crime, whether he or she has visited the scene, has been briefed, or knows nothing of the events. As each of the following steps is enacted, orientation and close-up photographs, with a scale included, must be taken of each point of interest. Many pathologists dictate their observations as they progress through each step. Others prefer to record only measurements and weights while at the table and dictate their report at the conclusion of the procedure.

*Inspection for subtle as well as obvious wounds.* The pathologist must inspect all the skin surface for any type of break. Injection sites and bite marks might be overlooked unless a good source of white light is used. Following that, the room should be darkened and the skin reexamined for all defects and debris using a UV lamp, a laser, or an alternative light source (ALS)—ideally, all three. Older trauma may also be visible using these light sources and be recognized by an aware pathologist. This process would not be repeated if, during the preautopsy examination, the body was nude and the pathologist was present to make the observations at that time.

It is critical to probe all the body's orifices for evidence of trauma, foreign objects, or debris. The vagina, the anus, the urethra (in the penis), the mouth—including under the tongue—the tongue and the teeth, the ears, and in and under the armpits. It is not uncommon to find objects inserted in the body's openings. Part or all of this step could be completed during the preautopsy examination.

*The Y-incision.* I have noticed that some pathologists make a tiny cut in the skin on the superior aspect of the body before making their major invasion into the body cavity. They are looking for bleeding. There should not be any. Bleeding under these circumstances means there is blood pressure. Bleeding means this person is still alive. It has happened.

The three cuts in a Y shape on a corpse are deep enough to cut through the skin, fat, and muscle down to the ribs in the chest area and through all the layers of the abdomen. The V-shaped area between the nipples is lifted bit by bit and undercut so all the ribs and connecting tissue are exposed. The entire front section of the ribs must be removed to open up the thorax. The ribs must be cut through with shears or a very sharp knife. Some pathologists use garden loppers (branch cutters), and sometimes linoleum knives are used for this process. The ribs are not cut away in the V shape. Two parallel cuts, about a foot apart on adults, are made and then connected by cutting across the top of the chest. Once cut and removed, this opens as large a working area as possible and exposed the thoracic cavity. The thorax contains the heart, lungs, and supporting vessels.

The single cut below the V shape down to the pubis exposes the entire abdominal cavity, sometimes referred to as the peritoneal cavity. The abdominal cavity contains the stomach, intestines, liver, kidneys, spleen, pancreas, and bladder, and in females it also contains the uterus and the other reproductive organs. The thorax and the abdomen are separated by the diaphragm muscle.

Be warned: If the body is at all decomposed or is a bit green or purple around the stomach, and particularly if the stomach is bulging, stand back when the abdomen is initially punctured. The smell can be pretty bad for a while. Some folks smear a dab of Vicks Vaporub on the tip of their nose. There is not enough Vicks in the entire world, as far as I'm concerned. I worked through a lot of these really bad ones, but I never got used to the smell. I'm sure the stuff bores into you somehow. Days later, when you sneeze or blow your nose, a little pocket of the smell that somehow got trapped up your nose breaks loose, and it's as if you are there again, standing over the decomp.

*Inspection of internal penetrating wounds.* The pathologist must examine them for the damage to organs, vessels, nerves, and bones. They can establish direction of travel and depth. Any debris can be removed and collected.

*Excising the wound.* It may be decided to retain the area around the wound. This may be critical in close gunshot wounds and in stabbing when the size and type of blade needs to be determined.

*Inspection of all organs.* All organs are removed and inspected for trauma, weighed, and dissected to inspect for signs of disease or previous damage. The organs that have the most value in demonstrating the cause of death are the heart, lungs, liver, and kidneys. The esophagus, stomach, and intestines, in some cases, may reveal the cause of death.

*The heart.* The normal heart, mostly muscle tissue, weighs about ten ounces, or 300 grams, but can weigh as much as 600 to 700 grams or more in extreme cases of cardiomegaly (enlarged heart). The heart is protected better than most organs because it is situated in the thoracic cavity, within the rib cage and surrounded by the lungs. Nevertheless, it is vulnerable to penetrating weapons such as knives and bullets. Further, the heart and its connecting veins and arteries can be damaged by the shock of blunt force to the chest or sudden deceleration. Any injury that makes a hole in just one of the four chambers or vessels supporting the heart can cause death in a very short time.

Another autopsy observation, not related to trauma, is occlusions in the coronary arteries, called stenosis, that sometimes are so complete they can be seen, cross section, with the naked eye. The outward appearance of some victims of cardiac failure with fair skin is a bluish discoloration around the face and upper chest that is independent of lividity. This means there was a shortage of oxygen for a period before death, causing the skin to look blue rather than pink. Many other problems can cause oxygen deficiency, for example, other disease, physical activity, some poisons, or an overdose of depressant drugs. Not all dead cardiac victims will have this appearance. If the death was very abrupt, the blood would not have enough time to become oxygen deficient.

Many sudden deaths are attributed to ventricular fibrillation of the heart muscle. But in most of those cases, just how the pathologist signs out the death to fibrillation may be a bigger mystery than the death itself. Fibrillations are spasms or irregular rapid contractions of muscle that are counterproductive to the muscle's normal activities.

In the case of the heart muscle, the pumping action is ineffective, limiting the blood supply to all vital organs, including the heart and brain, in particular. Death will result. But unless the patient is hooked up to an EKG and the electric signal of the heartbeat is being recorded, as soon as the victim dies, there are no more electric signals of any kind to measure. The muscle relaxes. There is no trauma. And there is no evidence to demonstrate fibrillation.

There are some circumstances in which fibrillation is likely, such as deaths resulting from electric shock. Certainly, some drug overdoses and certain poisons interrupt the normal electric signal of the central nervous system and cause fibrillations. But listing it as the cause of death is not appropriate because it can't be proved. Remember, this is forensic medicine.

*The lungs.* The lungs fill most of the thoracic cavity. Trauma to the lungs is often from external puncture wounds, but the lungs are also the passageway into the blood used by toxic gases, vapors, and dusts. Lungs are collected as evidence for specific reasons. The residue of some gases, such as methane and propane, can be identified if an entire lung is stored in an airtight container. After a short time the vapors of the gas will be in equilibrium in the air surrounding the lung, and a sample for testing can be removed with a syringe after punching a tiny hole in the cap of the jar.

The question of whether a person was alive during a fire can be answered by examining the airway, the trachea, the bronchi, and the lungs. If the victim was alive, there most likely will be soot or ash visible inside the airway and all the way into the lungs. The conclusion is verified by analyzing the victim's blood for the presence of carbon monoxide (CO), the product of combustion. This is called the carboxy-hemoglobin test and is extremely accurate. Our blood has a higher affinity for CO than it does for oxygen. In the presence of CO, even when there is adequate oxygen blood cells will become quickly saturated with CO and there is no space left for the transport of oxygen. When that happens, humans die. The lungs may not contain any soot or ash, although there is enough CO to kill. For example, someone who uses a charcoal burner inside a small room, camper, or boat can die from CO but have no visible soot.

The question of whether a victim of a heroin overdose was a longtime user can also be answered by studying the lungs. Heroin users will eventually absorb enough carbonate, a chemical used to mix the heroin, so that crystals of it can be found microscopically in the lung tissue. The pathologist prepares microscope slides and stains thin slices of the lung to see the crystals.

The question of whether a fetus was alive long enough to breathe has been answered by examining the lungs of the child. Once the infant has taken a breath, the lung will float. I have never seen this done, but many pathologists rely on it as a fact.

Natural deaths can be due to lung disease, TB, cancer, and a number of fibroses caused by the long-term inhalation of particles. Another cause of death involving the lung is caused by an embolism, a clot that blocks the blood circulation to a major portion of the lungs. The embolism can be a blood clot, a chunk of fat, a bubble of air, or anything else that breaks loose from within the circulatory system.

*The liver.* The liver is located at the top right of the abdominal cavity just below the diaphragm. A healthy adult liver weighs between two to three plus pounds or 960 to 1,500 grams. Visually it is similar to a cow's liver, sold in meat markets. Since the day I started doing coroner's toxicology in 1961, I have never again had fried liver and onions. Liver activity and functions are referred to as hepatic. Hepatitis, for example, is any ailment of the liver that alters its function. Hepatitis, malnutrition, and drug use, including alcohol use, are all causes of cirrhosis, a disease that actually hardens the liver tissue. At autopsy, a cirrhotic liver appears yellow to tan rather than the reddish-brown color of a healthy liver. The texture is actually hard and tough rather than the pliable soft feel of a healthy liver. Advanced stages of liver disease cause jaundice, a yellowing of the skin and tissues. The whites of the eyes appear yellow as the disease progresses. The victim in the case of "Blood Suckers Loose in Newport Beach" had the yellow discoloration of her skin.

Her liver was in the advanced stages of cirrhosis, in her case most likely due to continued alcohol abuse.

Because the liver tissue is soft and pliable, it is vulnerable to tearing or lacerating. Lacerations can be caused by blunt force, such as a solid blow to the gut with a fist, foot, or heavy object, or a sudden deceleration that occurs in some vehicular collisions.

*The kidneys.* The two kidneys are located inside the lower area of the rib cage at about the same orientation on each side of the spine. Each normally weighs about six ounces or 180 grams. "Renal" refers to the kidney's activities or problems that affect them. The kidneys maintain balance in blood by filtering out all the bad stuff, in particular the toxic by-products of protein metabolism. The liquid produced by the filtering process is urine. Drug addicts who have contracted hepatitis and as a result suffer from a cirrhotic liver may fail to metabolize proteins. The toxins that pass out of the liver damage the kidneys, and the addict dies from renal failure.

The tip-off is their jaundiced (yellowish) appearance, and a very high blood urea nitrogen (BUN) reading indicated by their blood chemistry test. High BUN indicates the kidneys are failing to eliminate uric acid and urea, products of protein metabolism, and cannot maintain a proper acid/base balance. Acidosis—too much acid—results, and the patient may die.

Kidneys are vulnerable to blunt force trauma and can rupture from transmitted shock. The term "kidney punch" implies a blow delivered to the back side of a boxer and is illegal by official boxing standards.

*Collection of heart blood.* Heart blood is most likely to be uncontaminated. It is divided into two samples with specific preservatives, one for typing and one to determine blood alcohol levels. There is always some amount of blood left in the heart, even when the victim has bled to death.

*Collection of stomach and its contents.* The contents of the stomach may be important in drug overdose cases. Collection and inspection of stomach contents also are important to establish the victim's activities prior to death. The inspection may be very helpful in narrowing down an estimated time of death if the time and menu of the last meal is known.

*The bowel.* The entire length of the bowel is sliced and stripped to inspect its contents and collect any objects that might be significant, as well as to inspect it for trauma and disease. The location of undigested food may help determine the time of death. Packages of drugs are found on occasion during this inspection and may be an indication of the cause of death.

*The reproductive organs.* These are removed and examined closely for trauma, pregnancy, disease, or surgical modification.

*The interior area of the neck.* A great deal of information is obtained from a detailed examination of the interior of the neck. This is the site of the thyroid gland, the carotid arteries, and the muscles of the neck that surround the esophagus (to the stomach), trachea (to the lungs), and the hyoid bone. Death due to strangulation is discussed on the following pages.

*The head.* The scalp is cut on a continuous line from behind the ears and pulled down over the forehead. This is called "reflecting the scalp." It makes everyone look just a bit like Moe of the Three Stooges. This exposes the inner lining of the scalp and the top of the skull, revealing any hemorrhaging. The skull is then cut open by encircling the upper half. The circular cut is interrupted by cutting two small V-shaped notches in the bone, one behind each ear, which will be used to reset the top of the skull at the conclusion of the autopsy. The skull cap can then be popped off, exposing the brain. After its outer surface is studied for trauma, the brain is removed in one piece, lacking severe damage, and weighed. It is then sectioned, checking for internal trauma.

At the conclusion of the autopsy the pathologist and assistants reposition the skull and suture the scalp in such a manner that, once the hair is combed in a natural style, none of this exploration is visible at later viewing.

After the autopsy is completed, the team members should review the events of the scene and the autopsy to determine what else, if anything, needs to be done. The cause of death, if it was determined at the autopsy, should be discussed so no member misunderstands or misrepresents the conclusions reached during the autopsy. The last question should be: "Did we forget anything?"

If the team is in agreement that no other autopsy work is needed, the body should be embalmed and held for at least forty-eight hours. At that time the surface areas of the body should be reexamined for new information. Embalming denatures the tissues and blood. Marks and defects such as bruises, bite marks, and other indentations become darker in color and clearer in appearance. Marks that were not visible during the autopsy become apparent for the first time. Any new information should be documented by photographs and written descriptions.

The bottom line of the coroner's investigation is to get accurate information to fill in all the blanks on a death certificate. There are numerous ways a person dies, but death occurs when the oxygen supply to the brain is gradually slowed down or stopped suddenly. This is called *anoxia,* the lack of oxygen. For the purposes of the death certificate, what caused the anoxia is the cause of the death. Each death certificate has four lines that can be used to describe, in single words or short phrases, exactly why and how this person died, including any other conditions contributing but not related to the immediate cause of death (such as a driver's excessive blood alcohol content during the accident that killed him).

## CAUSES OF DEATH FROM HEAD TO TOE

Unless it is explained otherwise, all the traumatic causes of death discussed below can be due to accident, suicide, or homicide, and, where stated, can be natural. These are some, certainly not all, of the possible causes of death.

### Brain Damage

*Extradural and subdural hematoma.* The dura mater is a layer of tissue between the skull and the brain. A blow to the head, with or without visible external trauma or a fracture of the bone, can cause blood vessels to break and bleed. A hematoma—a blood clot—can grow large enough to put pressure on the brain, causing death. The extradural space is between the bone and the dura, and the subdural space is between the dura and the brain. These hematoma can occur due to ruptured aneurysms—natural breaks in weakened blood vessels.

*Subarachnoid hematoma.* The arachnoid is a thin layer of protective tissue between the dura and the brain. Trauma or ruptured aneurysms can release free blood, forming a clot and putting pressure on the brain, resulting in death.

*Intracerebral hematoma.* This hematoma refers to any mass of free blood within the brain tissue. The details are similar to the description of the subarachnoid hematoma, but trauma from a penetrating weapon, such as a bullet, may be required.

*Circle of Willis.* The circle of Willis is located just at the base of the brain and is, in fact, a circle of blood vessels carrying arterial blood to the brain, consisting of the internal carotids and the basilar artery. This area is as removed from external danger as any part of the body. An occlusion or an aneurysm can result in blockage and/or rupture and provoke some very bizarre behavior as a hematoma forms and puts pressure on the base of the brain and the brain stem. Death will occur within minutes, but in the interim the subject may do some unexpected things.

*Contra coup or counter blow.* A hematoma, usually intra-cerebral, may be found in the space opposite the location of force. The damage to the other side of the brain is due to the brain moving within the skull, in effect bouncing off the opposite side of the skull. There may be a hematoma or trauma at both locations.

*Massive brain damage.* This extreme damage can be the result of instant trauma, such as a gunshot to the head or great force applied by a blow or repeated blows sufficient to smash through the skull and decimate a major part of the brain. *Avulsion* describes the effect of forceful tearing of tissue, as when brain matter is visibly oozing from trauma to the skull.

## Suffocation

Any type of physical suffocation can be accidental, suicidal, or at the hands of another. Of all the traumatic methods of death, it is perhaps the most difficult to detect, since there may be no evidence of violence. The murder weapon can be a cupped hand, soft pillow, plastic bag, or anything else that would conform to the lines of the face.

*Sudden Infant Death Syndrome.* A classification of SIDS means that all known causes of death have been eliminated and the infant's death remains a mystery. Technically, SIDS is listed as the cause of death, but in fact there is no ascertainable cause. The victim is usually less than two years old.

Most crib deaths were once thought to be due to child neglect, leaving parents wondering what they did wrong. Some undoubtedly were accidental suffocation, but as more is learned about SIDS, it becomes obvious that it may have a variety of causes that are all beyond the immediate control of the parent. Nevertheless, each death must be autopsied to eliminate any known natural cause or any cause due to accident or homicide. When there is a cause of death, even if the death occurred in a crib, it is not a SIDS.

***Positional Asphyxiation.*** Some crib deaths are due to positional asphyxiation (PA) as are some unusual adult deaths. Infant PA can occur when the baby slips into a space face-down and cannot extract itself. The space between the crib frame and a mismatched or improperly fitted mattress is a potential death trap. Toys that allow the infants to crawl into them, or insert the head into a space in such a way that they cannot back out, can result in PA.

Adult PA is almost always a result of victims falling into an odd position or confined place while acutely intoxicated or too weak to extract themselves for other reasons. PA is occasionally the cause of industrial deaths when construction workers, for instance, are trapped by falling debris that renders them helpless or is too heavy for them to move. The asphyxiation may be due to a constriction across or around the front of the neck that compresses the larynx (the upper airway) or from the weight of an object pinned against the person's chest that is sufficient to inhibit breathing by compressing the chest. It was not exactly at the hands of another, but nevertheless, the victim of one murder I know of died due to PA, as the result of one assailant sitting on her chest while another raped her.

***Sudden Adult Death Syndrome.*** Soon after the end of the war in Southeast Asia, a large number of immigrants from that region moved into Orange County. With them came many wonderful new traditions that are now a part of Orange County life. But with that life came a strange form of death for no apparent reason, Sudden Adult Death Syndrome, known as SADS. Like the infant syndrome, the victims were otherwise healthy, and after a complete autopsy, no cause of death could be discovered. There is a major difference in investigating these occurrences. Babies can't tell us they had a bad night, for instance, a dream in which someone was chasing them. But adults who survive their dream can.

Adults who eventually died of SADS had previously reported that they had been visited by the angel of death during the night. One eventual SADS victim survived an earlier incident while napping in the presence of witnesses. One witness described him as jerking around and then turning blue. When shaken by the witness, he woke up and described the angel as many others had. A few weeks later this man died in his sleep. As with the other SADS, all autopsy results including toxicology were negative.

Turning blue is an indication that the heart had stopped momentarily. Whatever the reason, their deaths remain a mystery.

*Autoerotism.* Deaths due to autoerotic activities are as difficult for the family members to accept as the practice of autoerotism is to comprehend. The *American Heritage Dictionary*'s number one definition of autoerotism is "self satisfaction of sexual desire, as by masturbation." A second definition adds: "without external stimulus." Maybe that is a good definition since the act involves sexual stimulation, but in fatal cases there is always an external stimulus. It is just not what most people think of when they imagine a sexual stimulus. There is always some choking device, a device that limits the air supply, reducing the oxygen and increasing the carbon dioxide to oxygen ratio in the blood on the way to the brain. Carbon dioxide acts as a trigger to activate some natural physiological functions.

Death is almost always accidental and is due to suffocation, perhaps by hanging or some bondage devices around the neck. The victim is usually a young man, twelve to thirty years old. Until a case was reported in the late 1980s, I had never heard of any female victims.

Typically, autoerotic death scenes have some common factors that distinguish them from suicides. Foremost, suffocation is by a device or setup that has an escape system that failed, and usually some hint, if not blatant indication, of sexual fantasy.

Some cases of autoerotic death by hanging are classified

as suicides or murders by investigators unfamiliar with the practice. If they were familiar with the habits of the auto-erotic, they would know what to look for. In fact some of these deaths are not murders but suicides. In some cases the autoerotic has planned the death, leaving notes documenting the reasons for committing suicide and staging a very dramatic scene.

*Food Bolus.* Choking to death on a bolus—a soft mass—is almost always classified as an accident because a large chunk of food, usually a solid piece of meat, gets wedged in the throat. Until Dr. Henry J. Heimlich introduced his life-saving maneuver, there were many cases when onlookers stood by helplessly as a hurried eater choked on food that was not chewed adequately. Deaths still occur when the person choking is unattended or companions don't know what to do.

In many of the deaths that I reviewed, the victims, coincidentally, had a substantial blood alcohol level, in the range of 0.20. At that level, bad things happen. The victims lost much of their ability to make sound judgments and their gag reflex was depressed. The victims were attempting to swallow large chunks of food without chewing and were not receiving any gag warning that the volume of the food was too large to handle. There was nothing much the victims could do, drinking or not, once the bolus was wedged in the trachea.

Cases have been reported in which victims of robbery or kidnapping were gagged and died when unable to breathe. Even if the death was unintended, it most likely would be classified as murder, a death committed during the commission of a felony. In the Mark Hall case, Randy Kraft forced soil down the throat of his living victim. Cause of death: asphyxia due to foreign object in airway. Classification: at the hands of another.

A group of Orange County teenagers were convicted of murder in 1994 after they beat a crime-in-the-planning partner unconscious with a baseball bat. When that didn't kill him, they poured alcohol down his throat and taped his mouth shut with duct tape. Cause of death: suffocation due to foreign material forced down his throat.

## Drowning

A drowning death is due to anoxia or asphyxiation, with water acting as a fluid bolus. Most drownings are accidental, some are suicidal, and a few are homicides. A forensic laboratory can distinguish between fresh water and saltwater. Screenwriters have concocted many a plot around a bathtub murder where the body is transported to the shore and it is made to appear that the victim drowned in the ocean.

*Vomitos Amigos.* Not everyone drowns in water. Any fluid will do. Drunks, for example, have been known to drown in their own vomitus. I have already mentioned the loss of the gag reflex. Drunks vomit. Drunks pass out. Sometimes drunks pass out in their own vomit. Without a gag reflex, and if the vomit pools up—as on a leatherette auto seat—or is inhaled, asphyxiation can occur. The deaths are classified as accidental.

*Drowning Due to Drug Intoxication.* Some drowning, as well as other forms of death, have drugs as a condition contributing but not related to the immediate cause of death. In the case of PCP, cocaine, and some of the amphetamine-related drugs, intoxication is more of a reason for the drowning than you might at first guess. Most drugs, if used in excess, are known to cause confusion, which can result in a user accidentally falling into a body of water and drowning. But in the case of the drugs mentioned here, one of the side effects, actually compels the user to seek out any available water: hyperthermia, the elevation of the body's temperature. Although stupefied by the drug, the user senses the danger of the fever and perhaps instinctively heads for cooler pastures: water. The water doesn't have to be treacherous. There's a case where the victim drowned in less than a foot of water in a reflecting pool. Cause of death: drowning, due to fresh water immersion due to possible hyperthermia. Contributing but not directly related: PCP intoxication.

## Injuries to the Neck

*Strangulation.* The word "strangle" even sounds violent. Most strangulation deaths are in fact violent in nature, where something grabs hold of the victim's neck as he or she struggles for survival. Nevertheless, strangulation can be accidental, suicidal, as well as at the hands of another, as we see in the movies. Murderous strangulation can be manual, by hanging, or committed with a device such as a garrote, which can be any thin cord or wire that is convenient, such as a lamp or telephone cord. A garrote built for murder, an indication of premeditation, is equipped with handles on each end of the wire to assist in the grip.

Deaths due to strangulation could be caused by direct asphyxia when the larynx is compressed, withholding air from the lungs, or could be the result of obstructing the circulation of blood from the brain by compressing the jugular veins. Veins are usually closer to the body surface, while arteries are more secluded, protected by muscle. Nevertheless, focused or intense pressure can also cut off the flow of blood to the brain by compressing the carotid arteries. So there is an important difference. If only the veins are compressed, blood is still pumped into the head and brain but it can't exit. If both the veins and the arteries are compressed, blood flow may be stopped altogether. Death by most methods of strangulation takes time, a few minutes, so the difference in pressure can cause subtle trauma.

*Petechial Hemorrhage.* When blood continues to flow to the head but can't exit, there is additional internal pressure within all the vessels. At some point the pressure may be enough to cause some of the weaker points to rupture. These tiny ruptures in the capillaries, called "petechial hemorrhages" or *petechia*, are often visible, particularly in the transparent membrane that connects and protects the zone between the whites of the eye and the upper and lower eyelids, or conjunctiva.

Petechia are not exclusive to hangings. They may be found in the skin's or internal organs' capillaries in any area of the body where blood is being pumped but can't exit for some reason, an occlusion, for example. And there may be other causes of increased blood pressure preceding death—certain drugs, for instance—so the presence of petechia, even in the conjunctiva, without supporting evidence is not absolute proof of strangulation.

***Hyoid Bone.*** The hyoid is a small, thin, U-shaped bone embedded in the heavy muscle of the neck. Its purpose is to act as an anchor for the tongue's muscles. The bone is unique in that it is not connected to any other bone. It is fragile and can crack when compressed. You can locate the area of your hyoid bone by placing your thumb and index finger in the front area of your upper neck. As you slide your hand upward, your fingers will stop at the underside of your chin. Position your fingers about two inches apart and you are almost touching your hyoid bone.

Coincidentally, this area on the neck proximate to the hyoid is where the hand of a murderer would end up during the act of manual strangulation. The fracture usually occurs on one or both of the thinner arms of the U shape where they meet the sturdier base. It is likely that the fracture would be caused by the pressure of the thumbs, one or the other or both. The muscle supporting the hyoid will also likely be deeply bruised, and there can be visible marks on the skin of the victim. Some of those marks may be defense marks.

A broken hyoid with contiguous deep muscle bruising on only one side or the other could be an indicator of the hand used by the murderer. If the victim is unable to resist for any reason—a baby, already unconscious, or just weak, for example—thumb pressure of one hand could do the damage. Nevertheless, the relative position of the killer to the victim has to be known or established to predict a specific hand, and it usually isn't. Remember, if face-to-face, it is right thumb to right side, left to left, because the thumb crosses over the neck as it is gripped.

***Hanging.*** The major difference between suicidal hangings and the accidental autoerotic variety is the usual absence of an intentional escape system in suicides. On some occasions the victims will even tie their own hands together, making it impossible or difficult to escape should they have a change of mind. Finding a hanging victim with hands tied together certainly sounds suspicious, and indeed it is. But to me all suicides are suspicious and should be examined by the investigators with the same degree of curiosity as any questioned death.

The material used to make the ligature, and the nature of the knots, is critical. There must be some explanation of the source of the material. Jailhouse hangings, for example, are most often by an item of clothing belonging to the victim, or linens, sheets, or towels supplied by the jailers. If a rope or electric cord was found to be the ligature, that would require an additional explanation. In any case, the material needs to be identified. What is its source and how did it get to the scene?

There may be two knots to consider: one holding the material to a solid support, usually overhead, and the knot around the neck. These knots can be an indication of the knowledge and skills of the tier, and any unusual knot needs explaining. All knots found in place must be retained as evidence and should never be untied unless it is a matter of saving the victim's life. If it appears the subject is alive when the first officer arrives, the victim should be cut down first, to release the pressure of the body weight, and then the ligature cut off in a location away from the knot. As soon as possible, the officer who cut the rope should mark the material in such a way that would reestablish how it was positioned before being cut. When there is no emergency, or as time allows in any case, a string should be tied securely to each of the cut ends to document their relative position and to hold any loose or slip knots in place.

Hanging by a narrow material such as an electric or tele-

phone cord can cut into the neck enough to make characteristic impressions deep in the skin and supporting underlying
tissue (see top photo, insert page 11). If the body weight is
sufficient, the pressure can be great enough to compress the
arteries, stopping all blood from entering the head. In that
case, petechial hemorrhages may not be present. Wide materials such as sheets or a heavy rope or even narrow material
where there is not much weight on the ligature will usually reduce the flow of the exiting blood, and petechia will be present.

If the subject jumps from a sufficient height, then regardless of the material around the neck, if the material holds the
neck may break. Death may be very quick, even instant, if
the spinal cord is severed or damaged.

Most broken necks are due to accidental causes. Movie
villains or heroes fighting for their lives seem to be able to
break the other guy's neck, but in real murders you don't see
this as a cause of death too often.

*The Jugulars.* There are two sets of jugulars, one on each
side of the neck. In fact, the jugular vein is actually three
veins: internal, external, and superficial. The internal carries
the most blood from the brain and is very close to the carotid
arteries. The external and superficial are the most vulnerable
to trauma. Once a jugular vein is cut, the blood flow is difficult to stop, and without expert care death is imminent.
Death is due to loss of blood, and the classification can be
accidental, suicidal, or at the hands of another.

## Stab Wounds

### Sharp Force

Murder by knife is often accomplished by stabbing rather
than slicing, which tends to be superficial. Further, slices are
more apt to be defensive (see top photo, insert page 11),
whereas stabs are likely to be intended to kill, as in the coup
de grace of the sword fighters. Stabs may puncture a vital organ or blood vessel that otherwise is well-protected. The
pathologist may be able to describe the knife by examining

the cut—for example, two-edged rather than single-edged—and the width and length of the blade (see bottom photo, insert page 12; insert page 13). It is unusual to find the weapon stuck in the wound. Artistically, the visual impact of a knife sticking in the back tells a story to moviegoers or readers of cartoons, but in real life the stabber usually withdraws the blade.

*Blunt Force*

Blunt force may be the mode of any number of traumatic deaths. Blunt force trauma is caused by being struck by the wide surface of an object being propelled with great energy, or by falling, for whatever reason, onto a flat surface. Homicide cases may involve a heavy weapon with a wide surface, such as a frying pan, a brick, a baseball bat, or a two-by-four. It can also be the result of a powerful blow with the fist, foot, or head of the assailant, as seen in variations of the martial arts. Blunt force trauma is often the cause of death of pedestrians and passengers involved in automobile collisions. Close examination of the trauma may reveal a recognizable pattern descriptive of the weapon. Further, material from the weapon may be embedded in the tissue surrounding the wound.

## Gunshot Wounds

Gunshot wounds can be from any distance, and in their simplest forms are equivalent to the puncture wounds in stabbing. In fact, most gunshot wounds are far from simple, since much modern-day ammunition is designed to do far more damage than merely puncture. Since the only purpose of shooting any live thing is to kill it, these bullets are designed to deliver the fullest effect possible by transferring all the kinetic energy to the target. For example, most ammunition manufacturers offer specialty bullets that expand or mushroom on contact for the purpose of immediately disabling the target. The information below describes the trauma created at close proximity—that is, at distances that are most common in handgun shootings—and the physical evidence that can be used to document the distance. The first example is when there is no distance between the muzzle and the target.

**Ballooning and Blow Back** describe the events that can occur when a round is fired from a weapon pressed tightly against any part of a body. A large volume of hot, expanding gases exits the barrel just after the bullet. In contact wounds, most if not all of the gases follow the bullet into the body. For a microsecond or two there is a huge expanding ball of flame and hot gas inside the body (see insert page 14). Something has to give, like a balloon blown up beyond its elastic limits. In many cases, particularly when there is resistance to inward expansion from bone, muscle, or other solid backing, the expanding gases push back in the direction of the weapon.

All skin has lines of stress that are perpendicular—90 degrees—and secondary lines of stress at 45 degrees to the primary lines. Ballooning can cause the skin to tear from inside out, first along the primary lines of stress and then, with greater pressure, along the secondary lines. The initial tearing looks very much like a cross, four tears, when the flaps of the wound are repositioned. This wound is described as a cruciform (cross) tear. The more complex wound looks like an eight-pointed star and is described as star-shaped. In either case, the escaping gases cause the wound to open up, as if it were an exit wound, and blow back tiny particles of blood, fat, skin, muscle tissue, or clothing fibers in the direction of the weapon. The wound is an entrance but also, in a sense an exit, though not for the bullet. Part of the gases and particles of debris blow back out of the wound.

Any material, such as clothing, that is pressed between the muzzle and the skin will also be affected by the blow-back gases. A standard weave of cotton or wool with threads woven at 90 degrees will tear in the cruciform shape. A jersey knit weave may just open up like a run, while some synthetics, such as orlon, melt. The tip ends of the damaged threads are forced out in the direction of the weapon and look somewhat like an erupted volcano.

***Entrance versus Exit Wounds.*** An unaware investigator, evidence examiner, or pathologist can mistake the surface appearance of a contact wound in cloth or skin for an exit wound. I have seen it happen. These authorities mistakenly believe the shooter and any witnesses are lying about the position of the shooter relative to the victim. Their thinking is 180 degrees off! And their undetected blunder could result in a miscarriage of justice.

For example, an aggressor charges an armed individual, such as a police officer, store employee, or resident, and in defense the armed individual fires the weapon at the aggressor at the last moment. The aggressor is in contact with the individual and the muzzle of the weapon when the shot is fired. The blow-back damage in the clothing and potentially in the body tissue can make the entrance appear as an exit. Combine this with a relatively clean exit wound and the uninformed examiner may claim the individual shot the aggressor in the back rather than in self-defense.

Demonstrating the presence of muzzle debris in the entrance wound and its predictable shape can avoid a bad arrest. When the initial close-up photography is completed and any particles of debris have been collected, the torn skin can be positioned, displaying the cross-shaped tear. The entire wound can then be incised as deep as needed to include all the affected underlying tissue, usually one to two inches.

If the investigator's urge is overpowering, it may be necessary to show the nonbelievers, on the spot, what happens inside a contact wound. It is better, scientifically, to wait and look at the wound under laboratory conditions. Regardless, the incised tissue should be X-rayed while still at the morgue. The barrels of many weapons may shave off small pieces of metal from the bullet as it passes through the lands and grooves. These particles will show up as opaque spots on the X ray, facilitating their location and removal.

The metal shavings, when present, along with the soot, partially burned and unburned gunpowder, will line the path of the bullet, confirming the entrance nature of the wound. There may be visible singeing caused by the flames of the burning gases. In some cases the sooting is extremely heavy, due to the nature of the gunpowder, masking the singed tissue. The unburned gunpowder should eventually be picked out of the tissue and confirmed to be nitrocellulose (see bottom photo, insert page 15; insert page 16).

I examined only one case in which the bullet path was void of any evidence of a witnessed contact wound. There was an explanation. The victim had bled out through the wound, flooding out any debris.

*Muzzle Imprint.* If the muzzle is held tight against the skin in some areas of the body, particularly the temple area, the ballooning effect forces the skin backward hard against the heated muzzle. The result resembles a cattle brand, clearly outlining the design details of the muzzle.

Actually, the underlying imprint is caused more from a contusion than from heat. The back pressure of the gas on the ballooning tissue compresses and damages the blood capillaries just under the skin, causing some pattern hemorrhaging. Some blood cells are damaged and others clot at the site of the hemorrhage, creating a discoloration, a bruise, in the outline of the muzzle.

*Powder Burns* is a vague term that collectively describes the effect of close proximity gunshot wounds to bare skin. Two types of burns will occur if the muzzle is within a few inches of living skin: muzzle flash and tattooing. Beyond twelve inches, soot and unburned gunpowder can produce visible patterns that are classified as powder burns by some authorities. They are not actually burns at all, but tiny particles of chemical ash sprayed out in a cone shape. These patterns—flash, tattoo, and soot—are usually easily observable at a distance of twelve inches or less. With some handguns, depending on the ammunition, they may travel as much as twenty-four to thirty-six inches and still be seen with the unaided eye. In testing weapons and the patterns they produce, the contrast offered by white cotton cloth as a target facilitates locating the soot pattern. This test is explained in Chapter 5.

*Near Contact.* When the muzzle is within an inch of mature tissue, the gases can fan out, and tearing is not expected, although clothing over the wound may tear in a pattern similar to a contact shot. The appearance of a near contact is usually a tight dark circle of debris an inch or less in diameter that covers underlying burning or singeing of the skin. Depending on the gunpowder formulas, heavy soot may completely mask the underlining effects of the heat and individual burns. Regardless of the extent of sooting and masking, the collective appearance of the patterns formed are referred to as powder burns.

*Muzzle Flash* is a flame hot enough to burn or singe the skin or clothing if the muzzle is within six inches. The degree of visible damage can be subtle. Fortunately, it is not all that important to detect muzzle flash if heavy soot is present. The presence of either can be used to document close proximity if the suspect weapon and identical ammunition are available to create comparison patterns. Since different brands of ammunition, and to some extent various weapons, will make different patterns, controlled experiments must take place and comparisons must be made before any distance is reported. If soot is not present, burning and singeing of fine hairs on the skin or threads on cloth surfaces can be used to measure muzzle flash.

*Tattooing/Stippling.* Tattooing refers to permanent marks, and stippling is used to describe any pattern composed of tiny dots (see top photo, insert page 15). Either term is correct in describing the patterns of embedded materials surrounding an entrance wound. Handgun ammunition generally contains more gunpowder than can be burned in the short time between the primer ignition and the bullet exiting the barrel. Some of the excess powder gets hot and sticky enough to glow red, but does not ignite.

When red-hot particles of gunpowder (or tiny pieces of shaved lead) hit living skin at distances of less than nine inches, they can penetrate deep enough to damage the blood capillaries and cause tiny points of hemorrhage. The body reacts within seconds and the red blood cells clot at the site of the damage, creating small red or brownish dots. These dots are referred to as tattooing. If the victim survives, these marks will heal, lacking infection. In a fatal shooting these marks will be visible until the skin decomposes. If the body was already dead and then shot at close range, particles can still burn into the flesh, but the hemorrhage will not be visible.

Beyond nine inches, the particles cool down and slow down. Only lead shavings, if there are any in the muzzle debris, will make permanent tattoo marks beyond nine inches. Powder particles can remain red-hot and capable of burning into many types of surfaces at very close range. Within six inches, the particles can even burn through a single layer of clothing and still be hot enough to cause tattooing in living skin. At a range of somewhere between six and nine inches, most of the glowing hot gunpowder will cool down and may stick to the skin but won't burn it. As the range increases, the warm particles continue to spray out farther. They remain tacky enough to stick to any target surface reached, particularly clothing. If there are no intervening surfaces, most powder particles will lose their forward energy and fall to the ground after thirty-six to forty-eight inches. Sphere-shaped particles can go farther.

The particles of gunpowder, after photography, can be located and removed using a low-power binocular stereoscopic microscope. The pattern, although dependent to some extent on the nature of the collecting surface, is usually round in shape if viewed in line with the direction of fire. And remember, there is usually a bullet hole right in the middle.

*Trajectory.* Once the entrance/exit relationship has been confirmed by muzzle debris and grease wipes (described in Chapter 5), the bullet's trajectory into and through the body can be determined. The angle of travel is usually demonstrated by using long probes that have been inserted along the path the bullet traveled.

**The Bottom Line**

Death investigation can also be traumatic to the team of investigators assigned to the scene and the autopsy. It is difficult to assign potential long-range effects. I'm okay, I think. The sick humor you've encountered occasionally in *Crime Scene* may concern some readers. Perhaps you have considered an occasional joke or pun in poor taste or out of place, considering the gravity of the task. It is this gravity that necessitates a release, at least for some people. You can really get lost in the tragedy. So someone tells a joke.

**For more photographs go to crimescenetwo.com.**

# True Crime Sagas
# Ripped From Today's Headlines

## MURDER IN GREENWICH
### THE MARTHA MOXLEY CASE . . . SOLVED
*by Marc Fuhrman*
0-06-109692-X/ $7.99 US/ $10.99 Can

## KIDS WHO KILL
### BAD SEEDS AND BABY BUTCHERS—
### SHOCKING TRUE STORIES OF JUVENILE MURDERERS
*by Charles Patrick Ewing*
0-380-71525-2/ $6.99 US/ $9.99 Can

## SON OF A GRIFTER
### THE TWISTED TALE OF SANTE AND KENNY KIMES,
### THE MOST NOTORIOUS CON ARTISTS IN AMERICA
*by Kent Walker and Mark Schone*
0-06-103169-0/ $7.99 US/ $10.99 Can

## A WARRANT TO KILL
### A TRUE STORY OF OBSESSION, LIES AND A KILLER COP
*by Kathryn Casey*
0-380-78041-0/ $7.99 US/ $10.99 Can

## MAFIA WIFE
### MY STORY OF LOVE, MURDER, AND MADNESS
*by Lynda Milito with Reg Potterton*
0-06-103216-6/ $7.99 US/ $10.99 Can